TAKING SIDES

Clashing Views on Controversial
Global Issues

TAKING SIDES

Clashing Views on Controversial

Global Issues

Selected, Edited, and with Introductions by

James E. Harf
Ohio State University

and

Mark Owen Lombardi
University of Tampa

McGraw-Hill/Dushkin
A Division of The McGraw-Hill Companies

To my daughter, Marie: May your world conquer those global issues left unresolved by my generation. (J. E. H.)

For Betty and Marty, who instilled a love of education and need to explore the world. (M. O. L.)

Photo Acknowledgment
Cover image: © 2001 by PhotoDisc, Inc.

Cover Art Acknowledgment
Charles Vitelli

Library of Congress Cataloging-in-Publication Data
Main entry under title:
Taking sides: clashing views on controversial global issues/selected, edited, and with introductions by James E. Harf and Mark Owen Lombardi.—1st ed.
Includes bibliographical references and index.
1. Globalization. 2. International relations. 3. Global environmental change. 4. Population. 5. Emigration and immigration. I. Harf, James E., ed. II. Lombardi, Mark Owen, ed. III. Series.
303
0-07-240953-3

Printed on Recycled Paper

Preface

This volume reflects the changing nature of the international system. The personal reflections of its two editors bring this into sharp focus. We are both products of the separate environments in which we have been raised. Our 20-year age difference suggests that each of us brings to the study of international affairs a particular lens through which two distinct yet interconnected generations view contemporary world issues.

The elder editor began his formal schooling a few weeks after the United States dropped two atomic bombs on Japan. His precollegiate experience took place amid the fear that an evil enemy was lurking throughout the world, poised to conquer America and enslave its occupants. During his initial month in college, the Soviet Union launched the first space vehicle, *Sputnik,* forever changing the global landscape. Yet his 1961 international relations textbook assumed that, despite the bomb and the ability to exploit outer space, the driving forces behind national behavior had not changed very much. By the time he accepted his first university teaching position, the world had been locked in a protracted cold war for two decades. Yet evidence of a new global agenda of problems that were totally unrelated to the American-Soviet rivalry was beginning to appear. Soon this new set of issues would challenge the traditional agenda for the world's attention and also occupy the editor's research agenda during much of his career.

As the elder editor now moves on to the twilight of his career, the cold war exists no more. And the set of problems that have occupied his and others' attention for some time—population growth, resource scarcities, environmental degradation, and the like—are being transformed by the overarching presence of globalization. The Internet and other advances in communication and transportation signal an entirely new environment in which global actors design and carry out their policies. This was brought home in a rather graphic way in December 2000, as this editor joined others in Kiev, Ukraine, to watch the newspapers debate the pending closure of the remaining operating nuclear power plant at Chernobyl. To this elder editor, his world has now undergone three major changes, from a traditionalist, realist paradigm where military power dominated, to a new global agenda where problems demanded the attention and cooperation of a kaleidoscope of actors, to yet another set of problems and a transformation of existing issues brought on by globalization.

The younger editor began his formal schooling just after the United States and the Soviet Union had settled "comfortably" into the era of mutual assured destruction (MAD). He entered his university studies as increased tensions and U.S.-Soviet rivalry threatened to tear apart the fragile fabric of détente. As he embarked on his teaching career, the communist empire was taking its first steps toward total disintegration. Amid this revolutionary change, deeper and more complex issues of security, technology, development, and ethnic conflict became more pronounced and increasingly present in the consciousness of actors and scholars alike. Now at the midpoint of his academic life, this younger editor contemplates the speed and force of globalization and how the issues that this phenomenon has brought forth will affect the lens through which he observes world affairs, influencing his and other research agendas over the next few decades.

The decision of this book's publisher to embark on a text on global issues reflects how the nature of international affairs has changed. Many textbooks on world politics and American foreign policy address longstanding, important concerns of the student of world events, employing for the most part the traditional paradigm of the past century. Simply put, this traditional scholarly view assumed a world where power, particularly military might, dominated the world picture. Nation-states, the only really important world actors, focused on pursuing power and then using it in conventional ways to become a larger presence on the international scene. The specific problems of the day might have changed, but the fundamental principles that guided the international system remained the same. Most books in these fields reflect this outlook.

But the field of international affairs is ever changing, and this new volume takes into account the fact that the age of globalization has accelerated, transforming trends that began over three decades ago. No longer are nation-states the only actors on the global stage. Moreover, their position of dominance is increasingly challenged by an array of other actors—international governmental organizations, private international groups, multinational corporations, and important individuals—who might be better equipped to address newly emerging issues (or who might also be the source of other problems). This new agenda took root in the late 1960s, when astute observers began to identify disquieting trends: quickening population growth in the poorer sectors of the globe, growing disruptions in the world's ability to feed its population, increasing shortfalls in required resources, and expanding evidence of negative environmental impacts, such as a variety of pollution evils. The global agenda's current transformation, brought about by globalization, demands that our attention turn toward the latter's consequences.

The format of *Taking Sides: Clashing Views on Controversial Global Issues* follows the successful formula of other books in the Taking Sides series. The book begins with an introduction to the emergence of global issues and the new age of globalization. It then presents 20 current global issues grouped into five parts. Population takes center stage in Part 1 because it not only represents a global issue by itself, but it also adversely affects the parameters of most other global issues. Part 2 addresses a range of problems associated with global resources. Parts 3, 4, and 5 feature issues borne out of the emerging agenda of the twenty-first century, including the increased movement of peoples and ideas across national boundaries and new security issues in the post–cold war era.

Each issue has two readings, one pro and one con. The readings are preceded by an issue *introduction* that sets the stage for the debate and briefly describes the two readings. Each issue concludes with a *postscript* that summarizes the issues, suggests further avenues for thought, and provides additional *suggestions for further reading*. Also, Internet site addresses (URLs) have been provided on the *On the Internet* page that accompanies each part opener, which should prove useful as starting points for further research. At the back of the book is a listing of all the *contributors to this volume* with a brief biographical sketch of each of the prominent figures whose views are debated here.

A word to the instructor   An *Instructor's Manual With Test Questions* (multiple-choice and essay) is available through the publisher for the instructor using *Taking Sides* in the classroom. A general guidebook, *Using Taking Sides in the Classroom,* which discusses methods and techniques for integrating the pro-con approach into any classroom setting, is also available. An online version of *Using Taking Sides in the Classroom* and a correspondence service for *Taking Sides* adopters can be found at http://www.dushkin.com/usingts/.

    Taking Sides: Clashing Views on Controversial Global Issues is only one title in the Taking Sides series. If you are interested in seeing the table of contents for any of the other titles, please visit the Taking Sides Web site at http://www.dushkin.com/takingsides/.

James E. Harf
Ohio State University

Mark Owen Lombardi
University of Tampa

Contents In Brief

Contents

Author Michael Tobias argues that there can be no doubt that under virtually all plausible scenarios of future global population growth, such growth will continue at unprecedented levels and will cause accelerated damage to the planet. Max Singer, cofounder of the Hudson Institute, a public policy research organization, contends that the world's population will be declining in 50 years as a consequence of an increasing number of countries' achieving a higher level of modernity.

Robert S. McNamara, former president of the World Bank, argues that the developed countries of the world and international organizations should help the countries of the developing world to reduce their population growth rates. The late professor of economics and business administration Julian L. Simon maintains that international organizations seek to impose birth control methods on developing nations in the misguided name of "virtuous and humanitarian . . . motives."

Don Hinrichsen, an environmental reporter and a consultant for the United Nations Population Fund, argues that the planet's natural systems and ecological systems are having increasing difficulty withstanding the negative consequences of continuing population growth. Economics professor N. Gregory Mankiw maintains that, assuming each additional person on Earth creates resources, if the amount created by each new individual is greater than the amount used by that individual, then the Earth's quality is enhanced by the presence of that individual.

Peter G. Peterson, chairman of the Blackstone Group, a private investment bank, argues that global aging will dominate the public-policy agenda of the developed world as it attempts to cope with a vast array of problems associated with such aging. Adjunct professor of demography Leon F. Bouvier and Jane T. Bertrand, chair of the Department of International Health and Development at Tulane University School of Public Health and Tropical Medicine, argue that a future developed society will be quite less able to cope with declining growth rates.

PART 2   GLOBAL RESOURCES AND THE ENVIRONMENT   69

The United Nations Environment Programme presents a comprehensive and gloomy assessment of the global environment at the turn of the millennium. Peter Huber, a senior fellow of the Manhattan Institute, contends that humankind is saving the Earth with the technologies that the "soft greens" most passionately oppose.

Christopher Flavin and Seth Dunn, researchers at the Worldwatch Institute, argue that a new energy system is emerging, in part because of a series of revolutionary new technologies and approaches, that will cause a transition away from reliance on oil as the primary energy source. Francis R. Stabler, a technology planner for General Motors, contends that technology and free enterprise will combine to allow the human race to continue its reliance on oil far into the future.

The late professor of economics and business administration Julian L. Simon asserts that the world has always been able to grow food to meet demand and that new technologies will accelerate that ability in the future. Bioscientist David Pimentel and his colleagues argue that many scholarly groups are increasingly concerned about the ability of the Earth's resource base to feed the planet's growing population.

Adil Najam, an assistant professor in the Department of International Relations at Boston University, argues that consumption control among developed countries is a major key to avoiding continuing environmental crises. Lester R. Brown, Gary Gardner, and Brian Halweil, researchers at the Worldwatch Institute, examine 16 dimensions of population growth in the areas of food and agriculture, environment and resources, and economic impacts and quality of life, and they indicate that the effects of such growth are mainly adverse.

Journalist Ross Gelbspan points to a variety of scientific evidence, including a 1995 announcement from 2,500 scientists, indicating that the planet is warming. Brian Tucker, a senior fellow of the Institute for Public Affairs, argues that there are still too many uncertainties to conclude that global warming has arrived.

Joe Stork, advocacy director of Human Rights Watch/Middle East, contends that an International Criminal Court (ICC) for war crimes is vital to U.S. and global security. He argues that the only way to prevent war crimes is to have the full weight of the international community, including the United States, behind such a court. Lee A. Casey and David B. Rivkin, Jr., who both practice law in Washington, D.C., contend that the International Criminal Court is against U.S. national interests and would be used as a political weapon by nations that are opposed to American policies. They argue that it should not be established or recognized by the United States.

Issue 20.   Are Cultural Rivalries and Ethnic Conflicts the Next Great Threats to International Security?   338

Political scientist Samuel P. Huntington argues that the emerging conflicts of the twenty-first century will be cultural and not ideological. He identifies the key fault lines of conflict and discusses how these conflicts will reshape global policy. John R. Bowen, a professor of sociocultural anthropology, rejects the idea that ethnic and cultural conflicts are decisive. He argues that political choices made by governments and nations, not cultural divides and intercultural rivalry, dictate much of global international affairs.

Introduction

Global Issues in the Twenty-First Century

James E. Harf

Mark Owen Lombardi

The Emergence of the Age of Globalization

The cold-war era, marked by the domination of two superpowers in the decades following the end of World War II, has given way to a new era of globalization. This new epoch is characterized by a dramatic shrinking of the globe in terms of travel and trade, increased participation in global policy making of national and nonstate actors, and an exploding volume of problems with growing consequences. While the tearing down of the Berlin Wall over a decade ago dramatically symbolizes the end of the cold war era, the creation of the Internet illustrates the emergence of the globalization era in the new century.

Early signs of this transition were manifested during the latter part of the last century by a series of problems that transcended national boundaries. These problems caught the attention of policymakers who demanded comprehensive analyses and solutions. The effects of significant population growth in the developing world, for example, called for multilateral action by leaders in developed and developing nations alike. Acid rain, created by emissions from smokestacks upwind, was the precursor of a host of environmental crises that appeared with increasing frequency, challenging the traditional political order. Finally, many began to perceive the planet as "Spaceship Earth" with finite resources in danger of being exhausted.

These global concerns remain today. Some are well on their way to being addressed successfully, while others languish amid a lack of consensus about the nature of the problem and how to solve it. With the final shattering of the cold war system and the advent of the globalization age, new issues have emerged to broaden our conception of the global agenda. In the past ten years, the freedom of people to move has expanded and with this freedom are concerns about refugees and displaced persons within the developing world, and about the brain drain from the poorer nations to those countries most able to provide a better life.

However, the increase in the movement of people pales in comparison with the accelerated movement of information and ideas, which has ushered in global concerns about cultural imperialism, individual privacy, and freedom.

The ability both to retrieve and to disseminate information will have an impact in this new century as great as if not greater than, the seminal inventions of the past—the printing press, telegraph, the telephone, radio, and television. The potential for global good or ill is endless. Finally, traditional notions of great-power security embodied in the cold war rivalry have given way to concerns about terrorism, genocide, nuclear proliferation, cultural conflict, and the expansion of international law.

Globalization by definition heightens our awareness of a vast array of issues that will challenge individuals, as well as governmental and nongovernmental actors. With the demise of the cold war world, analysts and laypersons are free to define, examine, and explore solutions to such issues on a truly global scale. This text seeks to identify those issues central to the discourse on globalization. The issues in this volume provide a broad overview of the mosaic of global issues that will impact students' daily lives.

What Is a Global Issue?

We begin by addressing what a "global issue" is.[1] By definition, the word *issue* is characterized by disagreement along several related dimensions:

1. disagreement about whether a problem exists;
2. disagreement about the characteristics of the problem;
3. disagreement about preferred future alternatives or solutions; and/or
4. disagreement about how preferred futures are to be obtained.

These problems are real, vexing, and controversial because policymakers bring to their analyses different historical experiences, values, goals, and objectives. These differences impede, and can even prevent, successful problem solving.

The inclusion of the word *global* in the phrase *global issue* is what makes the set of problems confronting the human race today far different from those that challenged our ancestors. Historically, problems were confined to a village, city, or region. The capacity of the human race to fulfill its daily needs was confined to a much smaller space. When local resources were exhausted, humans moved elsewhere in search of another local environment better able to supply them. With the inventions of the locomotive and the automobile, however, humans were able to travel greater distances on a daily basis. National energy systems and agricultural systems emerged, freeing humans from a reliance on their local community. Problems then became national, as dislocations in the production or distribution system in one part of a country had repercussions.

With the advent of transoceanic transportation capabilities, national distribution systems gave way to global systems. The "breadbasket" countries of the world, those best able to grow food, expanded production to serve an ever-larger global market. Oil producing countries with vast reservoirs increased production to satisfy the needs of an ever-growing worldwide clientele. Countries best able to provide other resources to a larger part of the world entered the global trade system as well. These spatial changes were a consequence of significant increases in population and per capita consumption, both of which dramatically heightened the demand for resources.

Additionally, the larger machines of the Industrial Revolution were capable of moving greater quantities of dirt and of emitting greater amounts of pollutants into the atmosphere. With these new production and distribution capabilities came more prevalent manifestations of existing issues as well as new issues. Providers either engaged in greater exploitation of their own environment or searched further afield in order to satisfy additional resource requirements.

The character of these new issues is different from those of earlier eras. First, they transcend national boundaries and impact virtually every corner of the globe. In effect, these issues help make national borders increasingly meaningless. Environmental pollution and diseases such as acquired immunodeficiency syndrome (AIDS) do not recognize or respect national borders.

Second, these new issues cannot be resolved by the autonomous or individual action of a single actor, be it a national government, international organization, or multinational corporation. A country cannot guarantee its own energy or food security without participating in a global energy or food system.

Third, these issues are characterized by a wide array of value systems. To a family in the developing world, giving birth to a fifth or sixth child may contribute to the family's immediate economic well-being. But to a research scholar at the United Nations Population Fund, the consequence of such an action multiplied across the entire developing world leads to expanding poverty and resource depletion.

Fourth, these issues will not go away. They require specific policy action by a consortium of local, national, and international leaders. Simply ignoring the issue cannot eliminate the threat of chemical or biological terrorism, for example. If global warming does exist, it will not disappear unless specific policies are developed and implemented.

Finally, these issues are characterized by their persistence over time. The human race has developed the capacity to manipulate its external environment and, in so doing, has created a host of opportunities and challenges. The accelerating pace of technological change suggests that global issues will proliferate and will continue to challenge human beings throughout the next millennium.

In the final analysis, however, a global issue is defined as such only through mutual agreement by a host of actors within the international community. Some may disagree about the nature, severity, or presence of a given issue and these concerns become areas of focus only after a significant number of actors (states, international organizations, the United Nations, and others) begin to focus systematic and organized attention to the issue.

The Creation of the Global Issues Agenda

Throughout the first part of the cold war, the international community found itself more often as an observer of, rather than a player, in the superpower conflict for global domination being waged by the United States and the Soviet Union. Other forces and trends were at work during this period that competed for the attention of world leaders. Economic development exploded in many parts of the globe, while other areas floundered in poverty. Resource consumption expanded alongside economic growth throughout the developed world, creating both pollution and scarcity. Population growth rates increased dramatically in societies unable to cope with the consequences of a burgeoning population. New forms of violence replaced traditional ways of employing force.

As the major participants in the cold war settled into a system of routinized behavior designed to avoid catastrophic nuclear war, other actors in the international system began to worry about the disquieting effects associated with exploding population and consumption. Nation-states, international governmental organizations, and private groups sought to identify these growth-related problems and to seek solutions. The United Nations (UN) soon became the principal force to which those affected by such global behavior turned.

International community members soon began to join forces under the auspices of the UN to design comprehensive strategies. Such plans became known as international regimes—a set of agreements, structures, and plans of action involving all relevant global actors in addressing specific issues before them.

For example, in response to concerns of the Swedish government in the early 1970s about the discovery of a significant amount of dead fish in its lakes, the UN brought together relevant parties to discuss the problem, assumed to be caused by acid rain. This 1972 conference, called the United Nations Conference on the Human Environment, represented the first major attempt of the international community to address the global ecological agenda. Representatives from 113 countries appeared in Stockholm, Sweden. (The Soviet-bloc countries boycotted the conference for reasons unrelated to the environmental issue.) Over 500 international nongovernmental organizations from disparate interests such as environment, science, women, religion, and business also sent delegates. Members of the United Nations Secretariat and specialized international governmental organizations within the UN such as the World Bank and the Food and Agricultural Organization (FAO) were present, as well. Experts from all walks of life—scientists, environmentalists, and others—attended.

The conference in Stockholm ushered in a new age of thinking about issues in their global context and became the model for future conferences on global issues. Position papers were prepared for delegates and preparatory committees hammered out draft declarations and plans of action. These served as the starting point for conference deliberations. The final plan of action included the establishment of a formal mechanism, the United Nations Environmental Programme (UNEP), for addressing environmental issues in the future.

The most significant outcome of the conference was the creation of awareness among national government officials regarding the severity of ecological issues, the extent to which these issues cross national boundaries, and the need for international cooperation in order to solve these issues. The era of global issues identification, analysis, and problem solving was born.

Twenty years later, the global community reconvened in Rio de Janeiro, Brazil, at the UN Conference on Environment and Development, more popularly known as the Earth Summit. This meeting produced Agenda 21, a report that outlined a plan of action for achieving development throughout the world while at the same time avoiding environmental degradation.

Another example of the international community's venture into this emerging agenda focused on the global population problem. In the early 1970s, the UN responded to the pleas of a variety of groups to consider the negative consequences of exploding birth rates in many developing countries. The reason for such concern grew out of the belief that such growth was deterring economic growth in those areas of the world that were the most poverty stricken.

The result was the United Nations World Population Conference held in Bucharest, Romania, in 1974, and attended by delegates from 137 countries as well as representatives of numerous governmental and nongovernmental organizations. The principal result of the conference was the placement of population on the global agenda and the development of a formal plan of action. The international community has continued its formal attention to the population issue, and has convened every ten years since Bucharest—in Mexico City, Mexico, in 1984 and in Cairo, Egypt, in 1994—to evaluate strategy and assume new tasks to lower growth rates.

These kinds of conferences, where a myriad of experts join a wide range of governments of all levels, private groups, and individuals, is now characteristic of how the global community is addressing the emerging global agenda. But the international community was far less certain of the wisdom of this strategy in 1972. However, the success of the United Nations Conference on the Human Environment led to similar strategies in a host of other environmental areas and provided the blueprint for the analysis of unforeseen global issues. For most of the issues in this text, the international community is either now formally addressing the problem or is considering its first steps.

The Nexus of Global Issues and Globalization

In 1989 the Berlin Wall fell, and with it a variety of assumptions, attitudes, and expectations of the international system. This event did not usher in a utopia, nor did it irrevocably change all existing ideas. It did, however, create a void. As a dominant cold war system entrenched since the end of World War II was broken apart, alternative views, issues, actors, and perspectives began to emerge to fill the void left by the collapse of the old system. What helped to bring down the previous era and what has emerged as the new dominant international construct is what we now call globalization.

Throughout the 1990s, scholars and policymakers have struggled to define this new era. Some have analyzed it in terms of the victory of Western or American ideals, the dominance of global capitalism, and the spread of democracy. Others have defined it in terms of the multiplicity of actors now performing on the world stage, and how states and their sovereignty have declined in importance and impact vis-à-vis others, such as multinational corporations and nongovernmental groups like Greenpeace and Amnesty International. Still others have focused on the vital element of technology and its impact in communications, information storage and retrieval, and global exchange.

Whether globalization reflects one, two, or all of these characteristics is not as important as the fundamental realization that globalization is the dominant element of a new era in international politics. This new period is characterized by several basic traits that greatly impact the definition, analysis, and solution of global issues. They include the following:

- an emphasis on information technology;
- the increasing speed of information and idea flows;
- a need for greater sophistication and expertise to manage such flows;
- the control and dissemination of technology; and
- the cultural diffusion and interaction that comes with information expansion and dissemination.

Each of these areas has helped shape a new emerging global issues agenda. Current issues remain important and, indeed, these factors help to understand them on a much deeper level. Yet, globalization has also created new problems and has brought them to the fore such that significant numbers of actors now recognize their salience in the international system.

For example, the spread of information technology has made ideas, attitudes, and information more available to people throughout the world. Americans in Dayton, Ohio, had the ability to log onto the Internet and speak with their counterparts in Kosovo to discover when NATO bombing had begun and to gauge its accuracy to later news reporting. Norwegian students can share values and customs with counterparts in South Africa, experiencing cultural attitudes firsthand without the filtering mechanisms of governments, or even parents and teachers. Scientific information available through computer technology can now be used to build sophisticated biological and chemical weapons of immense destructive capability. Ethnic conflicts and genocide between groups of people are now global news, forcing millions to come to grips with issues of intervention, prevention, and punishment.

Globalization is an international system and it is also a rapidly changing trend in global society. Because of the fluid nature of this system and the fact that it is both relatively new and largely fueled by the amazing speed of technology, continuing issues are constantly being transformed and new issues emerge on a regular basis. The nexus of globalization and global issues has now become, in many ways, the defining dynamic of understanding global issues. Whether it is new forms of terrorism, new conceptions of security, expanding international law, solving ethnic conflicts, dealing with mass migration, coping with individual freedom and access to information, or addressing cultural clash and cultural imperialism, the transition from a cold war world to a globalized world helps us understand in part what these issues are and why they are important.

Identifying the New Global Issues Agenda

The analysis of global issues by scholars and policymakers has changed. Our assumptions, ideas, and conceptions of what makes a problem a global issue has expanded. New technologies and actors within a changing global order have made the study of global issues a broader and more complex undertaking.

The organization of this text reflects these phenomena. Parts I and II focus on the continuing global agenda of the post-cold war era. The emphasis is on global population and environmental issues and the nexus between these two phenomena. Is world population out of control or is it a regional phenomenon centered only in the poorer sectors of the globe? What, if anything, should the international community do about this problem? Does population affect the environment, and if so, how? Should humanity be concerned with resource availability, be they food, oil, and/or pristine land? Do the activities of the human race account for the degradation of the environment or is such change part of a natural evolution to be embraced, not feared?

Parts III, IV, and V address the emerging global agenda of the globalization age. Is human migration a positive development or a sign of growing human desperation for economic and social well-being? The new age of globalization has facilitated the flow of ideas worldwide. Is this dissemination of knowledge a force for good or a form of indoctrination by one culture over another? Will this greater flow of information promote human empowerment or serve to restrict human freedom?

Has the end of the cold war brought a chance for global peace or has it unleashed a set of forces that will pose greater and more insidious dangers than those faced during the last century? Has the threat of nuclear war been replaced by a new struggle between terrorist groups using more dangerous weapons of mass destruction? Have the horrors of the Holocaust been revisited through ethnic cleansing and genocide? Can the international community prevent and police such conflicts through international forums? Can we diminish the threat of nuclear war by banning all testing of nuclear weapons? And finally, can the world overcome the debilitating effect of ethnic conflicts across the globe?

The revolutionary changes of the last few decades present us with serious challenges unlike any in human history. However, as in all periods of historic change, we possess significant opportunities to overcome problems. The task ahead is one of defining these issues, exploring their context, and developing solutions that are comprehensive in scope and effect. The role of all researchers in this field, or any other, is to analyze objectively such problems and search for workable solutions. As students of global issues, your task is to educate yourselves about these issues and become part of the solution.

Note

1. The five characteristics are extracted from James E. Harf and B. Thomas Trout, *The Politics of Global Resources,* Duke University Press, 1986, pp. 12–28.

On the Internet ...

Population Reference Bureau

The Population Reference Bureau provides current information on international population trends and implications from an objective viewpoint. The PopNet section of this Web site offers maps with regional and country-specific population information as well as information divided by selected topics.

http://www.prb.org

United Nations Population Fund (UNFPA)

The United Nations Population Fund (UNFPA) was established in 1969 and was originally called the United Nations Fund for Population Activities. This organization works with developing countries to educate about reproductive and sexual health as well as family planning. UNFPA also supports population and development strategies that will benefit developing countries and works to advocate for the resources needed to accomplish these tasks. Explore this site to learn more about UNFPA, including the organization's support of allowing the right of individuals to decide the number and spacing of their children without outside coercion.

http://www.unfpa.org/index.html

Zero Population Growth (ZPG)

Zero Population Growth (ZPG) is a nonprofit organization that seeks to educate about the benefits of slowing population growth and conserving natural resources. This site provides information about the organization itself as well as current demographic facts for the United States and the world. Quality of life is addressed on this site.

http://www.zpg.org

The CSIS Global Aging Initiative

The Center for Strategic and International Studies (CSIS) is a public policy research institution and approaches the issue of the aging population in developed countries in a bipartisan manner. CSIS is involved in a two-year project to explore the global implications of aging in developed nations and to seek strategies on dealing with this issue. This site includes a list of publications presented at previous events.

http://www.csis.org/gai/

PART 1

Global Population Growth

*I*t is no coincidence that many of the global issues in this volume emerged at about the same time as the world population exploded. No matter what the issue, the presence of a large and fast-growing population along with it exacerbates the issue and transforms its basic characteristics. The ability of the global community to respond is diminished by certain population conditions, be it an extremely young consuming population in a developing country in need of producers, or a large working-age group in a nation without enough jobs, or a rapidly growing, resource-consuming population in an area without sufficient food and water.

Thus we begin this text with a series of issues directly related to various aspects of population growth. This section serves to illuminate the issues in and of themselves and as a context within which other issues are examined.

- Is World Population Growth Out of Control?

- Should the International Community Attempt to Curb Population Growth in the Developing World?

- Does Population Growth Significantly Harm the Earth's Quality of Life?

- Will Declining Population Growth Rates in the Developed World Lead to Major Problems?

1

ISSUE 1

Is World Population Growth Out of Control?

YES: Michael Tobias, from *World War III: Population and the Biosphere at the End of the Millennium* (Continuum, 1998)

NO: Max Singer, from "The Population Surprise," *The Atlantic Monthly* (August 1999)

ISSUE SUMMARY

YES: Author Michael Tobias argues that there can be no doubt that under virtually all plausible scenarios of future global population growth, such growth will continue at unprecedented levels and will cause accelerated damage to the planet.

NO: Max Singer, cofounder of the Hudson Institute, a public policy research organization, contends that the world's population will be declining in 50 years as a consequence of an increasing number of countries' achieving a higher level of modernity.

In the context of global issues, a broad debate rages among policymakers and scholars about the respective consequences of increasing population levels and consumption patterns on the Earth's biosphere. The debate is politically charged because recent population growth has been confined primarily to the world's poorer regions, while consumption excesses are typically identified with rich countries.

Although an objective analysis of any specific global problem will likely suggest that increases in both human numbers and per capita consumption patterns play important roles, the rhetoric of most observers typically points to one or the other of these two macroinfluences as the predominant determinant of the magnitude of the problem.

Clearly, population numbers are critical to any global issue, perhaps more critical than any other factor. They affect the issue in both degree and kind. Population levels may serve as a threshold, above which a nonissue suddenly is transformed into a problem. For example, demographers allude to the *demographic threshold*, suggesting that once the percentage of the population below age 15 reaches 50 percent of the total, a country is hard-pressed to provide all the necessary services—education, food, housing, etc.—to this young consuming group prior to their becoming producers of goods and services (a problem of *kind*). But the extent of the problem is also a function of numbers. It is far easier to feed a country of 10 million than one of 20 million (a problem of *degree*). Without high population levels, consumption patterns would have far less impact.

So numbers do matter. Population size is important. And population growth rates are even more significant. They contain a potential built-in momentum that, if left unchecked, creates a geometric increase in births. A simple example illustrates the point. Let us assume that a young mother in a developing nation gives birth to three daughters before the age of 20. In turn, these three daughters each have three daughters before they reach the age of 20. The result of such fertility behavior is a ninefold (900 percent) increase in the population (minus a mortality-rate influence that is much lower than that in the developed world) within 40 years, or two generations. Contrast this pattern with that of a young mother in the developed world, who is currently reproducing at or slightly above replacement level. In the developed world, daughters replace mothers, and granddaughters replace daughters. Add a third generation of fertility, and the developing-world family has increased 27-fold within 60 years, while the developed-world family's size will likely remain virtually unchanged. A comparison of the consumption patterns of 27 new developing-world individuals with one new developed-world individual suggests that the overall increases in consumption may not be as different as originally assumed.

Looking at the potential problem at the macro level, consider the impact of the average annual growth rate of 2 percent for low-income countries (excluding China and India) during most of the 1990s. Those countries must also experience an annual 2 percent growth rate in food production, schools, jobs, housing, hospital beds, and all other basics in order to maintain the same quality of life, let alone improve it.

Thus, problems relating to population growth may, in fact, be at the heart of most global issues. If growth is a problem, control it, and half the ecological battle is won. Fail to control it, and global problem solvers will be swimming upstream against an ever-increasing current. The importance of out-of-control population growth is irrefutable. Its overarching impact is undeniable. The only area of dispute is whether or not the global community has turned the corner in its efforts to curb the high birth rates of the past 30–40 years throughout the developing world.

In the following selections, the authors reach competing conclusions regarding if and when growth has or will slow down in the developing world and then level off. For Michael Tobias, 40 years of global population control efforts have not yielded the desired results, and the resultant damage to the biosphere during this period has been unprecedented and will only accelerate in the future. Max Singer, on the other hand, argues that the twenty-first century will witness rapid downsizing in the numbers. Not only will population growth level off, he asserts, but the actual size of the population will begin to decline within 50 years.

Demographic Madness

Chomolungma

It is estimated that every second more than twenty-eight people are born and ten die; that every hour nearly eleven thousand newborns cry out. Each day more than one million human conceptions are believed to come about, accompanied by some 150 thousand abortions. Among those newborns, every day thirty-five thousand will die by starvation, twenty-six thousand of them children. Meanwhile, every twenty-four hours the pace of war against the planet increases, sometimes in major affronts, other times imperceptibly, at least by our limited perceptual standards. That war includes the loss of fifty-seven million tons of topsoil and eighty square miles of tropical forest and the creation of seventy square miles of virtually lifeless desert every day. At current birth and death rates, the world is adding a Los Angeles every three weeks. If average human growth rates were to continue at their present course (the so-called "constant fertility variant" or rate of natural increase) the world's population would reach at least ten billion by the year 2030, twenty billion by 2070, forty billion by 2110, and eighty billion by the year 2150. Most social scientists believe the figure will be, at worst, between eleven and twelve billion. But some have not ruled out a population between fifteen and twenty billion.

While I have felt the oppressive weight of people—whether I envision them raging across the countryside, teeming over the concrete, slaughtering other species, burning down forests, or raping one another—I am still not quite conversant with the paradox of my own complicity. That, by association, as one more member of that species, I am as guilty, as out of control and blind as the next man. While my wife and I have had no child, we are two westerners, equal in ecologically destructive impact, I imagine, to at least four hundred of our brethren in the developing world. My response to that estimated ratio should be colossal guilt. Yet, in truth, I cannot trace, or visualize the known burden of myself upon nature. The quantum leap from my personal conduct and lifestyle to an imperiled world is vastly diffused and muted. Yet, there is no doubting the insoluble dilemma, that incessant proximity to more and more members of our own kind, who are at the crux of this biological configuration, of absolutely tragic dimensions. Such bipedal, carnivorous masses are unique in the

From Michael Tobias, *World War III: Population and the Biosphere at the End of the Millennium* (Continuum, 1998). Copyright © 1998 by Michael Charles Tobias. Reprinted by permission of Continuum Publishing Company. Notes omitted.

annals of earthly experience, and surely outweigh all feeble, academic efforts to grapple with demographic theory. Even the theological struggle to explain, and resist, evil falls short of the psychological mayhem, the omnipresent paradox of so many *Homo sapiens*. "There is a concept which corrupts and upsets all the others," writes Jorge Luis Borges. "I refer not to Evil whose limited realm is that of ethics, I refer to the infinite." So many people: six, twelve, fifteen billion people; ever dwindling privacy; the volatility of competing demands, desires, and information. The psyche is overrun by these many components of congestion, this malaise of contagion, these very doubts as to our own nature, and the meaning of so many separate human lives.

So far, in the span of my own life, we have more than doubled our number as a species. Over 90 percent of the growth of the human population has taken place in less than one tenth of 1 percent of our whole species' history. And because half the world's population is now under the age of twenty-four, a third younger than fifteen, it is clear that we have currently reached the base—not the top—of a demographic Mount Everest, or Chomolungma, as those Buddhists dwelling directly beneath the mountain call it.

Though this century has already witnessed an unprecedented human population explosion, we are presently poised to proliferate as never before. Three billion young people will enter their reproductive years in the next twenty years. To sustain even a *nonpetroleum*-based, well-fed economy at current levels of affluence, it has been pointed out that the U.S. population should exceed no more than one hundred million people. We are, as of late 1997, at a petroleum-based population of 270 million. I can think of no better image of this steadfast pyramid of human consumers, this total population dynamic, than that of a mountain like Chomolungma (29,032 feet), cresting above the surrounding Himalayan roof of the world. Where the analogy abruptly ends, however, is with the adjectives appropriate to such a sacred mountain as Chomolungma: wild, free, and magnificent, descriptions that no longer apply to most of the world. Ironically, already Chomolungma herself is showing signs of wear. The effects of overpopulation are starkly clear. Since 1951, thousands of climbers and trekkers to the mountain have left some forty thousand pounds of nondecomposing refuse strewn upon what is, in fact, one of the most fragile of ecosystems, an eight thousand meter peak.

Some social scientists continue to ask, "At what point does the real population crisis set in? Or does it ever set in?" In parts of Egypt, that crisis has meant that school children obtain no more than three hours per day of instruction, so as to make way for incoming shifts of other students; in the Pacific Caroline Islands, the Yapese people were said to have been so overpopulated, and consequently destitute, that "families lived miserably on rafts in the mangrove swamps... and that sometimes four hungry men had to make a meal from a single coconut." In 1722, 111 people were left on Easter Island. Polynesians had settled there as early as the third century A.D., and had attained a stable population size of seven thousand. But excessive deforestation meant that no more fishing boats could be constructed, and the eventually malnourished population split into two warring tribes that only succeeded, ultimately, in virtually wiping one another out. Water scarcity in Pakistan, the absolute lack of new arable land in Kenya and Madagascar, are all crisis-level circumstances.

There is absolutely no doubting the links between human population growth—the daunting number of consumers—and environmental turmoil. It is known that, at a minimum, 75 percent of all global demand for fuelwood is the specific function of increasing numbers of consumers. By the year 2030, at least eight billion people will reside in countries previously—but no longer—containing tropical rain forests from which their primary sustenance had once been extracted. Global reforestation is occurring at only a fraction of what would be necessary to ensure long-term fuelwood supplies as against the exponential growth of human numbers. Ninety-four percent of all population growth in the coming decades will likely occur in those developing countries with the most impoverished resource base. In Pakistan, even by the late 1970s there was fuelwood scarcity. Yet Pakistan's population is poised to more than triple in size in the coming two generations, while only 2 to 3 percent of the country's forest cover remains. Where population is increasing most rapidly—from Myanmar to Cameroon—ecological deterioration tends to be the worst; and infant and child mortality, maternal mortality, and the extent of malnutrition and hunger, tend to be the highest.

The trends have long declared themselves. At present, for example, while the world population is growing by 1.8 percent per year, net grain output is growing at less than 1 percent per year. By the end of this century, the amount of arable land per person on the planet will be less than half of what it was in 1951. According to one model, because of the cumulative environmental impacts of overpopulation, global grain harvests will plummet by as much as 10 percent every forty months, on average, in the coming decades, and between fifty and four hundred million additional people will die from starvation.

Nor has this net food deficit been mollified by the nearly eight billion tons of additional artificial fertilizer spewed into the atmosphere each year in the form of carbon dioxide emissions, at least two-thirds of which are the explicit result of overpopulation (i.e., more automobiles and electrification). While future fossil fuel generation in the developed countries may be modified by gains in efficiency and the implementation of best available technologies, in the developing world per capita CO_2 emissions are projected to double in the coming generation. For governments in sub-Saharan Africa, where agricultural production has declined by more than 2 percent annually during the past twenty-four years, condemning at least thirty million people to starvation and chronic malnutrition, and 320 million others, or 65 percent of the total sub-Saharan population to "absolute poverty," such indicators are bewildering.

The sheer habit of finitude plagues any mind that attempts to reconcile seemingly irreconcilable conflict. We use the zero almost as casually as common change. But by 10^5—or one hundred thousand—we are no longer capable of visualizing the size. And this is precisely the point at which Aristotle, writing in Book VII of his *Politics*, suggested the emergence of a crisis in numbers. Human population, he said, is only in balance when it is "both self-sufficient and surveyable." Beyond that surveyable, self-sufficient size, Aristotle advocated, by any standards, hideous alternatives—compulsory abortion, and the mercy killing of children born deformed, though he did not stipulate what kind of deformities. But what does "surveyable" mean in the twentieth century? A man surveys his property. But what about a place like Macao, the most densely human-populated corner of the planet, with 61,383 individuals per square mile over a region of ten square miles? In an essay he named "Despair Viewed under the Aspects of Finitude and Infinitude," (part of his larger work, *On Fear and Trembling*), Soren Kierkegaard psychoanalyzed an individual attempting to survey the unsurveyable. We can't see in the infrared, hear ultrahigh frequencies, nor single ourselves out from a cluster of 5.8 billion other people. The effort leads to loneliness, a kind of ecological existentialism, or insanity.

All of our physical capabilities, desires, and metaphors are conditioned by the need for stability, a precursor of so many of our formulations, general principles, hypotheses, and behavior. Hence, demographers have tended to establish rather arbitrarily a point of stabilization for the human population, much in the manner of Hegel, whose "dialectic" presupposed eventual synthesis and resolution in the human psyche. The World Bank and United Nations have each predicated their respective population projections according to this general impulse, appropriating a formulaic optimism as a means of asserting the inevitability of classic demographic transition. But the whole mental image of humanity's developmental triumphs, the very hope of family planning, is totally absorbed by blue sky. While there is some exceedingly good news (the increasing number of countries showing fertility replacement trends, for example), there is just as much reason for a sinking heart, if not outright panic.

Global Shock

The bomb is now ticking. Every organism dimly perceives the growing shadow. In Oceanic Vanuatu the 1990 population of 151 thousand is expected to reach 205 thousand by the end of the 1990s. And, with its current high TFR [total fertility rate] of 5.53, the island population is expected to double by the year 2015, a mere generation away. Ten years later, in 2025 Vanuatu may well contain 348 thousand people. To feed and house such an increase in so small a region can only have the most devastating environmental consequences, reminiscent of Easter Island. Vanuatu is a surveyable problem. A dot in the ocean. And yet, even in this one workable microcosm, no solution to the population–environment collision has come to light.

Presently, eight to ten Paris-size cities a year are being added to the world's urban population. There is no way, as yet, to conduct real time population audits of these new megalopolises; no method by which the ecological or psychological impacts may be adequately measured. Too much is happening, too fast. Thought of differently, every eight months there is another Germany, every decade, another South America. And while TFRs throughout the developing world (China excluded) have declined from 6.1 to 4.0 on average, and overall population growth from 2.1 to 1.7–1.8 percent per year, getting these numbers down any further is appearing next to impossible. In fact, because the base population is so much huger than ever before, runaway growth is outstripping the aforementioned declines. The numbers, then, are tragically deceptive. For the human race to check its growth even at 16.5 billion, it will have to reach a two-child (replacement) family by the year 2080. In the United States, at present, only 23 percent of the population actually conforms to a two-child norm.

A global demographic transition assumes that declining fertility will follow declining mortality, an assumption that is proving to be less and less tenable in most low-income countries like Indonesia and India. These countries are stricken with an average sixty-two-year life expectancy, and a mean infant mortality of ninety-four per one thousand, versus eight per one thousand in the industrialized countries. More than half of the poor populations live in ecological zones that are biodiversity hotspots, those particularly vulnerable to further economically induced disruption. Eighty-five percent of all future megacities—ecological tinderboxes—are in the developing world. Each year, for example, Egypt, Ethiopia, and Nigeria add more people to the world than all of Europe combined. What we are seeing is the breakup of any predictability, just at the time when more and more government agencies and administrations are depending upon that presumed underlying orderliness to fulfill donor country targets, meet international treaty mandates, pay back loans, and get reelected. But ecological and economic fragmentation are rendering obsolete all classical demographic transition theory. Postindustrial fertility declines required a century in northwest Europe, but only thirty-five years throughout much of the Pacific Rim and Cuba. In Sri Lanka, China, and Costa Rica, diminished fertility did not coincide with noteworthy industrial development, whereas in Brazil and Mexico zealous industrialization has had little impact on continually escalating fertility rates.

By the year 2000, projections show that 1.2 billion women of reproductive age will have three children on average, and the number of those children under fifteen will have risen to 1.6 billion. By 2025 reproductive-age women will number 1.7 billion and their offspring also 1.7 billion. As technology enables women to conceive later in life, TFR data—sampled, typically, at one time—will tend to be less and less reliable. Moreover, male TFRs are yet to be accounted for. What this all means is that projections for future stabilization—be they population-oriented or ecological—are fraught with uncertainty.

Yet, according to the U.N., the U.S. Bureau of the Census, and the World Bank, demographic transition will effect a global human population stabilization in the middle of the coming century. According to an executive summary of a U.N. document from its Population Division, the range of human stabilization is between six billion (clearly impossible) and nineteen billion for the year 2100. These revised figures are based upon a replacement fertility rate of 2.06. But if fertility stabilization were just minutely higher, at 2.17, the world's population would hit nearly twenty-one billion in the year 2150! What is clearly terrifying to consider is that so minuscule an increase, multiplied by the human population over time, given all the current trends and variables, seems not only plausible, but dreadfully conservative. Demographers play a roulette game of chance. Yet, few people in government, or in science, dare to speak about a human population of twenty-one billion. Only the Vatican continues to uphold a belief that the world could carry on, even with forty billion people. Most scientists consider such convictions absurd. What is certain is the fact that human fertility is more combustible than ever before; its extent, advantage, brain power, carnivorous habits, footprint, hedonism, and malevolence, far in excess of the whole biological past combined.

What if, as outlined earlier, even the 2.17 figure is nothing more than demographic dreaming? What if a global average TFR of 3.0 persists, as it has for the past decade? After all, Africa is projected to remain at a TFR of six, its population expected to triple to 1.6 billion by 2025. And as of 1995, fifty-three countries still showed child mortality rates at or above one hundred per thousand. (In Europe, the average is thirteen.) Twenty countries in 1999 will still be officially considered malnourished, providing less than 90 percent of those respective populations' caloric requirements, engendering "stunting" and "wasting," as the conditions are known. And remarkably, sixty-eight countries containing 18 percent of the world's population are currently either maintaining or actually encouraging a rise in their fertility rates. The major population centers—India, China, Indonesia, and the U.S., which until recently prided themselves on family planning—are all losing ground to wave after wave of new baby booms. Given the enormity of the world's present fertility base, the triggers seem to be transcending culture or technology. They are purely mathematical. In spite of all the talk of environmental mediation, international family planning, and the very best intentions, such mathematics indicate a war that has gotten totally out of our control.

Projecting Into the Future?

Population projections are based upon a host of assumptions. If the assumptions are off to any extent, so are the projections. The variables are exasperating. For example, population momentum ensures that all growth will continue for many decades before any assumed new norms are likely to set in. Human disaster tends to work in favor of more and more people. In many countries, economic success is also translating into higher fertility rates, as witnessed in Singapore and China. And, as for the much-touted principle of education, in Kerala it has had a major impact on fertility, but less so in California, Mexico, or Malaysia. And in poor Mali, the literacy rate has actually declined in the past two decades, not risen.

The biggest contradiction inherent to all stablization projections is the very assumption that the human population will ever stabilize; or that the human condition is inevitably headed toward more wealth, more leisure, more security, when in fact all indications suggest the opposite. The standard of living, the so-called quality of life package, is rapidly diminishing for more and more people—billions of people in fact. Against such trends, how can anyone trust that fertility and mortality will eventually fall into some heavenly harmony? Economic and educational advantages are slipping for more people. On what grounds, then, can demography assume anything about demographic resolution?

Population experts have presumed that the conditions making for the most progressive region within a country will spread to all other regions in due time. In India and China these are doubtful deductions. For example, the replicability of the Tamil Nadu/Kerala TFRs, literacy rates, and IMRs [infant mortality rates] may not be possible in any other Indian states, in which case, if India continues to grow, it will double, triple, and quadruple its size within a time-frame that is projected, instead, to stabilize. Zimbabwe has achieved a rather progressive contraceptive prevalence rate of over 30 percent and yet its TFR is still a high 4.4. The region of Chogoria in central Kenya is a good percentile point below the rest of the country in terms of TFR, but its success does not appear to be spreading elsewhere throughout that nation.

The entire North American growth rate of an annual 0.9 is projected to decrease to 0.3 by 2025 as a result of diminished net migration from Latin America. Yet statistics from California, the country's most populous state, show a doubling of numbers (comparable to Uttar Pradesh) and an enormous increase in migration (not unlike the situation in India's Bihar state). The notion that the world's total fertility rate is projected to decline from 3.3 to 2.9 in seven years, and then to 2.4 by 2025 is based upon nothing more than vague institutional optimism. "For countries with high fertility, the trend is assumed to be downward, and substantial fertility decline is projected." Just like that!

Fifty countries currently show incomes under $610 per capita per year. Another fifty-five or so are lower-middle income, from $610 to $2399. Still another thirty-three countries are, by any Western standards, poor. These include the Czech Republic and Brazil. All of these nations demonstrate the very economic adversity that has traditionally lent itself to higher and higher birthrates, not declines. While declining fertility assumptions by the World Bank and others are said to have no predictive relationship to socioeconomic factors, those are precisely the factors that have held sway during the initial fertility transitions in the two most populous countries in the world, and now appear to be doing so, contrary to most expectations, in Kenya. And if one assumption is incorrect, many probably are. For example, a higher TFR value will skew the anticipated decline in the proportion of individuals under the age of fifteen, meaning a larger percentage of childbearing females, and thus a larger built-in population momentum than expected. Optimism on this stage of life is a house of cards. Thus, the editors of the World Bank Working Papers caution a "universal qualifer that population will follow the indicated path if the assumptions prove to be correct." And if the assumptions prove to be incorrect? Add a global recession and the mounting "trigger" of ecological collapse throughout the world, and all such population assumptions and projections go up in smoke.

To appreciate the sense of discrepancy that prevails within the demographic community, note that the World Bank Working Papers project that China will "remain the most populous country until 2120." Yet dozens of independent demographers all predict that India will overtake China within two generations. Like some macabre game of chicken: two conflicting sets of data race toward a brink, crossing over the domains of urban and rural health care, ecology, religion, anthropology, politics, the world market economy, the shifting geopolitical landscape, the engineering, biotechnology, and military sectors, even ecotourism and telecommunications. The falling market for coconuts, the rising value of tennis shoes, the Pope's travel itinerary, new emergent contraceptive technologies, the age of certain political leaders, the extent of groundwater pollution, the death of mackerel, daily calorie supply, the scope of infant immunization, secondary school enrollment, the rate of inflation, political freedom, and civil rights, all enter into the equation of demographic projection.

In a recent study of women in twelve countries, it was shown that breast-feeding beyond the resumption of menstruation and sexual relations, following a birth had a "considerable contraceptive effect." UNICEF says that breast-feeding could save 1.5 million lives a year, as well as sparing the 250 thousand children who are permanently blinded from vitamin A deficiency disease. Yet, few hospitals or doctors normally advocate breast-feeding as a form of contraception. And the same bias prevails with regard to the "rhythm method" which can be 97.5 percent effective, according to the World Health Organization. Even periodic abstinence has an 80 percent effectiveness rate, better than spermicides or sponges, about the same as a diaphragm, and just slightly less than the condom.

And yet, despite forty years of concentrated family planning worldwide, neither breast-feeding (which of course requires no genius, no literacy, no technology whatsoever) nor other natural methods have exerted the kind of population controls that many have hoped for. Experts argue it is because the educational component is lacking. Others attribute this missed opportunity to maternal morbidity, economic fallout, ecological stress, or lack of access to family planning services affecting at least three hundred million couples. During the decade of the 1990s, another one hundred million couples will need family planning services just to maintain the status quo. According to a WHO/UNFPA/UNICEF statement, every year thirteen million children die before their fifth birthday and five hundred thousand women die from pregnancy complications, but "with current technology, the majority of these deaths could be prevented."

There is no question that new technologies, and the greater application of existing ones, could alter the demographic outlook. UNICEF saves nearly two million children each year through the administering of measles vaccinations. Breast-feeding traditionally saves lives. But the demographic dangling modifier is more intractable than anyone ever imagined: Will such technologies and techniques increase or decrease the overall size of the human population, keeping in mind that it is precisely the advances in medical technology, the best-laid plans of humanitarianism, for example, that paved the way for India's and Africa's population booms?

Such data leaves the question wide open as to whether or not new technologies are likely to have any impact on curtailing fertility in the future.

Every factor influencing demographic projections confronts the same unknowable forces. Disaster breeds disaster. Medical technology devised and applied compassionately can inadvertently invoke even greater pain and suffering by keeping more people alive for longer periods and setting the groundwork for more and more children. Healthier children are understood to be the secret to few children. And yet, just the opposite can also be argued. There are no rules. Human nature, like every other force of nature, defies consistency.

And even where the highest TFRs might be expected eventually to come down (i.e., Rwanda from 6.2, Yemen from 7.2) other high TFRs are now going even higher—in Mozambique, Tanzania, and Niger, for example. And there are a host of other crucial quantitative observations that defy certitude or predetermination. For example, the World Bank estimates that by the year 2000 the developing world will suddenly start declining in growth—just like that. Why should it, coming right after the largest population growth rate in world history? And there are now the largest proportion of childbearing females ever! How can it be assumed that within one generation, twenty-two million fewer children will be born every year? The reason, of course, is that it simply "has to be" that way if fertility and mortality are going to even out, or harmonize, by the year 2150. This "harmony" is an arbitrary goal that says more about the human psyche and its perennial faith in the future, than it does about any hard science of numbers.

A good indication of the inherent vulnerability of such data is the total number of females in their childbearing years (fifteen to forty-four) as calculated in 1995 and again in 2150. In every significant country, there will be many more such women 155 years hence. Unless all other assumptions are fulfilled in the domains of health care, education, environmental remediation, and economic equality, these numbers indicate anything but stabilization.

In countries like Iran, Iraq, Pakistan, Egypt, India, Indonesia, Brazil, Mexico, Nigeria, the Philippines, Vietnam, and China, these inherent fertility faults in the smooth surface of mathematics—inherent volatilities of culture and economics, politics and religion, ecology and healthcare—provide no sure indication whatsoever of the planet's future. In China, 1998 will see 44 million girls added to the "teenage" sector, but in the year 2150, 53 million of them will be added. In India, overall there will be 260 million teenage girls in 1998, but in 2150, 370 million of them. In Malaysia, 1998 will see 3.5 million teenage girls, but the year 2150 will see over 8 million of them. In Pakistan, the gap is enormous: from a 1995 figure of 33 million teenage females to nearly 80 million females of childbearing age in 2150. Officials in many of these countries may insist all they like that there are no teen pregnancies, but the fact remains that millions of teenage girls are having babies and in nearly every country such teen pregnancies are on the rise, as they are dramatically in a place like Los Angeles.

Many of these young people, in over forty countries, in countless interviews and discussions with me, have expressed their common depression, sense of futility, and fatalism about the planet as they view it, adding fuel to their determination to enjoy life while they can. There are very few good arguments to dissuade them from having sex in a world where tigers and chimpanzees are going extinct. Even the prescriptions for "safe sex" lose cogency in a world so fraught with decay. Add to these intuitive syndromes one other astonishing fact: worldwide the average age of first menstruation is dropping! This trend corresponds with what must be seen as a global emphasis on earlier sex. Throughout Latin America, birthrates among teen mothers are extremely high—15 percent in El Salvador, for example. By the year 2000, there will be nearly 130 million teenagers in Latin America. Only 10 percent of them use any form of contraception, often erratically and hence, ineffectively. In Africa, 40 percent of all women have their first child before the age of eighteen. In at least one coastal district of Kenya, a country that has until recently placed a premium on female education, girls are getting married as early as the age of nine.

Only Brazil, among the fastest growing of large nations, will have a slightly lower fertile female count in the twenty-second century than it does now—by a few million. Yet, Brazil's population will have doubled from its 1990 figure of 150 million to over 300 million by then. Again, according to the "harmony" (stabilization) scenario, China's and India's populations are expected to become stable by the year 2150, at 1.8 and 1.85 billion respectively, while Indonesia is expected to reach 375 million at that time. *The Working Papers* see Indonesia's population doubling by the year 2110, yet some government officials within Indonesia see it happening by the year 2040. Even in a defined, relatively small area—Shenyang, China, for example—projections are at odds. Shenyang's Environmental Protection Bureau has declared the city's annual population growth rate to be 1.5 percent. The U.N., however, estimates a growth rate of exactly double that.

In sum, future contraceptive technologies and medical breakthroughs, increasing economic disparities, massive urbanization, emerging viruses susceptible to ecological disruption, a fast-growing population base among teenagers, and the unpredictability of fertility rebounds following disasters, all bode of population instability.

But, regardless of the imprecision and huge discrepancies of demographic projections, one unambiguous fact remains: the current size of the human population has wreaked unprecedented damage on the biosphere, and is going to accelerate that damage. Millions of plant and animal species will be driven to extinction. Hundreds of millions of innocent children, women, and men have been, and will be, slaughtered, in one form or another. A billion people are hungry. The ozone layer is thinning, with consequences that are lethal for every living organism. The air, water, and soil across the planet have been fouled. The forests in many countries are gone or nearly gone. And the mammary glands of every mother on Earth are now infiltrated with DDT and other harmful chemicals. These essential facts—truths that distinguish this century from any other in our history—are all the result of uncontrolled human fertility and thoughtless behavior. Even if we should somehow manage to merely double our population size by the next century, attaining, in other words, a number of twelve billion, the ecological damage will be catastrophic.

Oddly, despite this litany of woes, there is a new sense of ecological consciousness and stewardship throughout the world; a spirit of environmental community that is rapidly trying to mobilize in order to meet this disaster head-on. Whether a similar mobilization to meet the even more difficult crisis of as yet unborn children can be accomplished quickly, humanely, and firmly, will determine whether any kind of qualitative human future is even possible.

Max Singer

 NO

The Population Surprise

Fifty years from now the world's population will be declining, with no end in sight. Unless people's values change greatly, several centuries from now there could be fewer people living in the entire world than live in the United States today. The big surprise of the past twenty years is that in not one country did fertility stop falling when it reached the replacement rate—2.1 children per woman. In Italy, for example, the rate has fallen to 1.2. In Western Europe as a whole and in Japan it is down to 1.5. The evidence now indicates that within fifty years or so world population will peak at about eight billion before starting a fairly rapid decline.

Because in the past two centuries world population has increased from one billion to nearly six billion, many people still fear that it will keep "exploding" until there are too many people for the earth to support. But that is like fearing that your baby will grow to 1,000 pounds because its weight doubles three times in its first seven years. World population was growing by two percent a year in the 1960s; the rate is now down to one percent a year, and if the patterns of the past century don't change radically, it will head into negative numbers. This view is coming to be widely accepted among population experts, even as the public continues to focus on the threat of uncontrolled population growth.

As long ago as September of 1974 *Scientific American* published a special issue on population that described what demographers had begun calling the "demographic transition" from traditional high rates of birth and death to the low ones of modern society. The experts believed that birth and death rates would be more or less equal in the future, as they had been in the past, keeping total population stable after a level of 10–12 billion people was reached during the transition.

Developments over the past twenty years show that the experts were right in thinking that population won't keep going up forever. They were wrong in thinking that after it stops going up, it will stay level. The experts' assumption that population would stabilize because birth rates would stop falling once they matched the new low death rates has not been borne out by experience. Evidence from more than fifty countries demonstrates what should be unsurprising: in a modern society the death rate doesn't determine the birth rate. If

From Max Singer, "The Population Surprise," *The Atlantic Monthly*, vol. 284, no. 2 (August 1999). Copyright © 1999 by Max Singer. Reprinted by permission of *The Atlantic Monthly* and the author.

in the long run birth rates worldwide do not conveniently match death rates, then population must either rise or fall, depending on whether birth or death rates are higher. Which can we expect?

The rapid increase in population during the past two centuries has been the result of lower death rates, which have produced an increase in worldwide life expectancy from about thirty to about sixty-two. (Since the maximum—if we do not change fundamental human physiology—is about eighty-five, the world has already gone three fifths as far as it can in increasing life expectancy.) For a while the result was a young population with more mothers in each generation, and fewer deaths than births. But even during this population explosion the average number of children born to each woman—the fertility rate—has been falling in modernizing societies. The prediction that world population will soon begin to decline is based on almost universal human behavior. In the United States fertility has been falling for 200 years (except for the blip of the Baby Boom), but partly because of immigration it has stayed only slightly below replacement level for twenty-five years.

Obviously, if for many generations the birth rate averages fewer than 2.1 children per woman, population must eventually stop growing. Recently the United Nations Population Division estimated that 44 percent of the world's people live in countries where the fertility rate has already fallen below the replacement rate, and fertility is falling fast almost everywhere else. In Sweden and Italy fertility has been below replacement level for so long that the population has become old enough to have more deaths than births. Declines in fertility will eventually increase the average age in the world, and will cause a decline in world population forty to fifty years from now.

Because in a modern society the death rate and the fertility rate are largely independent of each other, world population need not be stable. World population can be stable only if fertility rates around the world average out to 2.1 children per woman. But why should they average 2.1, rather than 2.4, or 1.8, or some other number? If there is nothing to keep each country exactly at 2.1, then there is nothing to ensure that the overall average will be exactly 2.1.

The point is that the number of children born depends on families' choices about how many children they want to raise. And when a family is deciding whether to have another child, it is usually thinking about things other than the national or the world population. Who would know or care if world population were to drop from, say, 5.85 billion to 5.81 billion? Population change is too slow and remote for people to feel in their lives—even if the total population were to double or halve in only a century (as a mere 0.7 percent increase or decrease each year would do). Whether world population is increasing or decreasing doesn't necessarily affect the decisions that determine whether it will increase or decrease in the future. As the systems people would say, there is no feedback loop.

❦

What does affect fertility is modernity. In almost every country where people have moved from traditional ways of life to modern ones, they are choosing to have too few children to replace themselves. This is true in Western and in Eastern countries, in Catholic and in secular societies. And it is true in the richest parts of the richest countries. The only exceptions seem to be some small religious communities. We can't be sure what will happen in Muslim countries, because few of them have become modern yet, but so far it looks as if their fertility rates will respond to modernity as others' have.

Nobody can say whether world population will ever dwindle to very low numbers; that depends on what values people hold in the future. After the approaching peak, as long as people continue to prefer saving effort and money by having fewer children, population will continue to decline. (This does not imply that the decision to have fewer children is selfish; it may, for example, be motivated by a desire to do more for each child.)

Some people may have values significantly different from those of the rest of the world, and therefore different fertility rates. If such people live in a particular country or population group, their values can produce marked changes in the size of that country or group, even as world population changes only slowly. For example, the U.S. population, because of immigration and a fertility rate that is only slightly below replacement level, is likely to grow from 4.5 percent of the world today to 10 percent of a smaller world over the next two or three centuries. Much bigger changes in share are possible for smaller groups if they can maintain their difference from the average for a long period of time. (To illustrate: Korea's population could grow from one percent of the world to 10 percent in a single lifetime if it were to increase by two percent a year while the rest of the world population declined by one percent a year.)

World population won't stop declining until human values change. But human values may well change—values, not biological imperatives, are the unfathomable variable in population predictions. It is quite possible that in a century or two or three, when just about the whole world is at least as modern as Western Europe is today, people will start to value children more highly than they do now in modern societies. If they do, and fertility rates start to climb, fertility is no more likely to stop climbing at an average rate of 2.1 children per woman than it was to stop falling at 2.1 on the way down.

In only the past twenty years or so world fertility has dropped by 1.5 births per woman. Such a degree of change, were it to occur again, would be enough to turn a long-term increase in world population of one percent a year into a long-term decrease of one percent a year. Presumably fertility could someday increase just as quickly as it has declined in recent decades, although such a rapid change will be less likely once the world has completed the transition to modernity. If fertility rises only to 2.8, just 33 percent over the replacement rate, world population will eventually grow by one percent a year again—doubling in seventy years and multiplying by twenty in only three centuries.

The decline in fertility that began in some countries, including the United States, in the past century is taking a long time to reduce world population because when it started, fertility was very much higher than replacement level. In addition, because a preference for fewer children is associated with modern societies, in which high living standards make time valuable and children financially unproductive and expensive to care for and educate, the trend toward lower fertility couldn't spread throughout the world until economic development had spread. But once the whole world has become modern, with fertility everywhere in the neighborhood of replacement level, new social values might spread worldwide in a few decades. Fashions in families might keep changing, so that world fertility bounced above and below replacement rate. If each bounce took only a few decades or generations, world population would stay within a reasonably narrow range—although probably with a long-term trend in one direction or the other.

The values that influence decisions about having children seem, however, to change slowly and to be very widespread. If the average fertility rate were to take a long time to move from well below to well above replacement rate and back again, trends in world population could go a long way before they reversed themselves. The result would be big swings in world population—perhaps down to one or two billion and then up to 20 or 40 billion.

Whether population swings are short and narrow or long and wide, the average level of world population after several cycles will probably have either an upward or a downward trend overall. Just as averaging across the globe need not result in exactly 2.1 children per woman, averaging across the centuries need not result in zero growth rather than a slowly increasing or slowly decreasing world population. But the long-term trend is less important than the effects of the peaks and troughs. The troughs could be so low that human beings become scarcer than they were in ancient times. The peaks might cause harm from some kinds of shortages.

One implication is that not even very large losses from disease or war can affect the world population in the long run nearly as much as changes in human values do. What we have learned from the dramatic changes of the past few centuries is that regardless of the size of the world population at any time, people's personal decisions about how many children they want can make the world population go anywhere—to zero or to 100 billion or more.

POSTSCRIPT

Is World Population Growth Out of Control?

The population growth issue can be most simply structured as one of an insurmountable built-in momentum versus dramatic change in fertility attitudes and behavior. Tobias is correct when he asserts that "the world is adding [the equivalent of] a Los Angeles every three weeks." Furthermore, he is on target when he suggests that the population explosion of the latter part of the twentieth century has the potential of future fertility disaster because of the high percentage of the population that is either in the middle of or about to enter the reproductive years.

The key word here is *potential*. Its relevance grows out of the built-in momentum that has caused the developing world's actual population to rise substantially in the last 30 years despite a decline in the growth rate. According to the UN report *Population Growth, Structure and Distribution: The Concise Report* (1999), although the population growth rate dropped from a high of 2.04 percent in the late 1960s to 1.3 percent at the turn of the century, the world's population grew from a little over 3.5 billion people to 6 billion. Over 95 percent of this growth occurred in the developing world, where the rate of growth at its peak reached over 2.5 percent several decades ago. In 1998 the world population's net increase was about 78 million people every year.

Tobias suggests that the growth rate could continue on its present course, yielding 10 billion people by the year 2030, 20 billion by 2070, and 80 billion by 2150. He acknowledges, however, that a leveling-off figure advocated by most scientists of between 11 and 12 billion is a more realistic figure, although some have focused on a number closer to 20 billion. He likely overstates the probability of massive growth rates unseen in human history, however, when he suggests that "we have currently reached the base—not the top—of a demographic Mount Everest" and that "we are presently poised to proliferate as never before." Tobias bases his assessment on the large percentage of the world's population that is under the age of 24 (50 percent) or younger than 15 (one-third).

Singer contends that these latter groups of individuals will not produce at the same level as their parents and grandparents based on the evidence of the last quarter century. Two factors are at work here. The demographic transition is evident in those countries of the developing world that are experiencing economic growth. Birth rates have dropped significantly, leading to lowered growth rates. But while the rates are higher than those for the newly industrializing countries of the developing world, growth rates for the remaining developing countries have also dropped in a large number of cases. In the latter situation, policy intervention lies at the heart of the lowered rates. The latter effort has been spearheaded by the United Nations and includes the work of many nongovernmental organizations as well. In global conferences held every 10 years (1974, 1984, and 1994), the entire international community has systematically addressed the problem of fertility in the developing world, admittedly from different perspectives.

For Singer, the key is a change in human values: "Values, not biological imperatives, are the unfathomable variable in population predictions." The United Nations and other organizations have bought into this idea and are pursuing many initiatives to change the views of individuals in developing countries about the desirability of having large numbers of children.

The United Nations serves as an authoritative source on various population data, whether historical, current, or future oriented. One UN agency, the United Nations Population Fund (UNFPA), issues an annual *State of the World Population,* as well as other reports. Two private organizations, the Population Reference Bureau and the Population Institute (both based in Washington, D.C.), publish a variety of booklets, newsletters, and yearly reports. Admittedly, these sources tend to emphasize the continued urgency rather than the seeds of progress. Others focus on either success stories or the potential for success growing out of recent policy intervention. The Population Council (New York) and the Population Research Institute (Virginia) fall into the latter category.

For over a decade (until the death of one of the participants) two individuals took center stage in the debate over population growth and its implications. Paul R. Ehrlich led the call for vigorous action to curb population growth. His books *The Population Bomb* (Ballantine Books, 1968) and *The Population Explosion,* coauthored with Anne H. Ehrlich (Simon & Schuster, 1990) advanced the notion that the Earth's resource base could not keep pace with population growth; thus, the survival of the planet was brought into question. The late Julian L. Simon's *Population Matters: People, Resources, Environment, and Immigration* (Transaction, 1990) and *The Ultimate Resource 2* (Princeton University Press, 1996) challenge Ehrlich's basic thesis.

A succinct, centrist, and easily understandable analysis of the future of world population and its implications can be found in Leon F. Bouvier and Jane T. Bertrand, *World Population: Challenges for the Twenty-First Century* (Seven Locks Press, 1999). For an analysis of the different perspectives of the current population debate, see Frank Furedi, *Population and Development: A Critical Introduction* (St. Martin's Press, 1997).

ISSUE 2

Should the International Community Attempt to Curb Population Growth in the Developing World?

YES: Robert S. McNamara, from "The Population Explosion," *The Futurist* (November–December 1992)

NO: Julian L. Simon, from *The Ultimate Resource 2* (Princeton University Press, 1996)

ISSUE SUMMARY

YES: Robert S. McNamara, former president of the World Bank, argues that the developed countries of the world and international organizations should help the countries of the developing world to reduce their population growth rates.

NO: The late professor of economics and business administration Julian L. Simon maintains that international organizations seek to impose birth control methods on developing nations in the misguided name of "virtuous and humanitarian... motives."

The history of the international community's efforts to lower birth rates throughout the developing world goes back to the late 1960s, when the annual population growth rate hovered around 2.35 percent. At that time, selected individuals in international governmental organizations, including the United Nations, were persuaded by a number of wealthy national governments as well as by international nongovernmental population agencies that a problem of potentially massive proportions had recently emerged. Quite simply, demographers had observed a pattern of population growth in the poorer regions of the world quite unlike that which had occurred in the richer countries during the previous 150–200 years.

Population growth in the developed countries of the globe has followed a rather persistent pattern during the last two centuries. Prior to the Industrial Revolution, these countries typically experienced both high birth rates and death rates. As industrialization took hold and advances in the quality of life for citizens of these countries occurred, death rates fell, resulting in a period of time when the size of the population rose. Later, birth rates also began to decline, in large part because the newly industrialized societies were better suited to families with fewer children. After awhile, both birth and death rates leveled off at a much lower level than during preindustrial times. This changing pattern of population growth is known as the *demographic transition.*

This earlier transition throughout the developed world differed, however, from the newer growth pattern in the poorer regions of the globe observed by demographers in the late 1960s. First, the transition in the developed world occurred over a long period of time, allowing the population to deal more readily with such growth. On the other hand, more recent growth in the developing world has taken off at a much faster pace, far outstripping the capacity of these societies to cope with the changes accompanying such growth.

Second, the earlier growth in the developed world began with a much smaller population base and a much larger resource base than the developing world did, again allowing the richer societies to cope more easily with the dislocations caused by such growth. The developing world of the 1960s, however, found percentages of increase based on a much higher base. Coping under the latter scenario proved much more difficult. Moreover, available resources to assist in this coping, such as arable land, were far more abundant in the earlier period than today.

Finally, industrialization accompanied population change in the developed world, again allowing for those societies to address resultant problems more easily. Today's developing world has no such luxury. New jobs are not available, expanded educational facilities are nonexistent, unsatisfactory health services remain unchanged, and modern infrastructures have not been created.

The international community formally placed the population issue—defined primarily as excessive birth rates in the developing world—on the global agenda in 1974 with the first major global conference on population, held in Bucharest, Romania. But most of the poor countries resisted the argument of the wealthier nations that they had a problem. Those that accepted the notion pointed to economic development, not to formal fertility reduction programs, as the solution. Both sides eventually came to accept the other's description of the cause and cure of the problem and pledged to work together. Each bought into the assumption that "the best contraceptive was economic development," but until development was achieved, national family planning programs would help lower growth rates. This compromise was not universally accepted by all poor nations; some saw the motives of the developed world in this matter to be less than pure, a kind of ethnic genocide in its extreme.

In the first of the following selections, Robert S. McNamara argues that high population growth is exacerbating an already dire set of conditions in the developing world and that the industrialized countries of the globe should embark on a massive assistance program to help the "have not" countries reduce fertility. In the second selection, Julian L. Simon argues that organizations such as the United Nations Population Fund seek to impose birth control methods on the developing world in the misguided name of "virtuous and humanitarian . . . motives" while attacking the motives of their opponents.

Robert S. McNamara

 YES

The Population Explosion

For thousands of years, the world's human population grew at a snail's pace. It took over a million years to reach 1 billion people at the beginning of the last century. But then the pace quickened. The second billion was added in 130 years, the third in 30, and the fourth in 15. The current total is some 5.4 billion people.

Although population growth rates are declining, they are still extraordinarily high. During this decade, about 100 million people per year will be added to the planet. Over 90% of this growth is taking place in the developing world. Where will it end?

The World Bank's latest projection indicates that the plateau level will not be less than 12.4 billion. And Nafis Sadik, director of the United Nations Population Fund, has stated that "the world could be headed toward an eventual total of 14 billion."

What would such population levels mean in terms of alleviating poverty, improving the status of women and children, and attaining sustainable economic development? To what degree are we consuming today the very capital required to achieve decent standards of living for future generations?

More People, Consuming More

To determine whether the world—or a particular country—is on a path of sustainable development, one must relate future population levels and future consumption patterns to their impact on the environment.

Put very simply, environmental stress is a function of three factors: increases in population, increases in consumption per capita, and changes in technology that may tend to reduce environmental stress per unit of consumption.

Were population to rise to the figure referred to by Sadik—14 billion—there would be a 2.6-fold increase in world population. If consumption per capita were to increase at 2% per annum—about two-thirds the rate realized during the past 25 years—it would double in 35 years and quadruple in 70 years. By the end of the next century, consumption per capita would be eight times greater than it is today.

Some may say it is unreasonable to consider such a large increase in the per capita incomes of the peoples in the developing countries. But per capita income in the United States rose at least that much in this century, starting from a much higher base. And today, billions of human beings across the globe are now living in intolerable conditions that can only be relieved by increases in consumption.

A 2.6-fold increase in world population and an eightfold increase in consumption per capita by 2100 would cause the globe's production output to be 20 times greater than today. Likewise, the impact on non-renewable and renewable resources would be 20 times greater, assuming no change in environmental stress per unit of production.

On the assumptions I have made, the question becomes: Can a 20-fold increase in the consumption of physical resources be sustained? The answer is almost certainly "No." If not, can substantial reductions in environmental stress—environmental damage—per unit of production be achieved? Here, the answer is clearly "Yes."

Reducing Environmental Damage

Environmental damage per unit of production can—and will—be cut drastically. There is much evidence that the environment is being stressed today. But there are equally strong indications that we can drastically reduce the resources consumed and waste generated per unit of "human advance."

With each passing year, we are learning more about the environmental damage that is caused by present population levels and present consumption patterns. The superficial signs are clearly visible. Our water and air are being polluted, whether we live in Los Angeles, Mexico City, or Lagos. Disposal of both toxic and nontoxic wastes is a worldwide problem. And the ozone layer, which protects us all against skin cancer, is being destroyed by the concentration of chlorofluorocarbons in the upper atmosphere.

But for each of these problems, there are known remedies—at least for today's population levels and current consumption patterns. The remedies are costly, politically difficult to implement, and require years to become effective, but they can be put in place.

The impact, however, of huge increases in population and consumption on such basic resources and ecosystems as land and water, forests, photosynthesis, and climate is far more difficult to appraise. Changes in complex systems such as these are what the scientists describe as nonlinear and subject to discontinuities. Therefore, they are very difficult to predict.

A Hungrier Planet?

Let's examine the effect of population growth on natural resources in terms of agriculture. Can the world's land and water resources produce the food required to feed 14 billion people at acceptable nutritional levels? To do so would require a four-fold increase in food output.

Modern agricultural techniques have greatly increased crop yields per unit of land and have kept food production ahead of population growth for several decades. But the costs are proving to be high: widespread acceleration of erosion and nutrient depletion of soils, pollution of surface waters, overuse and contamination of groundwater resources, and desertification of overcultivated or overgrazed lands.

The early gains of the Green Revolution have nearly run their course. Since the mid-1980s, increases in worldwide food production have lagged behind population growth. In sub-Saharan Africa and Latin America, per capita food production has been declining for a decade or more.

What, then, of the future? Some authorities are pessimistic, arguing that maximum global food output will support no more than 7.5 billion people. Others are somewhat more optimistic. They conclude that if a variety of actions were taken, beginning with a substantial increase in agricultural research, the world's agricultural system could meet food requirements for at least the next 40–50 years.

However, it seems clear that the actions required to realize that capacity are not now being taken. As a result, there will be severe regional shortfalls (e.g., in sub-Saharan Africa), and as world population continues to increase, the likelihood of meeting global food requirements will become ever more doubtful.

Similar comments could be made in regard to other natural resources and ecosystems. More and more biologists are warning that there are indeed biological limits to the number of people that the globe can support at acceptable standards of living. They say, in effect, "We don't know where those limits are, but they clearly exist."

Sustainability Limits

How much might population grow and production increase without going beyond sustainable levels—levels that are compatible with the globe's capacity for waste disposal and that do not deplete essential resources?

Jim MacNeil, Peter Winsemaus, and Taizo Yakushiji have tried to answer that question in *Beyond Interdependence,* a study prepared recently for the Trilateral Commission. They begin by stating: "Even at present levels of economic activity, there is growing evidence that certain critical global thresholds are being approached, perhaps even passed."

They then estimate that, if "human numbers double, a five- to ten-fold increase in economic activity would be required to enable them to meet [even] their basic needs and minimal aspirations." They ask, "Is there, in fact, any way to multiply economic activity a further five to ten times, without it undermining itself and compromising the future completely?" They clearly believe that the answer is "No."

Similar questions and doubts exist in the minds of many other experts in the field. In July 1991, Nobel laureate and Cal Tech physicist Murray Gell-Mann and his associates initiated a multiyear project to try to understand how "humanity can make the shift to sustainability." They point out that "such a change, if it could be achieved, would require a series of transitions in fields ranging from technology to social and economic organization and ideology."

The implication of their statement is not that we should assume the outlook for sustainable development is hopeless, but rather that each nation individually, and all nations collectively, should begin now to identify and introduce the changes necessary to achieve it if we are to avoid costly—and possibly coercive—action in the future.

One change that would enhance the prospects for sustainable, development across the globe would be a reduction in population growth rates.

Population and Poverty

The developing world has made enormous economic progress over the past three decades. But at the same time, the number of human beings living in "absolute poverty" has risen sharply.

When I coined the term "absolute poverty" in the late 1960s, I did so to distinguish a particular segment of the poor in the developing world from the billions of others who would be classified as poor in Western terms. The "absolute poor" are those living, literally, on the margin of life. Their lives are so characterized by malnutrition, illiteracy, and disease as to be beneath any reasonable definition of human dignity.

Today, their number approaches 1 billion. And the World Bank estimates that it is likely to increase further—by nearly 100 million—in this decade.

A major concern raised by poverty of this magnitude lies in the possibility of so many children's physical and intellectual impairment. Surveys have shown that millions of children in low-income families receive insufficient protein and calories to permit optimal development of their brains, thereby limiting their capacity to learn and to lead fully productive lives. Additional millions die each year, before the age of five, from debilitating disease caused by nutritional deficiencies.

High population growth is not the only factor contributing to these problems; political organization, macroeconomic policies, institutional structures, and economic growth in the industrial nations all affect economic and social advance in developing countries. But intuitively we recognize that the immediate effects of high population growth are adverse.

Our intuition is supported by facts: In Latin America during the 1970s, when the school-age population expanded dramatically, public spending per primary-school student fell by 45% in real terms. In Mexico, life expectancy for the poorest 10% of the population is 20 years less than for the richest 10%.

Based on such analyses, the World Bank has stated: "The evidence points overwhelmingly to the conclusion that population growth at the rates common in most of the developing world slows development.... Policies to reduce population growth can make an important contribution to [social advance]."

A Lower Plateau for World Population?

Any one of the adverse consequences of the high population growth rates—environmentally unsustainable development, the worsening of poverty, and the negative impact on the status and welfare of women and children—would be reason enough for developing nations across the globe to move more quickly to reduce fertility rates. Taken together, they make an overwhelming case.

Should not every developing country, therefore, formulate long-term population objectives—objectives that will maximize the welfare of both present and future generations? They should be constrained only by the maximum feasible rate at which the use of contraception could be increased in the particular nation.

If this were done, I estimate that country family-planning goals might lead to national population-stabilization levels that would total 9.7 billion people for the globe. That is an 80% increase over today's population, but it's also 4.3 billion fewer people than the 14 billion toward which we may be heading. At the consumption levels I have assumed, those additional 4.3 billion people could require a production output several times greater than the world's total output today.

Reducing Fertility Rates

Assuming that nations wish to reduce fertility rates to replacement levels at the fastest possible pace, what should be done?

The Bucharest Population Conference in 1974 emphasized that high fertility is in part a function of slow economic and social development. Experience has indeed shown that as economic growth occurs, particularly when it is accompanied by broadly based social advance, birth rates do tend to decline. But it is also generally recognized today that not all economic growth leads to immediate fertility reductions, and in any event, fertility reduction can be accelerated by direct action to increase the use of contraceptives.

It follows, therefore, that any campaign to accelerate reductions in fertility should focus on two components: (1) increasing the pace of economic and social advance, with particular emphasis on enhancing the status of women and on reducing infant mortality, and (2) introducing or expanding comprehensive family-planning programs.

Much has been learned in recent years about how to raise rates of economic and social advance in developing countries. I won't try to summarize those lessons here. I do wish to emphasize, however, the magnitude of the increases required in family planning if individual countries are to hold population growth rates to levels that maximize economic and social advance.

The number of women of childbearing age in developing countries is projected to increase by about 22% from 1990 to 2000. If contraception use were to increase from 50% in 1990 to 65% in 2000, the number of women using contraception must rise by over 200 million.

That appears to be an unattainable objective, considering that the number of women using contraception rose by only 175 million in the past *two* decades, but it is not. The task for certain countries and regions—for example, India, Pakistan, and almost all of sub-Saharan Africa—will indeed be difficult, but other nations have done as much or more. Thailand, Indonesia, Bangladesh, and Mexico all increased use of contraceptives at least as rapidly. The actions they took are known, and their experience can be exported. It is available to all who ask.

Financing Population Programs

A global family-planning program of the size I am proposing for 2000 would cost approximately $8 billion, with $3.5 billion coming from the developed nations (up from $800 million spent in 1990). While the additional funding appears large, it is very, very small in relation to the gross national products and overseas development assistance projected for the industrialized countries.

Clearly, it is within the capabilities of the industrialized nations and the multilateral financial institutions to help developing countries finance expanded family-planning programs. The World Bank has already started on such a path, doubling its financing of population projects in the current year. Others should follow its lead. The funds required are so small, and the benefits to both families and nations so large, that money should not be allowed to stand in the way of reducing fertility rates as rapidly as is desired by the developing countries.

The developed nations should also initiate a discussion of how their citizens, who consume seven times as much per capita as do those of the developing countries, may both adjust their consumption patterns and reduce the environmental impact of each unit of consumption. They can thereby help ensure a sustainable path of economic advance for all the inhabitants of our planet.

Julian L. Simon **NO**

The Rhetoric of Population Control

Inflammatory Terminology and Persuasion by Epithet

Fear of population growth has been inflamed by extravagant language. Examples are the terms "population explosion," "people pollution," and "population bomb." These terms are not just the catchwords of popular wordsmiths, whose rhetoric one is accustomed to discount. Rather, they have been coined and circulated by distinguished scientists and professors. One example comes from demographer Kingsley Davis, who began a recent article in a professional journal, "In subsequent history the Twentieth Century may be called either the century of world wars or the century of the population plague." (Margaret Sanger also wrote of China that "the incessant fertility of her millions spread like a plague.") Davis also has said that "Over-reproduction—that is, the bearing of more than four children—is a worse crime than most and should be outlawed." Or biologist Paul Ehrlich: "We can no longer afford merely to treat the symptoms of the cancer of population growth; the cancer itself must be cut out." And it was in his Nobel Peace Prize speech, of all places, that agronomist Norman Borlaug spoke of "the population monster" and the "population octopus."

Writers vie with each other to find the ugliest possible characterization of human beings. From a Greenpeace leader, "[O]ur species [is] the AIDS of the Earth: we are rapidly eroding the immune system of the Earth." . . .

Such language is loaded, pejorative, and unscientific. It also reveals something about the feelings and attitudes of contemporary antinatalist writers. Psychiatrist Frederick Wertham pointed out that many of these terms have overtones of violence, for example, "bomb" and "explosion," and many show contempt for other human beings, such as "people pollution." Referring to expressions such as "these days of the population explosion and the hydrogen bomb" and "both nuclear weapons and population growth endanger mankind," he wrote, "The atomic bomb is the symbol, the incarnation, of modern mass violence. Are we justified in even speaking in the same vein of violent death and birthrate? And is it not a perverse idea to view population destruction and population growth as twin evils?"

There is no campaign of counter-epithets to allay the fear of population growth, perhaps because of a Gresham's law of language: Ugly words drive out sweet ones. Reasoning by epithet may well be part of the cause of the fear of population growth in the United States.

Not only epithets but also value-smuggling neologisms have been used against fertility. The term "childfree" is a neologism coined by NON—the National Organization for Non-Parents—as a replacement for "childless." Their intention is to substitute a positive word, "free," for a negative word, "less." This neologism is an interesting example of skillful propaganda. Whereas the term "less" is only slightly pejorative—you can have less of something good (love) *or* of something bad (acne)—the term "free" *always* seems better than "unfree," and one can only be free of something bad. If not having children makes you "free," then this clearly implies that children are bad. In a similar vein, you now hear people speak with pain of "wetlands lost," a phenomenon earlier referred to with pleasure as "swamps drained."

Phony Arguments, Crude and Subtle

Some of the antinatalist propaganda is subtle. While seeming to be only straightforward birth-control information, in reality it is an appeal to have fewer children. Planned Parenthood was responsible for such a campaign on television and radio. The campaign was produced by the Advertising Council as a "public service" and shown on television during time given free by the broadcasters as part of their quid pro quo to the public in return for their licenses; that is, it was indirectly paid for by taxpayers. The following is drawn from a letter written in complaint to the Advertising Council decision makers —the only letter they said that they had ever received.

> You may have seen an advertising campaign staged by Planned Parenthood that ran on radio, television, and in many national magazines. There were a number of specific ads in the campaign including one that was headlined "How Many Children Should You Have? Three? Two? One?"; another that adduced "Ten Reasons for Not Having Children" and, finally, the most offensive one was called the "Family Game": the game was staged on a great monopoly board and every time the dice of life were thrown and a child was born—rather like going to jail without passing "go"—the background audio announced the disasters that came in the wake of children—"there goes the vacation," or "there goes the family room. . . ."
>
> One of the ads enjoins young people to "enjoy your freedom" before, by having children, you let some of that freedom go. Such a theme . . . continues the view that the contribution children make to persons and to society is a purely negative one. In this view children are a loss: they take space, constrict freedom, use income that can be invested in vacations, family rooms, and automobiles. We find no consideration here of how children enhance freedom, and of how the advantages of freedom itself are realized when shared rather than prized as a purely personal possession. Finally, one of the ads encapsulates the spirit of the entire campaign: "How many children should a couple have? Three? Two? One? None?" Such an ad belies the claim that the advertising avoids the designation of any specific number of

children as "preferred." Why not 12? 11? 10? or six? five? four? In the same ad, in order to lead audience thinking, it is noted that the decision to have children "could depend on their concern for the effect population growth can have on society." The direction of the effect on society is implied, but nowhere is the effect analyzed, or even clearly stated.

In summary, the ads not only teach family planning but recommend population control. Moreover, they do this by defining the range of acceptable family size as between zero and three, by placing children as negative objects alongside the positive goods supplied by industry, by equating the bringing up of children with merely equipping them with these same goods, by viewing children as an essential constriction of human freedom, and by suppressing a view of life and children that might lead people to think that having more children is a positive and rewarding act. There are values, not just techniques embodied in those ads.

Not all antinatality rhetoric is that subtle. Some is crude name calling, especially the attacks on the Catholic church and on people with Catholic connections. An example is the bold black headline on the full-page ad that was run in national magazines: "Pope denounces birth control as millions starve." Another example is the dismissal of opposing views by referring to the happenstance that the opponent is Catholic. Consider, for example, the religion-baiting of Colin Clark—a world-respected economist who presented data showing the positive effects of population growth—by sociologists Lincoln and Alice Day: "Colin Clark, an internationally known Roman Catholic economist and leading advocate of unchecked population growth..." (Lincoln Day also likened me to a "defrocked priest.") And Jack Parsons writes, "Colin Clark, the distinguished Roman Catholic apologist... refrains from discussing optimization of population at all... an extraordinary omission." Gunnar Myrdal is not a Catholic and is a Nobel prize winner, and yet *he* called the concept of an optimum population level "one of the most sterile ideas that ever grew out of our science." But Parsons feels free to attribute religious motives to Clark's choice of technical concepts and vocabulary when Clark does not mention this "optimization" concept. And in the widely read text of Paul Ehrlich and others, *Population, Resources, and Environment*, we find a reference to Clark as an "elderly Catholic economist," an innovation in the name calling by referring to Clark's age as well as to his religion.

As a firsthand example in the same vein, my own views... were described by Paul Silverman, a biologist, before a packed auditorium on the first and greatest Earth Day, in 1970, as "inspired by Professor Simon's contact with the Bible.... Indeed, a new religious doctrine has been enunciated in which murder and abstinence from sex are not distinguishable."

Grabbing Virtue, Daubing With Sin

A rhetorical device of the antinatalists (as of all rhetoricians, I suppose) is to attribute to themselves the most virtuous and humanitarian of motives, while attributing to their opponents motives that are self-serving or worse. Biologist Silverman again: "... people such as Paul Ehrlich and Alan Guttmacher and presumably myself... out of our great concern for the future of the world and the threat to the quality of life... have urged that voluntary means be adopted for bringing about restraints on the overburdening of our environment by overpopulation.... We must, we can, and we will achieve a fine and beautiful world for ourselves and our children to inherit.... We can realize a new quality of life, free from avarice which characterizes our current society." (A few minutes before, the same speaker had said, "If voluntary restraints on population growth are not forthcoming, we will be faced with a need to consider coercive measures"—similar to Ehrlich's "by compulsion if voluntary methods fail.") (See my 1991 book, selection 58, for more discussion of how the population-control organizations assume the moral high ground and deny it to others.)

Why Is Population Rhetoric So Appealing?

Let us consider some of the reasons that antinatality rhetoric has won the minds of so many people. (For more extended discussion, see my 1991 book, selection 52.)

Short-Run Costs Are Inevitable, Whereas Long-Run Benefits Are Hard to Foresee

In the very short run, the effects of increased births are negative, on the average. If your neighbor has another child your school taxes will go up, and there will be more noise in your neighborhood. And when the additional child first goes to work, per-worker income will be lower than otherwise, at least for a short while.

It is more difficult to comprehend the possible long-run benefits. Increased population can stimulate increases in knowledge, pressures for beneficial changes, a youthful spirit, and the "economies of scale."... That last element means that more people constitute bigger markets, which can often be served by more efficient production facilities. And increased population density can make economical the building of transportation, communication, educational systems, and other kinds of "infrastructure" that are uneconomical for a less-dense population. But the connection between population growth and these beneficial changes is indirect and inobvious, and hence these possible benefits do not strike people's minds with the same force as do the short-run disadvantages.

The increase in knowledge created by more people is especially difficult to grasp and easy to overlook. Writers about population growth mention a greater number of mouths coming into the world, and even more pairs of hands, but they never mention more brains arriving. This emphasis on physical consumption and production may be responsible for much unsound thinking and fear about population growth.

Even if there are long-run benefits, the benefits are less immediate than are the short-run costs of population growth. Additional public medical care is needed even before the birth of an additional child. But if the child grows up to discover a theory that will lead to a large body of scientific literature, the economic or social benefits may not be felt for a hundred years. All of us tend to put less weight on events in the future compared with those in the present, just as a dollar that you will receive twenty years from now is worth less to you than is a dollar in your hand now.

The above paragraphs do not imply that, on balance, the effect of increased population will surely be positive in any longer-run period. The fact is that we do not know for sure what the effects will be, on balance, in fifty or one hundred or two hundred years. Rather, I am arguing that the positive effects tend to be overlooked, causing people to think—without sound basis—that the long-run effects of population growth *surely* are negative, when in fact a good argument can be made that the net effect *may* be positive.

Intellectual Subtlety of Adjustment Mechanisms

In order to grasp that there can be long-run benefits from additional people, one must understand the nature of a spontaneously ordered system of voluntary cooperation, as described by Mandeville, Hume, Smith, and their successors. But this is a very subtle idea, and therefore few people understand its operation intuitively, and believe explanations based on it.

Not understanding the process of a spontaneously ordered economy goes hand-in-hand with not understanding the creation of resources and wealth. And when a person does not understand the creation of resources and wealth, the only intellectual alternative is to believe that increasing wealth must be at the cost of someone else. This belief that our good fortune must be an exploitation of others may be the taproot of false prophecy about doom that our evil ways must bring upon us. (See below on the prophetic impulse.)

Apparent Consensus of Expert Judgment

Antinatalists convey the impression that *all the experts* agree that population is growing too fast in the United States and that it is simply a *fact* that population is growing too fast. An example from Lester Brown: "There are few if any informed people who any longer deny the need to stabilize world population." Other examples come from Paul Ehrlich, "Everyone agrees that at least half of the people of the world are undernourished (have too little food) or malnourished (have serious imbalances in their diet)." And, "I have yet to meet anyone familiar with the situation who thinks India will be self-sufficient in food by 1971, if ever." And from a *Newsweek* columnist and former high State Department official: "Informed men in every nation now know that, next to population growth and avoidance of nuclear war, the despoiling of nature is the biggest world problem of the next 30 years."

These "everyone agrees" statements are just plain wrong. Many eminent experts did not agree with them when they were made (and now the consensus disagrees with them . . .). But such assertions that "everyone agrees" may well be effective in manipulating public opinion. Which nonspecialist is ready to pit his or her own opinion against that of all the "informed people"?

Population as a Cause of Pollution

Fear of population growth is surely heightened by the linking of population and pollution issues. It has come to seem that if one is for pollution control then one must be against population growth. And pollution control in itself appeals to everyone, for very substantial reasons.

To understand why the link-up of population control and pollution control has occurred with such force, we must understand the nature of the rhetoric on both sides of the argument. One can directly demonstrate that more people increase the flow of a pollutant—for example, more cars obviously make more emissions. The argument that more people may reduce pollution is less direct and not so obvious. For example, as more people create a worse auto-emission pollution problem, forces of reaction arise that may eventually make the situation better than ever before.

Furthermore, the ill effects of people and pollution can be understood deductively. More people surely create more litter. But whether the endpoint after a sequence of social steps will be an even cleaner environment can only be shown by an empirical survey of experiences in various places: Are city streets in the United States cleaner now than they were one hundred years ago? Such empirical arguments are usually less compelling to the imagination than are the simplistic deductive arguments.

Population, Natural Resources, and Common Sense

With respect to natural resources, the population-control argument apparently makes perfect "common sense." If there are more people, natural resources will inevitably get used up and become more scarce. And the idealistic, generous side of young people responds to the fear that future generations will be disadvantaged by a heavy use of resources in this generation.

Perhaps such a doomsday view of natural resources is partly accounted for by the ease of demonstrating that more people will cause some particular negative effects—for example, if there are more Americans there will be less wilderness. The logic of the rebuttal must be global and much more encompassing than the logic of the charge. To show that the loss of wilderness to be enjoyed in solitude is not an argument against more people, one must show that an increase in people may ultimately lead to a general expansion of the "unspoiled" space available to each person—through easier transportation to the wilderness, high-rise buildings, trips to the moon, plus many other partial responses that would not now be possible if population had been stationary 100 years ago. It is obviously harder to show how good is the sum effect of these population-caused improvements than it is to show how bad is the partial effect of a decrease in this or that wilderness area that one may enjoy in solitude. Hence the result is a belief in the ill effects of population growth.

Judgments About People's Rationality

At the bottom of people's concern about population growth often lies the belief that other people will not act rationally in the face of environmental and resource needs. Arguments about the need to stop population growth now often contain the implicit premise that individuals and societies cannot be trusted to make rational, timely decisions about fertility rates. This is the drunkard model of fertility behavior. . . .

One of the themes that runs through much of the population movement is that the experts and the population enthusiasts understand population economics better than other persons do. As John D. Rockefeller III put it, "The average citizen doesn't appreciate the social and economic implications of population growth."

It is not obvious why a politician or businessman—even though a very rich one—should have a clearer understanding of the costs of bearing children than "an average citizen." But Rockefeller has much power to convert his opinion into national action.

Forces Amplifying the Rhetoric

Media Exposure

Antinatality views get enormously more exposure than pro-natality or neutralist views. Paul Ehrlich has repeatedly been on the Johnny Carson show for an unprecedented hour; no one who holds contrary views gets such media exposure. This is also clear from a casual analysis of the titles of articles listed in the *Reader's Guide to Periodical Literature.*

Money

The leaders of population agencies that have vast sums of money at their disposal—UNFPA and USAID—take as their goal the reduction of population growth in the poorer countries. Scientists who work in population studies and who have a reasonable degree of career prudence are not likely to go out of their way to offend such powerful potential patrons. Individuals and organizations hitch all kinds of research projects to this money-star. Furthermore, various agencies such as UNFAO realize that their own budgets will be larger if the public and government officials believe that there are fearsome impending dangers from population growth, environmental disaster, and starvation. Therefore, their publicity organs play up these threats.

Standards of Proof and of Rhetoric

The standard of proof demanded of those who oppose the popular view is much much more exacting than is the standard of proof demanded of those who share the popular view. One example: Decades ago the scientific procedure of the *Limits to Growth* study was condemned by every economist who reviewed it, to my knowledge. Yet its findings are still acclaimed and retailed by the "population community." But if I say that the world food situation has been improving year by year, you will either say "Prove it," or "I won't believe it." . . .

Furthermore, anti-doomsday people are in a double bind rhetorically. The doomsdayers speak in excited, angry, high-pitched voices, using language such as *Famine 1975!* They say that such tactics are acceptable because "we are faced with a crisis... the seriousness of which cannot be exaggerated." The fears they inspire generate lots of support money from the UN, AID, and popular fund-raising campaigns in full-page advertisements.

Many anti-doomsday people, on the other hand, speak in quiet voices—as reassurance usually sounds. They tend to be careful people. And they are totally ignored. The great geologist Kirtley F. Mather wrote a book called *Enough and To Spare* in 1944 that reassured the public that resources would be plentiful; it was withdrawn from the University of Illinois library just twice—in 1945 and 1952—prior to my 1977 withdrawal. But there are literally armfuls of books such as Fairfield Osborn's 1953 *Limits of the Earth* that have been read vastly more frequently. Even a book published by a vanity press and written by a retired army colonel who has Malthus's first name as "Richard" and who believes that *Overpopulation* (the title of the book) is a plot of the "Kremlin gangsters" had been withdrawn ten times between 1971 and 1980 (when I checked), and untold more times between its 1958 publication and 1971, when the charge slip was changed.

Finally—The Piper

Many of those in favor of population control are frank to admit the use of emotional language, exaggerated arguments, and political manipulation.... They defend these practices by saying that the situation is very serious.

Would the environment have gotten cleaner without the exaggerated and untrue scary statements made by the doomsayers starting in the late 1960s? Perhaps they helped speed the cleanup of our air and water—perhaps. But without false alarms, Great Britain started on its cleanup earlier than did the United States, and went further, faster. And even granting some credit to the doomsayers, were the benefits worth the costs? Billions of dollars were wasted preparing the airplane industry for $3-per-gallon gasoline, and tens of billions wasted worldwide on raw materials purchased in fear that metal prices would soar.

Much more expensive was the loss of public morale and the spirit of adventurous enterprise due to false environmental scares. And most costly, in my view, has been the inevitable loss of trust in science and in our basic institutions as people realized that they had been systematically fooled.

Exaggeration and untruth run up debts with the piper, who eventually gets paid. Philip Handler, president of the National Academy of Sciences, was a strong supporter of environmental and population control programs. But even he worried about the piper.

> It is imperative that we recognize that we know little and badly require scientific understanding of the nature and magnitude of our actual environmental difficulties. The current wave of public concern has been aroused in large measure by scientists who have occasionally exaggerated the all-too-genuine deterioration of the environment or have overenthusiastically made demands which, unnecessarily, exceed realistically realizable—or even desirable—expectations....

> The nations of the world may yet pay a dreadful price for the public behavior of scientists who depart from ... fact to indulge ... in hyperbole.

As far back as 1972, John Maddox, the long-time editor of *Nature*, warned that

> [T]here is a danger that much of this gloomy foreboding about the immediate future will accomplish the opposite of what its authors intend. Instead of alerting people to important problems, it may seriously undermine the capacity of the human race to look out for its survival. The doomsday syndrome [the name of his book] may in itself be as much a hazard as any of the conundrums which society has created for itself.

This may already have come to pass. In 1992 Theodore Roszak refers to himself as one of "those of us who presume to act as the planet's guardians" and who agrees that "the important thing is to spread the alarm" because "there is no question in my mind that these problems are as serious as environmentalists contend." He finds himself taken aback by physician Helen Caldicott's warning that "every time you turn on an electric light you are making another brainless baby" because nuclear power is the cause of anencephalic births along the Mexican border. "Despite my reservations, I do my best to go along with what Dr. Caldicott has to say—even though I suspect ... that there is no connection between light bulbs and brainless babies." But he worries that "a fanatical antienvironmental backlash [is] now under way" because of the exaggerations and falsehoods.

Were it occurring, a fanatical backlash would not be a good thing; fanaticism of any kind will be destructive in these matters, where cool scientific consideration of the evidence is so desperately needed to assess dangers of all kinds. But this is what Handler and Maddox warned of—the piper that will finally be paid for untruths about population, resources, and environment.

This raises the question: To what extent is the current public belief that the U.S. economy and society are on the skids related to false doomsday fears that we are running out of minerals, food, and energy? And to the unfounded belief that the United States is an unfair plunderer of the world's resources, a supposed "exploitation" that people believe must bring grave consequences for the United States?

And when we count the costs of the doomsayers' excesses we must remember the tragedy of the human lives not lived because countries such as China and Indonesia prevent births in the name of the now-discredited doctrine that population growth slows economic development. It will fall to the future historian to balance the questionable benefits against those undeniable costs.

POSTSCRIPT

Should the International Community Attempt to Curb Population Growth in the Developing World?

There are at least two basic dimensions to this issue. First, ought the international community involve itself in reducing fertility throughout the developing world? That is, is it a violation of either national sovereignty (a country should be free from extreme outside influence) or human rights (an individual has the right to make fertility decisions unencumbered by outside pressure, particularly those from another culture)? Second, can the international community be successful in such policy intervention, or is it just a waste of money?

McNamara assumes that the answer to the first question is "yes" and addresses the second by linking population growth and increases in resource consumption. For McNamara, a 2.6-fold increase in population and an 8-fold increase in consumption per capita (by the end of the twenty-first century) would result in a 20-fold impact on nonrenewable and renewable resources. He cites the projected agricultural needs to demonstrate that the Earth cannot sustain such consumption levels. Additionally, McNamara suggests that other consequences include environmentally unsustainable development, worsening of poverty, and negative impacts on the welfare of women and children.

Those who oppose such intervention point to several different reasons. The first, originally articulated at the 1974 Bucharest conference, argues that economic development is the best contraceptive. The demographic transition worked in the developed world, and there is no reason to assume that it will not work in the developing world. Second, some who oppose intervention simply do not see the extreme negative environmental consequences of expanding populations. For them, the pronatalists (those favoring fertility reduction programs) engage in inflammatory discourse, exaggerated arguments, and scare tactics devoid of much scientific evidence. Simon suggests why such approaches are appealing at first but fall apart upon further analysis. For him, humans have always found a way to fulfill increased resource needs: technological fixes have been the norm since the start of the industrial age.

An excellent account of the 1994 Cairo population conference's answer to how the international community ought to respond can be found in Lori S. Ashford's "New Perspectives on Population: Lessons From Cairo," *Population Bulletin* (March 1995). Other sources that address the question of the need for international action include William G. Hollingsworth's *Ending the Explosion: Population Policies and Ethics for a Humane Future* (Seven Locks Press, 1996) and Elizabeth Liagin's *Excessive Force: Power, Politics, and Population* (Control Information Project for Africa, 1996).

ISSUE 3

Does Population Growth Significantly Harm the Earth's Quality of Life?

YES: Don Hinrichsen, from "6,000,000,000 Consumption Machines," *International Wildlife* (September/October 1999)

NO: N. Gregory Mankiw, from "Be Fruitful and Multiply," *Fortune* (September 7, 1998)

ISSUE SUMMARY

YES: Don Hinrichsen, an environmental reporter and a consultant for the United Nations Population Fund, argues that the planet's natural systems and ecological systems are having increasing difficulty withstanding the negative consequences of continuing population growth.

NO: Economics professor N. Gregory Mankiw maintains that, assuming each additional person on Earth creates resources, if the amount created by each new individual is greater than the amount used by that individual, then the Earth's quality is enhanced by the presence of that individual.

Intuitively, many people, perhaps even a significant majority, are likely to agree that population growth significantly harms the Earth's quality of life. After all, one need look no further than the highway during morning rush hour to find a poignant reminder of the effects of an ever-increasing population. "No vacancy" signs at popular destinations seem to appear with increasing frequency. The waiting lines at the checkout counter, the movie theater, and the amusement park appear to be evidence of a growing population. The list seems endless.

Scholars and policymakers in certain quarters mirror the initial intuition displayed by most people who find themselves in situations like those mentioned above. These activists point to many presumed consequences of population growth as evidence of a declining quality of life associated with such growth. Other researchers argue that a particular population characteristic, such as an absolute size or a certain rate of growth, is neither good nor bad. It is only when this characteristic is combined with something else—too few jobs, insufficient food, inadequate housing, overcrowded schools—that the population condition is vilified. In these circumstances, cries abound to "do something" so that the corresponding nonpopulation condition can be eliminated and one's quality of life can be improved.

Indeed, population growth rates in the developing world were such a cause for concern that the global community formally placed the issue on its agenda in 1974 by holding the first major global conference on population in Bucharest, Romania, and it has continued to expend substantial resources in addressing the problem. Simply put, it was the belief that population growth at both personal and national levels is strongly associated with poverty and a lack of development that spurred world leaders to take action.

It is instructive that the international community has recently revisited its original thesis about the link between growth rates and poverty. For example, an increasing "revisionist" literature that questions whether or not growth and poverty are as intertwined as previously thought is emerging. Also, if the 1974 population conference was informally called an economic development conference because of its emphasis on such development, the 1994 population conference, which was held in Cairo, might properly be termed a women's empowerment conference. One would have been hard-pressed at Cairo, for example, to find mention of the growth-poverty nexus. Instead, the more recent conference focused almost entirely on giving women control of their "minds, bodies and pocketbooks."

This viewpoint about the lack of an association between the rather specific condition of poverty and underdevelopment on the one hand and high population growth on the other repeats itself in more general terms in countless ways. However, the arguments take two basic forms. One, the impact of growth is difficult to measure precisely, and examples presented by its advocates are simply random impressions. Critics who utilize this reasoning argue that the world is much too complex to suggest such a simple paradigm. To them, poverty can just as easily be explained by the lack of capital, bad physical environment, unscrupulous leaders, or the "luck of the draw."

The line of reasoning in the second argument takes the dispute to a higher level of disagreement. To this group of critics, not only is increased population not harmful to one's quality of life, its consequences are essentially positive. For example, more people means more consumption, which means more jobs and more profits. More people also suggests more minds at work solving humankind's major problems, such as finding a cure for cancer. And more American workers means a more secure social security system.

The following selections are at opposite ends of the argument about population growth and quality of life. Don Hinrichsen uses the occasion of the recent birth of "Earth's six billionth human," the one putting the planet's present population over the 6 billion mark, to highlight the strains placed by continuing growth on the planet's vital systems. N. Gregory Mankiw, in contrast, advances the position that the one factor that is clearly associated with world population increases has been and continues to be higher standards of living for Earth's inhabitants.

Don Hinrichsen

 YES

6,000,000,000 Consumption Machines

Sometime on October 12, 1999—most likely in China or India, according to demographic probabilities—the Earth's six billionth human [was] born.

As a consumer of water and food, forest products and clean air, animals and the ocean's bounty, this newborn will make but a tiny dent on natural resources during its sojourn on the planet. But put Baby Six Billion together with all the other human consumption machines already here, and alarm bells go off.

Can Earth's natural resources and ecological systems withstand the additive impact of this latest member of our species? Worse yet, what will happen in the year 2025, when Baby Eight Billion is projected to be born?

If this latest addition to the human family arrives in a developed country —say, the United States—he or she will automatically be in the top 20 percent of the human race, at least in terms of good housing, potable water, proper sanitation, a high school or college education, sound medical care, jobs, disposable income and leisure time. But Baby Six Billion will also be part of an elite that consumes in record numbers. In all, 270 million Americans use up nearly 10 billion metric tons of materials a year, 30 percent of the planet's total. And the world's one billion richest people—which also include Europeans and Japanese, among others—consume 80 percent of the Earth's resources.

If, on the other hand, Baby Six Billion is indeed born in the Third World, where three-quarters of humanity is already concentrated, he or she stands a good chance of being thrown into misery and deprivation. One-third of Earth's people—two billion of them—already subsist on just $2 a day or less. Half of all people on Earth have improper sanitation facilities. A quarter have no access to clean water. A third live in substandard housing, many in tin-roofed shacks with dirt floors. A sixth will never learn to read, and 30 percent who enter the global workforce will never get adequate job opportunities. The other five billion people on Earth make do with just 20 percent of the planet's resources.

Rising expectations and the inevitable quest for improved living conditions in the Third World are likely to exacerbate this assault on resources. The average American consumes 37 metric tons of fuels, metals, minerals, food and forest products each year. By contrast, the average Indian consumes less than one metric ton. According to the United Nations, if the entire population of the Earth were to have the same level of consumption as the average American or West European, it would take three Planet Earths to supply the necessary resources.

Regardless of where Baby Six Billion [was] born, he or she will contribute to the relentless collective consumption that continues to devour global resources at rates most experts say are nonsustainable. And in the process, the human newcomer—along with his 5,999,999,999 companions—will produce enormous quantities of waste.

Whether Earth has the ability to absorb more people and provide for their ever-growing needs is not a closed question. Some technocrats have argued that the Earth's greatest resource is the innate capacity of human beings to invent or engineer their way out of population and resource crises. If that is so, however, human ingenuity is not keeping pace with human consumption as measured in the degradation of virtually every natural system—from the chilly North Atlantic with its vital fisheries to the steamy rain forests of Amazonia with their incomparable array of plants and animals.

When all is said and done, human activities caused by population growth and consumption patterns are taking a heavy toll on our planet's life-support systems—and on Earth's other species, which are disappearing at record rates as human numbers rise. The following report looks at the collective effect of six billion consumption machines on six aspects of the natural world. It is a grim picture, with only flashes of hope.

Water

Squandering the Planet's Lifeblood

Water is the liquid of life. Without it, the blue planet would be a dead and barren wasteland. Fresh water is also the most finite of Earth's resources. There is no more water on Earth now than there was 2,000 years ago when the human population was less than 3 percent of its current size. But population growth and rising use have put the squeeze on available resources.

Today, 31 countries with a collective population of half a billion people are experiencing chronic water shortages for all or part of the year. But within just 25 years, that figure will explode to 50 countries and 3 billion people—35 percent of all the people projected to be living on Earth in 2025.

Experts cite two reasons for this drastic increase: population growth plus the increasing demands of agriculture, industry and urban areas. During this century, the world's population has tripled, while the amount of water withdrawn from the planet's finite total has increased by more than six times. Since 1940, annual use of water has grown twice as fast as global population.

While population growth and escalating consumption patterns mean there is less water available per person, water resources are increasingly fouled with all manner of wastes. These include raw sewage and garbage from urban areas, toxic industrial effluents and such agricultural runoffs as fertilizers, pesticides and animal wastes. The UN Food and Agriculture Organization (FAO) estimates that each year roughly 450 cubic kilometers of wastewater—an amount equal to the entire renewable freshwater resources available to Malaysia on a yearly basis—are discharged into rivers, streams and lakes. More than 13 times that amount of clean water is required just to dilute and transport this dirty water. If current trends continue, the FAO projects, the world's entire river flow will be needed just for pollution transport and dilution by the middle of the twenty-first century.

As a global average, agriculture accounts for the lion's share (70 percent) of water taken for human use. Farming also accounts for the largest amount (70 percent in the U.S. and Europe, 50 to 60 percent in developing countries) of pollution to surface and ground waters. Disease carried by dirty water kills more than 12 million people a year, mostly women and children. And nearly all these deaths take place in the Third World.

There is another sinister side to the water crisis. As of 1996, the world's human population was expropriating 54 percent of all the accessible fresh water contained in rivers, lakes and underground aquifers. By 2025, population growth alone will push this figure to 70 percent. As humankind withdraws more and more water to satisfy its unquenchable thirst, less is available to maintain vital wetlands, like the Everglades in Florida.

The wholesale loss and degradation of life-giving riverine, lake and wetland habitats translates to a dramatic decline in populations of other species. Globally, close to one-quarter of all freshwater fish species are either endangered, vulnerable or on their way to extinction. Southeast Asia's Mekong River alone reports a two-thirds drop in fish catch due to dams, deforestation and the conversion of nearly 4,000 square miles of mangrove swamps into rice paddies and fish ponds.

Caught between finite and increasingly polluted water supplies on one hand and rapidly rising demand from population growth and development on the other, many countries face uneasy choices. The World Bank warns that the lack of fresh water is likely to be one of the major factors limiting economic development in the decades to come. It is also likely to spawn wars.

Forests

Earth's Green Lungs Begin to Fade

The earth's green mantle of forests provides humankind with multiple benefits. Forests absorb carbon dioxide and produce oxygen, regulating climate. They anchor soils and prevent erosion. They regulate water flow and protect watersheds. And they provide habitat for countless species of plants and animals. Yet over the course of the past half century, this green mantle has been reduced to tattered remnants.

Currently, about 39.5 million acres of forest, an area roughly the size of Nepal, are cut, bulldozed or burned each year. According to the World Resources Institute (WRI), an environmental think tank based in Washington, D.C., half of the world's original forest cover has been lost, with most of the destruction taking place during the last four decades. WRI reports that only one-fifth of the world's remaining forests are classified as "frontier forests"—pristine areas that have not been disturbed or degraded by human activities.

In Europe, despite green belts and conservation areas, only a tiny patch of the continent's original forest remains, cloistered in Bialowieza National Park in southeast Poland, hard against the border with Belarus. Here 1,000-year-old linden, oak and hornbeam stand cathedral-like—silent reminders of what has been lost irrevocably. Old-growth forests in the United States have been decimated, too; in the contiguous 48 states, 99 percent of frontier forests are gone —an empty echo of what once was.

Most experts link the loss of such forests, directly or indirectly, to human population growth and the insatiable demands of people. Lester Brown of the Washington-based Worldwatch Institute, which monitors human use of resources, reckons that 75 percent of the historical growth of population and 75 percent of the loss in global forest cover has taken place in the twentieth century. "The correlation makes sense," reasons Brown, "given the additional need for farmland, pastureland and forest products as human numbers expand. But since 1950, the advent of mass consumption of forest products has quickened the pace of deforestation."

In the Third World, conversion of forest resources to meet everyday human needs is significant. Dirk Bryant, a senior researcher at WRI, estimates that fuelwood collection and overgrazing by domestic animals are now responsible for degrading about 14 percent of the world's remaining frontier forests, nearly all of which—disregarding northern Canada and Russia—are found in developing countries.

But the relentless and rapidly escalating consumption of forest products by rich countries is also responsible for whittling away much of the remaining pristine forests. The use of paper and paperboard per person has nearly tripled since 1960, with the developed countries of North America, Europe and Asia accounting for most of it. North America, Europe and Japan, with just 16 percent of the global population, consume two-thirds of the world's paper and paperboard and half of its industrial wood.

Researchers at Friends of the Earth in the United Kingdom have determined that humanity's demand for forest products is already 25 percent beyond the point of sustainable consumption. What this means is that given population and income growth in the developing world and continued demand for forest products in the industrialized world, the future of the world's frontier forests and all the ecosystem benefits they provide to humankind are in jeopardy.

Soils

From Bare Earth: Hunger Amid Plenty

The world's topsoils, the "bottom line" in food production, are increasingly eroded and degraded by the demands both of large-scale mechanized agriculture and the desperate needs of subsistence farmers. We could be entering what some experts call the "century of scarcity," as rising demand for food is paralleled by a corresponding drop in supply.

Food shortages may seem an incredulous idea to those who subscribe to the "horn of plenty" scenario of agricultural productivity. After all, since the end of World War II, food production has tripled while population has only doubled. And the daily calories available per person in the Third World have increased from an average of 1,925 in 1961 to 2,540 in 1992.

Yet the prospects are unsettling. Much of the expansion of food production since the post-war days is explained by the adoption of crop rotation, mass production, use of petroleum-based fertilizers, chemical pesticides and expanded irrigation. Since the early 1960s, the introduction of genetically superior, disease-resistant cultivated crops—a signature part of what is known as the Green Revolution—also contributed heavily to food-production gains. But many of these successes have been accompanied by a downside—widespread land abuse and inappropriate agricultural policies, including $228 billion worth of subsidies spent on price supports and outright payments.

The gains in food output are not universal either: There is still widespread hunger in the midst of this plenty. The world has 840 million chronically malnourished people, mostly women and children, while an additional one billion suffer from protein malnutrition. Also, despite slower rates of population growth over the past decade, grain supplies per capita have actually fallen worldwide.

Declines in food production are particularly critical in many poor countries. Between 1985 and 1995, food production lagged behind population growth in 64 out of 105 developing countries. Africa, where food production per person fell in 31 out of 46 nations, fared the worst of all. It now produces nearly 30 percent less food per person than it did in 1970.

The change in direction in food availability in these areas is due primarily to two trends. On the one hand, rapid population growth and changing diets have increased demand. On the other, higher population densities in traditional agricultural areas, fragmentation of small farmsteads, poor land management and inappropriate agricultural and economic policies have suppressed supply.

Together, population growth, rapid urbanization and land degradation have also combined to reduce the amount of food-producing land available for each person on Earth. In developing countries as a whole, the average amount of arable land per person fell from about 0.3 hectares (a hectare equals 2.47 acres) in 1961 to less than 0.2 hectares in 1992.

On top of these alarming developments, nearly 2 billion hectares of crop and grazing land—an area larger than the United States and Mexico combined—suffer from moderate to severe soil degradation. The main causes are soil erosion, loss of nutrients, damage from inappropriate farming practices (including poorly built irrigation systems) and the misuse of agricultural chemicals. In the Philippines, for instance, nearly one-quarter of all cropland has been severely degraded.

According to WRI projections, by 2025 about 3 billion people, 35 percent of the global population, will live in land-short countries, with less than 0.07 hectares of fertile land per person. That is roughly the size of two tennis courts.

Air

Dark Skies, Changing Climates

Clean air is the life-giving resource most people take for granted. Yet increasingly, as human population spirals and consumption rises, the air we breathe is becoming both an agent of illness and the vehicle for modifying Earth's climate.

Few experts dispute the simple fact that more people means more air pollution. Even with the availability of vastly improved technologies to limit pollution, population growth translates directly into more use of energy, more cars on the road, more factories and hence more dirty urban air.

In turn, that often results in severe health problems. Today, more than one billion people suffer from dangerously high air-pollution levels. Most of those live in sprawling Third World cities where industries and power plants have few, if any, pollution controls and where traffic jams are a perpetual feature of urban life. Up to 700,000 of those people die every year from the air they breathe.

Cities such as Bangkok, Manila and Beijing are often entombed in a sickening pall spewed out from a rapidly growing fleet of vehicles and uncontrolled industrial emissions. In these cities and 17 others, air pollution—most commonly in the form of sulfur oxides, oxides of nitrogen, carbon monoxide and ozone—is one of the leading causes of respiratory infections and premature death. Just breathing the air in Mexico City has the same health effect as smoking three packs of cigarettes a day.

On the consumption side, the distribution of energy is uneven. Currently, the richest fifth of humanity consumes close to 60 percent of the world's energy, while the poorest fifth uses just 4 percent. The benefits of the fossil-fuel revolution, which drives industrial nations, have still not reached a full third of humanity—the two billion people who must burn fuelwood and organic waste for heating, cooking and lighting.

The other side of the atmospheric pollution problem is climate change, often called global warming. When carbon from burning of wood, coal, oil and other fossil fuels is released into the atmosphere, it combines with oxygen to form carbon dioxide, the gas responsible for two-thirds of human-induced changes in the world's climate. Atmospheric concentrations of carbon dioxide in 1997 reached 363.6 parts per million, the highest in more than 160,000 years. Altogether, carbon emissions are rising faster than the rate of population growth. In 1997, according to the Worldwatch Institute, global emissions of carbon totaled 6.3 billion tons. Since 1950, world carbon emissions have increased fourfold. Though western industrialized countries currently account for close to half this output, developing countries have increased their share dramatically in the past decade and are collectively responsible for 40 percent of global carbon emissions. China is now the world's second largest emitter, after the United States, with a 14 percent share.

Over the course of the next century, atmospheric concentrations are expected to double, triggering potentially devastating climatic changes on a regional and global scale. By 2100, according to the U.S. National Academy of Sciences, sea levels may rise by up to one meter, inundating vast swaths of coastal land, while average surface temperatures may increase by up to 3.5 degrees Celsius. Destabilization of the Earth's climate engine is expected to result in more intense heat waves, more severe droughts and floods, more devastating storms (tornadoes and hurricanes) and more frequent forest fires. These events, in turn, can add to the problem. The six months of extensive forest fires in Asia in 1997 and 1998 released more carbon into the atmosphere than Western Europe emits in an entire year.

Oceans

Trouble in Earth's Liquid Heart

Oceans, where life first evolved 3.5 billion years ago, cover 70 percent of the globe's surface. They wrap around the planet like an insulating blanket, making life possible on Earth today.

Oceans are the engines that drive the climate, defining weather and storing huge quantities of solar energy. They also make up the liquid heart of the planetary hydrological cycle, enabling roughly 430,000 cubic kilometers of water to evaporate every year.

But even this vast watery world is coming under increasing pressure from human activities. Just over half of humanity—some 3.2 billion people, according to some estimates—live and work within 120 miles of a sea coast, on just 10 percent of the Earth's land area. Two-thirds live within 250 miles of a coast.

These mounting human numbers and the development that follows in their wake have taken a grim toll on ocean resources nearby. Half the world's coastal wetlands, including salt marshes, for instance, have disappeared. And close to 70 percent of the world's beaches are eroding at rapid rates because of human impacts.

Coastal ecosystems, valuable because they function as nurseries for fish and other sea life, have been especially hard hit. Over the past century alone, 25 million hectares of mangrove forests—multi-rooted trees on the edge of the sea —have been destroyed or grossly degraded. Seagrass beds—underwater meadows in coastal shallows—have fared little better and are in retreat near virtually all inhabited coastal areas.

Coral reefs, the rain forests of the sea with perhaps 1 million species, are being pillaged as well. They are poisoned by sewage outfalls, overfished, dynamited, pummeled by ship's anchors, broken by recreational divers and bleached by unseasonally warm temperatures. Of the world's 230,000 square miles of reef-building corals, 60 percent could be lost within 40 years, marine biologists fear. Over 80 percent of the reefs in Southeast Asia alone are in peril.

One of the biggest threats to the integrity of ocean ecosystems is directly attributable to people and their insatiable demand for protein: the relentless hunt for fish. Of the world's 15 major oceanic fisheries, 11 are in decline. The catch of Atlantic cod has dropped 70 percent since 1970, while bluefin tuna stocks have declined by 80 percent over the same period.

A fivefold growth in seafood consumption since 1950 has pushed these and other fisheries to the brink and beyond. Between 1991 and 1995 the world's commercial fleets hauled in, on average, 84 million tons of seafood a year. Since seafood provides close to 20 percent of the world's total animal protein intake —up to 90 percent in the South Pacific and parts of Southeast Asia—the decline in fish catches is eroding food security for a number of poor countries in the tropics.

The overcapacity of the world's fishing fleets has itself become a threat to the integrity of ocean ecosystems. Currently, 5.8 million square miles of ocean bottom are trawled each year, the marine equivalent of strip-mining. Since bottom trawls are indiscriminate harvesters of marine life, the by-catch from these operations constitutes a horrendous waste of potential food. Every year, 10 pounds of fish and shellfish are discarded for every person on Earth— up to 40 million tons.

In too many places, the sea has also become a dumping ground for oil and a giant cesspool to collect the runoff of poisons from inland sources. Each year, for instance, effluents flowing from the Mississippi River system leave a lifeless dead zone 30 miles out into the Gulf of Mexico.

Animals

Plundering the Planet's Species

Human life cannot exist in the absence of complicated interactions of millions of species in biological systems. Yet we live in a period of the greatest loss of plant and animal species since the mega-extinctions of the Jurassic Period 65 million years ago.

Every year over the course of the coming decades, 50,000 plant and animal species are likely to disappear, ecologists warn. The percentage of birds, mammals, fish, reptiles and amphibians threatened with extinction is now in double digits, and the loss of insects and microorganisms is incalculable. Overall, human-induced habitat loss, killing by bushmeat hunters in the Tropics and the introduction of nonnative species, among other problems, have conspired to change the lineup of species on Earth.

Loss of biodiversity is not limited to wildlife. Since 1900, about threequarters of the genetic diversity of agricultural crops have also disappeared, according to FAO estimates, along with half the wild gene pool upon which domestic cattle are dependent for improving their resistance to diseases, pests and changing environmental conditions.

Increasing population density and pressure for faster but unmanaged economic development are largely to blame. In a study of 50 countries in Asia and Africa, the United Nations Population Fund found that the loss of natural habitat was greatest in high-density areas and least in low-density areas. In the 10 countries that had lost the most habitat, population density averaged close to 200 people per square kilometer. In the 10 countries that had lost the least amount of habitat, the population density averaged just 29 people per square kilometer.

The outlook is particularly bleak in some of the most biologically rich countries of the Third World, where population growth and unsustainable exploitation of natural resources is savaging habitat in "biodiversity hotspots" —ecosystems with a superabundance of plant and animal species. So far, 24 of these hotspots containing half the planet's land species have been identified. Overall, five of the six most biologically diverse countries could see more than two-thirds of their original habitat destroyed or grossly degraded by the middle of the next century.

Meantime, the world's last great expanses of pristine, mostly uninhabited tropical forests now face imminent destruction. These large tracts of land —in the Guayana Shield region of northern South America, Amazonia, Africa's Congo and the island of New Guinea—are prime targets for logging. Together, they are about the size of the state of Alaska.

In other areas, the introduction of nonnative, or exotic, species contributes to extinction woes. Hawaii's native fauna and flora have been decimated by species brought in, deliberately or by accident, by people. On the U.S. mainland, exotics have been implicated in close to 70 percent of all fish extinctions this century. In Europe, much of the Black Sea's fauna has been eliminated by a combination of overfishing, pollution and exotics. Its commercially valuable fish species have declined from 26 to 5 in a decade.

On top of all that, an ominous new term has been added recently to the biologists' lexicon of threats to animals: "defaunation," also referred to as "the empty forest." From Laos to Congo, Brazil to Madagascar, impoverished people desperate to put food in the pot are killing whatever moves. Now, vast areas of tropical forest have been scoured nearly clean by hunters of bushmeat. For the first time, there are large areas of available habitat with few birds or mammals to live in them.

NO

N. Gregory Mankiw

Be Fruitful and Multiply

Iconfess: My wife and I are about to commit what some people consider a socially irresponsible act. Toward the end of the summer, we will bring our third child into the world.

A third child means, of course, that my wife and I are contributing to the world's population explosion, and to some people this makes our decision more than personal. To see how guilty I should feel, I just read the recent book by nature writer Bill McKibben, *Maybe One: A Personal and Environmental Argument for Single-Child Families*. McKibben tries to accomplish through persuasion what China has done through government fiat—make one child per couple the norm. The book wasn't published in time to change my family size, but even if it had been, it wouldn't have persuaded me to abstain from reproduction.

As McKibben is well aware, fear of overpopulation has a long and embarrassing history. Two centuries ago, Thomas Malthus argued that an ever-increasing population would continually strain society's ability to produce goods and services. As a result, mankind was doomed to forever live in poverty —a prediction that led Thomas Carlyle to label economics "the dismal science."

Fortunately, Malthus was far off the mark. Although the world population has increased about sixfold over the past two centuries, living standards are much higher. The reason is that growth in mankind's ingenuity has far exceeded growth in population. New ideas about how to produce and even about the kinds of goods to produce have led to greater prosperity than Malthus—or anyone else of his era—could have ever imagined.

The failure of Malthus' prediction, however, has not stopped others from repeating it. The most famous modern Malthusian is biologist Paul Ehrlich, whose 1968 book, *The Population Bomb*, warned of impending worldwide shortages in food and natural resources. Thirty years later, however, most natural resources are in abundant supply and are available at low prices. Even the famines that sometimes ravage less-developed countries are rarely due to overpopulation—civil war is a more common cause. Nonetheless, the fear of worldwide shortages because of overpopulation remains widespread.

Among the wealthy, reducing population growth is a popular cause. When David Packard, co-founder of Hewlett-Packard and father of four, died leaving $9 billion to his foundation, he specified that the foundation's highest priority

From N. Gregory Mankiw, "Be Fruitful and Multiply," *Fortune* (September 7, 1998). Copyright © 1998 by Time, Inc. Reprinted by permission.

should be lowering global birth rates. Packard's efforts may someday be dwarfed by those of investor Warren Buffett, father of three. Buffett claims he will give away most of his vast wealth, and according to some reports, the problem that most moves Buffett is the population explosion.

Those who fear overpopulation share a simple insight: People use resources. They eat food, drive cars, and take up space. Because resources are scarce, the only way to improve living standards, Malthusians argue, is to limit the number of people with whom we have to share these resources.

The rebuttal to this argument is equally simple: People create resources. They bring into the world their time, effort, and ingenuity. Before deciding whether world population growth is a curse or a blessing, we have to ask ourselves whether an extra person added to the planet uses more or less resources than he or she creates.

Environmentalists such as McKibben view humans as rapacious consumers who devour as much as they can get their hands on. About this, the environmentalists are largely right. But there is no problem as long as people pay for what they consume. In a market economy, the price system ensures that no one can consume resources without first creating some of equal or greater value.

Problems do arise when important resources fail to have prices attached to them. For instance, consider the issue that most concerns McKibben—global warming caused by the use of fossil fuels. Because people burning gasoline in their cars or oil in their furnaces do not pay for their impact on climate, they burn too much. The solution, according to McKibben, is fewer people. A more direct solution is a tax on fossil fuels.

Perhaps the most important resource without a price is society's pool of ideas. Every time a baby is born, there is some chance that he or she will be the next Newton, Darwin, or Einstein. And when that happens, everyone benefits. Although the government can easily protect the environment with a well-designed tax system, spurring the production of great ideas is much harder. The best way to get more geniuses is to have more people.

As a serial procreator, therefore, I make no apologies. When I welcome Peter Mankiw onto our planet, I will do so without a shred of guilt. I don't guarantee that he will find a cure for cancer or a solution to global warming, but there is always a chance. And in that chance lies the hope for our species.

POSTSCRIPT

Does Population Growth Significantly Harm the Earth's Quality of Life?

Research scholars and policymakers have not reached a conclusion about the role that population growth precisely plays in affecting our resource base or our quality of life in general. Nonetheless, observers of change, whether local or global, typically acknowledge that population plays a significant role. The problem is determining how much of the diminished quality is due specifically to population factors.

Sources abound that address the link between population and environmental factors. One recent addition to this huge body of literature is U.S. State Department official Richard E. Benedick's article "Human Population and Environmental Stresses in the Twenty-First Century," in the Woodrow Wilson Center's *Environmental Change and Security Project Report* (Summer 2000). In it, Benedick proclaims that "inhabitants of planet Earth find themselves threatened by environmental dangers that would have been unimaginable" earlier. He explores his thesis with reference to three different links to population: forests, freshwater, and climate change.

Hinrichsen uses the same strategy in exploring the consequences of increased population growth for quality of life. People use resources. More people probably use more resources. Water, forests, soils, air, oceans, and animals are adversely affected by each additional person. Resource depletion is intimately tied up with quality of life. Hinrichsen may be right, but he has not been able to isolate the magnitude of population's effect on the systems that ensure a good quality of life.

Those who challenge the conventional wisdom, like Mankiw, suggest that quality of life is more about living standards than one's natural surroundings. The human race has managed to have its ingenuity grow faster than its numbers, Mankiw says, so all may benefit. Moreover, he argues that most natural systems are in abundant supply. He suggests that while it is true that people use resources, they also produce resources.

Lester R. Brown, Gary Gardner, and Brian Halweil outline the effects of population growth along 19 dimensions in *Beyond Malthus: Nineteen Dimensions of the Population Challenge* (Worldwatch Institute, 1999). The results of a Vatican-sponsored conference on the relationships of human and material resources to population growth can be found in Bernardo Colombo, Paul Demeny, and Max F. Perutz, eds., *Resources and Population: Natural, Institutional, and Demographic Dimensions of Development* (Oxford University Press, 1996). Finally, Julian L. Simon's *Ultimate Resource 2* (Princeton University Press, 1996) provides an alternative view to conventional wisdom.

ISSUE 4

Will Declining Population Growth Rates in the Developed World Lead to Major Problems?

YES: Peter G. Peterson, from "Gray Dawn: The Global Aging Crisis," *Foreign Affairs* (January/February 1999)

NO: Leon F. Bouvier and Jane T. Bertrand, from *World Population: Challenges for the Twenty-First Century* (Seven Locks Press, 1999)

ISSUE SUMMARY

YES: Peter G. Peterson, chairman of the Blackstone Group, a private investment bank, argues that global aging will dominate the public-policy agenda of the developed world as it attempts to cope with a vast array of problems associated with such aging.

NO: Adjunct professor of demography Leon F. Bouvier and Jane T. Bertrand, chair of the Department of International Health and Development at Tulane University School of Public Health and Tropical Medicine, argue that a future developed society will be quite less able to cope with declining growth rates.

While the poorer nations of the world have endured over 30 years of huge birthrates, the richer sectors of the globe have witnessed the opposite phenomenon for an even longer period. The demographic transition began far earlier in the then newly industrialized countries of Western Europe and the United States. And for almost half a century, these nations have witnessed the third and final stage of this transition—low birth and death rates. The drop in the death rates in these countries has been a function of several factors. One major factor has been the dramatic decline in both infant mortality (within the first year of birth) and child mortality (within the first five years) due to women being healthier during pregnancy and nursing periods and to the virtually universal inoculation of children against principal childhood diseases. A second factor is that once people reach adulthood, they are living longer, in large part because of medical advances against key adult illnesses, such as cancer and heart disease.

Declining mortality rates yield an aging population in need of a variety of services—heath care, housing, and guards against inflation, for example —provided, in large part, by the tax dollars of the younger, producing sector of society. As the "gray" numbers of society grow, the labor force is increasingly called upon to provide more help for this class. Moreover, the decline of infant and child mortality suggests that a potentially larger group will live to adulthood and become part of the producing class, with the potential to produce more children who will continue the cycle.

Declining birth and death rates in developed countries means that significantly more services will be needed to provide for the aging populations of these countries, while at the same time, fewer individuals will be joining the workforce to provide the resources to pay for these services. However, some experts say that the new workforce will be able to take advantage of the skills of the more aged, unlike in previous eras. In order for national economies to grow in the information age, an expanding workforce may not be as important a prerequisite as it once was. While automation replaced many sectors of the labor force in the heyday of industrialization, the global information age takes it one step further. Expanding minds, not bodies, may be the key to expanding economies and increasing abilities to provide public services.

However, the elderly and the young are not randomly distributed throughout society, which is likely to create regional problems. In the United States, for example, the educated young are likely to leave the "gray belt" of the north for the Sun Belt of the south, southwest, and west. Who will be left in the older, established sectors of the country that were originally at the forefront of the industrial age to care for the disproportionately elderly population? As more and more young adults rush to the cities in search of high-paying jobs in the new economy, who will take care of rural and small-town America? What will happen 30 or 40 years from now, when the respective sizes of the young and the elderly populations throughout the developed world will yield a much larger population at the twilight of their existence?

In the following selection, Peter G. Peterson presents the conventional argument about the doomsday condition of "gray America." He introduces the phrase "the Floridization of the developed world," alluding to the fact that retirees in the United States continue to flock to Florida in unprecedented numbers, in order to capture the essence of the problems associated with the changing age composition in industrial societies. Leon F. Bouvier and Jane T. Bertrand look at the problem somewhat differently in the second selection. While they acknowledge that the developed world is on the "brink of an entirely new age" because of the leveling off of its population, they do not assume that the future society will be less able to cope with the changing demographics. To them, the information age will be knowledge-intensive, not labor-intensive. That is, labor's traditional role in production—the hands and backs of a younger workforce—will be replaced by those who are best able to use their minds, no matter what age.

Peter G. Peterson

 YES

Gray Dawn: The Global Aging Crisis

Daunting Demographics

The list of major global hazards in the next century has grown long and familiar. It includes the proliferation of nuclear, biological, and chemical weapons, other types of high-tech terrorism, deadly super-viruses, extreme climate change, the financial, economic, and political aftershocks of globalization, and the violent ethnic explosions waiting to be detonated in today's unsteady new democracies. Yet there is a less-understood challenge—the graying of the developed world's population—that may actually do more to reshape our collective future than any of the above.

Over the next several decades, countries in the developed world will experience an unprecedented growth in the number of their elderly and an unprecedented decline in the number of their youth. The timing and magnitude of this demographic transformation have already been determined. Next century's elderly have already been born and can be counted—and their cost to retirement benefit systems can be projected.

Unlike with global warming, there can be little debate over whether or when global aging will manifest itself. And unlike with other challenges, even the struggle to preserve and strengthen unsteady new democracies, the costs of global aging will be far beyond the means of even the world's wealthiest nations —unless retirement benefit systems are radically reformed. Failure to do so, to prepare early and boldly enough, will spark economic crises that will dwarf the recent meltdowns in Asia and Russia.

How we confront global aging will have vast economic consequences costing quadrillions of dollars over the next century. Indeed, it will greatly influence how we manage, and can afford to manage, the other major challenges that will face us in the future.

For this and other reasons, global aging will become not just the transcendent economic issue of the 21st century, but the transcendent political issue as well. It will dominate and daunt the public-policy agendas of developed countries and force the renegotiation of their social contracts. It will also reshape foreign policy strategies and the geopolitical order.

From Peter G. Peterson, "Gray Dawn: The Global Aging Crisis," *Foreign Affairs*, vol. 78, no. 1 (January/February 1999). Copyright © 1999 by The Council on Foreign Relations, Inc. Reprinted by permission of *Foreign Affairs*.

The United States has a massive challenge ahead of it. The broad outlines can already be seen in the emerging debate over Social Security and Medicare reform. But ominous as the fiscal stakes are in the United States, they loom even larger in Japan and Europe, where populations are aging even faster, birthrates are lower, the influx of young immigrants from developing countries is smaller, public pension benefits are more generous, and private pension systems are weaker.

Aging has become a truly global challenge, and must therefore be given high priority on the global policy agenda. A gray dawn fast approaches. It is time to take an unflinching look at the shape of things to come.

The Floridization of the developed world. Been to Florida lately? You may not have realized it, but the vast concentration of seniors there—nearly 19 percent of the population—represents humanity's future. Today's Florida is a demographic benchmark that every developed nation will soon pass. Italy will hit the mark as early as 2003, followed by Japan in 2005 and Germany in 2006. France and Britain will pass present-day Florida around 2016; the United States and Canada in 2021 and 2023.

Societies much older than any we have ever known. Global life expectancy has grown more in the last fifty years than over the previous five thousand. Until the Industrial Revolution, people aged 65 and over never amounted to more than 2 or 3 percent of the population. In today's developed world, they amount to 14 percent. By the year 2030, they will reach 25 percent and be closing in on 30 in some countries.

An unprecedented economic burden on working-age people. Early in the next century, working-age populations in most developed countries will shrink. Between 2000 and 2010, Japan, for example, will suffer a 25 percent drop in the number of workers under age 30. Today the ratio of working taxpayers to nonworking pensioners in the developed world is around 3:1. By 2030, absent reform, this ratio will fall to 1.5:1, and in some countries, such as Germany and Italy, it will drop all the way down to 1:1 or even lower. While the longevity revolution represents a miraculous triumph of modern medicine and the extra years of life will surely be treasured by the elderly and their families, pension plans and other retirement benefit programs were not designed to provide these billions of extra years of payouts.

The aging of the aged: the number of "old old" will grow much faster than the number of "young old." The United Nations projects that by 2050, the number of people aged 65 to 84 worldwide will grow from 400 million to 1.3 billion (a threefold increase), while the number of people aged 85 and over will grow from 26 million to 175 million (a sixfold increase)—and the number aged 100 and over from 135,000 to 2.2 million (a sixteenfold increase). The "old old" consume far more health care than the "young old"—about two to three times as much. For nursing-home care, the ratio is roughly 20:1. Yet little of this cost is figured in the official projections of future public expenditures.

Figure 1

Just Thirty Years From Now, One in Four People in the Developed World Will Be Aged 65 or Older, up From One in Seven Today.

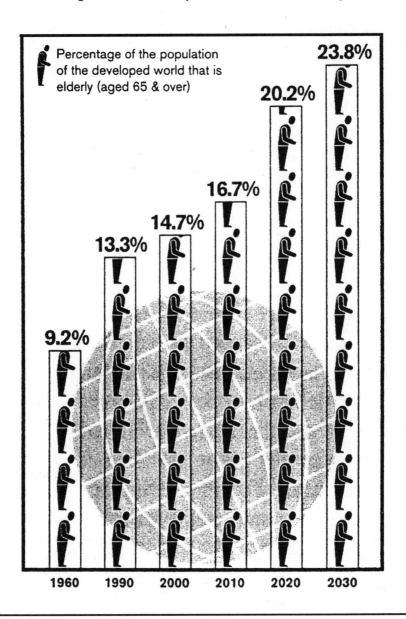

Falling birthrates will intensify the global aging trend.   As life spans increase, fewer babies are being born. As recently as the late 1960s, the worldwide total fertility rate (that is, the average number of lifetime births per woman) stood at about 5.0, well within the historical range. Then came a behavioral revolution, driven by growing affluence, urbanization, feminism, rising female participation in the workforce, new birth control technologies, and legalized abortion. The result: an unprecedented and unexpected decline in the global fertility rate to about 2.7—a drop fast approaching the replacement rate of 2.1 (the rate required merely to maintain a constant population). In the developed world alone, the average fertility rate has plummeted to 1.6. Since 1995, Japan has had fewer births annually than in any year since 1899. In Germany, where the rate has fallen to 1.3, fewer babies are born each year than in Nepal, which has a population only one-quarter as large.

A shrinking population in an aging developed world.   Unless their fertility rates rebound, the total populations of western Europe and Japan will shrink to about one-half of their current size before the end of the next century. In 1950, 7 of the 12 most populous nations were in the developed world: the United States, Russia, Japan, Germany, France, Italy, and the United Kingdom. The United Nations projects that by 2050, only the United States will remain on the list. Nigeria, Pakistan, Ethiopia, Congo, Mexico, and the Philippines will replace the others. But since developing countries are also experiencing a drop in fertility, many are now actually aging faster than the typical developed country. In France, for example, it took over a century for the elderly to grow from 7 to 14 percent of the population. South Korea, Taiwan, Singapore, and China are projected to traverse that distance in only 25 years.

From worker shortage to rising immigration pressure.   Perhaps the most predictable consequence of the gap in fertility and population growth rates between developed and developing countries will be the rising demand for immigrant workers in older and wealthier societies facing labor shortages. Immigrants are typically young and tend to bring with them the family practices of their native culture—including higher fertility rates. In many European countries, non-European foreigners already make up roughly 10 percent of the population. This includes 10 million to 13 million Muslims, nearly all of whom are working-age or younger. In Germany, foreigners will make up 30 percent of the total population by 2030, and over half the population of major cities like Munich and Frankfurt. Global aging and attendant labor shortages will therefore ensure that immigration remains a major issue in developed countries for decades to come. Culture wars could erupt over the balkanization of language and religion; electorates could divide along ethnic lines; and émigré leaders could sway foreign policy.

Graying Means Paying

Official projections suggest that within 30 years, developed countries will have to spend at least an extra 9 to 16 percent of GDP [gross domestic product] simply to meet their old-age benefit promises. The unfunded liabilities for pensions (that is, benefits already earned by today's workers for which nothing has been saved) are already almost $35 trillion. Add in health care, and the total jumps to at least twice as much. At minimum, the global aging issue thus represents, to paraphrase the old quiz show, a $64 trillion question hanging over the developed world's future.

To pay for promised benefits through increased taxation is unfeasible. Doing so would raise the total tax burden by an unthinkable 25 to 40 percent of every worker's taxable wages—in countries where payroll tax rates sometimes already exceed 40 percent. To finance the costs of these benefits by borrowing would be just as disastrous. Governments would run unprecedented deficits that would quickly consume the savings of the developed world.

And the $64 trillion estimate is probably low. It likely underestimates future growth in longevity and health care costs and ignores the negative effects on the economy of more borrowing, higher interest rates, more taxes, less savings, and lower rates of productivity and wage growth.

There are only a handful of exceptions to these nightmarish forecasts. In Australia, total public retirement costs as a share of GDP are expected to rise only slightly, and they may even decline in Britain and Ireland. This fiscal good fortune is not due to any special demographic trend, but to timely policy reforms—including tight limits on public health spending, modest pension benefit formulas, and new personally owned savings programs that allow future public benefits to shrink as a share of average wages. This approach may yet be emulated elsewhere.

Failure to respond to the aging challenge will destabilize the global economy, straining financial and political institutions around the world. Consider Japan, which today runs a large current account surplus making up well over half the capital exports of all the surplus nations combined. Then imagine a scenario in which Japan leaves its retirement programs and fiscal policies on autopilot. Thirty years from now, under this scenario, Japan will be importing massive amounts of capital to prevent its domestic economy from collapsing under the weight of benefit outlays. This will require a huge reversal in global capital flows. To get some idea of the potential volatility, note that over the next decade, Japan's annual pension deficit is projected to grow to roughly 3 times the size of its recent and massive capital exports to the United States; by 2030, the annual deficit is expected to be 15 times as large. Such reversals will cause wildly fluctuating interest and exchange rates, which may in turn short-circuit financial institutions and trigger a serious market crash.

As they age, some nations will do little to change course, while others may succeed in boosting their national savings rate, at least temporarily, through a combination of fiscal restraint and household thrift. Yet this too could result in a volatile disequilibrium in supply and demand for global capital. Such imbalance could wreak havoc with international institutions such as the European Union [EU].

In recent years, the EU has focused on monetary union, launched a single currency (the euro), promoted cross-border labor mobility, and struggled to harmonize fiscal, monetary, and trade policies. European leaders expect to have their hands full smoothing out differences between members of the Economic and Monetary Union (EMU)—from the timing of their business cycles to the diversity of their credit institutions and political cultures. For this reason, they established official public debt and deficit criteria (three percent of GDP for EMU membership) in order to discourage maverick nations from placing undue economic burdens on fellow members. But the EU has yet to face up to the biggest challenge to its future viability: the likelihood of varying national responses to the fiscal pressures of demographic aging. Indeed, the EU does not even include unfunded pension liabilities in the official EMU debt and deficit criteria—which is like measuring icebergs without looking beneath the water line.

When these liabilities come due and move from "off the books" to "on the books," the EU will, under current constraints, be required to penalize EMU members that exceed the three percent deficit cap. As a recent IMF report concludes, "over time it will become increasingly difficult for most countries to meet the deficit ceiling without comprehensive social security reform." The EU could, of course, retain members by raising the deficit limit. But once the floodgates are opened, national differences in fiscal policy may mean that EMU members rack up deficits at different rates. The European Central Bank, the euro, and a half-century of progress toward European unity could be lost as a result. The total projected cost of the age wave is so staggering that we might reasonably conclude it could never be paid. After all, these numbers are projections, not predictions. They tell us what is likely to happen if current policy remains unchanged, not whether it is likely or even possible for this condition to hold. In all probability, economies would implode and governments would collapse before the projections ever materialize. But this is exactly why we must focus on these projections, for they call attention to the paramount question: Will we change course sooner, when we still have time to control our destiny and reach a more sustainable path? Or later, after unsustainable economic damage and political and social trauma cause a wrenching upheaval?

A Graying New World Order

While the fiscal and economic consequences of global aging deserve serious discussion, other important consequences must also be examined. At the top of the list is the impact of the age wave on foreign policy and international security.

Will the developed world be able to maintain its security commitments?   One need not be a Nobel laureate in economics to understand that a country's GDP growth is the product of workforce and productivity growth. If workforces shrink rapidly, GDP may drop as well, since labor productivity may not rise fast enough to compensate for the loss of workers. At least some developed countries are therefore likely to experience a long-term decline in total production of goods and services—that is, in real GDP.

Economists correctly focus on the developed world's GDP per capita, which can rise even as its workforce and total GDP shrink. But anything with a fixed cost becomes a national challenge when that cost has to be spread over a smaller population and funded out of shrinking revenues. National defense is the classic example. The West already faces grave threats from rogue states armed with biological and chemical arsenals, terrorists capable of hacking into vulnerable computer systems, and proliferating nuclear weapons. None of these external dangers will shrink to accommodate our declining workforce or GDP.

Leading developed countries will no doubt need to spend as much or more on defense and international investments as they do today. But the age wave will put immense pressure on governments to cut back. Falling birthrates, together with a rising demand for young workers, will also inevitably mean smaller armies. And how many parents will allow their only child to go off to war?

With fewer soldiers, total capability can be maintained only by large increases in technology and weaponry. But boosting military productivity creates a Catch-22. For how will governments get the budget resources to pay for high-tech weaponry if the senior-weighted electorate demands more money for high-tech medicine? Even if military capital is successfully substituted for military labor, the deployment options may be dangerously limited. Developed nations facing a threat may feel they have only two extreme (but relatively inexpensive) choices: a low-level response (antiterrorist strikes and cruise-missile diplomacy) or a high-level response (an all-out attack with strategic weapons).

Will Young/Old become the next North/South fault line?   Historically, the richest industrial powers have been growing, capital-exporting, philanthropic giants that project their power and mores around the world. The richest industrial powers of the future may be none of these things. Instead, they may be demographically imploding, capital-importing, fiscally starving neutrals who twist and turn to avoid expensive international entanglements. A quarter-century from now, will the divide between today's "rich" and "poor" nations be better described as a divide between growth and decline, surplus and deficit, expansion and retreat, future and past? By the mid-2020s, will the contrast between North and South be better described as a contrast between Young and Old?

If today's largest low-income societies, especially China, set up fully funded retirement systems to prepare for their own future aging, they may well produce ever larger capital surpluses. As a result, today's great powers could someday depend on these surpluses to keep themselves financially afloat. But how should we expect these new suppliers of capital to use their newly acquired leverage? Will they turn the tables in international diplomacy? Will the Chinese, for example, someday demand that the United States shore up its Medicare system the way Americans once demanded that China reform its human rights policies as a condition for foreign assistance?

As Samuel Huntington recently put it, "the juxtaposition of a rapidly growing people of one culture and a slowly growing or stagnant people of another culture generates pressure for economic and/or political adjustments in both societies." Countries where populations are still exploding rank high on any list of potential trouble spots, whereas the countries most likely to lose population—and to see a weakening of their commitment to expensive defense and global security programs—are the staunchest friends of liberal democracy.

In many parts of the developing world, the total fertility rate remains very high (7.3 in the Gaza Strip versus 2.7 in Israel), most people are very young (49 percent under age 15 in Uganda), and the population is growing very rapidly (doubling every 26 years in Iran). These areas also tend to be the poorest, most rapidly urbanizing, most institutionally unstable—and most likely to fall under the sway of rogue leadership. They are the same societies that spawned most of the military strongmen and terrorists who have bedeviled the United States and Europe in recent decades. The Pentagon's long-term planners predict that outbreaks of regional anarchy will occur more frequently early in the next century. To pinpoint when and where, they track what they call "youth bulges" in the world's poorest urban centers.

Is demography destiny, after all? Is the rapidly aging developed world fated to decline? Must it cede leadership to younger and faster-growing societies? For the answer to be no, the developed world must redefine that role around a new mission. And what better way to do so than to show the younger, yet more tradition-bound, societies—which will soon age in their turn—how a world dominated by the old can still accommodate the young.

The Demographic Challenges of the Twenty-First Century

The Developed World

Low fertility in developed nations seems here to stay. Whereas demographic "predictions" are hazardous, the evolution in fertility rates over the past 30 years in developed nations provides strong evidence of a trend that is unlikely to reverse itself in the current social and economic climate.

This trend began in 1973, when a momentous new demographic phenomenon began to unfold throughout most of the developed world: fertility fell below the level of 2.1 births per woman needed to replace the population in the long run *and remained there*. Country after country—Canada, the then two Germanys, the United Kingdom, the United States—all reported fertility rates under two births per woman in 1983 and still lower rates in the early 1990s. Actual population size did not begin to fall immediately because all of the nations experienced a rise in their fertility rates after World War II—some for just a few years, others (such as Australia, Canada, and the United States) for 10 to 15 years. As a result, the number of young couples of childbearing ages was quite large in the 1970s, so that even with extraordinarily low fertility *per woman*, births continued to outnumber deaths each year, reflecting population *momentum*....

But by the late 1970s, the effect of that momentum had subsided in many European countries, and in some, deaths began to outnumber births by the mid-1980s. Population decline was noted in Austria and East and West Germany. Continued immigration and the higher fertility of immigrants warded off decline for a time in other countries, but by the early 1980s, France and the United Kingdom were losing population, as was Hungary.

In the younger developed nations—the United States, Canada, Australia, New Zealand—the trend toward actual population decline will occur later than in Europe because of the reverberating impact of the tremendous post–World War II baby boom generation and because immigration levels have remained high. Nevertheless, the U.S. Census Bureau has projected that its population would stop growing at about 309 million by 2050 and then begin to decline, given continued below-replacement fertility and if net immigration was limited to 450,000 per year.

Espenshade, Bouvier, and Arthur calculated that even with net immigration of 400,000 per year, the U.S. population would be reduced to 109 million before achieving zero growth in some 200 years, if the national fertility rate continued below replacement.

This low fertility pattern, first noted some 20 years ago, continues to this date in most European countries as well as the United States, Canada, Australia, New Zealand, and Japan. According to the most recently published data, Italy, Spain, Romania, and the Czech Republic have fallen to 1.2 and below, the lowest in the world. Other nations in this group are not far behind. (See table 1.)

Table 1

Total Fertility Rates in Selected Developed Countries, 1970, 1975, 1982, 1998

Country	1970	1975	1982	1998
Europe				
Austria	2.3	1.8	1.7	1.4
Belgium	2.2	1.7	1.6	1.6
Denmark	2	1.9	1.4	1.8
France	2.5	1.9	1.9	1.7
Germany, East	2.2	1.5	1.9	-
Germany, West	2	1.5	1.4	1.3*
Hungary	2	2.4	1.8	1.4
Italy	2.4	2.2	1.6	1.2
Netherlands	2.6	1.7	1.5	1.5
Norway	2.5	2	1.7	1.8
Spain	2.9	2.8	2	1.2
Sweden	1.9	1.8	1.6	1.6
Switzerland	2.1	1.6	1.6	1.6
United Kingdom	2.4	1.8	1.8	1.7
Other Areas				
Australia	2.9	2.2	1.9	1.8
Canada	2.3	1.9	1.7	1.6
Japan	2.1	1.9	1.7	1.4
United States	2.5	1.8	1.9	2

Note: *This rate is for the combined Germanys.

Source: World Population Data Sheets, selected years (Washington, D.C.: Population Reference Bureau).

By 1995, Ireland (1.8 in 1998) and Portugal (1.4 in 1998) had joined the European low fertility groups and were accompanied by most of the new republics carved out of the erstwhile USSR. Thus, it is clear that fertility is remaining extremely low in all of Europe, Japan, and the former English colonies such as the United States, Canada, and Australia. It is also interesting to note that a slight increase in fertility has occurred in some Scandinavian countries. This may be a precursor of future trends and suggests that fertility could rise ever so slightly in other European countries in years to come.

Short-lived periods of low fertility have occurred in the past. During the Great Depression of the 1930s, fertility fell below replacement in most western European countries and in the United States. But the rates began to climb again by the late 1930s in the United States and during World War II in western Europe. Never before in modern history has fertility been so low in so many countries for such a long period as has been the case since 1973. And as of the late 1990s, the rates in most developed countries show little evidence of climbing back to the point where population growth, or at least population replacement, can be assured over the long run.

End of Growth in the Developed World

The significance of this new demographic pattern throughout most of the developed world suggests adaptation to a new era. The developed nations of the planet may well be poised on the brink of an entirely new age when the quantitative demands for labor will be modest, although the qualitative demands will be great.

We have seen harbingers of this momentous change. For example, John Naisbitt noted in his 1982 book, *Megatrends*: "In 1956 for the first time in American history, white-collar workers and technical-managerial positions outnumbered blue-collar workers. Industrial America was giving way to a new society where for the first time in history most of us worked with information rather than producing goods." Naisbitt named this the "information society." Sociologist Daniel Bell called it the "postindustrial society." These social observers, however, did not identify an end to population growth as an important ingredient in this emerging new society.

We are at the onset of a social upheaval as great as that touched off by the Industrial Revolution that began some 200 years ago. Interestingly, a demographic revolution occurred then also. With the improved living conditions resulting from the Industrial Revolution, mortality began to fall gradually from the end of the 18th century. Couples took a while to adjust to the fact that more of their children were surviving, so fertility generally did not begin to fall until late in the 19th century. During this interim period, population growth rose to over 1 percent a year in many western European countries, rates unprecedented in world history at that time. This growth helped supply workers needed for the cities' burgeoning industries, as well as immigrants to the "New World." Then western European couples realized that they could take advantage of improving social and economic opportunities by having fewer, but better educated, children. Today's population actors—at least those in developed nations—are once again responding appropriately to meet the needs of a new era.

This "information society," benefitting from high technology—and by 1990, from robotic technology and more recently from the Internet—will be knowledge-intensive rather than labor-intensive. The pattern of shifting the production of shoes and textiles, for example, to lower-wage developing countries is now being followed with the sophisticated "tools" of the information age. The 1983 decision by California-based Atari to move assembly-line work for its microcomputers to Hong Kong and Taiwan was but an early example of what has become standard practice. To some extent, that practice was behind the General Motors strike in 1998. The union argued that too many jobs were being sent to cheap labor countries such as Mexico. Even many service occupations may be eliminated in developed countries. Economist and Nobel prize winner Wassily Leontief has suggested that "the ability of the service sector to absorb displaced workers will diminish." He added, "As soon as not only the physical but also the controlling 'mental' functions involved in the production of goods and services can be performed without the participation of human labor, labor's role as an indispensable 'factor of production' will progressively diminish."

The Logical Result: Increased International Immigration

The current and future demographic scenarios are increasingly shaped by the prospect of increased international migration. Perhaps more than at any time in the past, residents of the poorest nations are making the decision to move across international borders sometimes legally, sometimes illegally in search of a better life. Humans have always been peripatetic, but with the emergence of nation-states and political barriers in the late 19th and early 20th centuries, migration had become relatively controlled. However, with recent spectacular advances in communications and transportation facilities, added to the staggering poverty in developing nations (aggravated by rapid population growth), more and more people are ignoring these constraints and are moving despite the possibly dire consequences. This is happening all over the world, not only between developing and developed nations but also between the less affluent and more affluent developed countries, as from Portugal to France and Italy to Germany, and between the poorest developing countries and their somewhat better-off neighbors, as from Egypt to Saudi Arabia and Colombia to Venezuela.

[Elsewhere] we quoted the eminent American demographer, Kingsley Davis. He asked, "One wonders how long the inequalities of growth between the major regions can continue without an explosion?" Davis's question is now being answered by millions upon millions of people who are giving up their long-accepted ways of life in search of something better. They may be legal immigrants whose decision to move resulted from considerable discussion and thought. They may be refugees forced to abandon their homeland because of political strife. They may be illegal immigrants who surreptitiously enter a country and lead guarded lives for fear of deportation.

It is evident that life in the 21st century will be greatly influenced by these three demographic phenomena: (1) the historically unprecedented levels of fertility decline in certain developed nations; (2) sustained population growth in the developing world over the past 40 years, which has created a "surplus population" in many nations; and (3) massive international migration by individuals in search of what they hope might be a better life.

POSTSCRIPT

Will Declining Population Growth Rates in the Developed World Lead to Major Problems?

The issue of the changing age composition in the developed world is a relatively recent one. With the successful demographic transition in the industrial world, the percentage of citizens above age 60 is on the rise, while the labor force is decreasing. In 1998, 19 percent of the developed world fell into the post-60 category (10 percent worldwide). Children under age 15 also make up 19 percent of the developed world's population, while the labor force is at 62 percent. With birthrates hovering around 1 percent or less and life expectancy increasing, the percentages will likely continue to grow toward the upper end of the scale.

For Peterson, not only will the costs of global aging outweigh the benefits but the capacity of the developed world to pay for these costs is questionable at best. The economic burden on the labor force, he contends, will be "unprecedented." And Peterson takes to task governments of the developed world for failing to plan for the consequences of this phenomenon.

For Bouvier and Bertrand, there seems to be a potential silver lining on the horizon. Although future increases in immigration will counterbalance the decline of the indigenous population, they assert, the real advance will be the decoupling of productivity expansion and workforce increases. The information age is knowledge-intensive, and becoming more so, not labor-intensive. Bouvier and Bertrand maintain that knowledge will continue to explode and that it will not be simply the reserve of the workforce. The aged will presumably be just as capable of contributing to the knowledge base.

One author who accepts Bouvier and Bertrand's thesis is the noted scholar of management Peter Drucker. In "The Future That Has Already Happened," *The Futurist* (November 1998), Drucker predicts that retirement age for healthy people in the developed world will soon rise to 75 primarily because their greatest skill, knowledge, will become even more of an asset. He maintains that knowledge resources will become the most important commodity.

Although the percentage is smaller (8 percent), the developing world will also experience a graying cycle. While the problem is most evident in the developed world, people are living longer in the developing world primarily because of the diffusion of modern medical practices. But unless society can accommodate their skills of later years, they may become an even bigger burden in the future for their national governments.

On the Internet . . .

World Conservation Monitoring Centre

The World Conservation Monitoring Centre Web site contains information on conservation and sustainable use of the globe's natural resources. This center provides information to policymakers concerning global trends in conservation, biodiversity, loss of species and habitats, and more. This site includes a list of publications and environment links.

http://www.wcmc.org.uk

Renewing India

Renewing India is a comprehensive Web site promoting new and renewable sources of energy in India. One can find case studies, articles, links, and a list of organizations and businesses involved in renewable energy technologies, as well as an on-line discussion group.

http://www.renewingindia.org

The Hunger Project

The Hunger Project is a nonprofit organization that seeks to end global hunger. This organization asserts that society-wide actions are needed to eliminate hunger and that global security depends on ensuring that everyone's basic needs are fulfilled. Included on this site is an outline of principles that guide the organization, information on why ending hunger is so important, and a list of programs sponsored by the Hunger Project in 11 developing countries across South Asia, Latin America, and Africa.

http://www.thp.org

Global Warming Central

The Global Warming Central Web site provides information on the global warming debate. Links to the best global warming debate sites are included as well as key documents and reports. Explore the recent news section to find the latest articles on the subject.

http://www.law.pace.edu/env/energy/globalwarming.html

PART 2

Global Resources and the Environment

T
he availability of resources and the manner in which the planet's inhabitants use them characterize another major component of the global agenda. Many state that renewable resources are being consumed at a pace that is too fast to allow for replenishment. Many also contend that nonrenewable resources are being consumed at a pace that is faster than our ability to find suitable replacements.

The production, distribution, and consumption of these resources also leave their marks on the planet. This section examines whether these impacts are permanent, too degrading to the planet, too damaging to one's quality of life, or simply beyond a threshold of acceptability.

- Is Environmental Degradation Worsening?

- Are Alternative Sources of Energy the Best Solution to the World Oil Crisis?

- Will the World Be Able to Feed Itself in the Foreseeable Future?

- Is Global Environmental Stress Caused Primarily by Increased Resource Consumption Rather Than Population Growth?

- Is the Threat of Global Warming Real?

ISSUE 5

Is Environmental Degradation Worsening?

YES: United Nations Environment Programme, from *Global Environment Outlook 2000* (Earthscan, 1999)

NO: Peter Huber, from "Wealth Is Not the Enemy of the Environment," *Vital Speeches of the Day* (April 1, 2000)

ISSUE SUMMARY

YES: The United Nations Environment Programme presents a comprehensive and gloomy assessment of the global environment at the turn of the millennium.

NO: Peter Huber, a senior fellow of the Manhattan Institute, contends that humankind is saving the Earth with the technologies that the "soft greens" most passionately oppose.

T his issue focuses on a global arena that has occupied much newsprint and air time in the last 30 years: the global environment. The production, distribution, and consumption of the resources that are vital to our daily lives take place in the context of a set of constraints placed on every one of us by the environment in which we live. Its influence crosses every kind of human endeavor, from our ability to grow enough food to our capacity to enjoy clean air and water.

It is not surprising, therefore, that early in the post–World War II period the international community came to appreciate that modern technology had given the human race the ability to "move mountains" literally and figuratively, and so humans did, for better and for worse. Problems that were previously confined to a small geographical area—soot from steam engines, pollution downstream and downwind from local factories, the clearing away of a small tract of land for a village's agricultural needs, the Dust Bowl of the 1930s—now manifested themselves in larger and more pervasive ways. Because factories started erecting larger smokestacks, the air pollution that had rained down on the towns adjacent to the local factories was now carried much further downwind, even across national boundaries. Moreover, this pollution was transformed during its journey into a much more insidious monster: acid rain.

It was the effects of this last pollutant that forced the international community to consider whether or not other human activities had a similar price associated with them. In the early 1970s the United Nations answered a plea from the Scandinavian countries to investigate the mysterious death of millions of fish in their lakes and streams. The formal gathering, termed the 1972 Conference on the Human Environment and held in Stockholm, ushered in a new global strategy for addressing what was to become a new set of global issues.

Since Stockholm, the international community has been much more sensitive to the potentially adverse effects of modern human behavior on the Earth's natural and ecological systems. The Stockholm model has been replicated well over 20 times since 1972 in the global community's efforts to ensure that the human race survives the various onslaughts on its planet.

No serious observer now disputes that human activity leaves its mark on the Earth's various systems. The question is whether or not the impact is within an acceptable range and whether or not the planet can recover within a reasonable period of time. The term *Spaceship Earth* has become part of our lexicon, and its visual image, the brilliant photograph of Earth from an early NASA mission, has been forever embedded on many people's minds. The implication of this new addition to our vocabulary is that everyone on this planet must collectively endure the consequences of human activity across the globe. As a result, it is easy for some people to be seduced by cries of "the sky is falling, the sky is falling," uttered by doomsayers who see the demise of the planet in every expanded human endeavor. Others, far fewer in number, respond as small voices in the wilderness, accusing the doomsayers of having "Chicken Little syndrome." Between these two extremes, though, are the majority of the international community's leaders. These officials have embarked on a series of steps in each environmental area to ascertain whether or not a problem really exists and, if so, the nature and degree of the problem, what a preferred future alternative should look like, and how policymakers might successfully address the problem and achieve the desired end state.

The two selections for this issue address the general question of the state of the environment. The first source is a major report of the United Nations Environment Programme (UNEP), the official UN agency created at Stockholm in 1972 to monitor the environment. This report was prepared with the participation of over 850 individuals and more than 30 environmental institutes worldwide, as well as with every other relevant UN organization. As such, it represents the current official scorecard for the state of the planet's national and ecological systems. The picture it paints is one of grave concern. The second selection is much different in both its message and method of delivery. Peter Huber offers an alternative view of the effects of much modern human activity in a speech before the Harvard Club. To Huber, science and technology have combined to allow the human race to make a rather positive footprint on much of the planet.

Synthesis

Two over-riding trends characterize the beginning of the third millennium. First, the global human ecosystem is threatened by grave imbalances in productivity and in the distribution of goods and services. A significant proportion of humanity still lives in dire poverty, and projected trends are for an increasing divergence between those that benefit from economic and technological development, and those that do not. This unsustainable progression of extremes of wealth and poverty threatens the stability of the whole human system, and with it the global environment.

Secondly, the world is undergoing accelerating change, with internationally-coordinated environmental stewardship lagging behind economic and social development. Environmental gains from new technology and policies are being overtaken by the pace and scale of population growth and economic development. The processes of globalization that are so strongly influencing social evolution need to be directed towards resolving rather than aggravating the serious imbalances that divide the world today. All the partners involved—governments, intergovernmental organizations, the private sector, the scientific community, NGOs [nongovernmental organizations] and other major groups—need to work together to resolve this complex and interacting set of economic, social and environmental challenges in the interests of a more sustainable future for the planet and human society.

While each part of the Earth's surface is endowed with its own combination of environmental attributes, each area must also contend with a unique, but interlinked, set of current and emerging problems. GEO-2000 [*Global Environmental Outlook 2000*] provides an overview of this range of issues. This synthesis provides a summary of the main conclusions of *GEO-2000*.

The State of the Environment: A Global Overview

Climate Change

In the late 1990s, annual emissions of carbon dioxide were almost four times the 1950 level and atmospheric concentrations of carbon dioxide had reached their highest level in 160 000 years. According to the Intergovernmental Panel on Climate Change, 'the balance of evidence suggests that there is a discernible human influence on global climate'. Expected results include a shifting of climatic zones, changes in species composition and the productivity of ecosystems, an increase in extreme weather events and impacts on human health.

Through the United Nations Framework Convention on Climate Change and the Kyoto Protocol, efforts are under way to start controlling and reducing greenhouse gas emissions. During the Third Conference of the Parties in Buenos Aires in 1998, a plan of action was developed on how to use the new international policy instruments such as emission trading and the Clean Development Mechanism. However, the Kyoto Protocol alone will be insufficient to stabilize carbon dioxide levels in the atmosphere.

Stratospheric Ozone Depletion

Major reductions in the production, consumption and release of ozone-depleting substances (ODS) have been, and continue to be, achieved by the Montreal Protocol and its related amendments. The abundance of ODS in the lower atmosphere peaked in about 1994 and is now slowly declining. This is expected to bring about a recovery of the ozone layer to pre-1980 levels by around 2050.

Illegal trading, still a problem, is being addressed by national governments but substantial quantities of ODS are still being smuggled across national borders. The Multilateral Fund and the Global Environment Facility are helping developing countries and countries in transition to phase out ODS. Since 1 July 1999, these countries have, for the first time, had to start meeting obligations under the Montreal Protocol.

Nitrogen Loading

We are fertilizing the Earth on a global scale through intensive agriculture, fossil fuel combustion and widespread cultivation of leguminous crops. Evidence is growing that the huge additional quantities of nitrogen being used are exacerbating acidification, causing changes in the species composition of ecosystems, raising nitrate levels in freshwater supplies above acceptable limits for human consumption and causing eutrophication in many freshwater habitats. In addition, river discharges laden with nitrogen-rich sewage and fertilizer run-off tend to stimulate algal blooms in coastal waters, which can lead to oxygen starvation and subsequent fish kills at lower depths, and reduce marine biodiversity through competition. Nitrogen emissions to the atmosphere contribute to global warming. Consensus among researchers is growing that the scale of disruption to the nitrogen cycle may have global implications comparable to those caused by disruption of the carbon cycle.

Chemical Risks

With the massive expansion in the availability and use of chemicals throughout the world, exposure to pesticides, heavy metals, small particulates and other substances poses an increasing threat to the health of humans and their environment. Pesticide use causes 3.5 to 5 million acute poisonings a year. Worldwide,

400 million tonnes of hazardous waste are generated each year. About 75 per cent of pesticide use and hazardous waste generation occurs in developed countries. Despite restrictions on toxic and persistent chemicals such as DDT, PCBs and dioxin in many developed countries, they are still manufactured for export and remain widely used in developing countries. Efforts are under way to promote cleaner production, to limit the emissions and phase out the use of some persistent organic pollutants, to control waste production and trade, and improve waste management.

Disasters

The frequency and effects of natural disasters such as earthquakes, volcanic eruptions, hurricanes, fires and floods are increasing. This not only affects the lives of millions of people directly, through death, injury and economic losses, but adds to environmental problems. As just one example, in 1996–98 uncontrolled wildfires swept through forests in Brazil, Canada, China's north-eastern Inner Mongolia Autonomous Region, France, Greece, Indonesia, Italy, Mexico, Turkey, the Russian Federation and the United States. The health impacts of forest fires can be serious. Experts consider a pollution index of 100 $\mu g/m^3$ unhealthy; in Malaysia, the index reached 800 $\mu g/m^3$. The estimated health cost of forest fires to the people of Southeast Asia was US$1 400 million. Fires are also a serious threat to biodiversity, especially when protected areas are burnt. Early warning and response systems are still weak, particularly in developing countries; there is an urgent need for improved information infrastructures and increased technical response capabilities.

El Niño

Unusual weather conditions over the past two years are also attributed to the *El Niño* Southern Oscillation (ENSO). The 1997/98 *El Niño* developed more quickly and resulted in higher temperatures in the Pacific Ocean than ever recorded before. The presence of this mass of warm water dominated world climate patterns up to mid-1998, causing substantial disruption and damage in many areas, including temperate zones. Extreme rainfall and flooding, droughts and forest fires were among the major impacts. Forecasting and early warning systems, together with human, agricultural and infrastructural protection, have been substantially improved as a result of the most recent *El Niño*.

Land, Forests and Biodiversity

Forests, woodlands and grasslands are still being degraded or destroyed, marginal lands turned into deserts, and natural ecosystems reduced or fragmented, further threatening biodiversity. New evidence confirms that climate change may further aggravate soil erosion in many regions in the coming decades, and threaten food production. Deforestation continues at high rates in developing countries, mainly driven by the demand for wood products and the need for land for agriculture and other purposes. Some 65 million hectares of forest were lost between 1990 and 1995, out of a total of 3500 million hectares. An increase of 9 million hectares in the developed world only slightly offset this loss. The quality of the remaining forest is threatened by a range of pressures including acidification, fuelwood and water abstraction, and fire. Reduced or degraded habitats threaten biodiversity at gene, species and ecosystems level, hampering the provision of key products and services. The widespread introduction of exotic species is a further major cause of biodiversity loss. Most of the threatened species are land-based, with more than half occurring in forests. Freshwater and marine habitats, especially coral reefs, are also very vulnerable.

Freshwater

Rapid population growth combined with industrialization, urbanization, agricultural intensification and water-intensive lifestyles is resulting in a global water crisis. About 20 per cent of the population currently lacks access to safe drinking water, while 50 per cent lacks access to a safe sanitation system. Falling water tables are widespread and cause serious problems, both because they lead to water shortages and, in coastal areas, to salt intrusion. Contamination of drinking water is mostly felt in megacities, while nitrate pollution and increasing loads of heavy metals affect water quality nearly everywhere. The world supply of freshwater cannot be increased; more and more people depend on this fixed supply; and more and more of it is polluted. Water security, like food security, will become a major national and regional priority in many areas of the world in the decades to come.

Marine and Coastal Areas

Urban and industrial development, tourism, aquaculture, waste dumping and discharges into marine areas are degrading coastal areas around the world and destroying ecosystems such as wetlands, mangroves and coral reefs. Climatic changes also affect the quality of ocean water as well as sea levels. Low-lying areas, including many small islands, risk inundation. The global marine fish catch almost doubled between 1975 and 1995, and the state of the world's fisheries has now reached crisis point. About 60 per cent of the world's fisheries are at or near the point at which yields decline.

Atmosphere

There is a major difference between air pollution trends in developed and developing countries. Strenuous efforts have begun to abate atmospheric pollution in many industrialized countries but urban air pollution is reaching crisis dimensions in most large cities of the developing world. Road traffic, the burning of coal and high-sulphur fuels, and forest fires are the major causes of air pollution. People in developing countries are also exposed to high levels of indoor pollutants from open fires. Some 50 per cent of chronic respiratory illness is now thought to be associated with air pollution. Large areas of forest and farmland are also being degraded by acid rain.

Urban Impacts

Many environmental problems reinforce one another in small, densely-populated areas. Air pollution, garbage, hazardous wastes, noise and water contamination turn these areas into environmental hot spots. Children are the most vulnerable to the inevitable health risks. Some 30–60 per cent of the urban population in low-income countries still lack adequate housing with sanitary facilities, drainage systems and piping for clean water. Continuing urbanization and industrialization, combined with a lack of resources and expertise, are increasing the severity of the problem. However, many local authorities are now joining forces to promote the concept of the sustainable city.

Policy Responses: A Global Overview

As awareness of environmental issues and their causes develops, the focus of policy questions shifts towards the policy response itself: what is being done, is it adequate and what are the alternatives? *GEO-2000* includes a unique assessment of environmental policies worldwide.

Environmental laws and institutions have been strongly developed over the past few years in almost all countries. Command and control policy via direct regulation is the most prominent policy instrument but its effectiveness depends on the manpower available, methods of implementation and control, and level of institutional coordination and policy integration. In most regions, such policies are still organized by sector but environmental planning and environmental impact assessment are becoming increasingly common everywhere.

While most regions are now trying to strengthen their institutions and regulations, some are shifting towards deregulation, increased use of economic instruments and subsidy reform, reliance on voluntary action by the private sector, and more public and NGO participation. This development is fed by the increasing complexity of environmental regulation and high control costs as well as demands from the private sector for more flexibility, self-regulation and cost-effectiveness.

GEO-2000 confirms the overall assessment of *GEO-1*: the global system of environmental management is moving in the right direction but much too slowly. Yet effective and well tried policy instruments do exist that could lead much more quickly to sustainability. If the new millennium is not to be marred by major environmental disasters, alternative policies will have to be swiftly implemented.

One of the major conclusions of the policy review concerns the implementation and effectiveness of existing policy instruments. The assessment of implementation, compliance and effectiveness of policy initiatives is complicated and plagued by gaps in data, conceptual difficulties and methodological problems.

Multilateral environmental agreements (MEAs) have proven to be powerful tools for attacking environmental problems. Each region has its own regional and sub-regional agreements, mostly relating to the common management or protection of natural resources such as water supply in river basins and transboundary air pollution. There are also many global-level agreements, including those on climate change and biodiversity that resulted from the United Nations Conference on Environment and Development, held in Rio de Janeiro, Brazil, in 1992.

In addition to the binding MEAs, there are non-binding agreements (such as *Agenda 21*) and environmental clauses or principles in wider agreements (such as regional trade treaties). A major trend in MEAs over the years has been a widening focus from issue-specific approaches (such as provisions for shared rivers) to trans-sectoral approaches (such as the Basel Convention), to globalization and to the general recognition of the linkage between environment and development. Another trend is still unfolding: the step-by-step establishment of common principles (such as the Forest Principles) in different sectors.

The *GEO-2000* review of MEAs highlights two issues:

- the effectiveness of MEAs depends strongly on the institutional arrangements, the financial and compliance mechanisms, and the enforcement systems that have been set up for them;
- it is still difficult to assess accurately the effectiveness of MEAs and non-binding instruments because of the lack of accepted indicators.

Regional Trends

Africa

Poverty is a major cause and consequence of the environmental degradation and resource depletion that threaten the region. Major environmental challenges include deforestation, soil degradation and desertification, declining biodiversity and marine resources, water scarcity, and deteriorating water and air quality. Urbanization is an emerging issue, bringing with it the range of human health and environmental problems well known in urban areas throughout the world. Growing 'environmental debts' in many countries are a major concern because the cost of remedial action will be far greater than preventive action.

Although many African countries are implementing new national and multilateral environmental policies, their effectiveness is often low due to lack of adequate staff, expertise, funds and equipment for implementation and enforcement. Current environmental policies are mainly based on regulatory instruments but some countries have begun to consider a broader range, including economic incentives implemented through different tax systems. Although cleaner production centres have been created in a few countries, most industries have made little effort to adopt cleaner production approaches. However, some multinational corporations, large-scale mining companies and even local enterprises have recently voluntarily adopted precautionary environmental standards.

There is growing recognition that national environmental policies are more likely to be effectively implemented if they are supported by an informed and involved public. Environmental awareness and education programmes are expanding almost everywhere, while indigenous knowledge receives greater recognition and is increasingly used. Environmental information systems are still weak.

There is fairly high interest in many of the global MEAs, and several regional MEAs have been developed to support the global ones. The compliance and implementation rate is, however, quite low, mainly due to lack of funds.

Asia and the Pacific

Asia and the Pacific is the largest region and it is facing serious environmental challenges. High population densities are putting enormous stress on the environment. Continued rapid economic growth and industrialization is likely to cause further environmental damage, with the region becoming more degraded, less forested, more polluted and less ecologically diverse in the future.

The region, which has only 30 per cent of the world's land area, supports 60 per cent of the world population. This is leading to land degradation, especially in marginal areas, and habitat fragmentation. Increasing habitat fragmentation has depleted the wide variety of forest products that used to be an important source of food, medicine and income for indigenous people. Forest fires caused extensive damage in 1997–98.

Water supply is a serious problem. Already at least one in three Asians has no access to safe drinking water and freshwater will be the major limiting factor to producing more food in the future, especially in populous and arid areas. Energy demand is rising faster than in any other part of the world. The proportion of people living in urban centres is rising rapidly, and is focused on a few urban centres. Asia's particular style of urbanization—towards megacities—is likely to increase environmental and social stresses.

Widespread concern over pollution and natural resources has led to legislation to curb emissions and conserve natural resources. Governments have been particularly active in promoting environmental compliance and enforcement although the latter is still a problem in parts of the region. Economic incentives and disincentives are beginning to be used for environmental protection and the promotion of resource efficiency. Pollution fines are common and deposit-refund schemes are being promoted to encourage reuse and recycling. Industry groups in both low- and high-income countries are becoming increasingly sensitive to environmental concerns over industrial production. There is keen interest in ISO14 000 standards for manufacturing and in eco-labelling.

In most countries, domestic investment in environmental issues is increasing. A major thrust, particularly among developing countries, is on water supply, waste reduction and waste recycling. Environment funds have also been established in many countries and have contributed to the prominent role that NGOs now play in environmental action. Many countries are in favour of public participation, and in some this is now required by law. However, education and awareness levels amongst the public are often low, and the environmental information base in the region is weak.

Whilst there is uneven commitment to global MEAs, regional MEAs are important. They include a number of important environmental policy initiatives developed by sub-regional cooperative mechanisms.

One of the greatest challenges is to promote liberal trade yet maintain and strengthen the protection of the environment and natural resources. Some governments are now taking action to reconcile trade and environmental interests through special policies, agreements on product standards, enforcement of the Polluter Pays Principle, and the enforcement of health and sanitary standards for food exports.

Europe and Central Asia

Environmental trends reflect the political and socio-economic legacy of the region. In Western Europe, overall consumption levels have remained high but measures to curb environmental degradation have led to considerable improvements in some, though not all, environmental parameters. Sulphur dioxide emissions, for example, were reduced by more than one-half between 1980 and 1995. In the other sub-regions, recent political change has resulted in sharp though probably temporary reductions in industrial activity, reducing many environmental pressures.

A number of environmental characteristics are common to much of the region. Large areas of forests are damaged by acidification, pollution, drought and forest fires. In many European countries, as much as half the known vertebrate species are under threat and most stocks of commercially-exploited fish in the North Sea have been seriously over-fished. More than half of the large cities in Europe are overexploiting their groundwater resources. Marine and coastal areas are susceptible to damage from a variety of sources. Road transport is now the main source of urban air pollution, and overall emissions are high—Western Europe produces nearly 15 per cent of global CO_2 emissions and eight of the ten countries with the highest per capita SO_2 emissions are in Central and Eastern Europe.

Regional action plans have been effective in forging policies consistent with the principles of sustainable development and in catalysing national and local action. However, some targets have yet to be met and plans in Eastern Europe and Central Asia are less advanced than elsewhere because of weak institutional capacities and the slower pace of economic restructuring and political reform.

Public participation in environmental issues is considered satisfactory in Western Europe, and there are some positive trends in Central and Eastern Europe. Many countries, however, still lack a proper legislative framework for public participation although the Convention on Access to Environmental Information and Public Participation in Environmental Decision Making signed by most of the ECE [Economic Commission for Europe] countries in 1998 should improve the situation. Access to environmental information has significantly increased with the formation of the European Environment Agency and other information resource centres in Europe. The level of support for global and regional MEAs, in terms of both ratification and compliance, is high.

There has been significant success, particularly in Western Europe, in implementing cleaner production programmes and eco-labelling. Within the European Union, green taxation and mitigating the adverse effects of subsidies are important priorities. Legislation is being adopted on entirely new subjects. Examples include the Nitrates Directive, the Habitat Directive and the Natura 2000 plan for a European Ecological Network. Implementation is, however, proving difficult.

The transition countries need to strengthen their institutional capacities, improve the enforcement of fees and fines, and build up the capacity of enterprises to introduce environmental management systems. The major challenge for the region as a whole is to integrate environmental, economic and social policies.

Latin America and the Caribbean

Two major environmental issues stand out in the region. The first is to find solutions to the problems of the urban environment—nearly three-quarters of the population are already urbanized, many in mega-cities. The air quality in most major cities threatens human health and water shortages are common. The second major issue is the depletion and destruction of forest resources, especially in the Amazon basin. Natural forest cover continues to decrease in all countries. A total of 5.8 million hectares a year was lost during 1990–95, resulting in a 3 per cent total loss for the period. This is a major threat to biodiversity. More than 1,000 vertebrate species are now threatened with extinction.

The region has the largest reserves of cultivable land in the world but soil degradation is threatening much cultivated land. In addition, the environmental costs of improved farm technologies have been high. During the 1980s, Central America increased production by 32 per cent but doubled its consumption of pesticides. On the plus side, many countries have substantial potential for curbing their contributions to the build-up of greenhouse gases, given the region's renewable energy sources and the potential of forest conservation and reforestation programmes to provide valuable carbon sinks.

During the past decade, concern for environmental issues has greatly increased, and many new institutions and policies have been put in place. However, these changes have apparently not yet greatly improved environmental management which continues to concentrate on sectoral issues, without integration with economic and social strategies. The lack of financing, technology, personnel and training and, in some cases, large and complex legal frameworks are the most common problems.

Most Latin American economies still rely on the growth of the export sector and on foreign capital inflows, regardless of the consequences to the environment. One feature of such policies is their failure to include environmental costs. Economic development efforts and programmes aimed at fighting poverty continue to be unrelated to environmental policy, due to poor inter-agency coordination and the lack of focus on a broader picture. On the industrial side, some producers have adopted ISO 14 000 standards as a means of demonstrating compliance with international rules.

An encouraging aspect is the trend towards regional collaboration, particularly on transboundary issues. For example, a Regional Response Mechanism for natural disasters has been established with telecommunication networks that link key agencies so that they can make quick assessments of damage, establish needs and mobilize resources to provide initial relief to affected communities. There is considerable interest in global and regional MEAs, and a high level of ratification. However, the level of implementing new policies to comply with these MEAs is generally low.

North America

North Americans use more energy and resources per capita than people in any other region. This causes acute problems for the environment and human health. The region has succeeded, however, in reducing many environmental impacts through stricter legislation and improved management. Whilst emissions of many air pollutants have been markedly reduced over the past 20 years, the region is the largest per capita contributor to greenhouse gases, mainly due to high energy consumption. Fuel use is high—in 1995 the average North American used more than 1600 litres of fuel a year (compared to about 330 litres in Europe). There is continuing concern about the effects of exposure to pesticides, organic pollutants and other toxic compounds. Changes to ecosystems caused by the introduction of non-indigenous species are threatening biodiversity and, in the longer term, global warming could move the ideal range for many North American forest species some 300 km to the north, undermining the utility of forest reserves established to protect particular plant and animal species. Locally, coastal and marine resources are close to depletion or are being seriously threatened.

The environmental policy scene is changing in North America. In Canada, most emphasis is on regulatory reform, federal/provincial policy harmonization and voluntary initiatives. In the United States, the impetus for introducing new types of environmental policies has increased and the country is developing market-based policies such as the use of tradeable emissions permits and agricultural subsidy reform. Voluntary policies and private sector initiatives, often in combination with civil society, are also gaining in importance. These include voluntary pollution reduction initiatives and programmes to ensure responsible management of chemical products. The region is generally active in supporting and complying with regional and global MEAs.

Public participation has been at the heart of many local resource management initiatives. Environmental policy instruments are increasingly developed in consultation with the public and the business community. Participation by NGOs and community residents is increasingly viewed as a valuable part of any environmental protection programme.

Increasing accountability and capacity to measure the performance of environmental policies is an overarching trend. Target setting, monitoring, scientific analysis and the public reporting of environmental policy performance are used to keep stakeholders involved and policies under control. Access to information has been an important incentive for industries to improve their environmental performance.

Despite the many areas where policies have made a major difference, environmental problems have not been eliminated. Economic growth has negated many of the improvements made so far and new problems—such as climate change and biodiversity loss—have emerged.

West Asia

The region is facing a number of major environmental issues, of which degradation of water and land resources is the most pressing. Groundwater resources are in a critical condition because the volumes withdrawn far exceed natural recharge rates. Unless improved water management plans are put in place, major environmental problems are likely to occur in the future.

Land degradation is a serious problem, and the region's rangelands—important for food security—are deteriorating, mainly as a result of overstocking what are essentially fragile ecosystems. Drought, mismanagement of land resources, intensification of agriculture, poor irrigation practices and uncontrolled urbanization have also contributed. Marine and coastal environments have been degraded by overfishing, pollution and habitat destruction. Industrial pollution and management of hazardous wastes also threaten socio-economic development in the region with the oil-producing countries generating two to eight times more hazardous waste per capita than the United States. Over the next decade, urbanization, industrialization, population growth, abuse of agrochemicals, and uncontrolled fishing and hunting are expected to increase pressures on the region's fragile ecosystems and their endemic species.

The command and control approach, through legislation, is still the main environmental management tool in almost all states. However, several new initiatives, such as public awareness campaigns, have been taken to protect environmental resources and control pollution. In addition, many enterprises such as refineries, petrochemical complexes and metal smelters have begun procedures for obtaining certification under the ISO 14 000 series. Another important approach to resource conservation has been a growing interest in recycling scarce resources, particularly water. In many states on the Arabian Peninsula, municipal wastewater is subjected at least to secondary treatment, and is widely used to irrigate trees planted to green the landscape.

Success in implementing global and regional MEAs in the region is mixed and commitment to such policy tools quite weak. At a national level there has, however, been a significant increase in commitment to sustainable development, and environmental institutions have been given a higher priority and status.

Polar Regions

The Arctic and Antarctic play a significant role in the dynamics of the global environment and act as barometers of global change. Both areas are mainly affected by events occurring outside the polar regions. Stratospheric ozone depletion has resulted in high levels of ultraviolet radiation, and polar ice caps, shelves and glaciers are melting as a result of global warming. Both areas act as sinks for persistent organic pollutants, heavy metals and radioactivity, mostly originating from other parts of the world. The contaminants accumulate in food chains and pose a health hazard to polar inhabitants. Wild flora and fauna are also affected by human activities. For example, capelin stocks have collapsed twice in the Arctic since the peak catch of 3 million tonnes in 1977. In the Southern Ocean, the Patagonian toothfish is being over-fished and there is a large accidental mortality of seabirds caught up in fishing equipment. On land, wild communities have been modified by introductions of exotic species and, particularly in northern Europe, by overgrazing of domestic reindeer.

In the Arctic, the end of Cold War tensions has led to new environmental cooperation. The eight Arctic countries have adopted the Arctic Environmental Protection Strategy which includes monitoring and assessment, environmental emergencies, conservation of flora and fauna, and protection of the marine environment. Cooperation amongst groups of indigenous peoples has also been organized. The Antarctic environment benefits from the continuing commitment of Parties to the Antarctic Treaty aimed at reducing the chance of the region becoming a source of discord between states. The Treaty originally focused on mineral and living resources but this focus has now shifted towards broader environmental issues. A similar shift is expected in the Arctic, within the broader context of European environmental policies. In both polar areas, limited financial resources and political attention still constrain the development and implementation of effective policies.

Peter Huber **NO**

Wealth Is Not the Enemy of
the Environment

I thought I'd focus my remarks... on trying to prove to you how very green New York really is. And I don't mean Central Park. I mean the skyscrapers.

But let me begin by stepping back from the city and saying one or two contrarian things about the continent and the planet.

Begin with a little publicized environmental fact. The prevailing winds blow west to east across North America. On the continent itself, we burn enough fossil fuel to release some 1.6 billion metric tons of carbon a year into the air. Yet—as best anyone can measure these things, carbon dioxide levels drop as you move across the continent. One estimate in *Science* magazine puts America's terrestrial uptake of carbon at about 1.7 billion metric tons. What's going on?

Besides burning fossil fuels, we're building suburbs and roads and cities. Suburban sprawl is much in the news these days. Estimates again vary widely, but without doubt, a lot of what used to be farmland around cities is being transformed into suburb. Our cities occupy over twice as much land today as they did in 1920.

Which, on its own, would certainly be making the carbon balance even worse. If we're leveling forest to make room for sprawling cities, it has to be getting worse, right? But we aren't leveling forests. We're reforesting this continent.

U.S. forest cover reached a low of about 600 million acres in 1920. It has been rising ever since. Precisely how fast is hard to pin down. But all analyses show that America's forest cover today is somewhere between 20 million and 140 million acres higher than it was in 1920. At least 10 million acres have been reforested in the last decade alone.

Now how can we square these facts?

We burn huge amounts of fossil fuel, but atmospheric carbon levels drop. Our cities sprawl, but we have more forest. Am I making all this up? No. The facts are what they are. The interesting question is: how come?

Understanding these apparent paradoxes sharply defines, the two types of green I want contrast, hard green and soft green.

From Peter Huber, "Wealth Is Not the Enemy of the Environment," *Vital Speeches of the Day*, vol. 66, no. 12 (April 1, 2000). Copyright © 2000 by Peter Huber. Reprinted by permission of *Vital Speeches of the Day* and the author.

Now let's work our way back to these facts from where we now sit, which is right here, in the heart of [Manhattan].

Here's something the Sierra Club and I agree on almost perfectly: the skyscraper as America's great green gift to the planet. It packs more people on to less land, which leaves more wilderness, undisturbed, in other places, where the people aren't. The city gets Wall Street, Saks, The Met, and the Times Square crowds, which leaves more fly-over country for bison and cougars. It's Saul Steinberg's celebrated *New Yorker* cover, painted green.

Conserve land and you conserve environment. Save "earth"—land itself—and you save the wilderness. There are other things to consider too, and I'll get to them. But if you're honestly interested in wilderness and environmental quality, land is the most important. When I say land, of course, I mean surface —including stream, river, lake and coastal waters, as well.

This is just basic ecology. Life on earth lives at the surface. The less humans disturb the surface—the land—the better for all other species. It's as simple as that.

That's why the Sierra Club and I basically agree about the city: though profligate in its consumption of most everything else, is very frugal with land. The one thing your average New Yorker does not occupy is 40 acres and a mule.

The original conservationists and Theodore Roosevelt [T. R.] had the focus just right. Recognize: to conserve wilderness, you have to conserve wilderness. Not trash. Not aluminum. Not zinc. Not energy. But rather forest, river, stream, coastal waters.

Today's soft say the two go hand in hand—conserve trash—stop using plastics—or conserve energy—ride a bike, not a car—and you conserve wilderness further up the line. But do you?

So how do humans destroy wilderness?

Lots of ways. We build cities and highways, of course. But in fact, they're quite secondary. Our cities, towns, suburbs, roads, and all the interstate highways currently cover under 3 percent of the U.S. land mass—under 60 million acres.

But for every acre of land we occupy ourselves, we use 6 acres for crops. Another 8 acres are designated as range—larders for our livestock. Most of the wilderness loss worldwide is to third-world agriculture.

However bucolic they may appear, farms aren't green. Endless miles of wheat are not bio-diverse prairie. Rangeland isn't pristine wilderness. Cattle denude it of native perennial grasses, to be replaced by sagebrush, mesquite, and juniper, or simply reduce it to desert. Acres of cassava are not acres of rain forest.

Shrinking agriculture is best, and we've done it.

Shrink the footprint of agriculture, and you can really save or restore a lot of wilderness. A 7 percent shrinkage in our agricultural footprint would return as much land to wilderness as wiping all our cities, suburbs, highways and roads off the map.

And shrinking agriculture is exactly what we've been doing, since about 1920. The result has been truly remarkable. Roughly 80 million more acres of

North American cropland were harvested sixty years ago than are harvested today.

That explains one of the paradoxes I started with. Yes, our cities are sprawling. People are leaving the country and moving to the city. The cities themselves have negative population growth. They sprawl because they draw people off the rest of the land. We've flipped from a population that was 80 percent rural two centuries ago, to one that is 80 percent urban today. Sprawling cities absorb a bit of farmland nearby, but return a lot more land to the wilderness farther away.

Most "soft" greens—like the Sierra Club—have the right instincts about cities. They recognize that cities pack a lot of people into a small amount of space. That leaves more wilderness undisturbed.

But what they get right about cities, soft greens get wrong about almost everything else. Most of the policies soft greens prescribe are environmental disasters, because most force us to use more land.

Let me put this as bluntly as I can. From Al Gore to the Sierra Club, the green establishment strives to make the human footprint on the wilderness ... bigger. If we do what they urge us to do with agriculture, our footprint on the land will at least double. If we do what they urge us to do with energy, it will more than double again.

We are saving the earth on this continent with the technologies that the soft greens most passionately oppose.

Until quite recently, humanity's advance meant retreat for the wilderness. The surface—land, river, and shallow coastal waters—supplied all our food, building materials, and fuel. The more we grew, the more land we seized.

In 1850, with one-tenth today's population, the United States cultivated as much cropland as we do today. Almost all of it was managed just as the modern soft would prefer: organic, pesticide-free, and genetically pure. For all that, the plows and the farmer wiped out the perennial grasses, crowded out the last ranges of the bison, eradicated the cougars and wolves, and created the dust bowl.

For much of this century, however, that process has been reversed. With genetic seed improvements, fertilizers, pesticides, and the relentless efficiencies of corporate farming, we almost trebled the land-to-food productivity of our agriculture.

Pesticides, packaging, preservatives, and refrigeration dramatically reduce the agricultural footprint, too.

One of the things that most concerned T.R. when he was pressing for forest conservation in 1905 was the future supply of lumber for railroad ties. Railroads were essential to the economy, and ties consumed enormous amounts of wood.

But that same year—1905—the railroads began coating their ties with creosote. That stopped the termites. The chemical preservative effectively slashed demand by two-thirds, by tripling their lifespan. Since then, wood preservatives and termite eradication have done far more to save forests in America than the recycling of newspapers.

Pesticides, preservatives, food irradiation, and plastic packaging all have comparable effects: they sharply reduce losses along the food chain, from farmer's field to dining room table, with commensurate reductions in agricultural sprawl.

Far more is still possible. The sun delivers an average energy density of roughly 180 watts per square meter of the United States. Wild plants currently convert about 0.35 w/m2 of that into stored energy, a dreadful 1:500 energy conversion efficiency.

Biotechnology could now double and redouble the agricultural productivity of land, in much the same way as silicon technology has doubled and redoubled the informational productivity of sand.

We've done even better with construction. A British frigate in 1790 required some 3,000 trees to build; the Exxon Valdez required none. Concrete, steel, and plastics substitute for hardwoods in our dwellings and furniture, which leaves the wood itself to the forest.

Far more substitution of this kind could be achieved. The total current U.S. wood harvest—90 percent of which is for construction, not energy—exceeds by several-fold the tonnage of all of the steel, copper, lead, nickel, zinc and other metals extracted in the United States. The raw materials for concrete are not at all scarce, and limitless amounts can be extracted from comparatively minuscule areas of land.

Soft greens endorse a few of these opportunities, but oppose most of them. They urge us to eat less meat, because letting cows eat our food before we do creates agricultural sprawl, but they oppose pesticides and preservatives, without which fungi, insects, and rodents do the cow's job instead. They urge us to improve the efficiency of motors and engines, but they oppose biotechnology, which improves the solar conversion efficiency of corn and cow. Sorts prefer natural, organic, free-range, wild—all of which require more land for less food.

The one solar technology that perennially fascinates soft greens is Pholtovoltaics (PV). Indeed, I owe my hard/soft taxonomy of green to Amory Lovins, of the Rocky Mountain Institute, who gained fame in the 1970s promoting what he called "soft" sources of energy like wind and solar over "hard" ones like uranium and coal.

Compared to a green plant, PV is certainly impressive technology. Selenium-doped silicon wafers mounted in glass or plastic can convert sunlight to useful energy better than chlorophyll in a typical leaf. About 60 times better: current PV technology can capture about 20 w/m2 in the United States.

New York, unfortunately, consumes 55 w/m2 of energy. So to power New York with PV, you have to cover every square inch of the city's horizontal surface with wafer—and then extend the PV sprawl over at least twice that area again, somewhere or other upstate.

PV technology could improve, of course. But the laws of nature and physics never allow anything approaching 100 percent capture; a reliable and economical 20 percent would be extraordinary, and would still require enormous amounts of ancillary material and space for energy storage, to keep the lights up when the sun is down.

The numbers for liquid fuels are even worse. The soft alternative here is "biomass." Shifting the prefix from "agri" to "bio" does make things sound greener from the get-go. "Tilling, not drilling. Biology, not geology. Living carbon, not dead carbon. Vegetables, not minerals." I am quoting here from the institute for local self reliance, which exhorts us to return to what it calls the "carbohydrate economy."

Which is to say: agriculture. We are to burn wood, garbage, bacterial mats, sunflower oil, buffalo gourd, peanut shells, chicken droppings, and tallow from lambs.

Farmers love the idea, which makes it doubly attractive to politicians. Green acres in your tank: natural, organic, free range, and wild. "Our goal," declare carbohydrate-economy pundits, "should be to get back to the ratio of 1920 when plant matter constituted one-third of all materials."

We know what the carbohydrate energy economy would look like: we've already lived it. In 1790, agriculture employed over 80 percent of the people; the founding fathers obtained 80 percent of their energy from wood. They had a "renewable" source of oil, too: the sperm whale. Their children and grandchildren almost fished it to extinction, until colonel Edwin Drake finally thought to mount his harpoon on a derrick in Titusville, Pennsylvania. Well into this century, vast areas of woods and forest were still being cut down, just to warm homes and cook food. The forests retreated steadily.

Any return to that way of life would mean resuming the retreat. Your car engine consumes far more calories than your muscles do.

No conceivable mix of solar, biomass, or wind technology could meet even half our current energy demand without (at the very least) doubling the human footprint on the surface of the continent. Sunlight is a thin, diffuse form of energy, and it's found nowhere but on the surface. Humanity burns the energy equivalent of about 1/7th of all the energy captured by all the green plants every year through photosynthesis. And that energy is already being used —to power the wilderness.

How did we escape from the carbohydrate economy in the first place? We began to dig. All U.S. oil wells and refineries together cover about 160,000 acres of land, or about one-fifth the area of King Ranch in southeastern Texas. All coal mines, including all strip mines, cover some two million acres, or well under 1 percent of the area occupied by U.S. crop land.

How did our energy footprint ever get so small?

Coal is dead trees—fossilized biomass. A coal mine yields something like 5000 w/m2 of land, an oil field more like 10,000. This makes them 5 to 10 thousand times more land frugal than existing PV technology, and 100 times more frugal than the highest PV or biomass efficiency even theoretically attainable.

There's no great mystery to why the numbers shake out that way: oil and coal are three-dimensional, sub-surface sources of energy; sunlight is all two-dimensional surface.

The environmental implications are enormous. For every acre occupied by dwellings and offices, we need about 14 acres of farm and range to produce the quite modest amount of energy—edible food—required by the people on that original acre. But we need a mere 0.3 acres of land to deliver the much greater quantities of energy people use as fuel.

In sum, it takes far less land to dig up energy than to grow it. That's what's so dreadfully wrong with all "renewables." By definition, renewables tap energy flow: solar and its immediate byproducts, plant growth or wind. But plant growth is either wilderness we should aim to conserve, or it's a farmer's field already under the plow, that the wilderness might otherwise reclaim.

Real estate on rooftops does offer some ecologically dead surface for solar capture, but there's nowhere near enough of it, and it isn't economical.

Technology won't ever close the gap. Biotechnology is young, which suggests great potential for improving the biomass energy economy. But conventional hard fuels are so much more concentrated forms of energy, and so much more profitable that they attract far more investment, which drives continuous innovation. Soft does improve, but hard improves even faster.

It just isn't a fair race, and it never can be. Sunlight is too thin, and it starts out spread across the surface—exactly where the wilderness is. Going after the sunlight means going after the energy that fuels the wilderness. It means overbuilding the wilderness itself.

Coal, oil, and gas, by contrast, represent ancient biomass already concentrated by nature, and buried in vast, three-dimensional reservoirs. From which it can now be extracted quite easily, through comparatively tiny incisions in the skin of earth. Given a choice, the wilderness will prefer the keyhole surgery every time.

A first soft green response is to suggest that renewables can be harvested interstitially, from within the sprawl that has already occurred. Mount PV arrays on existing rooftops. Process agricultural "waste" into usable fuels. Erect 400 foot-tall wind turbines amongst the rolling vineyards.

These are good rejoinders, so far as they go, but they don't go very far. Despite decades of subsidy and government promotion, "renewables" (other than conventional hydro) now generate barely 0.7 percent of our electricity. Add in the forest industry's on-site burning of waste wood, and renewables contribute perhaps 3 percent of all the energy we consume.

The economics just don't wash. Again, this isn't very surprising—it is, in fact, exactly the same reason that makes hard fuels kinder to the environment. It's just a lot cheaper to gather highly concentrated forms of energy, than dispersed ones.

A second soft rejoinder has nothing to do with the environment, really— it's a purely economic argument. We're going to run out of the stuff under the ground.

They've been saying that about energy since the '70s, just as they said it about food since the time of Thomas Malthus. But the fact is, we don't run out, and all serious economists understand why. Human ingenuity stretches resources and finds substitutes.

What terrifies the honest softs isn't that we're going to run out of fossils, but that we aren't. If we were going to run out any time soon, we wouldn't have to worry so much about global warming, would we? Running out would stop our emissions better than Al Gore possibly could.

In fact, we still have enormous reserves of fossil fuels, coal most especially. And beyond coal lie vast reservoirs of heavy oils in tar sands, which bio-engineered bacteria may make economically accessible. And uranium, and more.

Overall, the price of hard energy keeps dropping, which tells us all we can or need to know about the depths. Meanwhile, the price of land on the environmentally critical surface, and the value we attach to wilderness, keep rising.

The softs' last and most emphatic rejoinder is that hard fuels just devour surface in other, more insidious ways. Uranium becomes Chernobyl. Oil destroys Prince William Sound or—by way of global warming—the whole planet. Hard agriculture's real footprint includes all the land and water contaminated by fertilizers, pesticides, or wayward genes that kill monarch butterflies.

These are valid arguments. But to win the debate they have to be pushed further than they reasonably can be. Hard agriculture and hard fuels start out with footprints at least ten times smaller than the soft alternatives, and more often hundreds or thousands of times smaller. Their secondary sprawl, from pollution and such, has to be very bad indeed to make it as bad as soft alternatives.

And soft alternatives entail secondary sprawl of their own. Technologies that use more material and more surface are generally going to end up polluting more, as well.

The bicyclist emits greenhouse gas, as he puffs along the road—a lot of it, per pound of useful payload moved. Soft agriculture has run-offs, and relies on all-natural pesticides, bred into the pest-resistant crops themselves, and designed to kill predatory insects in much the same way as the chemicals Dow or Dupont would have us spray on less hardy plants. PV's are manufactured from toxic metals. More eagles have been killed by wind turbines than were lost in the Exxon Valdez oil spill. The Audubon Society labeled Enron's proposed wind farm in the Tehachapi mountains north of L.A. the "condor Cuisinart." The carbohydrate economy is the deforestation economy: third world practices make that quite clear.

All the while, hard technology keeps getting cleaner and more efficient. And in one very important sense, it's the hard fuels that are "renewable," not the soft ones.

Much of the land used when we extract fuels from beneath the surface is restored to wilderness after the fuels have been mined. Not so with soft "renewables": the surface-intensive technologies they depend on have to stay in place permanently—that's essential to the "renewing." Only the subsurface fuels are "renewable" so far as renewing the surface of the land is concerned.

Finally, when we have to allow for offsetting environmental benefits, too, soft alternatives certainly have their share, many of them purely aesthetic.

But hard technologies have their secondary benefits as well. Returning land to wilderness, as hard technologies do, can take care of a lot of pollution. Whatever impact pesticides have, freeing up 100 million acres to be reclaimed by forest will likely protect more birds than trying to bankrupt Dow Chemical through Superfund. The most beautiful way to purify water is probably the most effective too: maintain unfarmed, unlogged watersheds.

Carbon vividly illustrates this. As I mentioned at the outset, America is apparently sinking more carbon out of the air than it is emitting into it. What's doing the sinking? In large part, regrowth of forests on land no longer farmed or logged, and faster growth of existing plants and forests, which are fertilized by nitrogen oxides and carbon dioxide "pollutants."

The total forest ecosystem in the United States holds about 52 billion metric tons of carbon. Net growth rate of 3 percent a year is enough to consume all carbon emissions of the U.S. economy, and either in forests themselves or on surrounding grasslands and farms, that is about the net growth rate we seem to have.

Our carbon-energy cycle, begins with carbon sequestered in fossil fuels, and ends with carbon sequestered in trees. The sun supplied the energy that first converted atmospheric carbon to become fossil fuel, and today again, the sun supplies the energy that takes the carbon back out of the air and into the trees. Give it geologic time, and today's new biomass will eventually end up back in the depths once again, as new coal and oil. Well sealed landfills will help advance that process.

The soft green establishment would have us believe that wealth is the enemy of the wilderness. The facts are the opposite.

Wealth limits our residential sprawl: it urbanizes us.

Wealth makes possible hard technologies, which drastically reduce our agricultural and energy footprints on the land. Finally, and perhaps most importantly, wealth is the only means yet discovered to limit human fecundity. The richer people grow, the fewer children they bear.

The city itself is a center of negative population growth.

Western industrial nations have stabilized their population growth overall. And, of course, it is the wealthy nations, not the poor, that pour their land into wilderness conservation.

Wealth is green. Poverty isn't.

I started off by saying you're sitting in the greenest spot on earth, but I misspoke. The greenest spot is just south of here. It's Wall Street.

POSTSCRIPT

Is Environmental Degradation Worsening?

Since the human race developed the capacity to move mountains, both literally and figuratively, it has done so, for both good and ill. Thus, environmental degradation, once confined to the local community, has moved into the global arena, beginning with the 1972 Stockholm conference. Since then, various environmental problems have been the subject of much debate. Is there a problem? If so, what is its origin? How should it be addressed? For each environmental issue, the global community is at different stages in its fight to prevent, minimize, or eliminate some condition. For example, global warming remains a controversy despite an international agreement, the Kyoto Protocol of 1997. Greater progress has been made with respect to ozone layer depletion, in that 126 countries agreed to action in 1992. Acid rain has been the focus of regional action because of its regional character. And biodiversity issues have begun to be addressed, as have desertification, deforestation, and many others.

The point is that the international community must first reach some satisfactory level of consensus on the existence and nature of a problem before it can begin to find agreeable solutions. Thus, at any given moment in time, global policymakers might be at the problem identification stage (does it exist and, if so, what are its parameters?), the solution identification stage (choosing from a range of policy options), or the policy implementation stage (action undertaken to solve the problem).

The latter circumstance makes it difficult for the thoughtful reader to make some summary judgments about where we are in addressing questions of environmental degradation. Nonetheless, the *Global Environment Outlook 2000* report was an impressive undertaking. Admittedly, the individuals and groups who took part in the process brought to the table a concern about the environment and, presumably, a belief that it is in trouble. But given the complexity of the terrain and the distinctiveness of the issue areas, one is hard pressed to pass off the report as the work of a small group of individuals who brought their own agenda to the enterprise while ignoring paradigms that were inconsistent with their own beliefs. Accordingly, rejecting the essence of their findings, not to mention specific conclusions, requires an effort of the same magnitude.

But one need not reject the basic premise of the Huber article either. Much smaller in scope and ambition, it suggests that hard agriculture (substantial technological inputs) and hard fuels (nonrenewable sources) make an imprint "at least 10 times smaller than the soft alternatives." For Huber, a major way of creating a much more environmentally friendly planet is to continue to utilize science in the pursuit of fulfilling food and energy needs, and environmental degradation might just take care of itself.

Marvin S. Soroos's *The Endangered Atmosphere: Preserving a Global Commons* (University of South Carolina Press, 1997) addresses the entire range of threats to the atmosphere posed by various external factors. *Global Environmental Politics*, 2d ed., by Gareth Porter and Janet Welsh Brown (Westview Press, 1996) examines environmental policy making across a wide range of issues. Lynton K. Caldwell's *International Environmental Policy: From the Twentieth to the Twenty-First Century*, 3rd ed., in collaboration with Paul S. Weiland (Duke University Press, 1996) represents the contribution of the seniormost scholar in the field of environmental policy making.

Lester R. Brown and his colleagues at the Worldwatch Institute publish periodic studies of the environment, including an annual *State of the World* volume, which examines the contemporary environmental scene of that year. Finally, Stephen Collett's "Environmental Protection and the Earth Summit: Paving the Path to Sustainable Development," in Michael T. Snarr and D. Neil Snarr, eds., *Introducing Global Issues* (Lynne Rienner, 1998), presents a succinct and easily readable description of current global environmental policy-making efforts.

ISSUE 6

Are Alternative Sources of Energy the Best Solution to the World Oil Crisis?

YES: Christopher Flavin and Seth Dunn, from "Reinventing the Energy System," in Lester R. Brown et al., *State of the World 1999* (W. W. Norton, 1999)

NO: Francis R. Stabler, from "The Pump Will Never Run Dry!" *The Futurist* (November 1998)

ISSUE SUMMARY

YES: Christopher Flavin and Seth Dunn, researchers at the World-watch Institute, argue that a new energy system is emerging, in part because of a series of revolutionary new technologies and approaches, that will cause a transition away from reliance on oil as the primary energy source.

NO: Francis R. Stabler, a technology planner for General Motors, contends that technology and free enterprise will combine to allow the human race to continue its reliance on oil far into the future.

T he new millennium witnessed an oil crisis almost immediately, the third major crisis in the last 30 years (1972–1973 and 1979 also saw energy problems). The crisis of 2000 manifested itself in the United States via much higher gasoline prices and in Europe via both rising prices and shortages at the fuel pumps. Both were caused by the inability of national distribution systems to adjust to the Organization of Petroleum Exporting Countries' (OPEC's) changing production levels. By 2001 panic had subsided, but the issue is far from resolved.

These three major fuel crises are discrete episodes in a much larger problem facing the human race, particularly the industrial world. That is, oil, the Earth's current principal source of energy, is a finite resource that ultimately will be totally exhausted. And unlike earlier energy transitions, where a more attractive source invited a change (such as from wood to coal and from coal to oil), the next energy transition is being forced upon the human race in the absence of an attractive alternative. In short, we are being pushed out of our almost total reliance on oil toward a new system with a host of unknowns.

What will the new system be? Will it be a single source or some combination of sources? Will it be a more attractive source? Will the source be readily available at a reasonable price, or will a new cartel emerge that will control much of the supply? Will its production and consumption lead to major new environmental consequences? Will it require major changes to our lifestyles and standards of living?

There are prior questions to be asked, however. Are the calls for a viable alternative to oil premature? Are we simply running scared without cause? Did we learn the wrong lessons from the earlier energy crises? More specifically, were these crises artificially created or a consequence of the physical unavailability of the energy source? Have these crises really been about running out of oil globally, or were they due to other phenomena at work, such as poor distribution planning by oil companies or the use of oil as a political weapon by oil-exporting countries?

For well over half a century now, Western oil-consuming countries have been predicting the end of oil. Using a model known as Hubbert's Curve (named after the U.S. geologist who designed it in the 1930s), policymakers have predicted that the world would run out of oil at various times; the most recent prediction is that oil will run out a couple of decades from now. Simply put, the model visualizes all known available resources and the patterns of consumption on a time line until the wells run dry. Despite such prognostication, it was not until the crisis of the early 1970s that national governments began to consider ways of both prolonging the oil system and finding a suitable replacement. Prior to then, governments as well as the private sector encouraged energy consumption. "The more, the merrier" was an oft-heard refrain. Increases in energy consumption were associated with economic growth. After Europe recovered from the devastation of World War II, for example, every 1 percent increase in energy consumption brought a similar growth in economic output. To the extent that governments engaged in energy policymaking, it was designed solely to encourage increased production and consumption. Prices were kept low, and the energy was readily available. Policies making energy distribution systems more efficient and consumption patterns both more efficient and lowered were almost nonexistent.

But today the search for an alternative to oil continues. Nuclear energy, once thought to be the answer, may play a future role but at a reduced level. Both water power and wind power remain possibilities, as do biomass, geothermal, and solar energy. The question before us, therefore, is whether or not the international community has the luxury of some time before all deposits of oil are exhausted.

The two selections for this issue suggest different answers to this last question. Christopher Flavin and Seth Dunn argue that a new energy system will be fast upon us, the culmination of a global effort to find a better alternative to the principal system of the past century. Francis R. Stabler, on the other hand, maintains that predictions of a gas crisis fueled by the approaching end to fossil fuel on this planet are unfounded. To him, modern technology will do what it has always done—find a solution with the aid of free enterprise.

Christopher Flavin and Seth Dunn

Reinventing the Energy System

W hen the American Press Association gathered the country's "best minds" on the eve of the 1893 Chicago World's Fair and asked them to peer a century into the future, the nation's streets were filled with horse-drawn carriages and illuminated at night by gas lights that were still considered a high-tech novelty. And coal—whose share of commercial energy use had risen from 9 percent in 1850 to more than 60 percent in 1890—was expected to remain dominant for a long time to come.

The commentators who turned their crystal balls toward the nation's energy system foresaw some major changes—but missed others. They anticipated, for example, that "Electrical power will be universal.... Steam and all other sorts of power will be displaced." But while some wrote of trains traveling 100 miles an hour and moving sidewalks, none predicted the ascent of oil, the proliferation of the automobile, or the spread of suburbs and shopping malls made possible by cars. Their predictions also missed the many ways in which inexpensive energy would affect lives and livelihoods through the advent of air-conditioning, television, and continent-bridging jet aircraft. Nor did they foresee that oil and other fossil fuels would one day be used on such a scale as to raise sea levels, disrupt ecosystems, or increase the intensity of heat waves, droughts, and floods.

To most of today's energy futurists, the current system might seem even more solid and immutable than the nineteenth-century system appeared 100 years ago. The internal combustion engine has dominated personal transportation in industrial countries for more than eight decades, and electricity is now so taken for granted that any interruption in its supply is considered an emergency. Today the price of energy is nearly as low—in terms of consumer purchasing power—as it has ever been, and finding new energy sources that are more convenient, reliable, and affordable than fossil fuels is beyond the imagination of many experts. Former Eastern Bloc countries seek economic salvation in oil booms, while China and other developing nations are rushing to join the oil era—pouring hundreds of billions of dollars into the construction of coal mines, oil refineries, power plants, automobile factories, and roads.

Fossil fuels—coal, oil, and natural gas—that are dug or pumped from the ground, then burned in engines or furnaces, provide 90 percent or more of the

From Christopher Flavin and Seth Dunn, "Reinventing the Energy System," in Lester R. Brown et al., *State of the World 1999* (W. W. Norton, 1999). Copyright © 1999 by The Worldwatch Institute. Reprinted by permission of W. W. Norton & Company, Inc. Notes omitted.

energy in most industrial countries and 75 percent of energy worldwide. They are led by petroleum, the most convenient and ubiquitous among them—an energy source that has shaped the twentieth century, and that now seems irreplaceable. But as the Chicago World's Fair writings remind us, energy forecasts can overlook what later seems obvious. A close examination of technological, economic, social, and environmental trends suggests that we may already be in the early stages of a major global energy transition—one that is likely to accelerate early in [this] century.

To understand energy in world history is to expect the unexpected. And as we live in a particularly dynamic period, the least likely scenario may be that the energy picture 100 years from now will closely resemble that of today. Although the future remains, as always, far from crystal clear, the broad outlines of a new energy system may now be emerging, thanks in part to a series of revolutionary new technologies and approaches. These developments suggest that our future energy economy may be highly efficient and decentralized, using a range of sophisticated electronics. The primary energy resources for this system may be the most abundant ones on Earth: the sun, the wind, and other "renewable" sources of energy. And the main fuel for this twenty-first-century economy could be hydrogen, the lightest and most abundant element in the universe.

This transition would in some sense be a return to our roots. *Homo sapiens* has relied for most of its existence on a virtually limitless flow of renewable energy resources—muscles, plants, sun, wind, and water—to meet its basic needs for shelter, heat, cooking, lighting, and movement. The relatively recent transition to coal that began in Europe in the seventeenth century marked a major shift to dependence on a finite stock of fossilized fuels whose remaining energy is now equivalent to less than 11 days of sunshine. From a millennial perspective, today's hydrocarbon-based civilization is but a brief interlude in human history.

[This] century may be as profoundly shaped by the move away from fossil fuels as this [past] century was marked by the move toward them. Although it may take several decades for another system to fully develop, the underlying markets could shift abruptly in the next few years, drying up sales of conventional power plants and cars in a matter of years and affecting the share prices of scores of companies. The economic health—and political power—of nations could be sharply boosted or diminished. And our industries, homes, and cities could be transformed in ways we can only begin to anticipate.

Through the ages, the evolution of human societies has both influenced and been influenced by changes in patterns of energy use. But the timing of this next transition will be especially crucial. Today's energy system completely bypasses roughly 2 billion people who lack modern fuels or electricity, and underserves another 2 billion who cannot afford most energy amenities, such as refrigeration or hot water. Moreover, by relying on the rapid depletion of nonrenewable resources and releasing billions of tons of combustion gases into the atmosphere, we have built the economy on trends that cannot possibly be sustained for another century. The efforts made today to lay the foundations for a new energy system will affect the lives of billions of people in the twenty-first century and beyond.

Prime Movers

Energy transitions do not occur in a vacuum. Past shifts have been propelled by technological change and a range of social, economic, and environmental forces. Understanding these developments is essential for mapping out the path that humanity may follow in the next 100 years. The emergence of an oil-based economy at the beginning of this [past] century, for example, was influenced by rapid scientific advances, the growing needs of an industrial economy, mounting urban environmental problems in the form of smoke and manure, and the aspirations of millions for higher living standards and greater mobility.

Resource limits are one force that could help push the world away from fossil fuels in the coming decades. Oil is the main energy source today, accounting for 30 percent of commercial use; natural gas has emerged as an environmentally preferred alternative for many uses, and has a 23-percent share; coal has maintained a key role in power generation, and holds a 22-percent share of total energy use. Natural gas and coal are both available in sufficient amounts to last until the end of the twenty-first century or beyond—but oil is not. Just as seventeenth-century Britain ran out of cheap wood, today we face the danger of running out of inexpensive petroleum.

Although oil markets have been relatively stable for more than a decade, and real prices approached historical lows in 1998, estimates of the underlying resource base have increased very little. Most of the calm in the oil markets of the 1990s has been due to slower demand growth, not an increase in supply. Despite prodigious exploration efforts, known oil resources have expanded only marginally in the last quarter-century, though some nations have raised their official reserve figures in order to obtain larger OPEC [Organization of Petroleum Exporting Countries] production quotas. Approximately 80 percent of the oil produced today comes from fields discovered before 1973, most of which are in decline. Total world production has increased less than 10 percent in two decades.

In a recent analysis of data on world oil resources, geologists Colin Campbell and Jean Laherrere estimate that roughly 1 trillion barrels of oil remain to be extracted. Since 800 billion barrels have already been used up, this suggests that the original exploitable resource base is nearly half gone. As extraction of a nonrenewable resource tends to follow a bell-shaped curve, these figures can be extrapolated to project that world production will peak by 2010, and then begin to decline. Applying the more optimistic resource estimates of other oil experts would push back this production pinnacle by just a decade.

A peak in world oil production early in [this] century would reverberate through the energy system. The problem is not just the large amount of oil currently used—67 million barrels daily—but the intent of many developing countries, most lacking much oil of their own, to increase their use of automobiles and trucks. Meeting the growing needs of China, India, and the rest of the developing world in the way industrial countries' demands are met today would require a tripling of world oil production, even assuming no increases in industrial-country use. Yet production capacity in 2020 is unlikely to be much above current levels—and may well be declining.

Long before we completely run out of fossil fuels, however, the environmental and health burdens of using them may force us toward a cleaner energy system. Fossil fuel burning is the main source of air pollution and a leading cause of water and land degradation. Combustion of coal and oil produces carbon monoxide and tiny particulates that have been implicated in lung cancer and other respiratory problems; nitrogen and sulfur oxides create urban smog, and bring acid rain that has damaged forests extensively. Oil spills, refinery operations, and coal mining release toxic materials that impair water quality. Increasingly, oil exploration disrupts fragile ecosystems and coal mining removes entire mountains. Although modern pollution controls have improved air quality in most industrial countries in recent decades, the deadly experiences of London and Pittsburgh are now being repeated in Mexico City, São Paulo, New Delhi, Bangkok, and many other cities in the developing world. Each year, coal burning is estimated to kill 178,000 people prematurely in China alone.

Beyond these localized problems, it is the cumulative, global environmental effects that now are calling the fossil fuel economy into question. More than 200 years have passed since we began burning the sequestered sunlight of fossilized plants that took millions of years to accumulate, but only recently has it become evident that the carbon those fuels produce is disrupting the Earth's radiation balance, causing the planet to warm. Fossil fuel combustion has increased atmospheric concentrations of the heat-trapping gas carbon dioxide (CO_2) by 30 percent since preindustrial times. CO_2 levels are now at their highest point in 160,000 years, and global temperatures at their highest since the Middle Ages. Experts believe human activities could be ending the period of relative climatic stability that has endured over the last 10,000 years, and that permitted the rise of agricultural and industrial society.

In recent years scientists have extensively documented trends—receding glaciers, rising sea levels, dying coral reefs, spreading infectious diseases, migrating plants and animals—that are consistent with the projected effects of a warmer world. The extraordinary heat of 1998—on pace to hit a new record—was related to, but extended well beyond, an unusually strong El Niño phenomenon. This contributed to a range of extreme weather events, including droughts and rare fires in tropical and subtropical forests from Indonesia to Mexico; historic floods in China and Bangladesh; severe storms and epidemics in Africa and North, Central, and South America; and deadly heat waves in the United States, southern Europe, and India. The climate system is nonlinear and has in the past switched abruptly—even in the space of a few decades—to another equilibrium after crossing a temperature threshold. Such shifts have the potential to greatly disrupt both the natural world and human society. Indeed, previous changes have coincided with the collapse of several ancient civilizations.

Stabilizing atmospheric CO_2 concentrations at safe levels will require a 60–80 percent cut in carbon emissions from current levels, according to the best estimates of scientists. The Kyoto Protocol to the U.N. Framework Convention on Climate Change, agreed to in December 1997, is intended to be a small step on this long journey—which would eventually end the fossil-fuel-based economy as we know it today.

Energy transitions are also shaped by the changing needs of societies. Historians argue that coal won out over wood and other renewable resources during the eighteenth and nineteenth centuries in part due to the requirements of the shift from a rural, agrarian society to an urban, industrial one. Abundant and concentrated forms of energy were required for the new industries and booming cities of the period. In this view, coal did not bring about the transition but adapted to it more quickly. Ironically, the success of water mills and windmills in promoting early industrialization led to expanding energy demands that could only be met by the coal-fired stream engine.

Today's fast-growth economic sectors are not the production of food or automobiles, but software, telecommunications, and a broad array of services— from finance and news to education and entertainment. The Information Revolution will, like the Industrial Revolution, have its own energy needs—and will place a premium on reliability. Computer systems freeze up if power is cut off for a fraction of a second; heavy industries, such as chemical and steel production, now depend on semiconductor chips to operate. Yet the mechanical machines and networks of above-ground wires and pipelines that power current energy systems are vulnerable. Today's systems are also centralized, while much of the service economy can be conducted from far-flung locations that are connected through the Internet, and may require more localized, autonomous energy supplies than power grids or gas lines can provide. As with the water wheel, so with oil: the growing demands of the new economy might not be met by the energy system that helped launch it.

In the twenty-first century, the requirements of the developing world— where 80 percent or more of the new energy investment is expected to take place—are likely to be the leading driver of energy markets. Eighteenth-century Great Britain shifted to coal, and the twentieth-century United States to oil, in part to meet the demands of growing populations; similar changes might be expected as more than 5 billion people seek more convenient transportation, refrigeration, air-conditioning, and other amenities in the years ahead. Technologies that can meet the demands of developing nations at minimal cost may therefore assume prominent roles in the overall transition.

Systemic Change

The closing decades of the nineteenth century were a fertile period in the history of technology, as inventors applied novel scientific advances to a range of new devices. The incandescent light bulb, electric dynamo, and internal combustion engine were invented in the late 1800s but had relatively little effect on industry or daily life as the century ended. As they came into widespread use in later decades, however, it became clear in retrospect that the technological foundation for the transition was largely in place by 1900.

Today a new energy system is gestating in the late-twentieth-century fields of electronics, synthetic materials, biotechnology, and software. The silicon semiconductor chip, promising increased processing power and miniaturization of electronic devices, allows energy use to be matched more closely to need. Wider use of these chips offers efficiency gains in appliances, buildings, industry, and transport, making it possible to control precisely nearly all energy-using devices. Electronic controls also enable a range of small-scale, modular technologies to challenge the large-scale energy devices of the twentieth century.

Breakthroughs in chemistry and materials science are also playing key roles in energy, providing sophisticated, lightweight materials that operate without the wear and tear of moving parts. Modern wind turbines use the same carbon-fiber synthetic materials found in bullet-proof vests, "gore-tex" synthetic membranes line the latest fuel cells, and new "super-insulation" that reduces the energy needs of buildings relies on the same aluminum foil vacuum process that keeps coffee fresh. The latest electrochemical window coatings can be adjusted to reflect or absorb heat and light in response to weather conditions and the time of day.

A particularly fertile area of advance is in lighting, where the search is on for successors to Thomas Edison's incandescent bulb. Improvements in small-scale electronic ballasts have given rise to the compact fluorescent lamp (CFL), which requires one quarter the electricity of incandescent bulbs and last 10 times as long. Manufacturers are now working on even more advanced models with tiny ballasts that work with any light socket, and that cost half as much as today's models. Yet the new light-emitting diode (LED), a solid-state semiconductor device that emits a very bright light when charged, is twice as efficient as CFLs and lasts 10 times as long. Today's LEDs produce red and yellow light, which limits their market to applications such as traffic signals and automobile taillights, but scientists believe that white-light versions will soon become practical.

Late-twentieth-century technology has also revived an ancient source of energy: the wind. The first windmills for grinding grain appeared in Persia just over 1,000 years ago, and eventually spread to China, throughout the Mediterranean, and to northern Europe, where the Dutch developed the massive machines for which the country is still known. Wind power emerged as a serious option for generating electricity when Danish engineers began to apply advanced engineering and materials in the 1970s. The latest versions, which are also manufactured by companies based in Germany, India, Spain, and the United States, have variable-pitch fiberglass blades that are as long as 40 meters, electronic variable speed drives, and sophisticated microprocessor controls. Wind power is now economically competitive with fossil fuel generated electricity, and the market, valued at roughly $2 billion in 1998, is growing more than 25 percent annually.

Use of the sun as an energy source is also being renewed by modern technology. The solar photovoltaic cell, a semiconductor device that turns the sun's radiation directly into electric current, is widely used in off-grid applications as a power source for satellites and remote communications systems, as well as in consumer electronic devices such as pocket calculators and watches. Improvements in cell efficiency and materials have lowered costs by 80 percent in the past two decades, and the cells are now being built into shingles, tiles, and window glass—allowing buildings to generate their own electricity. Markets are booming. The cost of solar cells will need to fall by another 50–75 percent in order to be fully competitive with coal-fired electricity, but automated manufacturing, larger factories, and more-efficient cells promise further cost reductions in the near future. Semiconductor research is also nurturing the development of a close cousin of the solar cell, the "thermophotovoltaic" cell, which can produce electricity from industrial waste heat.

The technology that could most transform the energy system, the fuel cell, was first discovered in 1829, five decades before the internal combustion engine. The fuel cell attracted considerable interest at the turn of the century but required efficiency improvements before its first modern application in the U.S. space program in the 1960s. Fuel cells use an electrochemical process that combines hydrogen and oxygen, producing water and electricity. Avoiding the inherent inefficiency of combustion, today's top fuel cells are roughly twice as efficient as conventional engines, have no moving parts, require little maintenance, are nearly silent, and emit only water vapor. Unlike today's power plants, they are nearly as economical on a small scale as on a large one. Indeed, they could turn the very notion of a power plant into something more closely resembling a home appliance.

Although the first fuel cells now run on natural gas—which can be separated into hydrogen and carbon dioxide—in the long term they may be fueled by pure hydrogen that is separated from water by using electricity, a process known as electrolysis. Researchers are also testing various catalysts that, when placed in water that is illuminated by sunlight, may one day produce inexpensive hydrogen. Chemists have recently developed a solar-powered "water splitter" that nearly doubles the efficiency of converting solar energy to hydrogen. Some scientists note that finding a cheap and efficient way to electrolyze water could make hydrogen as dominant an energy carrier in the twenty-first century as oil was in the twentieth.

Many energy analysts argue that it will take a long time for such devices to become competitive with fossil fuels. But dwelling on the current cost gap ignores a principle that Henry Ford discovered earlier this [past] century. Mass production allowed Ford to cut the cost of a Model T by 65 percent between 1909 and 1923. As with the Model T, the costs of the new, modular energy devices are expected to fall dramatically as their markets expand.

Historically, energy innovations have first emerged in specialized "niches" where they were, for a variety of reasons, preferred to the conventional fuel. Petroleum's initial market was as a replacement for whale oil used in lighting kerosene lamps; what now seems a marginal use of oil was a powerful force in the late nineteenth century, sufficient to attract millions of dollars of investment. Today's emerging energy technologies are exploiting similarly small but growing niches that are spurring investment and larger-scale manufacturing. Shipments of solar cells doubled between 1994 and 1997 as a result of burgeoning niche markets such as powering highway signals and water pumps, as well as a half-million homes not connected to a grid, where solar power is the most economical source of electricity. Fuel cells are first appearing in buses, hospitals, military bases, and wastewater treatment plants, and are being developed for cellular phones, laptop computers, and cabin lamps. One day, they could be found in most buildings and automobiles.

As these examples suggest, downsizing and decentralization may become major features of the twenty-first century energy economy. While the twentieth century has seen a trend toward larger facilities and greater distances between energy source and use, the new technologies would place an affordable, reliable, and accessible power supply near where it is needed. This would retrace the computer industry's path from mainframe to desktop computers in the past two decades—and resurrect Thomas Edison's vision of decentralized, small-scale power generation. In contrast to today's monoculture of power generation, a distributed energy system would combine a range of new devices: small turbines in factories, fuel cells in basements, rooftop solar panels, wind turbines scattered across pastures, and power plants that can be carried in a briefcase.

The information age—itself downsized and decentralized—could help ensure the reliability of a distributed power system through instantaneous telecommunications and sophisticated electronic controls that coordinate millions of individual generators, much as the Internet works today. Computer and telecommunication companies are developing "intelligent" power systems that send signals over phone lines, television cables, and electric lines. Micro-generators and even home appliances can be programmed to respond to electronically relayed price information, providing power to the grid and storing it—in the form of hydrogen, or the kinetic energy of a flywheel—as demand fluctuates. This fine-tuning of the balance between electricity supply and demand would increase the efficiency of the new system—reducing pollution and saving energy and money.

Buildings were energy self-sufficient for much of history, but in the last century they have become dependent on increasingly distant sources of supply. A distributed energy system would allow buildings to once again meet most of their own energy needs with rooftop solar systems, fuel cells, and flywheels— even becoming net energy generators that sell excess power back to the grid. Basement fuel cells could provide electricity and heat during the day, while automobiles and electric bicycles might be replenished with household-generated hydrogen or electricity at night. "Zero net energy" buildings can be tightly designed to rely on passive solar energy and on the body heat of occupants. Buildings themselves may be made of mass-produced components and modules that can be shipped to a site and then assembled.

The automobile, too, is likely to be reshaped. Oil's automotive successors —be they batteries or turbines, flywheels or fuel cells—will likewise motivate engineers to make the rest of the vehicle as lightweight as possible, as demonstrated with the bulky lead-acid battery and sleek exterior of the first modern commercial electric car, designed by General Motors (GM). The first commercially available "hybrid-electric" vehicle, Toyota's Prius, uses engine and battery in tandem and is twice as fuel-efficient as the average U.S. car. (More than 7,700 sold in the first eight months, leading the company to double production during its first year; Toyota [had] plans to market the vehicle in North America and Europe by 2000.) In a combination of these two ideas, the first hybrid-electric fuel cell taxi has appeared on the streets of London. Trucks, locomotives, and other heavy vehicles may also soon shift—and adjust—to the new technologies.

Running a modular energy system on renewable resources will require adapting the system to their intermittent nature. A temporary measure might be to build backup generators using efficient gas turbines, fuel cells, or pumped water storage; new technologies such as compressed air, plastic batteries, flywheels, and other energy storage devices also have parts to play. But the key to a reliable, diversified energy system based on renewable sources will be the use of hydrogen as a major energy carrier and storage medium.

Developing a system for storing and transporting hydrogen will be a major undertaking. In the long run, materials that can store large amounts of hydrogen, such as metal hydrides or carbon nanotubes, are being developed for use in electric vehicles and other applications. And deriving hydrogen from natural gas for the initial generation of fuel cells would allow the early stages of a hydrogen economy to be based on the extensive natural gas pipelines and other equipment already in place. Small-scale reforming units that convert natural gas into hydrogen could be placed in homes, office buildings, and service stations. The carbon dioxide released from this conversion would be far less than from internal combustion engines, and could be turned into plastics or sequestered in underground or undersea reservoirs.

The use of natural gas as a "bridge" to hydrogen might allow for a relatively seamless transition to a renewable-energy-based system. Hydrogen could be mixed with natural gas and carried in the same pipelines, then later transported through rebuilt pipelines and compressors that are designed to carry pure hydrogen. Large amounts of hydrogen might be produced in remote wind farms or solar stations, and then stored underground; homeowners could produce hydrogen from rooftop solar cells and store it in the basement. Liquid hydrogen could find a niche in air transport—replacing the kerosene that figured prominently in the rise of oil and that still fuels most commercial jets.

Systemic change can begin slowly, but gather momentum quickly. The transition from gas to electric lighting proceeded quietly at first: in 1910, only 10 percent of U.S. houses had electricity. At the turn of the twentieth century, the gasoline-powered car was still competing with the horsedrawn carriage and the steam engine– and electric battery–powered car, while oil accounted for just 2.4 percent of U.S. energy use. Within a generation, however, the internal combustion engine had displaced the others; oil had surpassed coal by 1921; and by 1930, 80 percent of the country's houses had been electrified. The pace and direction of an energy transition, then, are determined not just by technological developments, but also by how industries, governments, and societies respond to them.

NO

Francis R. Stabler

The Pump Will Never Run Dry!

Experts have debated the fate of fossil-fuel supplies for the past 30 years. Doomsayers predict that economic disaster is just around the corner, as hydrocarbon fuel becomes increasingly scarce and prices rise beyond reach.

For the record, I say the pumps at local service stations will never go dry unless governments create an artificial shortage. I doubt that the citizens of the United States or those of most other nations will allow that to happen. Those who predict a cataclysmic fuel shortage underestimate the capabilities of mankind to utilize available resources.

Let's consider the petroleum supply: Since the 1970s, people have repeatedly said that we will run out of affordable petroleum in a few years—five, 10, or 20, depending on the writer. When we examine today's proven oil reserves, we find them to be at historically high levels: 40 to 50 years' supply at the current rate of usage. As demand has increased, the oil industry has responded by identifying additional supplies.

How long can this go on? I do not have an absolute answer, but even a slowly expanding supply will continue to meet the demand for many decades. In addition, oil shale and tar sands have a potential to provide petroleum supplies equivalent to or greater than the known oil reserves. The recovery of this resource is starting to look economically viable and could double our oil supply.

Fuel From Natural Gas and Methane

There are a number of reasons why the pumps will not go dry, even though petroleum is a finite resource.

Experts say that natural gas supplies far exceed potential oil reserves in total energy value. Many countries, including some that lack significant oil resources, have large natural gas supplies. But most cars do not run on natural gas.

Recent advances by oil company and related researchers have identified new processes, or enhanced old ones (such as the Fischer-Trope process), that can economically convert natural gas to diesel fuel and petrochemical feedstock. A side benefit is that the resulting fuel is a naturally clean, low-sulfur

From Francis R. Stabler, "The Pump Will Never Run Dry!" *The Futurist*, vol. 32, no. 8 (November 1998). Copyright © 1998 by The World Future Society. Reprinted by permission of The World Future Society, 7910 Woodmont Avenue, Suite 450, Bethesda, Maryland 20814.

variety needed for low-emission vehicles. A billion-dollar facility being constructed in Qatar by Exxon is evidence of the industry's faith in natural gas conversion. An operational Shell Oil plant in Malaysia provides fuel today, and seagoing facilities to convert drill platform flare gas to liquid fuel are being proposed.

Figure 1

Gas-to-Liquids Technology: Converting Natural Gas to Liquids

Source: Exxon Corporation

It is possible to convert natural gas into gasoline, but this process is currently more expensive than converting crude oil to gasoline. Remote sources of natural gas are increasing in value now that they can be converted to liquid fuel and transported to market by conventional means. Some countries with little crude oil but plenty of natural gas can potentially become fuel independent or even fuel exporters.

Methanol, also a liquid fuel derived from natural gas, is produced by many factories around the world. Its use may increase in some areas, but methanol has a distribution problem: It cannot be transported by the same pipelines that currently transport petroleum products. Even this plentiful supply of liquid fuel from natural gas cannot last forever, so how will we keep the pumps full in the future?

In the last few years, deposits of methane hydrate have been discovered under the sea floor. Methane gas is generated when organic material settling at the bottom of the ocean is decomposed by bacteria. At low temperatures and high pressure, this methane can be trapped in ice crystals below the ocean floor. These deposits may have as much as four times the energy value of the total natural gas supply. The methane energy supply could also be converted to liquid fuel using the same processes used for natural gas, which is primarily methane. Conversion at the recovery site, usually at sea, would make transportation of the fuel easier.

No one has yet invented an economical method for recovering methane from hydrate deposits, but the problem has only been studied for a short time. The economic stakes in harvesting this methane supply and converting it to liquid fuel are high enough to drive a lot of technical creativity. The challenge is similar to that of the economical recovery of oil from beneath the North Sea floor, a task considered impossible not long ago. Energy-poor countries such as Japan have a strong incentive to develop methods to harvest methane. But even this vast resource of clean energy will come to an end some day; therefore, it only postpones the day when the pumps could run dry. It will, however, buy us time to prepare for an alternate supply.

Fuel From Space

If it takes eons for hydrocarbons to form, at some point the earth's supply will be exhausted, the pumps will run dry, and the wheels of transportation will stop. Many otherwise rational people feel that, if we can no longer poke a hole in the ground and get vast supplies of "natural" hydrocarbons, all is lost for our civilization. Why not skip the eons it takes to form hydrocarbon deposits in the ground and make our own?

Sustainability does not mean we have to hoard our meager supplies or use valuable cropland and fertilizer to grow biomass for ethanol factories. This is an energy dead end. We can make our own hydrocarbons in other ways.

In looking for a way to explore Mars faster and cheaper, NASA has identified a novel way to make hydrocarbons. Several scientific papers and Robert Zubin's book, *Mars Direct,* describe a straightforward method for turning carbon dioxide (the primary constituent of the Martian atmosphere) into fuel. NASA would first send a small automatic chemical factory, a supply of hydrogen, and a nuclear-powered thermoelectric generator to Mars. The factory would use the hydrogen and electric power to turn the carbon dioxide in the Martian atmosphere into hydrocarbon fuel (methane), water, and oxygen for use by the explorers to follow. They could use the methane and oxygen to fuel their ground exploration vehicles and their rocket for return to Earth.

Why not use outer space technology right here at home? We can convert a waste product, carbon dioxide, into usable hydrocarbons (methane) by combining it with hydrogen from water. The source of carbon dioxide can be low-grade coal deposits, garbage, feed-lot waste, and many other currently neglected sources of carbon. It may be possible to collect carbon dioxide directly from the smokestacks of coal-fired power plants and factories and pipe it to fuel production facilities.

We might even achieve the ultimate in fuel sustainability by mimicking what plants do naturally: Take carbon dioxide from the atmosphere and recycle it into fuel. The process will require energy added into the loop, water as a raw material, and electricity to generate hydrogen from water using electrolysis. Thermal energy will be needed for parts of the chemical process of making liquid fuel.

We have several possible sources of electrical and thermal energy for this seemingly magical process. Off-peak power from current facilities, hydroelectric power, nuclear power plants, ground solar energy collectors, solar power satellites, and even that holy grail of energy sources—nuclear fusion—are all potential power sources for hydrocarbon manufacturing plants. We might even use hydrogen directly for transportation purposes, although distribution and storage for mobile applications are difficult obstacles. Converting hydrogen into liquid hydrocarbon fuel would make the new product compatible with the existing infrastructure and transportation fleet. This conversion process is in fact an inexpensive way to store electrical energy in chemical form for ease of transportation and later use. It could also supply service station pumps with a fuel source that keeps flowing for a long time.

Fueling Future Mobility

There are many potential sources of gasoline and diesel fuel for personal transportation in the future. There are also supply problems that we would be foolhardy to ignore. Fuel from sunlight, water, and air will not be free fuel. Huge capital investments will be required at every stage of development. These are the kinds of investments that are made each day to produce the goods and services that consumers are willing to pay for—and that provide a return on shareholders' investments.

These proposed fuel processes will not develop overnight, but neither will our current fuel supply be exhausted tomorrow. There may be short-term fuel shortages and spikes in prices during transition periods, but these disruptions are unlikely to be any more severe than the politically motivated ones we have experienced in the past.

I don't claim that any one of these fuel-generating processes is the best way to provide gasoline to your local service station. They are intended to show that it is possible to make liquid fuel in the form of gasoline or diesel fuel from many available resources. It is also feasible to produce liquid fuels using electric power in a sustainable process. Better, cheaper, cleaner processes may well be available. I leave it to the chemical, refining, and manufacturing experts to devise the best and least-expensive processes to generate fuel to keep our transportation system moving.

The investors in methane hydrate wells, desert solar collection farms, smokestack carbon dioxide recovery systems, and new fuel production complexes will eventually become wealthy, although they may have to wait until the petroleum supplies are reduced. In the meantime, researchers and entrepreneurs are honing their ability to make gasoline and diesel fuel at a lower cost than is currently done from petroleum. They must beat the costs of the oil companies that start with crude oil pumped from the ground the old-fashioned way. The alternative is to wait until the price of petroleum rises to a level where the new sources can compete.

The winners of the future will be the wealthy energy companies that do not wait too long. They may have familiar names, like Shell, Arco, BP, and Exxon —companies that want to continue making a profit by providing the world's fuel.

We should not permit a narrow view of the future to frighten us into no-growth practices that undermine civilization in general. Human ingenuity, if allowed to address the real problems, will provide sustainable solutions for our energy needs. While this prospect may be a bitter pill for the purveyors of doom and the advocates of limits on growth, I think that we have a bright future. We clearly have access to the energy sources necessary to continue fueling the economic engine of the world far into the future.

The fuel pump will not run dry if we can tap into the real source of our unlimited power: individuals and businesses with the freedom to use their intellectual resources.

POSTSCRIPT

Are Alternative Sources of Energy the Best Solution to the World Oil Crisis?

The twenty-first century ushered in another in a series of energy crises that have plagued the developed world since 1972. Gas prices jumped to record heights, and the prospects of a return to $1.00-a-gallon levels seem increasingly remote. Once again, cries for eliminating dependence on foreign oil and for developing alternatives to the twentieth century's principal energy source were heard.

The two articles featured in this issue were written prior to the summer 2000 crisis. But the most recent episode would not have changed their messages. For Stabler, the title of his article tells the reader everything: "The Pump Will Never Run Dry!" How can his conclusion be evaluated? He may not be a neutral observer, as he has worked as a systems engineer in the automotive and defense industries for 30 years and is currently a technology planner for General Motors. Stabler therefore has a vested interest in the internal combustion engine, with its fuel requirement of gasoline. Nonetheless, he lays out a systematic argument for his position, with an appropriate level of evidence in support of his conclusions. Moreover, as a technology planner for an automotive giant, it would not behoove him to suggest continual reliance on a technology that may become obsolete because of fuel limitations.

To be sure, Stabler's view of the future availability of gas is in the minority. One supporter is Julian L. Simon, who argues in *The Ultimate Resource 2* (Princeton University Press, 1996) that even God may not know exactly how much oil and gas are "out there." Chapter 11 of Simon's book is entitled "When Will We Run Out of Oil? Never!" In it, Simon takes the reader through a 12-step process to demonstrate that the doomsayers are wrong.

Flavin and Dunn follow conventional wisdom in their article. That is, because oil is a finite resource, its supply will end someday, and that day will be sooner rather than later. In fact, they argue that the world may already be in the early stages of a major global energy transition. They assert that the global economy has been built on the rapid depletion of nonrenewable resources and that such consumption levels cannot possibly be maintained throughout the twenty-first century. Although Flavin and Dunn's arguments probably have a receptive audience among scholars who are concerned with the increasing scarcity of nonrenewable resources, they require the reader to accept a set of assumptions about the acceleration of future energy consumption. But one can easily be seduced by the logic of their argument because it "just seems to make sense."

Lester R. Brown et al., in *Beyond Malthus: Sixteen Dimensions of the Population Problem* (Worldwatch Institute, 1998), suggest that most writers hold that world oil production will peak sometime between the years 2010 and 2025. The consequence, if that estimate is accurate, is a need for alternative sources. The student of energy politics, however, must be careful not to ignore how advances in energy source exploration and extraction have tended to expand known reserves. Is the future lesson that the tide has finally turned and no significant reserves remain to be discovered? Or is the lesson that history will repeat itself and modern science will yield more oil and gas deposits, as well as make their extraction cost effective?

ISSUE 7

Will the World Be Able to Feed Itself in the Foreseeable Future?

YES: Julian L. Simon, from *The Ultimate Resource 2* (Princeton University Press, 1996)

NO: David Pimentel et al., from "Impact of Population Growth on Food Supplies and Environment," *Population and Environment* (September 1997)

ISSUE SUMMARY

YES: The late professor of economics and business administration Julian L. Simon asserts that the world has always been able to grow food to meet demand and that new technologies will accelerate that ability in the future.

NO: Bioscientist David Pimentel and his colleagues argue that many scholarly groups are increasingly concerned about the ability of the Earth's resource base to feed the planet's growing population.

Visualize two pictures. The first snapshot, typical of photographs that have graced the covers of many of the world's magazines, reveals a group of people in Africa, including a significant number of small children, who show dramatic signs of advanced malnutrition and even starvation. The second picture (really several in sequence) shows an apparently wealthy couple finishing a meal at a rather expensive restaurant. The waiter removes their plates still half full of food, an untouched loaf of French bread, and assorted other morsels from the table and deposits them in the kitchen garbage can. These scenarios once highlighted a popular film about world hunger. The implication was quite clear: If only the wealthy would share their food with the poor, no one would go hungry.

This issue addresses the question of whether or not the world will be able to feed itself by the middle of the twenty-first century. A prior question, of course, is whether or not enough food is grown throughout the world today to handle the current needs of all the planet's citizens. News accounts of chronic food shortages somewhere in the world have been appearing regularly for about

20 years. This time has witnessed graphic accounts in news specials about the consequences of insufficient food, usually in sub-Saharan Africa. Also, several national and international studies have been commissioned to address world hunger. An American study organized by President Jimmy Carter, for example, concluded that the root cause of hunger was poverty.

One might deduce from all this activity that population growth had outpaced food production and that the planet's agricultural capabilities are no longer sufficient. Yet the ability of most countries to grow sufficient food has not yet been challenged. During the 1970–2000 period, only one region of the globe, sub-Saharan Africa, was unable to have its own food production keep pace with population growth. All other regions of the globe experienced food increases greater than human growth.

This is instructive because, beginning in the early 1970s, a number of factors conspired to lessen the likelihood that all humans would go to bed each night adequately nourished: Weather in major food-producing countries turned bad; a number of countries, most notably Japan and the Soviet Union, entered the world-grain importing business with a vengeance; the cost of energy used to enhance agricultural output rose dramatically; and less capital was available to poorer countries as loans or grants for purchasing agricultural inputs or the finished product (food) itself. Yet the world has had little difficulty growing sufficient food, enough to provide every person with two loaves of bread per day as well as other commodities. Major food-producing countries have even cut back the amount of acreage devoted to agriculture.

Why, then, have famine and other food-related maladies appeared with increasing frequency? The simple answer is that food is treated as a commodity, not a nutrient. Those who can afford to buy food or grow their own do not go hungry. However, the world's poor have become increasingly unable to afford to create their own successful agricultural ventures or to buy enough food.

The problem for the next half century, then, has several facets to it. First, can the planet physically sustain increases in food production equal to or greater than the ability of the human race to reproduce itself? This question can only be answered by examining both factors in the comparison—likely future food production levels and future fertility scenarios. A second question relates to the economic dimension associated with an efficient global food distribution system: Will the poorer countries of the globe that are unable to grow their own food have sufficient assets to purchase it, or will the international community create a global distribution network that ignores a country's ability to pay? And third, will countries that want to grow their own food be given the opportunity to do so?

The selections in this issue address the question of the planet's continuing ability to grow sufficient food to feed its growing population. The late Julian L. Simon argues that not only will the world's capacity to grow enough food fail to disappear but new technologies will likely make the task of feeding tomorrow's population easier. David Pimentel and his colleagues contend that population growth is more likely to follow a geometrical path (doubling every so often), which will increasingly challenge the Earth's arable land, water, energy, and biological systems to keep pace.

Julian L. Simon

 YES

What Are the Limits on Food Production?

The cost of food has been declining in recent decades—which means that world food supplies have grown faster than human population, despite the well-publicized dire predictions. What about the future?

The Short-Run Outlook

It is not necessary or useful to discuss whether there is an "ultimate" limit to the supply of any natural resource, including food.... We know for sure that the world can produce vastly more food than it now does, especially in such low-income countries as India and Bangladesh, even with conventional methods. If India were to produce only at the high present productivity of Japan and Taiwan (which have much less land and a shorter growing season), and if Bangladesh were to produce only at the rate of Holland (which has similar flooding problems and a much shorter growing season), food production would increase dramatically in India and Bangladesh.

More generally, with present technology and without moving toward the much higher yields found under experimental conditions, the world can more than feed any foreseeable population increase. There are a host of already well-proven techniques that could boost production immediately, including better storage facilities that would cut the perhaps 15–25 percent loss to pests and rot every year; improved production devices such as vacuums that suck up bugs instead of killing them with pesticides; and the host of individually small innovations that one can read about every month in farm magazines. Widespread adoption adds up to steady improvement, and yields seem to be accelerating rather than tapering off....

Of course an increase in consumption imposes costs in the short run. But in the long run, population pressure reduces costs as well as improves the food supply in accord with the general theory, which I'll repeat again: More people, and increased income, cause problems of increased scarcity of resources in the short run. Heightened scarcity causes prices to rise. The higher prices present opportunity, and prompt inventors and entrepreneurs to search for solutions. Many fail, at cost to themselves. But in a free society, solutions are eventually found. And in the long run the new developments leave us *better off than if the problems had not arisen.* That is, prices end up lower than before the increased scarcity occurred, which is the long-run history of food supply.

Some people wonder whether we can be sure that food production will increase, and whether it would be "safer" to restrict population growth until the increase is realized. But food production increases only in response to demand; farmers will not grow more food until the demand warrants it—either the number of mouths in a subsistence household, or the price in the market. Furthermore, one can predict with great confidence the *average* yields a few years hence in such countries as the United States by looking at the *record* yields for the present year; historically, the average catches up to the record yields only several years later.

The twin keys to this advancement in the agriculturally-productive countries are two-fold: 1) The existence of new knowledge, and educated people to take advantage of it. 2) Economic freedom. The ability of the world to increase production when there is a profitable opportunity to do so is amazing.

The Long-Run Outlook

In addition to the already-proven methods of raising output, there are many promising scientific discoveries at the research stage.... [A] decade ago, these methods included such innovations as (a) orbiting giant mirrors that would reflect sunlight onto the night side of the Earth and thereby increase growing time, increase harvest time, and prevent crop freezes, (b) meat substitutes made of soybeans that produce the nutrition and enjoyment of meat with much less resource input, and (c) hydroponic farming as described in the next paragraph. Such ideas may seem like unrealistic science fiction. But we should remember that tractors and wheeled irrigation pipes, which are making enormous contributions today, seemed quite unrealistic a hundred or fifty years ago. Furthermore, nowadays we have the capacity to estimate the chances of successful new developments much more accurately than we did in the past. When scientists predict that a process will be commercially successful within a given number of years, the likelihood of it being so is rather good.

Some radical improvements for the long run have already been well tested, and are not just a desperate last resort. In the environs of Washington, D.C., where I now live, there are a dozen or so small farms that raise vegetables hydroponically and sell them through supermarkets at premium prices because of their high quality. And this is commercially viable without subsidies from the government or from other divisions of a large firm. That is, this is not futuristic stuff, but right-now technology. You can read the names of the firms on the produce at the local supermarket. In fact, hydroponics is sufficiently practical that at least one supermarket has built a 10,000-square-foot vegetable garden inside its store to provide the freshest possible vegetables to its customers. If the scarcity of farmland—as measured by the price of farmland—were to increase greatly, the potential production by hydroponic farming is enormous.

In ... brief time ..., the capacity of food-factory production has expanded to a degree almost beyond belief. On a space of perhaps 36 *square meters*—that is, a "plot" six meters or 18 feet on each side—with the use of artificial light, enough food can be raised to supply the calories for a single person, day in and day out. (A less conservative estimate is that a plot ten feet square will suffice. That is, an average bedroom in an ordinary U.S. house, 20 feet by 20 feet, would contain enough area to feed a family of four.)

You might think that though this is possible in a laboratory, practical development might be far in the future, or might never become practical—the way people think of fusion energy now. But farming at almost this level of land efficiency is already in commercial operation. In DeKalb, Illinois, Noel Davis's PhytoFarm produces food—mainly lettuce and other garden vegetables—in a factory measuring 200 feet by 250 feet—50,000 square feet, one acre, 0.4 hectares, 1/640 of a square mile—at a rate of a ton of food per day, enough to completely feed 500 or 1,000 people. This is not substantially below the experimental laboratory rates stated above. And PhytoFarm now does this without government subsidies.

As a bonus, PhytoFarm produce is more attractive to chefs than other produce. It is unbruised, looks good, tastes good, and is more consistent day after day than crops grown in fields, especially in months when the produce must be brought from long distances.

Energy for artificial light is the key raw material in state-of-the-art hydroponics. Even at present electricity costs, PhytoFarm is profitable, and its food prices are affordable at ordinary American incomes. With improved power production from nuclear fission—or from fusion—costs will certainly drop in the future.

But let's go even further. With only a minor boost from artificial light—perhaps by a quarter of the total energy used by the plants—greenhouse tomato production in New Jersey is sufficiently profitable that only about a fiftieth of an acre is sufficient to feed a person fully. This is about a tenth as efficient as PhytoFarm, but still would allow food for the entire U.S. population to be produced on about a hundredth of present arable land, which is itself only a fraction of total U.S. land area. And if grain were raised instead of lettuce and tomatoes—which are now more profitable—much less space would be needed to supply the necessary nutrition.

This illustration makes irrelevant the assertion of some biologists that our food supplies are limited by the amount of sunlight falling on green plants. They claim that 40 percent of the sunlight's "net primary production" is "used, co-opted, or foregone as a direct result of human activity" such as logging, farming, or paving over land in urban areas. Those calculations seem to suggest that humans are already at the margin of existence, since we must share the remaining 60% of the sun's "net primary production" with millions of other species. But as we have seen, not only can humans get by with very little agricultural space, if needed, but sunlight is not an ultimate constraint, because of the availability of nuclear or even non-nuclear power to make light. Right now, green plants capture less than 1 percent of the solar energy that strikes the Earth's surface. If we indeed "co-opt" 40 percent of that 1 percent, we could give it *all* back to the plants and still draw plenty of "natural" energy from sources like solar cells, wind, ocean currents, and other reservoirs of the untapped 99 percent.

To dramatize the findings a bit (and without worrying about the exact arithmetic because it does not matter), we can imagine the matter thusly: At the current efficiency of PhytoFarm, the entire present population of the world can be supplied from a square area about 140 miles on a side—about the area of Massachusetts and Vermont combined, and less than a tenth of Texas. This represents only about a thousandth as much land as is needed for agriculture at present (give or take a factor of four; for illustrative purposes greater exactitude is unnecessary). And if for some reason that seems like too much space, you can immediately cut the land space by a factor of ten: just build food factories ten stories high, which should present no more problems than a ten-story office building. You could economize even more and build a hundred stories high, like the Empire State Building or the Sears Tower. Then the surface area needed would be no more than the space within the corporate limits of Austin, Texas, to pick the first alphabetically among the many U.S. cities large enough.

PhytyoFarm techniques could feed a hundred times the world's present population—say 500 billion people—with factory buildings a hundred stories high, on 1 percent of present farmland. To put it differently, if you raise your bed to triple bunk-bed height, you can grow enough food on the two levels between the floor and your bed to supply your nutritional needs.

Does this surprise you? It hasn't been front-page news, but the capacity to feed people with an ever smaller small land surface has been developing rapidly for decades. In 1967 Colin Clark estimated that the minimum space necessary to feed a person was 27 square meters, a then-optimistic figure that had not been proven in commercial practice or even large-scale experiment. Now a quarter of a century later there is commercial demonstration of land needs only a fifth or a tenth that large. It is most unlikely that this process of improvement will not continue in the future.

Only 200 years ago, half of the diet of Sauk and Mesquakie Native Americans came from hunting, and "It took 7,000 acres to support one human." Phytofarm's one acre, which supports 500 or 1,000 people, represents an increase in productivity per acre a million times over compared with the Native Americans.

Nor is this any "ultimate" limit. Rather, these gains are just the result of research over the past few decades, and there is no reason to think that future research in the next century or the next seven billion years could not greatly multiply productivity. It is likely that before the world gets to 500 billion people, or even to 10 billion, the maximum output per acre will be increased much beyond what PhytoFarm achieves now. The discussion so far does not take account of such existing technology as bovine growth hormone, which has no proven effect on humans yet greatly increases the yield of milk products. Nor does the above assessment reflect such innovations as genetically engineered plants, which will surely produce huge commercial gains in the next century. For example, rapeseed output can already be boosted 15 to 30 percent with genetic engineering.

The possibilities already shown to be feasible are astounding. For example, one might insert into a potato genes from a moth that affect the potato's coloring. Other genes might make proteins in a potato with the full complement of amino acids that humans need—giving the benefits of meat and potatoes by eating the potatoes alone. Please keep in mind that this technology has been developed after only a few decades of work on the topic, and only a little more than a century after the first scientific knowledge of genetics. Potential progress in the future—even within the next few decades and centuries—is awesome. Doomsaying forecasts about population growth outstripping the food supply that take no account of these possibilities surely are seriously inadequate.

Food From Fish

Fish crops are not fundamentally different from field crops. Based on a few years of data, the *Global 2000 Report* issued the influential forecast that the world fish catch had hit its limit—"leveled off in the 1970s at about 70 million metric tons a year." But by 1988 the catch had reached 98 million tons a year, and it is still rising rapidly.

No limit to the harvest of wild varieties of seafood is in sight. Yet fish farms have begun to produce at or near competitive prices. A newspaper in the 1990s in Washington, D.C., advertised perch fillets from the North Atlantic for $2.99, while aquacultured Tilapia and catfish were $3.99 and $4.99 respectively. The aquacultured products sell well enough at these prices to be displayed prominently. And there is every reason to believe that with additional experience, aquaculture costs and hence prices will fall. Indeed, the main obstacle to a rapid increase in aquaculture is that wild fish are too cheap to invite more competition. The price of cultured catfish has fallen greatly already. Farm-grown salmon has been so successful that it "has produced a glut of massive proportions, which has brought down the wholesale price of a gutted fish from $7 a pound to $4." By 1992, the price to the fish farmer was only 60 cents a pound.

Aquaculture capacity can be expanded almost indefinitely. Land is a small constraint, as catfish farming in Mississippi shows; present methods produce about 3,000 pounds of fish per acre, an economic return far higher than for field crops. (The biggest obstacle to a large increase in catfish farming in Texas is the federal subsidy to rice farmers that keeps them producing that product instead of shifting the land to fish farming.) And now systems that raise fish intensively by piping in the necessary nutrients and piping out the waste products, akin to hydroponic cropping, are being developed. The process goes on year-round indoors under controlled temperature conditions, and can provide fish to restaurants and stores only hours after the catch.

New technology can also expand the supply of seafood by producing artificial substitutes. Imitation lobster, made of Alaska pollock plus artificial lobster flavor and almost indistinguishable from the real thing, sells for $4.00 per pound—vastly less than the price of real lobster. The same is true of artificial crab.

Why Is the Food Outlook Made to Seem Gloomy?

The reasons why we hear and believe so much false bad news about resources, environment, and population are so many and so complex that they require another volume to discuss (forthcoming soon, I hope). But a couple of comments about food in particular are needed.

It is puzzling why competent biologists go so wrong in their assessments of the food situation. They charge that people like me who are not biologists are by training disqualified from writing such material as this. But why is this so? What is it that they know (or don't know) that makes them believe that they understand the situation better than the rest of us, and that our calculations are not sound? An explicit explanation by one of them would be helpful.

Another curiosity is that even people who should know best about the wonderful long-run prospects for food production often fail to see the larger picture. Typically, Noel Davis of PhytoFarm—which makes land almost irrelevant as a factor of food production—comments that "each year the United States is losing an area of farmland greater in size than the state of Rhode Island." . . . [W]hat nonsense this is. Of course, such an alarming assertion may be given as justification for the need to invest in one's own new technology. But still it reflects some belief in the conventional wisdom—which Davis's own work belies.

Still another cause of the common belief that food is a looming problem is the propensity for the news media to put a bad-news twist on even the best news. Catfish farming has been so successful in the United States in the 1980s that prices have fallen rapidly. This is a great boon to consumers, and is additional evidence of the long-run potential of fish farming. But the falling prices have naturally hurt the least efficient producers. So a front-page headline is "Fish Farms Fall Prey to Excess," and the story contains no suggestion that the overall impact is beneficial to American citizens and to all humanity.

Conclusions

The notion that we are facing a long-run food shortage due to increased population and a Malthusian shortage of land is now scientifically discredited. High-tech methods of producing vastly more food per acre will not be needed for decades or centuries. Only after population multiplies several more times will there be enough incentive to move beyond the present field cropping systems used in the more advanced countries. But beyond the shadow of a doubt, the knowledge now exists to support many times the present world's population *on less land than is now being farmed*—that is, even without expanding beyond our own planet.

Malthus might be rephrased thusly: Whether or not population grows exponentially, subsistence grows at an even faster exponential rate (largely but not entirely because of population growth). And capacity to improve other aspects of the standard of living, beyond subsistence, grows at a still faster exponential rate, due largely to the growth of knowledge.

The main reason why more food has not been produced in the past is that there was insufficient demand for more food. As demand increases, farmers work harder to produce crops and improve the land, and more research is done to increase productivity. This extra work and investment imposes costs for a while. But... food has tended in the long run to become cheaper decade after decade. That's why production and consumption per capita have been rising.

Will a "population explosion" reverse these trends? On the contrary. Population growth increases food demand, which in the short run requires more labor and investment to meet the demand. (There is always some lag before supply responds to additional demand, which may mean that some will suffer.) But in the foreseeable long run, additional consumption will not make food more scarce and more expensive. Rather, in the long run additional people actually cause food to be less scarce and less expensive.

Once again, the basic process portrayed [here] applied to food: More people increase scarcity of food for a while. The higher prices prompt agronomical researchers and farmers to invent. The solutions that are eventually found cause food to be more available than before....

This conclusion presupposes a satisfactory social and economic system that will not prevent progress.

David Pimentel et al.

Impact of Population Growth on Food Supplies and Environment

As the world population continues to grow geometrically, great pressure is being placed on arable land, water, energy, and biological resources to provide an adequate supply of food while maintaining the integrity of our ecosystem. According to the World Bank and the United Nations, from 1 to 2 billion humans are now malnourished, indicating a combination of insufficient food, low incomes, and inadequate distribution of food. This is the largest number of hungry humans ever recorded in history. In China about 80 million are now malnourished and hungry. Based on recent rates of increase, the world population is projected to double from roughly 6 billion to more than 12 billion in less than 50 years (Pimentel et al., 1994). As the world population expands, the food problem will become increasingly severe, conceivably with the numbers of malnourished reaching 3 billion.

Based on their evaluations of available natural resources, scientists of the Royal Society and the U.S. National Academy of Sciences have issued a joint statement reinforcing the concern about the growing imbalance between the world's population and the resources that support human lives (RS & NAS, 1992).

Reports from the Food and Agricultural Organization of the United Nations, numerous other international organizations, and scientific research also confirm the existence of this serious food problem. For example, the per capita availability of world grains, which make up 80% of the world's food, has been declining for the past 15 years (Kendall & Pimentel, 1994). Certainly with a quarter million people being added to the world population each day, the need for grains and all other food will reach unprecedented levels.

More than 99% of the world's food supply comes from the land, while less than 1% is from oceans and other aquatic habitats (Pimentel et al., 1994). The continued production of an adequate food supply is directly dependent on ample fertile land, fresh water, energy, plus the maintenance of biodiversity. As the human population grows, the requirements for these resources also grow. Even if these resources are never depleted, on a per capita basis they will decline significantly because they must be divided among more people.

From David Pimentel, Zuewen Huang, Ana Cordova, and Marcia Pimentel, "Impact of Population Growth on Food Supplies and Environment," *Population and Environment*, vol. 19, no. 1 (September 1997). Copyright © 1997 by Human Sciences Press, Inc. Reprinted by permission of Kluwer Academic/Plenum Publishers. References omitted.

At present, fertile cropland is being lost at an alarming rate. For instance, nearly one-third of the world's cropland (1.5 billion hectares) has been abandoned during the past 40 years because erosion has made it unproductive (Pimentel et al., 1995). Solving erosion losses is a longterm problem: it takes 500 years to form 25 mm of soil under agricultural conditions.

Most replacement of eroded agricultural land is now coming from marginal and forest land. The pressure for agricultural land accounts for 60 to 80% of the world's deforestation. Despite such land replacement strategies, world cropland per capita has been declining and is now only 0.27 ha per capita; in China only 0.08 ha now is available. This is only 15% of the 0.5 ha per capita considered minimal for a diverse diet similar to that of the United States and Europe. The shortage of productive cropland combined with decreasing land productivity is, in part, the cause of current food shortages and associated human malnutrition. Other factors such as political unrest, economic insecurity, and unequal food distribution patterns also contribute to food shortages.

Water is critical for all crops which require and transpire massive amounts of water during the growing season. For example, a hectare of corn will transpire more than 5 million liters of water during one growing season. This means that more than 8 million liters of water per hectare must reach the crop. In total, agricultural production consumes more fresh water than any other human activity. Specifically, about 87% of the world's fresh water is consumed or used up by agriculture and, thus, is not recoverable (Pimentel et al., 1996).

Competition for water resources among individuals, regions, and countries and associated human activities is already occurring with the current world population. About 40% of the world's people live in regions that directly compete for shared water resources. In China where more than 300 cities already are short of water, these shortages are intensifying. Worldwide, water shortages are reflected in the per capita decline in irrigation used for food production in all regions of the world during the past twenty years. Water resources, critical for irrigation, are under great stress as populous cities, states, and countries require and withdraw more water from rivers, lakes, and aquifers every year. A major threat to maintaining future water supplies is the continuing over-draft of surface and ground water resources.

Diseases associated with water rob people of health, nutrients, and livelihood. This problem is most serious in developing countries. For example, about 90% of the diseases occurring in developing countries result from a lack of clean water (Pimentel et al., 1996). Worldwide, about 4 billion cases of disease are contracted from water and approximately 6 million deaths are caused by water-borne disease each year. When a person is ill with diarrhea, malaria, or other serious disease, anywhere from 5 to 20% of an individual's food intake offsets the stress of the disease.

Disease and malnutrition problems in the third world appear to be as serious in rural areas as they are in urban areas, especially among the poor. This will intensify in the future. Furthermore, the number of people living in urban areas is doubling every 10 to 20 years, creating major environmental problems, including water and air pollution and increased disease and food shortages.

Fossil energy is another prime resource used for food production. Nearly 80% of the world's fossil energy used each year is used by the developed countries, and part of it is expended in producing high animal protein diets. The intensive farming technologies of developed countries use massive amounts of fossil energy for fertilizers, pesticides, irrigation, and for machines as a substitute for human labor. In developing countries, fossil energy has been used primarily for fertilizers and irrigation to help maintain yields rather than to reduce human labor inputs (Giampietro & Pimentel, 1993).

Because fossil energy is a finite resource, its depletion accelerates as population needs for food and services escalate. The United States is already importing more than 50 per cent of its oil, and projections from the U.S. Department of Energy indicate that the country will exhaust all of its oil reserves within the next 15 to 20 years (Pimentel et al., 1994). Oil imports will then have to increase, worsening the U.S. trade imbalance. As supplies of fossil energy dwindle, the cost of fuel increases everywhere. The impact of this is already a serious problem for developing countries where the high price of imported fossil fuel makes it difficult, if not impossible, for poor farmers to power irrigation and provide for their other agricultural needs. Worldwide, per capita supplies of fossil energy show a significant decline.

In general, developing countries have been relying heavily on fossil energy, especially for fertilizers and irrigation to augment their food supply. The current decline in per capita use of fossil energy, caused by the gradual decline in oil supplies and their relatively high prices, is generating direct competition between developed and developing countries for fossil energy resources.

Economic analyses often overlook the biological and physical constraints that exist in all food production systems. The assumption is that market mechanisms and international trade are effective insurances against future food shortages. A rich economy is expected to guarantee a food supply adequate to meet a country's demand despite existing local ecological constraints. In fact, the contrary is true. When global biological and physical limits to domestic food production are reached, food importation will no longer be a viable option for any country. At that point, food importation for the rich can only be sustained by starvation of the powerless poor.

These concerns about the future are supported by two observations. First, most of the 183 nations of the world are now, to some extent, dependent on food imports. Most of these imports are cereal surpluses produced only in those countries that have relatively low population densities and practice intensive agriculture. For instance, the United States, Canada, Australia, Oceania, and Argentina provide 81% of net cereal exports on the world market. If, as projected, the U.S. population doubles in the next 60 years (Pimentel et al., 1994), then its cereal and other food resources would have to be used domestically to feed 520 million hungry Americans. Then the United States would cease to be a food exporting country.

In the future, when exporting nations must keep surpluses at home, Egypt, Jordan, and countless other countries in Africa and Asia will be without the food imports that now help them survive. China, which now imports many tons of food, illustrates this problem. As the Worldwatch Institute has pointed out, if China's population increases by 500 million and their soil erosion continues unabated, it will need to import 200–400 million tons of food each year by 2050 (Brown, 1995). But by then, sufficient food imports probably will not be available on the international market.

Certainly improved technology will assist in more effective management and use of resources, but it cannot produce an unlimited flow of those vital natural resources that are the raw materials for sustained agricultural production. For instance, fertilizers enhance the fertility of eroded soils, but humans cannot make topsoil. Indeed, fertilizers made from finite fossil fuels are presently being used to compensate for eroded topsoil. Per capita fish catch has not increased even though the size and speed of fishing vessels has improved. On the contrary, per capita fish production is lower than ever before because greater efficiency led to overfishing. In regions like eastern Canada, overfishing has been so severe that cod fishermen have no fish to catch, and the economy of that region has been devastated. All of the world's fishing grounds are facing overfishing problems.

Consider also the supplies of fresh water that are available not only for agriculture but also for industry and public use. Water withdrawn from the Colorado River in several states for irrigation and other purposes results in the river being nearly dry by the time it reaches the Sea of Cortes, Mexico. No available technology can double the flow of the Colorado River, although effective water conservation would be a help. Similarly, the shrinking ground water resources stored in vast aquifers cannot be refilled by human technology. Rainfall is the only supplier.

A productive and sustainable agricultural system depends on maintaining the integrity of biodiversity. Often small in size, diverse species are natural enemies of pests, degrade wastes, form soil, fix nitrogen, pollinate crops, etc. For example, in New York State on one bright, sunny day in July, the wild and other bees pollinate an estimated 6,000,000 blossoms of essential fruits and vegetables. Humans have no technology to substitute for many of the services provided by diverse species in our environment.

Strategies for the future must be based first and foremost on the conservation and careful management of land, water, energy, and biological resources needed for food production. Our stewardship of world resources must change and the basic needs of people must be balanced with those resources that sustain human life. The conservation of these resources will require coordinated efforts and incentives from individuals and countries. Once these finite resources are exhausted they cannot be replaced by human technology. Further, more efficient and environmentally sound agricultural technologies must be developed and put into practice to support the continued productivity of agriculture.

Yet none of these measures will be sufficient to ensure adequate food supplies for future generations unless the growth in the human population is simultaneously curtailed. Several studies have confirmed that to maintain a relatively high standard of living, the optimum population should be less than

200 million for the United States and less than 2 billion for the world (Pimentel et al., 1994). This estimate assumes that from now until an optimum population is achieved, strategies for the conservation of land, water, energy, and biological resources are successfully implemented and a sound, productive environment is protected.

POSTSCRIPT

Will the World Be Able to Feed Itself in the Foreseeable Future?

Presumably, economist Thomas Robert Malthus was not the first to address the question of the planet's ability to feed its population. But his 1798 *Essay on the Principle of Population* is the most quoted of early writings on the subject. Malthus's basic proposition was that population, if left unchecked, would grow geometrically, while subsistence resources could grow only arithmetically. Malthus, who wrote his essay in response to an argument with his father about the ability of the human race to produce sufficient resources vital for life, created a stir back in the late eighteenth century. The same debate holds the public's attention today as population grows at a rate unparalleled at any other time in human history.

Pimentel et al. allude to the warnings of a number of groups concerning the world's future food situation. They cite the findings of the Royal Society, the U.S. National Academy of Sciences, the UN Food and Agricultural Organization, and numerous other international organizations, as well as scientific research to support their view of the pending danger. For them, two issues are significant. The first is the existence of enough agricultural inputs: water, land, energy, and the like. The second is a global economic system that treats food as a commodity rather than as a nutrient. For these authors, the bottom line is that population growth must be curtailed.

For Simon, on the other hand, the answer is simple: The world can produce vastly more food than it currently does, even in places that rely on conventional methods. The essence of his argument is this: More people with higher incomes cause scarcity problems in the short run, which, in turn, results in raised prices. Into the picture then come inventors and entrepreneurs, some of whom will succeed in finding appropriate solutions. To Simon, we will be better off in the long run because of the potential for profit on the part of the problem solvers.

A balanced look at the planet's capacity to feed the UN's projected 2050 population is L. T. Evans's *Feeding the Ten Billion* (Cambridge University Press, 1998). In it, the author takes the reader through the ages, showing how the human race has addressed the agricultural needs of each succeeding billion people. The biggest challenge during the next half century, according to Evans, is to solve two problems: producing enough food for a 67 percent increase in the population and eliminating the chronic undernutrition that afflicts so many people. Solving the first problem requires a focus on the main components of increased food supply. For Evans, these include "(1) increase in land under cultivation; (2) increase in yield per hectare per crop; (3) increase in the number of crops per hectare per year; (4) displacement of lower yielding crops by higher yielding ones; (5) reduction of post-harvest losses; [and] (6) reduced use as feed for animals."

The second problem brings into play many socioeconomic factors beyond those that are typically associated with agricultural production. Growing enough food worldwide is a necessary but not sufficient condition for eliminating problems associated with hunger. Many studies have indicated that the root cause of hunger is poverty. Addressing poverty, therefore, is a prerequisite for ensuring that the world's food supply is distributed such that the challenge of global hunger is met.

Another source is a 1995 study by the UN Food and Agricultural Organization, *World Agriculture: Towards 2000*. The central message of this study is that the planet will be able to feed a growing population in the foreseeable future.

Another optimistic viewpoint about future food prospects is *The World Food Outlook* by Donald O. Mitchell, Merlinda D. Ingco, and Ronald C. Duncan (Cambridge University Press, 1997). Their basic conclusion is that the world food situation has improved dramatically for most of the regions of the globe and will continue to do so. The only exception is sub-Saharan Africa, but there the problems go far beyond agriculture.

ISSUE 8

Is Global Environmental Stress Caused Primarily by Increased Resource Consumption Rather Than Population Growth?

YES: Adil Najam, from "A Developing Countries' Perspective on Population, Environment, and Development," *Population Research and Policy Review* (February 1996)

NO: Lester R. Brown, Gary Gardner, and Brian Halweil, from "Sixteen Impacts of Population Growth," *The Futurist* (February 1999)

ISSUE SUMMARY

YES: Adil Najam, an assistant professor in the Department of International Relations at Boston University, argues that consumption control among developed countries is a major key to avoiding continuing environmental crises.

NO: Lester R. Brown, Gary Gardner, and Brian Halweil, researchers at the Worldwatch Institute, examine 16 dimensions of population growth in the areas of food and agriculture, environment and resources, and economic impacts and quality of life, and they indicate that the effects of such growth are mainly adverse.

The Woodrow Wilson Center recently published an article entitled "Human Population and Environmental Stresses in the Twenty-First Century," *Environmental Change and Security Project Report* (Summer 2000). In it, Richard E. Benedick, a former U.S. State Department official responsible for population and environmental policies, summarized what he called the new generation of environmental problems: (1) changing climate, bringing on drought, flooding, and assorted other problems; (2) depletion of the ozone layer, which protects humans, plants, and animals from ultraviolet radiation; (3) loss of biological diversity due to mass extinctions of animal and plant species; (4) spread of arid lands, desertification, and soil erosion on a global scale; (5) pollution of marine and freshwaters, and overfishing; (6) destruction of forests; and (7) worldwide diffusion of hazardous substances.

This issue focuses on a fundamental debate that is currently occurring in both the environmental and population issue areas of the new global agenda. That is, is the apparent additional stress on the Earth's various systems—such as that reported by Benedick—caused by the arrival of more people on the planet, or is the dramatic increase in per capita consumption, primarily in the developed world, the principal cause of environmental stress and degradation?

In examining this issue, we first make the assumption that both increased consumption and population growth affect the environment in some fashion. Common sense dictates that both play some role, however insignificant. The basic question, then, is whether the impact of one or both factors is substantial enough to damage the environment beyond a certain "normal use" threshold to qualify as the source of environmental "stress."

It is probably useful to break down our analysis into two broad groups of cases—the developed world and the developing sector. The reason for such a division is that different forces are at work in these two sectors. Population growth is almost at a standstill in the industrial sector of the globe. At present growth rates, many wealthy countries will take well over a century to double their populations. On the other hand, most of these developed nations have witnessed huge increases in per-capita resource consumption; in many cases these rates have doubled or tripled in a matter of decades. Given these two characteristics—little or no population growth and large consumption increases —one must assume that any additional environmental stress occurring in the developed world can be attributed to increased resource consumption.

The situation in the developing world is somewhat more complicated. Population growth rates soared for about 30 years. Many developing countries doubled their size during that time, and they continue to add huge numbers each year (despite current declining growth rates because of the built-in momentum). If each individual continued to consume about the same amount of resources during this time, the environmental impact would have doubled during the 30-year period. In this case, more people, not more per-capita consumption, would have made the difference.

On the other hand, evidence suggests that as individuals and countries move up the development ladder, their ability and inclination to use more resources in their daily lives also escalates. Their per-capita resource consumption rises. This phenomenon was quite evident during the demographic transition in the developed world, and it also appears to be currently at work in developing countries that are making strides toward industrialization. Thus, the answer to the question of how much environmental stress in the developing world is attributable to increased resource consumption and how much to population growth requires a more elaborate research strategy.

The two selections for this issue take opposite ends of the argument. Adil Najam supports the position that population growth in the developing world should not be held accountable for global environmental stress. Lester R. Brown, Gary Gardner, and Brian Halweil focus on population growth as the most critical issue of the day.

Adil Najam **YES**

A Developing Countries' Perspective on Population, Environment, and Development

In ancient times, people were few but wealthy and without strife. People at present think that five sons are too many, and each son has five sons also and before the death of the grandfather there are already 25 descendants. Therefore people are more and wealth is less; they work hard and receive little. The life of a nation depends upon having enough food, not upon the number of people.

— Han Fei-Tzu (circa 500 BC)

The happiness of a country does not depend, absolutely, upon its poverty or its riches, upon its youth or its age, upon its being thinly or fully inhabited, but upon the rapidity with which it is increasing, upon the degree in which the yearly increase of food approaches to the yearly increase of an unrestricted population.

— Rev. Thomas Robert Malthus (1798)

The causal chain of the deterioration [of the environment] is easily followed to its source. Too many cars, too many factories, too much detergent, too much pesticide, multiplying contrails, inadequate sewage treatment plants, too little water, too much carbon dioxide—all can be traced easily to too many people.

— Paul R. Ehrlich (1968)

The pollution problem is a consequence of population.... Freedom to breed will bring ruin to all.

— Garrett Hardin (1968)

From Adil Najam, "A Developing Countries' Perspective on Population, Environment, and Development," *Population Research and Policy Review*, vol. 15 (February 1996). Copyright © 1996 by Kluwer Academic Publishers. Reprinted by permission of Kluwer Academic Publishers. Notes and references omitted.

Introduction

The perception of population growth as a 'problem' is not new. That the catastrophe predicted by so many has been averted till now does not necessarily disprove the arguments of these Cassandras. However, Pollyannas like Julian Simon (1981) have taken much pleasure in rubbing in this fact and insist that human ingenuity will continue to outpace human propensity for procreation. It is within this context that much of the debate on the subject has been historically framed, with occasional shifts in popular and scholarly sentiments towards one side or the other.

The recent growth of popular interest in environmental issues has generated a renewal of concern about rapid population growth, which is seen as being largely responsible for global trends of environmental degradation. The causal relationship between the two seems intuitively obvious. Yet, it is being contested by a number of critical interests. Although some in the population community may consider such views peripheral to the mainstream debate, the prevalence and persistence of the dissension of the environment-population linkage may be gauged from the fact that in 1987 the World Commission on Environment and Development, reached unanimous agreement on all issues except two—Antarctica and the causal significance of population growth (Shaw 1992). Again, at the 1992 United Nations Conference on Environment and Development (UNCED) population remained the most contentious issue (Najam 1993a).

Most surprising is the reaction of the developing countries. On the one hand, many of them have very high population growth rates and are most immediately vulnerable to its consequences. At the same time, many of them support strong domestic population policies, which have been in place over long periods of time, and are vigorously—and sometimes coercively—enforced. Yet, at the international level, these same states seem hesitant, and sometimes hostile, to the notion of accepting a direct causal link between global environmental degradation and population growth.

This paper attempts to understand why the developing countries of the South are so weary of international population policy in the name of the environment. It is essentially a study of the political behavior of Southern governments. It is argued that the South's response has been, and continues to be, shaped by five inter-related concerns:

1. *Responsibility:* For precedent and principle, the South resists any effort that implies holding population growth (largely in the South) responsible for global environmental stress. Hence, the insistence that 'population growth in the developing countries is a national, not a global problem' (Mahbub-ul-Haq 1976: 124). The South has consistently held that the environmental crisis is of the North's making and has based its demands for assistance/reparations on that 'history of guilt'. In accepting population growth as *the* causal motor of environmental degradation the South loses this perceived leverage.

2. *Efficiency:* From the perspective of international environmental policy, the South insists that if the international concern about population growth stems from its effects on global systems then it would be more efficient to focus on consumption patterns. The argument is that whatever effects population may have, they are only in relation to consumption. As Ramphal (1994) stresses, once consumption is factored in, the 1.2 billion people living in industrialized countries place a pressure equivalent to more than 24 billion living in the developing countries. Thus, it would be more efficient to focus on policies that curb consumption than on those that target procreation.

3. *Efficacy:* From the implementation end, developing countries argue that development is still the best contraceptive. Experience in both North and South shows that 'people in the developed condition do not have too many children' (Keyfitz 1991: 39–40). The South argues, therefore, that if the international community is truly interested in curbing population growth it should spend its dollars on assisting economic and human development rather than simply enhancing contraceptive provision. Although the argument that economic growth will automatically slow population *growth* is contested (e.g., Harrison 1994), the assertion that social *development* will enhance the efficacy of population policies is now widely accepted (e.g., Brower 1994; Chhabra 1994; Harrison 1994; Lutz 1994; Ness 1994). The South builds on this emerging consensus to reinforce and rearticulate its enduring call that development (now more broadly defined) remains the best contraceptive (see Mahbub-ul-Haq 1994; Najam 1993b; Ramphal 1994).

4. *Additionality:* Programatically, the South remains concerned that greater donor assistance for population may translate to a lesser focus on development assistance. Ever since US President Johnson's 1965 statement that 'less than five dollars invested in population control is worth a hundred dollars invested in economic growth', developing countries have doubted the motives behind the West's emphasis on population control. Developing countries want to be sure that in accepting donor priorities (i.e. environment) they would not be asked to forfeit their own (i.e. development). For the South, the end of the cold war means that the geopolitical strategic value of Southern states has diminished, and new claimants to the already shrinking international assistance pie have emerged. This has reinvigorated the urgency of the additionality argument for the South.

5. *Sovereignty:* Politically, the South sees no contradiction between actively pursuing population policies domestically, and resisting them internationally. It sees population as an issue of sovereignty and any interference from the international community as a breach thereof. While recognizing the domestic benefits of slowed population growth and pursuing policies to bring it about, the South is unprepared to hold its policies subservient to external pressure. As Stephen Krasner points out, 'the South has maintained its unity, despite major differences among individual countries, even in an issue area where the

North has offered additional resources' because 'Southern resistance to Northern efforts to develop international population norms is not simply a product of specific national values, of evidence of a concern that antinatalism may be a ploy for subordinating development aid, but is also a reflection of the deep adherence of Third World states to the prerogatives of sovereignty' (Krasner 1985; 276–278).

The rest of this paper will look at how the discussion on population-environment-development policies ignores the South's concerns and, in doing so, alienates the very group of countries that is being required to carry out such policies. . . .

The Population-Environment-Development Nexus

In its most simple articulation, the argument of the new 'green' Cassandras has flowed from two observations: (a) the planet has never had as many people as it has today, and (b) the planet has never seen as much environmental stress on its natural systems as it is experiencing today. The correlation between the two is then extrapolated to imply causality.

In fairness to its proponents, the argument has become far more sophisticated over time. The reigning view is best identified by the Holdren-Ehrlich (1974) identity:

I = PAT
(environmental Impact = Population × Affluence × Technology)

This identity, while not without serious limitations, is elegant in that it attempts to capture both the number of users and the rate of use of natural systems. However, most scholars who use this, or similar, formulations often end up focusing on the population variable rather than the other two. For example, Nazli Choucri (1991: 100) suggests that 'the population nexus as a whole—the interaction of population, resources, and technological change—must become the focus of global policy'. However, she is quick to add that while population policy alone is by no means sufficient it is nonetheless necessary, implying that it is here that the most emphasis should be invested. Others have made similar arguments on the grounds that population policies will 'help buy time' (Keyfitz 1991; Shaw 1992). Implicit in such arguments seems the belief that changing population patterns is somehow 'easier' than changing patterns of consumption or technology.

From the South's point of view, while the diagnosis suggests that both the number (i.e. population growth) and the rate (i.e. consumption patterns) are at least equally critical motors of causality, the prescription focuses unduly on the first and not enough on the later. For many in the developing world, such a conceptualization adds insult to injury in that the focus on population as the main cause of environment degradation implicitly places the responsibility for such degradation on their doorsteps, even though the 'benefits' have been reaped by those in the North.

Very often, then, the argument becomes merely a more sophisticated re-hash of the more simplistic conception introduced earlier. For example, Nathan Keyfitz (1991: 44, 77) writes:

> In 1950 the world contained 2.5 billion people, and there was little evidence of damage to the biosphere. Now with over 5 billion there is a great deal of evidence with another 2.5 billion and continuance of present trends of production and consumption, disaster faces us. The planet cannot over a long period support that many people; yet an even larger number is threatened.... Twice as many people cooking with the same wood stoves use up twice as much wood. Twice as many cars of a given kind and given condition of repair put twice as much carbon dioxide into the atmosphere. Twice as many fish eaters require twice as large a catch. *With all else constant,* the requirements are the simplest possible linear function of the number of people. (Emphasis added)

Ceteris, however, is not *paribus.* Keyfitz knows that all else is not constant. He prefaces the above by saying that 'with *given* technology and *given* style of life the requirements from the environment are proportional to the number of people' (p. 44). However, neither technology nor lifestyle is 'given'. Yet, he chooses (as do most other analysts) to hold consumption constant in arguing for policies that would control the population variable. The implication seems to be that the North's lifestyle as it relates to consumption is accepted as a 'given' because it cannot (or is it, 'should' not?) be changed, but the South's lifestyle as it relates to procreation is not because it can.

The South's Response

Such arguments have the dual implication of holding population growth *responsible* for environmental degradation and touting population control as the most *efficient* opinion for environmental amelioration.

On the first count, the South responds by pointing out, for example, that the average Bangladeshi uses 2 milligrams of CFCs [chlorofluorocarbons] per year in comparison to the average US citizen who uses 2 kilograms per year; as such the 'environmental impact of an extra Bengali, in CFC terms, is only 1/1000th that of an extra American. On the second, they reason that even if the policy focus is to be only on population and not on consumption, it makes more sense to do so in the North where one averted birth is likely to produce 1000 times the environmental 'benefit' that it would in the South. Further, Southern commentators challenge the assumption that it is somehow 'easier' to reduce population amongst the poor than to curb consumption amongst the rich. If environment is the main concern, they argue, would it be easier to change lifestyles (consumption) of the few who are very rich or the children preferences of the very many who are poor. Arguably, the lifestyle change involved in reducing CFC consumption for an individual in USA is no more difficult—in fact, it should be far easier—than changing the children preference demanded from a peasant in Bangladesh. See Mahbub-ul-Haq (1994), Najam (1993b) and Ramphal (1994).

While the question of efficiency relates to the relative importance of the various options to check environmental degradation, the issue of *efficacy* concerns the effectiveness of various means to curb population growth. Since the South nowhere questions the need for population policies per se—and actively pursues them domestically—the efficacy of such policies is crucial for implementation. This brings us to that critical question of why people in poor conditions have high population growth. Environmentalists tend to spend too much effort in arguing *why* population should be controlled, and population experts spend too much time in figuring out *how* it could be controlled, but way too little thought is invested in *why* people have as many children as they do.

Falling mortality rates, old-age security, religion, and the sheer inertia of the demographic momentum are all valid and important factors, but they offer little in way of policy advice. For example, maintaining high mortality is ethically unacceptable, quick changes in social or religious preferences cannot be legislated, nor can changes in the nature of demographic momentum.

For the poorest, the difference between having four children or five is often not the difference between four hungry mouths to feed or five, but that between eight hands to earn with or ten. The rational cost-benefit analysis of childbearing decisions yields very different results where children become earning members before age ten, from where parents have to factor in the escalating costs of an expensive college education before thinking about that extra child. The fundamental, still unbridged, gap between North and South in matters pertaining to population is that what people in the industrialized world see as a problem of 'too many people' is seen by those in the developing countries as the problem of 'too much poverty'. The most vivid exemplars of this persistent chasm remains the following (still relevant) quotes from Paul Ehrlich and Mahmood Mamdani:

> One stinking hot night in Delhi... as we crawled through the city [in a taxi], we entered a crowded slum area. The temperature was well over 100, and the air was a haze of dust and smoke. The streets seemed alive with people. People eating, people washing, people sleeping. People visiting, arguing and screaming. People thrusting their hands through the taxi window, begging. People defecating and urinating. People clinging to buses. People herding animals. People, people, people, people. As we moved slowly through the mob, hand horn squawking, the dust, noise, heat, and cooking fires gave the scene a hellish aspect. Would we ever get to our hotel? All three of us were, frankly, frightened... since that night I've known the *feel* of overpopulation. (Ehrlich 1968: 15)

> The fact is that a hot summer night on Broadway in New York or Picadilly Circus in London would put Ehrlich in the midst of a far larger crowd. Yet such an experience would not spur him to comment with grave concern about 'overpopulation'. On the other hand, with a little more concern and a little less fear he

would have realized that what disturbed him about the crowd in Delhi was not its numbers, but its 'quality'—that is, its poverty. To talk, as Ehrlich does, of 'overpopulation' is to say to people: you are poor because you are too many.... People are not poor because they have large families. Quite the contrary: they have large families because they are poor. (Mamdani 1972: 14)

NO

Lester R. Brown, Gary Gardner, and
Brian Halweil

Sixteen Impacts of Population Growth

The world's population has doubled during the last half century, climbing from 2.5 billion in 1950 to 5.9 billion in 1998. This unprecedented surge in population, combined with rising individual consumption, is pushing our claims on the planet beyond its natural limits.

The United Nations projects that human population in 2050 will range between 7.7 billion and 11.2 billion people. We use the United Nations' middle-level projection of 9.4 billion (from *World Population Prospects: The 1996 Revision*) to give an idea of the strain this "most likely" outcome would place on ecosystems and governments in the future and of the urgent need to break from the business-as-usual scenario.

Our study looks at 16 dimensions or effects of population growth in order to gain a better perspective on how future population trends are likely to affect human prospects:

Impacts on Food and Agriculture

1. Grain Production

From 1950 to 1984, growth in the world grain harvest easily exceeded that of population. But since then, the growth in the grain harvest has fallen behind that of population, so per-person output has dropped by 7% (0.5% a year), according to the U.S. Department of Agriculture.

The slower growth in the world grain harvest since 1984 is due to the lack of new land and to slower growth in irrigation and fertilizer use because of the diminishing returns of these inputs.

Now that the frontiers of agricultural settlement have disappeared, future growth in grain production must come almost entirely from raising land productivity. Unfortunately, this is becoming more difficult. The challenge for the world's farmers is to reverse this decline at a time when cropland area per person is shrinking, the amount of irrigation water per person is dropping, and the crop yield response to additional fertilizer use is falling.

From Lester R. Brown, Gary Gardner, and Brian Halweil, "Sixteen Impacts of Population Growth," *The Futurist*, vol. 33, no. 2 (February 1999). Copyright © 1999 by The World Future Society. Reprinted by permission of The World Future Society, 7910 Woodmont Avenue, Suite 450, Bethesda, Maryland 20814.

2. Cropland

Since mid-century, grain area—which serves as a proxy for cropland in general—has increased by some 19%, but global population has grown by 132%. Population growth can degrade farmland, reducing its productivity or even eliminating it from production. As grain area per person falls, more and more nations risk losing the capacity to feed themselves.

The trend is illustrated starkly in the world's four fastest-growing large countries. Having already seen per capita grain area shrink by 40%–50% between 1960 and 1998, Pakistan, Nigeria, Ethiopia, and Iran can expect a further 60%–70% loss by 2050—a conservative projection that assumes no further losses of agricultural land. The result will be four countries with a combined population of more than 1 billion whose grain area per person will be only 300–600 square meters—less than a quarter of the area in 1950.

3. Fresh Water

Spreading water scarcity may be the most underrated resource issue in the world today. Wherever population is growing, the supply of fresh water per person is declining.

Evidence of water stress can be seen as rivers are drained dry and water tables fall. Rivers such as the Nile, the Yellow, and the Colorado have little water left when they reach the sea. Water tables are now falling on every continent, including in major food-producing regions. Aquifers are being depleted in the U.S. southern Great Plains, the North China Plain, and most of India.

The International Water Management Institute projects that a billion people will be living in countries facing absolute water scarcity by 2025. These countries will have to reduce water use in agriculture in order to satisfy residential and industrial water needs. In both China and India, the two countries that together dominate world irrigated agriculture, substantial cutbacks in irrigation water supplies lie ahead.

4. Oceanic Fish Catch

A fivefold growth in the human appetite for seafood since 1950 has pushed the catch of most oceanic fisheries to their sustainable limits or beyond. Marine biologists believe that the oceans cannot sustain an annual catch of much more than 93 million tons, the current take.

As we near the end of the twentieth century, overfishing has become the rule, not the exception. Of the 15 major oceanic fisheries, 11 are in decline. The catch of Atlantic cod—long a dietary mainstay for western Europeans—has fallen by 70% since peaking in 1968. Since 1970, bluefin tuna stocks in the West Atlantic have dropped by 80%.

With the oceans now pushed to their limits, future growth in the demand for seafood can be satisfied only by fish farming. But as the world turns to aquaculture to satisfy its needs, fish begin to compete with livestock and poultry for feedstuffs such as grain, soybean meal, and fish meal.

The next half century is likely to be marked by the disappearance of some species from markets, a decline in the quality of seafood caught, higher prices, and more conflicts among countries over access to fisheries. Each year, the future oceanic catch per person will decline by roughly the amount of population growth, dropping to 9.9 kilograms (22 pounds) per person in 2050, compared with the 1988 peak of 17.2 kilograms (37.8 pounds).

5. Meat Production

When incomes begin to rise in traditional low-income societies, one of the first things people do is diversify their diets, consuming more livestock products.

World meat production since 1950 has increased almost twice as fast as population. Growth in meat production was originally concentrated in western industrial countries and Japan, but over the last two decades it has increased rapidly in East Asia, the Middle East, and Latin America. Beef, pork, and poultry account for the bulk of world consumption.

Of the world grain harvest of 1.87 billion tons in 1998, an estimated 37% will be used to feed livestock and poultry, producing milk and eggs as well as meat, according to the U.S. Department of Agriculture. Grain fed to livestock and poultry is now the principal food reserve in the event of a world food emergency.

Total meat consumption will rise from 211 million tons in 1997 to 513 million tons in 2050, increasing pressures on the supply of grain.

Environment and Resources

6. Natural Recreation Areas

From Buenos Aires to Bangkok, dramatic population growth in the world's major cities—and the sprawl and pollution they bring—threaten natural recreation areas that lie beyond city limits. On every continent, human encroachment has reduced both the size and the quality of natural recreation areas.

In nations where rapid population growth has outstripped the carrying capacity of local resources, protected areas become especially vulnerable. Although in industrial nations these areas are synonymous with camping, hiking, and picnics in the country, in Asia, Africa, and Latin America most national parks, forests, and preserves are inhabited or used for natural resources by local populations.

Migration-driven population growth also endangers natural recreation areas in many industrial nations. Everglades National Park, for example, faces collapse as millions of newcomers move into southern Florida.

Longer waiting lists and higher user fees for fewer secluded spots are likely to be the tip of the iceberg, as population growth threatens to eliminate the diversity of habitats and cultures, in addition to the peace and quiet, that protected areas currently offer.

7. Forests

Global losses of forest area have marched in step with population growth for much of human history, but an estimated 75% of the loss in global forests has occurred in the twentieth century.

In Latin America, ranching is the single largest cause of deforestation. In addition, overgrazing and over-collection of firewood—which are often a function of growing population—are degrading 14% of the world's remaining large areas of virgin forest.

Deforestation created by the demand for forest products tracks closely with rising per capita consumption in recent decades. Global use of paper and paperboard per person has doubled (or nearly tripled) since 1961.

The loss of forest areas leads to a decline of forest services. These include habitat for wildlife; carbon storage, which is a key to regulating climate; and erosion control, provision of water across rainy and dry seasons, and regulation of rainfall.

8. Biodiversity

We live amid the greatest extinction of plant and animal life since the dinosaurs disappeared 65 million years ago, at the end of the Cretaceous period, with species losses at 100 to 1,000 times the natural rate. The principal cause of species extinction is habitat loss, which tends to accelerate with an increase in a country's population density.

A particularly productive but vulnerable habitat is found in coastal areas, home to 60% of the world's population. Coastal wetlands nurture two-thirds of all commercially caught fish, for example. And coral reefs have the second-highest concentration of biodiversity in the world, after tropical rain forests. But human encroachment and pollution are degrading these areas: Roughly half of the world's salt marshes and mangrove swamps have been eliminated or radically altered, and two-thirds of the world's coral reefs have been degraded, 10% of them "beyond recognition." As coastal migration continues—coastal dwellers could account for 75% of world population within 30 years—the pressures on these productive habitats will likely increase.

9. Climate Change

Over the last half century, carbon emissions from fossil-fuel burning expanded at nearly twice the rate of population, boosting atmospheric concentrations of carbon dioxide, the principal greenhouse gas, by 30% over preindustrial levels.

Fossil-fuel use accounts for roughly three-quarters of world carbon emissions. As a result, regional growth in carbon emissions tend to occur where economic activity and related energy use is projected to grow most rapidly. Emissions in China are projected to grow over three times faster than population in the next 50 years due to a booming economy that is heavily reliant on coal and other carbon-rich energy sources.

Emissions from developing countries will nearly quadruple over the next half century, while those from industrial nations will increase by 30%, according to the Intergovernmental Panel on Climate Change and the U.S. Department of Energy. Although annual emissions from industrial countries are currently twice as high as from developing ones, the latter are on target to eclipse the industrial world by 2020.

10. Energy

The global demand for energy grew twice as fast as population over the last 50 years. By 2050, developing countries will be consuming much more energy as their populations increase and become more affluent.

When per capita energy consumption is high, even a low rate of population growth can have significant effects on total energy demand. In the United States, for example, the 75 million people projected to be added to the population by 2050 will boost energy demand to roughly the present energy consumption of Africa and Latin America.

World oil production per person reached a high in 1979 and has since declined by 23%. Estimates of when global oil production will peak range from 2011 to 2025, signaling future price shocks as long as oil remains the world's dominant fuel.

In the next 50 years, the greatest growth in energy demands will come where economic activity is projected to be highest: in Asia, where consumption is expected to grow 361%, though population will grow by just 50%. Energy consumption is also expected to increase in Latin America (by 340%) and Africa (by 326%). In all three regions, local pressures on energy sources, ranging from forests to fossil fuel reserves to waterways, will be significant.

11. Waste

Local and global environmental effects of waste disposal will likely worsen as 3.4 billion people are added to the world's population over the next half century. Prospects for providing access to sanitation are dismal in the near to medium term.

A growing population increases society's disposal headaches—the garbage, sewage, and industrial waste that must be gotten rid of. Even where population is largely stable—the case in many industrialized countries—the flow of waste products into landfills and waterways generally continues to increase. Where high rates of economic and population growth coincide in coming decades, as they will in many developing countries, mountains of waste will likely pose difficult disposal challenges for municipal and national authorities.

Economic Impacts and Quality of Life

12. Jobs

Since 1950, the world's labor force has more than doubled—from 1.2 billion people to 2.7 billion—outstripping the growth in job creation. Over the next half century, the world will need to create more than 1.9 billion jobs in the developing world just to maintain current levels of employment.

While population growth may boost labor demand (through economic activity and demand for goods), it will most definitely boost labor supply. As the balance between the demand and supply of labor is tipped by population growth, wages tend to decrease. And in a situation of labor surplus, the quality of jobs may not improve as fast, for workers will settle for longer hours, fewer benefits, and less control over work activities.

Table 1

The 20 Largest Countries Ranked According to Population Size (In Millions)

| | *1998* | | *2050* | |
Rank	*Country*	*Population*	*Country*	*Population*
1	China	1,255	India	1,533
2	India	976	China	1,517
3	United States	274	Pakistan	357
4	Indonesia	207	United States	348
5	Brazil	165	Nigeria	339
6	Pakistan	148	Indonesia	318
7	Russia	147	Brazil	243
8	Japan	126	Bangladesh	218
9	Bangladesh	124	Ethiopia	213
10	Nigeria	122	Iran	170
11	Mexico	96	The Congo	165
12	Germany	82	Mexico	154
13	Vietnam	78	Philippines	131
14	Iran	73	Vietnam	130
15	Philippines	72	Egypt	115
16	Egypt	66	Russia	114
17	Turkey	64	Japan	110
18	Ethiopia	62	Turkey	98
19	Thailand	60	South Africa	91
20	France	59	Tanzania	89

Source: United Nations, *World Population Prospects: The 1996 Revision.*

As the children of today represent the workers of tomorrow, the interaction between population growth and jobs is most acute in nations with young populations. Nations with more than half their population below the age of 25 (e.g., Peru, Mexico, Indonesia, and Zambia) will feel the burden of this labor flood. Employment is the key to obtaining food, housing, health services, and education, in addition to providing self-respect and self-fulfillment.

13. Income

Incomes have risen most rapidly in developing countries where population has slowed the most, including South Korea, Taiwan, China, Indonesia, and Malaysia. African countries, largely ignoring family planning, have been overwhelmed by the sheer numbers of young people who need to be educated and employed.

If the world cannot simultaneously convert the economy to one that is environmentally sustainable and move to a lower population trajectory, economic decline will be hard to avoid.

14. Housing

The ultimate manifestation of population growth outstripping the supply of housing is homelessness. The United Nations estimates that at least 100 million of the world's people—roughly equal to the population of Mexico—have no home; the number tops 1 billion if squatters and others with insecure or temporary accommodations are included.

Unless population growth can be checked worldwide, the ranks of the homeless are likely to swell dramatically.

15. Education

In nations that have increasing child-age populations, the base pressures on the educational system will be severe. In the world's 10 fastest-growing countries, most of which are in Africa and the Middle East, the child-age population will increase an average of 93% over the next 50 years. Africa as a whole will see its school-age population grow by 75% through 2040.

If national education systems begin to stress lifelong learning for a rapidly changing world of the twenty-first century, then extensive provision for adult education will be necessary, affecting even those countries with shrinking child-age populations.

Such a development means that countries which started population-stabilization programs earliest will be in the best position to educate their entire citizenry.

16. Urbanization

Today's cities are growing faster: It took London 130 years to get from 1 million to 8 million inhabitants; Mexico City made this jump in just 30 years. The world's urban population as a whole is growing by just over 1 million people each week. This urban growth is fed by the natural increase of urban populations, by net migration from the countryside, and by villages or towns expanding to the point where they become cities or they are absorbed by the spread of existing cities.

If recent trends continue, 6.5 billion people will live in cities by 2050, more than the world's total population today.

Actions for Slowing Growth

As we look to the future, the challenge for world leaders is to help countries maximize the prospects for achieving sustainability by keeping both birth and death rates low. In a world where both grain output and fish catch per person are falling, a strong case can be made on humanitarian grounds to stabilize world population.

What is needed is an all-out effort to lower fertility, particularly in the high-fertility countries, while there is still time. We see four key steps in doing this:

Assess carrying capacity.   Every national government needs a carefully artic-ulated and adequately supported population policy, one that takes into account the country's carrying capacity at whatever consumption level citizens decide on. Without long-term estimates of available cropland, water for irrigation, and likely yields, governments are simply flying blind into the future, allowing their nations to drift into a world in which population growth and environmental degradation can lead to social disintegration.

Fill the family-planning gap.   This is a high-payoff area. In a world where population pressures are mounting, the inability of 120 million of the world's women to get family-planning services is inexcusable. A stumbling block: At the International Conference on Population and Development in Cairo in 1994, the industrialized countries agreed to pay one-third of the costs for reproductive-health services in developing countries. So far they have failed to do so.

Educate young women.   Educating girls is a key to accelerating the shift to smaller families. In every society for which data are available, the more edu-cation women have, the fewer children they have. Closely related to the need for education of young females is the need to provide equal opportunities for women in all phases of national life.

Have just two children.   If we are facing a population emergency, it should be treated as such. It may be time for a campaign to convince couples everywhere to restrict their childbearing to replacement-level fertility.

POSTSCRIPT

Is Global Environmental Stress Caused Primarily by Increased Resource Consumption Rather Than Population Growth?

$\mathbf{B}$rown and his colleagues chose to hold constant the effect of changes in consumption patterns in their analysis of the adverse impacts of population. Their prescription for minimizing such impacts is for each national government to create its own population policy that allows the country to avoid exceeding its carrying capacity "at whatever consumption level citizens decide on." Thus, the article begs the question of the comparative blame of consumption and population growth.

Najam, on the other hand, includes the question of consumption patterns, particularly in the developed world, when examining population effects. He takes to task scholars who choose to focus on population rather than on affluence and technology. He maintains that focusing on population as the principal cause of environmental degradation "implicitly places the responsibility for such degradation on [the] doorsteps" of the developing world.

Najam offers a simple comparison to show where the blame should really lie. The average Bangladeshi uses two milligrams of chlorofluorocarbons (CFCs) per year in comparison to the average American, who uses two kilograms of CFCs per year. Thus, the former's impact is only 1/1000th that of an American's. Najam concludes by asserting that it should be far easier to change the consumption lifestyles of the few very rich than the reproductive preferences of the many very poor.

One way to gain some insight into this debate is to examine the Earth's carrying capacity. A work that addresses this question in the context of exploring the planet's ability to feed 10 billion people is Gerhard K. Heileg's "How Many People Can Be Fed on Earth?" in Wolfgang Lutz, ed., *The Future Population of the World: What Can We Assume Today?* 2d ed. (Earthscan, 1996). In it, Heileg concludes that it is much too difficult to answer the question definitively because carrying capacity "is not a natural constant (but)... a dynamic equilibrium, essentially determined by human action." And the future choices are far too many to allow a firm prediction. This view is echoed by Joel E. Cohen's *How Many People Can the Earth Support?* (W. W. Norton, 1995).

ISSUE 9

Is the Threat of Global Warming Real?

YES: Ross Gelbspan, from *The Heat Is On: The High Stakes Battle Over Earth's Threatened Climate* (Addison-Wesley, 1997)

NO: Brian Tucker, from "Science Friction: The Politics of Global Warming," *The National Interest* (Fall 1997)

ISSUE SUMMARY

YES: Journalist Ross Gelbspan points to a variety of scientific evidence, including a 1995 announcement from 2,500 scientists, indicating that the planet is warming.

NO: Brian Tucker, a senior fellow of the Institute for Public Affairs, argues that there are still too many uncertainties to conclude that global warming has arrived.

At the UN-sponsored Earth Summit in Rio de Janeiro in 1992, a Global Climate Treaty was signed. According to S. Fred Singer, in *Hot Talks, Cold Science: Global Warming's Unfinished Debate* (Independent Institute, 1998), the treaty rested on three basic assumptions: First, global warming has been detected in the climate records of the last 100 years. Second, a substantial warming in the future will produce catastrophic consequences—droughts, floods, storms, a rapid and significant rise in sea level, agricultural collapse, and the spread of tropical disease. And third, the scientific and policy-making communities know (1) which atmospheric concentrations of greenhouse gases are dangerous and which ones are not; (2) that drastic reductions of carbon dioxide (CO_2) emissions as well as energy use in general by industrialized countries will stabilize CO_2 concentrations at close to current levels; and (3) that such economically damaging measures can be justified politically despite there being no significant scientific support for the assertion that global warming is a threat.

Since the Earth Summit, it appears that scientists have opted for placement into one of three camps. The first camp buys into the three assumptions outlined above. Scientists in the second camp suggest that while global warming has occurred and continues at the present, the source of such temperature rise cannot be ascertained yet. The conclusions of the Earth Summit were misunderstood by many in the scientific community, the second camp would argue. For these scientists, computer models, the basis of much evidence for the first group, have not yet linked global warming to human activities.

A third group of scientists argues that we cannot be certain that global warming is even taking place, yet alone determine its cause. They present a number of arguments in support of their position. Among them is the contention that presatellite data (pre-1979) showing a century-long pattern of warming is an illusion because satellite data (post-1979) reveal no such warming. Furthermore, when warming *was* present, it did not occur at the same time as a rise in greenhouse gases. Scientists in the third camp are also skeptical of studying global warming in the laboratory. They suggest, moreover, that most of the scientists who have opted for one of the first two camps have done so because of laboratory experiments rather than evidence from the real world.

Despite what appear to be wide differences in scientific thinking about the existence of global warming and its origins, the global community has moved forward with attempts to achieve consensus among the nations of the world for taking appropriate action to curtail human activities thought to affect warming. The latest effort occurred at a 1997 international meeting in Kyoto, Japan, where an agreement was forged for reaching goals established at the Earth Summit.

Not surprisingly, the authors of the two selections for this issue fall into different scientific camps. In the first selection, Ross Gelbspan not only affirms the presence of global warming but also points to oil and gas consumption as the culprits. Brian Tucker's position, clarified in the second selection, is that other factors—such as the politics of population, development, and environment—are to blame for the current rush to seek alternatives to oil and gas. Although his article was written prior to the Kyoto conference, his message remains the same.

Ross Gelbspan **YES**

Climate Change Is Here. Now.

In January 1995 a vast section of ice the size of] Rhode Island broke off the Larsen ice shelf in Antarctica. Although it received scant coverage in the press, it was one of the most spectacular and nightmarish manifestations yet of the ominous changes occurring on the planet.

As early as the 1970s, scientists predicted that the melting of Antarctica's ice shelf would signal the accelerating heating of the planet as human activity pushed the temperature of the earth upward. They were not wrong.

Two months later, a three-hundred-foot-deep ice shelf farther north collapsed, leaving only a plume of fragments in the Weddell Sea as evidence of its twenty-thousand-year existence.

Dr. Rodolfo del Valle, an Argentine scientist who witnessed the disintegration of the ice shelves, had little doubt about the implications when he recalled the events to a reporter from Reuters. "If conditions remain unchanged," he said, rising global temperatures "could cause catastrophic flooding all over the world. We thought the flooding would occur over the course of several centuries, but the whole process has been much quicker than we anticipated."

The first indications of the massive fissures had occurred in mid-January, when del Valle was working at a research station on James Ross Island, just off the Antarctic peninsula. Colleagues at an Argentine base on the Larsen ice shelf radioéd him there to say that they were being shaken by constant ice quakes. A few days later they called with even more startling news.

"On the twenty-third of January, they called me over the radio and said: 'Rudi, something's happening, the ice shelf is breaking.' An enormous crack had opened from the edge of the shelf on the Weddell Sea up to the mountains," said del Valle, who heads the earth sciences department at Argentina's National Antarctic Institute. Flying six thousand feet overhead in a light plane, del Valle saw that the ice shelf, up to a thousand feet thick in places, was beginning to break up into smaller icebergs. "It was spectacular because what once was a platform of ice more than forty miles wide had been broken up into pieces that looked like bits of polystyrene foam... smashed by a child.

"The first thing I did was cry."

The second monstrous crack—a forty-mile-long fissure that occurred two months later—appeared in the northernmost part of the Larsen shelf, which runs six hundred miles up the Antarctic peninsula. The cracking was caused by a regional warming that began in the 1940s. Measurements in the Antarctic peninsula show that its average temperature has risen by nearly 20 degrees Fahrenheit in the last twenty years. Del Valle said that several months earlier he and his colleagues predicted that the ice barrier would crack in ten years. "But it happened in barely two months," he observed. "Recently I've seen rocks poke through the surface of the ice that had been buried under six hundred meters of ice for twenty thousand years."

Ice works like a mirror. Its surface reflects most of the heat radiated by the sun back into the atmosphere. As ice like the Larsen ice shelf breaks up and newly exposed rocks absorb heat and further warm the ice cap, the earth will reflect less heat and retain more of it.

While the breakup of the Antarctic ice shelf may be the most dramatic manifestation of global warming, other symptoms have been emerging around the world for several years.

While the experts supposedly debate whether global warming has been "proved," the recent weather record has been marked by more intense rainfalls and severe snowstorms; stronger hurricanes; unseasonal and prolonged droughts, resulting in crop failure and devastating forest fires from Texas to Mongolia; killer heat waves from India to Chicago; and record flooding from Yemen to Nepal.

All of these escalating climate extremes share a common source, according to the overwhelming consensus of scientific thought: they are nature's expressions of the early stages of the heating of the atmosphere.

But some individuals do not want the public to know about the immediacy and extent of the climate threat. They have been waging a persistent campaign of denial and suppression that has been lamentably effective.

Four months after the fracturing of the Larsen ice shelf, the Washington-based, ideologically conservative George C. Marshall Institute released its fourth consecutive report emphatically dismissing the notion of planetary warming. "Comparable temperature changes are commonplace in recent climate history," according to the institute, which conducts no original research itself and whose reports are viewed by the vast majority of scientists as political statements rather than as research contributions. Its own chairman has acknowledged that the institute's reports represent nothing more than opinion.

But in some circles the opinions of the Marshall Institute carry more weight than those of the world's leading scientists. In May 1996 the House Science Committee was about to make its final budget decisions for the year. Before that meeting, the committee chairman, Robert Walker, a Republican congressman from Pennsylvania, asked the National Research Council (NRC) whether Congress should continue to fully fund NASA's Mission to Planet Earth, a program designed to monitor changes in the global climate and their effects. The NRC strongly recommended full funding for the program. Walker then turned to the Marshall Institute for advice. When he successfully recommended cutting the funding for the program, he cited the Marshall Institute's denials of the climate crisis to justify his decision.

It was not Representative Walker, however, who controlled the front line of the climate battle in the 104th Congress. In 1995 Dana Rohrabacher, a dapper, small-town journalist turned Republican congressman from Orange County, California, presided over a series of hearings on climate change in a House subcommittee. Discussing sea level rise, a consequence of atmospheric heating that scientists estimate will reach three feet within the next century, an Environmental Protection Agency (EPA) official told Rohrabacher that such a rise "could drown [up to] 60 percent of our coastal wetlands." That rise in sea level, he said, "would inundate more than five thousand square miles of dry land in the United States, an area the size of Connecticut," and some of its consequences would be "potentially catastrophic and irreversible."

The 49-year-old, round-faced Rohrabacher, an avid surfer, was unmoved by the gravity of the situation. "I am tempted to ask," he responded, "what this will do to the shape of the waves and rideability of the surf. But I will not do that. I will wait until later, when we get off the record."

After hearing from some of the world's leading climate scientists—who testified that global warming has already begun and that its early symptoms are already upon us—Rohrabacher, who chaired the Subcommittee on Energy and Environment of the House Committee on Science, accused them of practicing religion rather than science. He proceeded to vote to defund several government research programs that monitor the escalating stresses on the global environment.

In so doing, the congressman accomplished a staggering assault on foundations of our scientific knowledge. But he could never have succeeded in pulling off this legislative equivalent of a book burning were it not for the unique power of the one interest his leadership was benefiting: the fossil fuel industry. In dismissing the findings of the world's leading scientists about climate change, Rohrabacher was carrying out the strategy of big oil and big coal —and oil and coal emissions are the major driving force behind the heating of the planet's atmosphere.

In the United States the truth underlying the increasingly apparent changes in global climate has largely been kept out of public view. As a result, what most Americans know about global warming is obsolete and untrue.

That is no accident. The reason most Americans don't know what is happening to the climate is that the oil and coal industries have spent millions of dollars to persuade them that global warming isn't happening.

Together, oil and coal constitute the biggest single industry in history. Big oil alone does well over a trillion dollars a year in business. Coal and oil products are used by every home, every car, every factory, and every building in most countries of the world. Moreover, the invisible and well-funded public relations apparatus of the oil and coal lobby reaches many, many minds.

Denying global warming is a clever strategy—but its short-sightedness carries the seeds of massive destruction.

In November 1995, 2,500 leading climate scientists announced that the planet is warming because all the emissions from coal and oil burning are trapping in more of the sun's heat than is normal for our climate. Even if that warming is not yet obvious, they warned, it is already generating bizarre and extreme changes in the weather. This new period of less stable climate we have entered, the scientists wrote, "is likely to cause widespread economic, social and environmental dislocation." Their report noted that "potentially serious changes have been identified, including an increase in some regions of the incidence of extreme high temperature events, floods, and droughts, with resultant consequences for fires, pest outbreaks and ecosystem[s]."

This is a very frightening prospect. Starting slowly, we may already have embarked on a profoundly horrifying journey. Almost every week international news wires carry stories about extreme, disruptive, and often record-setting weather events. Unfortunately, these stories normally get buried away in local newspapers, and powerful forces are at work to see that they remain obscure and their significance unrecognized.

In the late summer of 1995 the immediacy of climate change struck me as I was sitting on my ramshackle back porch outside Boston. What was then a wilted patch of straw had once been my lush, green lawn before that summer, which was one of the driest in New England history. Overhead, between my porch and the far boundary of the atmosphere twelve miles up, carbon dioxide, driven upward by the unceasing flow of emissions from burning coal and oil, continued its relentless increase. This invisible gas is gradually warming the planet by trapping the sun's heat and preventing it from being reflected back into space. Higher up, just beyond the boundary of our atmosphere, water vapor continued silently to accumulate, amplifying the heating of earth. Hot as it was as I sat on my porch, the temperatures on earth could have been even hotter: Some of the warming of the atmosphere was masked by an invisible umbrella, about five miles overhead, of sulfate pollution, which deflected the sun's heat back into space. But that cooling effect, I knew, was only temporary.

My porch faces east. Two miles dead ahead the Atlantic Ocean was rising at a faster rate than at any time in human history, approaching a tenth of an inch a year. While scientists caution that this rapid rate may be temporary, the general trend toward significantly higher sea levels is not. One-tenth of an inch seems like a small amount until you stop to think that the oceans cover more than 70 percent of the earth's surface. A sea level rise of even a few inches would wreak havoc on many of the world's coastal communities.

Beyond the Boston Harbor islands, I mused, beyond the horizon, on the far side of the Atlantic, alpine plants are migrating up the mountainsides of Europe, seeking ever higher altitudes to survive the rising temperatures. Two thousand miles south, people living in the mountains of Rwanda and Kenya suffer from malaria and yellow fever, brought by mosquitoes that have recently migrated from lower levels. Only a few years ago, these mountain areas were free of such disease-carrying insects, because it was too cold for their survival there.

Environmentalists have been warning us about global warming for years. What is news is that global warming is no longer merely a future possibility. The heat is on. Now. Its early impacts, in the form of more extreme and unstable climate, are being felt even as I write.

The purpose of this [selection] is not only to bring home the imminence of climate change but also to examine the campaign of deception by big coal and big oil that is keeping the issue off the public agenda. I will examine the various arenas in which the battle for control of the issue is being fought—a battle with surprising political alliances and infuriating episodes of relentless obstructionism. The story told here provides an ominous foretaste of the most likely political consequences of our continued denial of the gathering threat—political chaos and the spread of totalitarianism. And it will conclude by outlining a transition to the future that contains at least the possibility of continuity for our existence as an organized, civilized society.

Sitting on my porch, remnants of my daughters' childhood were still visible in the parched yard. The weather-shredded marker where they buried their beloved cat. The thick screw hooks in the four-trunked poplar tree where they once hung a hammock. The same sun that dried my yard has also parched the eroded cornfields in the Andes Mountains of southern Ecuador, where my oldest daughter worked in a remote village the previous summer. About five hundred miles south of that village of Cashapugro, the ancient mountain glaciers of Peru are retreating at a frightening rate.

The late summer afternoon warmth stirred lazy reveries of my own approaching old age. Along with the genetic material and psychological baggage of my wife and myself, our daughters, now in college, carry our deepest hopes for the future. I had once fantasized a world of peace, in which my grandchildren would thrive in secure and nurturing communities. But that daydream has been overwhelmed by my terrible knowledge of a reality that is advancing with a gathering vengeance.

The problem is not difficult to understand. Each year humans pump 6 billion tons of heat-trapping carbon into the lower atmosphere, which is only twelve miles high. Within a few decades the atmospheric levels of carbon dioxide will double from preindustrial levels. The world's temperature record is already bearing witness to global climate change: Since 1980 we have seen the ten hottest years in recorded history. The five hottest consecutive years on record began in 1991. The hottest year in the world's recorded weather history was 1995. The planet is warming at a faster rate than at any time in the last ten thousand years.

It is a problem of mind-boggling magnitude, marching inexorably toward a climax. "If the last 150 years had been marked by the kind of climatic instability we are now beginning to see," says one world-class scientist, "the world might never have been able to support its current population of five billion people."

As horrifying as it is, the nature of the problem is not mysterious; nor is its cause. But another part of the problem is harder to fathom. It is taking place offstage behind closed doors, where the affairs of state and industry are conducted. In the media, where public opinion is formed; in the halls of Congress, where laws are made; and in international climate negotiations, the facts of global warming are being denied with a disinformation campaign as ferocious as any in history.

A major battle is under way: In order to survive economically, the biggest enterprise in human history—the worldwide oil and coal industry—is at war with the ability of the planet to sustain civilization. The trillion-dollar-a-year coal and oil industry is pitted against the oceans, forests, ice caps, and mountains of the earth as we know them today.

With sales exceeding two billion dollars every day, the oil industry supports the entire economies of most of the nations of the Middle East and large segments of the economies of Russia, Mexico, Venezuela, Nigeria, Indonesia, Norway, and Great Britain, among others. It employs millions of workers and affects the fortunes of tens of millions of investors. Substantial cuts in oil and coal consumption could, according to some economists and oil industry studies, disrupt entire nations and cripple the global economy.

Eventually, since the unstable climate poses threats even more dire than these to the survival of civilization, we will have no choice but to replace coal, oil, and eventually natural gas with other energy sources. This will mean the extinction of the fossil fuel industry. Nevertheless, the coal and oil lobbyists figure that they can buy time against that inevitable extinction by mystifying the public, casting doubt on every new piece of evidence that confirms global warming. They have good financial back-up, not only in their own immense war chests but in the vast wealth of the oil-producing nations of the Persian Gulf.

To carry out their mystification campaign, the industry's public relations specialists have made extensive use of a tiny band of scientists whose views contradict the consensus of the world's experts. The deep-pocketed industry lobby has promoted their opinions through every channel of communication it can reach. It has demanded access to the press for these scientists' views, as a right of journalistic fairness. Unfortunately, most editors are too uninformed about climate science to resist. They would not accord to tobacco company scientists who dismiss the dangers of smoking the same weight that they accord to world-class lung specialists. But in the area of climate research, virtually no news story appears that does not feature prominently one of these few industry-sponsored scientific "greenhouse skeptics."

It is a most impressive campaign, this assault on our sense of reality. It has carried the day in Congress, where a group of highly ideological legislators successfully waged a war on science. It has been a potent weapon on the international stage, permitting the corporate coal and oil interests—in tandem with the Organization of Petroleum Exporting Countries (OPEC) and other coal and oil exporting nations—to frustrate diplomatic attempts to address the crisis meaningfully.

Most importantly, the campaign has exerted a narcotic effect on the American public. It has lulled people into a deep apathy about the crisis by persuading them that the issue of climate change is terminally stuck in scientific uncertainty.

It is not.

For the last few years, the ravages of the changing climate have been sending shock waves through the executive suites of insurance companies in Zurich, Washington, Munich, and London. The recent succession of floods, hurricanes, and other extreme weather disasters, if they continue as a long-term trend, could bankrupt the insurance industry as such, and these executives know it.

In the relatively calm decade between 1980 and 1989, the insurance industry paid out, on the average, less than $2 billion a year for nonearthquake, weather-related property damage. But in just the five years between 1990 and 1995, the hurricanes, cyclones, and floods in Europe, Asia, and North America have cost the industry an average of more than $30 billion a year, according to the large German-based reinsurance firm Munich Re.

Today insurers worry that a direct hit on, say, Miami or New Orleans by a warming-intensified hurricane could leave them with $50 billion in insured losses. In 1995 Andrew Dlugolecki, a manager for the United Kingdom branch of the insurer General Accident, told a conference of insurers, bankers, and pension managers that "there is no doubt that weather patterns are changing. There is also no doubt... that small climate changes have very big effects on society.... Looking forward, I am sure that climate change will speed up. I am also sure that there will be major consequences for insurers."

Others in the corporate world, outside the fossil fuel industry, are also beginning to realize that new climate extremes could abruptly curtail the growth of the global economy. Their concerns do not derive from altruism. They are not in the business of environmental protection. What motivates them is a desire to protect their own industries or to increase their current market share. But as they mobilize in opposition to the relentless efforts of big oil and big coal to protect their commerce at any cost, the emerging alliances between insurers and non-oil big business hold significant promise as a positive force for large-scale change.

The spokesmen for big oil and big coal claim that "greenhouse hysteria" threatens to undermine the world's economic foundations. Taking action to reduce atmospheric warming, they say, would plunge humanity into a regressive and dramatically impoverished state. Even conceding the scientific validity of the climate threat, they say, would be the first step down a slippery slope toward desolate poverty and the living standards of our cave-dwelling ancestors.

But the consequences of planetary warming are even more terrifying—a cascade of environmental effects that could shake our civilization off its foundations altogether.

The catalog of anticipated effects is familiar—it reads like the biblical apocalypse. Scientists say these consequences will include not only more extreme temperatures, with hotter heat and colder cold, but also more intense rain and snowstorms, extraordinarily destructive hurricanes, and protracted, crop-destroying droughts, particularly in the interior regions of continents. Island nations and low-lying coastal regions everywhere might disappear under rising seas. These ecological shifts would trigger outbreaks of infectious diseases, as they have already begun to do.

If this scenario isn't hair-raising enough, researchers warn that the feedback effects of global warming could fuel even more nightmarish ones, in which initial warming would cause changes that would themselves intensify and, in turn, speed the warming even more. For example, higher temperatures could lead to drought and wildfires that would burn vast areas of forest. Since vegetation acts to absorb carbon dioxide, that burning would accelerate the accumulation of greenhouse gases—leading, in turn, to more warming-driven climate destabilization. As the greenhouse gases accumulate, the stress could catapult the global climate system into an epoch of wild instability, accompanied by a further rapid and uncontrollable surge of heating.

These feedback effects could cause more than ecological dislocations. They could ripple, as well, through our social fabric.

However insulated we may seem from nature, our planetary environment shapes the way we live. Our interactions reflect the variety of its geography; our institutions mirror its abundances and its stresses. Under the pressure of intensifying instabilities, climate changes and their feedback effects could very likely overwhelm the foundations of democracy. They could well mean a return to the age-old plague of totalitarianism.

In poorer and more environmentally vulnerable countries, the antidemocratic threat is easy to foresee. One of the first casualties of a succession of ecological disasters would likely be individual liberties and governmental democracy and their replacement by a permanent state of eco-emergency.

In wealthier countries like the United States, the impacts of a changing climate are very likely to catch both government and the corporate sector unprepared. And since carbon dioxide lingers in the atmosphere for one to two hundred years, it will continue to disturb the global climate long after we drastically cut our fuel emissions—whether we do so voluntarily or involuntarily. By the time we actually feel the heavy brunt of climate-driven catastrophes, it may well be too late for us to preserve any semblance of democratic order. Governments would likely be forced to resort to martial law in order to respond to weather-related homelessness, disease outbreaks, food shortages, and economic disruptions.

Add the advent of totalitarianism to the scenario of a disturbed climate and the collapse of much of the world's economy, and you get a sense of the stakes of the battle.

There is, moreover, a further complication to this conflict—the yawning chasm of economic inequality between rich and poor. It is an issue of morality to some and irrelevant to others. But in the context of earth's changing climate, the consequences of global economic inequality are as critical as the carbon in the air. Any solution to climate change must address this economic gulf. Regardless of whether it holds a place in one's moral or economic accounting system, addressing it is a critical prerequisite of any solution. Any cutback in oil and coal use by the wealthy countries will be dwarfed by a surge in carbon dioxide production—not to speak of the continuing destruction of the world's CO_2-absorbing forests—by China, India, Brazil, Mexico, and others. Unless they are provided with renewable, climate-friendly energy sources, the developing economic giants will likely be forced to accelerate their burning of fossil fuels to survive the relentless expansion of that poverty, driven by their expanding populations.

On the front of international diplomacy, the large developing nations have viewed with suspicion any initiative that might limit the supply of energy they need to feed and house and employ their citizens. At the same time, the oil- and coal-producing nations have been very successful in obstructing attempts to reduce the world's use of coal and oil But even in the face of this resistance, an unlikely coalition is prodding the world's governments into the beginnings of meaningful action. A number of small island nations—stretching from the Philippines to Jamaica—fear being flooded out of existence by rising sea levels and increasingly severe hurricanes; they have found common cause with Germany, Britain, Ghana, and other nations that fear the disastrous consequences of unchecked climate change. And they are beginning to force the world's negotiators to confront the problem.

Then there is this perversely good news: As the crisis becomes increasingly severe, the intensity of its destructive impacts will force us to overcome the current plague of disinformation—and the resistance of the deepest-pocketed, biggest private interest in history—to address the problem.

Despite the gravity of this cosmic squeeze we are in, solutions are within our reach. Creating a new energy economy is not a question of science; neither is it a question of technology. Armies of inventors and engineers, fascinated by the challenges of energy, have already supplied us with the devices and designs we need.

For hundreds of years, the engines of economic production have been powered by carbon-based fossil fuels. But in the last few decades, coal and oil have themselves turned into humanity's greatest unintended weapon of mass destruction. It is a happy coincidence of history that at the same time, the climate-friendly energy technologies that we need in order to begin to stabilize the atmosphere have already been created. We have at hand all the technology and knowledge we need to replace the world's supply of coal and oil and, eventually, of natural gas. They need only to be taken to the level of mass production and deployed throughout the world.

The escalating alarm signals emanating from our increasingly disturbed planet contain the seeds for a sweeping transformation. It is not hard to understand that nature is holding a gun to our head. What is harder to understand, at first, is that this moment also presents an opportunity for extraordinary positive change.

Historically, our energy transitions have occurred by accident. This time, as global citizens responsible for a common future, we can actively plan and manage the transition into our next energy epoch. What it requires is taking control of a natural resource-turned-hazard—before it trashes our planet and truncates our history.

NO

Brian Tucker

Science Friction:
The Politics of Global Warming

As everyone knows, there has been much sound and fury over the past decade about the threat of global warming, a condition held to be the result of "greenhouse" gas emissions caused by human activity. Indeed, the argument over global warming has been the main set piece of the international environmental culture wars for several years, with activist Cassandras and conservative Pollyannas both trying to marshal the authority of science as justification for their views. The ensuing battle has reminded us of a key truth of the sociology of knowledge, that while everyone may be entitled to his own opinions, none is entitled to his own facts.

In Kyoto this coming December [1997] a major UN-sponsored international conference on global warming is scheduled to take place; it is the culmination of several run-up meetings in Berlin, Geneva, and New York that have seen the various players rehearsing for the big event. From these precursor meetings, several things have become clear: that politics and emotions have distorted what is scientifically known about the phenomenon itself; that the issue is far more politically and morally complex than many realize or are prepared to admit; and that governments find themselves besieged by conflicting interests and pressures, both domestically and internationally. In light of all this, the outlook for anything very useful happening at Kyoto is mixed at best. An examination of the real science, the real issues, and the real choices before us shows why.

The Real Science

Many if not most non-expert observers assume that the greenhouse effect necessitates major and relatively rapid reductions in greenhouse gas emissions, particularly carbon dioxide, lest dire climatic changes imperil the biosphere. Typical of much media comment on the issue is the assertion, this one from *The Australian* newspaper, that " . . . some scientists are increasingly worried that greenhouse gases could wreak havoc with the earth's climate in future generations, creating huge floods and droughts from global warming." But those who

From Brian Tucker, "Science Friction: The Politics of Global Warming," *The National Interest*, no. 49 (Fall 1997). Copyright © 1997 by *The National Interest*. Reprinted by permission. Notes omitted.

157

believe such things do not get their data from the international consortium of climatologists who are continually collating results from recent studies.

Much of the scientific theory about greenhouse gas emissions is well founded, but it does not support the conclusion that calamitous effects from global warming are nigh upon us. The work of the Inter-governmental Panel on Climate Change (IPCC), established in 1988 by the World Meteorological Organization (WMO) and the United Nations Environmental Program, has yielded a worldwide scientific consensus that has become generally, if not universally, accepted as a balanced state-of-knowledge assessment. In essence, its conclusion is that while human activity has caused no significant direct increase of the major greenhouse gas—namely, water vapor—there is no doubt that other such gases are increasing. The most important of these is carbon dioxide, followed by methane and nitrous oxide. Fossil fuel burning is the main reason for the increase of carbon dioxide, and agricultural methods play a major role in the increase of methane and nitrous oxide. It follows that the energy and food requirements resulting from increases in world population together with the demands of the existing population make it inevitable that these gases will continue to accumulate in the foreseeable future. The rate at which this will occur, however, is still unclear.

Although scientific progress has occurred on several fronts, the timing, magnitude, and geographical distribution of climate change due to higher greenhouse gas levels can be estimated only inexactly and in limited detail. Climate scientists know that many important processes are inadequately treated in their models; notable difficulties include specifying the roles of clouds and ocean currents, and imprecise representation of precipitation processes. While sensible and careful attempts are being made to effect improvements, doubts remain as to how accurate our models can become anytime soon at representing the real atmosphere. Hence, the simulation of any but the broadest aspects of climate in a world with higher greenhouse gas levels is an exercise of uncertain validity.

In view of these uncertainties and the cautious way in which the scientists carrying out climate change studies regard their results, it is unfortunate that some on the periphery of this knowledge extrapolate so freely as to predict calamitous consequences even within the next century. There is no scientific justification for such a view. Only one prediction can be hazarded with any reasonable degree of confidence: that when an effective doubling of current greenhouse gases occurs, probably toward the end of [this] century, average near-surface air temperatures will be 2 degrees or 3 degrees C higher than they are at present. This represents the middle range of estimates, with some models predicting one or two degrees higher and others one or two degrees lower. Even this limited prediction depends on a correct treatment of climate processes represented in the models, and we are still not sure of their accuracy extrapolated out as far as eighty or ninety years.

Associated with these air temperature increases are higher near-surface sea temperatures and, with somewhat less confidence, sea level rises of up to half a meter due to thermal expansion of sea water. These changes would be superimposed upon vertical land movements of similar magnitude due to tectonic processes; in some cases, such movements would exacerbate the effects of higher sea levels, in other cases they would mitigate them. Another century on, that is to say around the year 2200, at a time when greenhouse gases may be three times their present concentration, models indicate a total climate change from the present of an additional 50 percent beyond the above-cited figures.

There is scientific consensus on little else. The belief that events such as the January 1995 and summer 1997 floods in Western Europe and the January/February 1996 cold spell in central and eastern parts of the United States were caused by higher greenhouse gas levels is taken seriously by many environmental activists. But they are, strictly speaking, scientifically unjustified. Indeed, all assertions that climate models indicate progressively extreme weather are highly questionable. Suggestions that global warming is increasing the frequency of tropical cyclones or of droughts are unfounded; indeed, some data suggest that a decrease in extreme weather is more likely. Analyses of recent climate model results do reveal a small rise in the frequency of high rainfall events in the presence of twice as much carbon dioxide as currently exists in the atmosphere, but this may be accepting too much detail from the surrogate model's crude spatial resolution and very inexact grasp of rainfall processes.

The Real Issues

Misconstrued science, however, is perhaps the least of the problems associated with the global warming scare. Far more significant is the misconstruction of the underlying politics of the thing.

Casual observers have a very truncated notion of what is at stake in the global warming debate. The typical newspaper reader appears to think that what is at issue is the extent to which the earth's ambient temperature is increasing and what needs to be done to prevent presumed calamity. If the problem were really that simple, we could expect that an objective consensus of qualified experts would suggest the path to prevention and remediation. But even if all the necessary unambiguous scientific facts were available—and as we have seen, this is not so simple a task—the very wording of the main objective of the Framework Convention on Climate Change (FCCC), negotiated at the 1992 Earth Summit at Rio de Janeiro, suggests the key complication. Article 2 of the FCCC commits signatories to achieve " . . . stabilization of greenhouse gas concentrations in the atmosphere at a level that would prevent dangerous anthropogenic interference with the climate system. Such a level should be achieved within a time frame sufficient to allow ecosystems to adapt naturally to climate change, to ensure that food production is not threatened, and to enable economic development to proceed in a sustainable manner."

This is an illuminating formulation for two reasons. First, no empirical definition is given (here or elsewhere in the FCCC) of what constitutes "dangerous" anthropogenic interference with the climate system, or a time frame "sufficient" to allow ecosystems to adapt naturally to climate change. What is dangerous or sufficient in these contexts is not obvious, short of extreme cases. And the entire statement begs the question of the extent to which any measurable change in the climate system has in fact been caused by humans. Not only has this proved difficult to determine, but, thanks to one of the most astonishing scientific episodes of the century, we know something in 1997 that we did not know in 1992: that a slight increase in water vapor, the most plentiful of the greenhouse gases, may come from a constant bombardment of the earth by small ice comets.

Second, and more important for our purposes, the FCCC acknowledges that the greenhouse gas emissions said to cause global warming are to a large extent a consequence of efforts to meet the energy and food requirements of a growing world population. In short, it suggests, obliquely at least, that there are trade-offs to be reckoned. And so there are: The only realistic way to reduce greenhouse gases sharply is to burn less fossil fuel, and the only way to do that without jeopardizing living standards, particularly in the poorest countries, is to rely far more heavily on nuclear-generated electricity. But many of the meliorist-minded political activists who are concerned about the environmental damage caused by modern industrialism are equally concerned about the poverty of the less developed parts of the world, and equally adamant opponents of generating electricity from nuclear power.

We can add to this already vexatious equation the contentious issue of world population control, which is part and parcel of the issue of world poverty. As the failure of the September 1994 World Population Summit at Cairo showed, there is no general international agreement on realistic plans to limit world population increases any more than there is general agreement on a plan to attack poverty in the world's poorer lands. Indeed, this entire melange of issues defines the current standoff between the OECD [Organisation for Economic Co-operation and Development] countries and what used to be called generically the Third World. Many relatively poor countries with high population growth rates have seen population control as a ploy of the advanced countries to deny them their future power, or to fob off responsibility for sharing global prosperity. Representatives of the more advanced countries, with generally more moderate rates of population growth, see such arguments as highly self-defeating and often unjustifiably conspiratorial in inspiration. The global warming argument between rich and poor countries is a variation on the same theme: Efforts by the industrialized powers to impose greenhouse gas emission limits on developing countries are seen by the governments of those countries as an alternative means of reducing their rates of economic growth and hence their national power; while the developing countries' refusal to accept limits on themselves is seen by the developed countries as cynical and self-serving.

The global warming controversy is therefore bound up not only with uncertainties about the objective causes and extent of the phenomenon, but also with impassioned arguments over global development, power, and morality. While most of the relevant government officials appreciate these complexities, many environmentalists have difficulty acknowledging that the Framework Convention objective itself begs the question of what is desirable, let alone what is possible. Having to make painful trade-offs between desirable but irreconcilable objectives is precisely what true believers of all stripes are temperamentally incapable of doing. In this instance, they are extremely reluctant to pose the crucial question: Which is worse, embracing nuclear power with its potential dangers and costs, imposing poverty-inducing restrictions on world energy consumption and agriculture, or accepting the costs of adjustment to climate change?

It is not surprising, therefore, that since the Rio meeting strong emotion has led many governments, including that of the United States, to try to capture the high moral ground of domestic politics by making promises that are, at least for the foreseeable future, manifestly impossible to keep. Indeed, several governments have adopted national interim targets even more ambitious than those of the United States. Germany, for example, aims for a 25 percent reduction of 1990 carbon dioxide emissions by 2005. Of the more than 150 national signatories that have ratified the FCCC and accepted its aim to stabilize greenhouse gas concentrations in the atmosphere, most have adopted national targets that are highly unlikely to be achieved. As Kyoto approaches, these governments find themselves caught in a crisis of wishing, suspended between the short-term political expediency of affirming such goals and the reality of actual limits to achieving them in light of the conflicting political and moral interests at stake.

Why the Alarm?

The scientific evidence thus far suggests that adjusting to what is liable to be rather moderate and very gradual climate change—with some conversion from fossil fuels to nuclear power to provide time for adjustment to a more moderate level and pace of change—is the most sensible answer to the question of trade-offs posed above. But this is not likely to be the conclusion reached in Kyoto. Instead, a combination of international beggar-thy-neighbor politics and a rush of millenarian fear seems to be taking over.

If there is so little evidence to support the notion of calamitous climate change associated with global warming, why has so much alarm been generated? The answer lies in part in the sky-is-falling perspective that seems to characterize the views of environmental activists, and their success at imparting this perspective to the general public through a media industry more interested in selling its wares than it is adept at understanding basic science. Not only is the magnitude of change exaggerated, but environmental activists have also been able to popularize the unwarranted assumption that all change must be deleterious.

Fear is as hardwired into human thought processes as the temptations of utopia, and both have influenced social development throughout human history. No doubt the increased popularity of declinist thought among intellectuals these last few decades owes at least a little something to an awareness of the finite nature of the physical world, and to a keener appreciation that humanity has prospered materially only because we have exploited this finite environment. As a result of these fears, the precautionary principle has become a major plank in many environmental platforms as a means of stopping environmental degradation. This principle states that, when faced with development proposals, regulators should anticipate environmental harm and act to ensure that such harm does not occur.

This sounds innocuous enough; surely no rational person would advocate deliberate and needless environmental degradation. But, as suggested above, there is not just one moral imperative at issue—the environment—but competing moral imperatives, or at least competing desired objectives, including the right to life, food, and comfort, and concern for both international and intergenerational equity. The precautionary principle of environmentalism, however, assumes that any developmental activity has a latent tendency to do more harm than good, and that whatever societal benefit may come from such activity cannot justify further environmental alteration. The key to such an assumption is that the environmental value necessarily takes precedence over all others because if the biosphere is wrecked beyond redemption, then no other value can be served. This key assumption, however, reflects an excessive fear of the future and a highly timorous view of the relationship between humanity and the environment.

The application of this gloomy perspective to the subject of climate change is much encouraged by a tendency to focus on potential damage to systems based on the present climatic state. Yet adaptation has been a hallmark of human resilience throughout history, and opportunities actually to benefit from prospective climate change are consistently ignored. Typically, for example, a broad indication of more rain tends to be regarded as likely to result in more floods rather than fewer droughts, and of less rain as causing more droughts rather than fewer floods. Such misplaced anxiety has caused one senior scientist to bemoan, "We have created the most unnecessarily fearful generation of humankind that ever populated the earth."

Fear of climate change has also been bolstered unwittingly by the development of "scenarios", a term that describes sets of climate change parameters regarded as feasible in the light of emerging model results. Scenarios were first prepared by climate scientists to provide a benchmark for estimating the sensitivity of different sectors of society and the economy to possible climate change. From their inception such scenarios were tagged with strong caveats indicating that they should not be regarded as forecasts, and were openly acknowledged to be based on models widely considered inadequate in many ways. But such warnings and qualifications have often been ignored, partly because many environmentalists feel happiest when they assume the worst, and partly because the explanatory notes issued with early scenarios were sufficiently ambiguous to imply forecasts to the non-expert.

A gradually changing climate may well be the inevitable consequence of human activity, and it may indeed pose serious problems of adaptation. It bears repeating that the evidence does not support the dismissive view that those concerned about global warming are spinning fantasies from thin air. But dramatic descriptions of potential calamity are hyperbole, and the assumption that all change will be for the worse is less a sign of perspicacity than paranoia.

The Real Choices

It is sometimes said that realism is the impact of thinking upon wishing. With world population rising more rapidly than at any previous time in history, and with industrialization spreading fast to formerly impoverished regions, the prospect of reducing world emission of the greenhouse gases necessarily involved in the industrial programs of developing nations and in world food production is, to put it mildly, not good.

It is important to distinguish between greenhouse gas emissions, which are what is put into the atmosphere, and gas concentrations, which are what stay there. An approach to stable emissions will be possible only when world population and associated development expectations have themselves stabilized —probably a century or more hence, or when alternatives to fossil fuel become widely available and commercially competitive. To stabilize concentrations of gases in the atmosphere would require worldwide emission reductions in excess of 50 percent, and that over a time interval during which world population is expected to double.

The situation is not totally irredeemable, however. Fossil fuel combustion accounts for some 75 percent of worldwide carbon dioxide emissions, and substitute means of generating electrical power on a large scale already exist. The most dramatic recent example of a national effort to reduce fossil fuel burning emissions is the French conversion to nuclear energy. France achieved a 40 percent reduction in carbon dioxide emissions during the 1980s, largely by increasing its nuclear-powered electricity generating capacity from about 10,000 to 56,000 megawatts. By 1994, about 78 percent of France's electricity was generated by nuclear power. No other country has undertaken such a massive transfer from fossil fuel to nuclear energy, although several other industrialized countries have moved in this direction. As a result, Sweden, South Korea, Switzerland, and Spain now have some of the lowest per capita rates of carbon dioxide emissions. For the United States, with the highest per capita emissions, carbon dioxide emissions in 1993 would have been 30 percent more than occurred had it not been for 109 nuclear-powered electricity generating stations. For the world as a whole, the amount of carbon dioxide accumulating in the atmosphere would be some 10 percent greater than at present without the existing nuclear production of electricity.

It is clear that policies fostering energy conservation, energy efficiency, and renewable energy alone cannot stabilize worldwide emissions, let alone reduce atmospheric concentrations of greenhouse gases. Nor is the drastic decrease in consumption required for such reductions remotely in prospect, for it would lead to a politically unacceptable reduction in living standards in the economically advanced countries, and to a politically unacceptable limit on development in the less advanced countries. The stabilization of emissions might be achieved, however, within about fifty years if there were an immediate international push to maximize nuclear-powered electricity production. But that, of course, raises concern about cost and safety—and here we come back to another difficult trade-off.

Concerns regarding the safety of nuclear power station operations are not something idly to be dismissed, even if one were satisfied that safe disposal of low, intermediate, and high-level wastes had been achieved. It is not fabricated paranoia to take such problems seriously, nor is it trivial to note that waste disposal problems have still not been solved. But nearly 450 nuclear power reactors in some 30 countries currently supply approximately 17 percent of the world's electricity needs, and nuclear power is today safer and less of an environmental threat than other means of generating electricity, at least as long as there is a willingness to pay the costs of safe reactor operation and waste management procedures. Such costs make nuclear-generated electricity more expensive than the fossil fuel method, but if we seek rapid reductions of carbon dioxide emissions, it is clear that any extra costs involved with nuclear power would be less than those of the only other alternative—namely, the economic and social disruption consequent upon drastic food and energy curtailment.

Political realities being what they are, there is no way that the FCCC objective of reducing emissions—which is likely to be reaffirmed in Kyoto—will be reached within the time frames agreed so far. There is no rapid way either to curtail emissions or to achieve substitution of nuclear-powered electricity generation capacity. The international scientific establishment knows this, having declared two years after Rio that even the "stabilization at present carbon dioxide concentrations . . . obviously is an impossible option." It is even clearer today that the direct economic costs of the magnitude of emission reduction being contemplated as we move toward the Kyoto meeting are enormous. To the extent that there is any political willingness to achieve the Rio targets, it is likely to be soon smothered by realization of the staggering price tag that comes with it.

Perhaps this is just as well since the actual extent of climate change is going to be much less dramatic than most non-experts think. It is important that emotions not lead governments into chasing non-existent solutions to highly exaggerated problems, if only because that will make it harder to achieve less daunting but still necessary solutions to real problems. If dispassionate analysis cannot put an end to the current alarmism, then perhaps the inevitability of failure to meet unrealistic goals will eventually induce a greater sense of realism.

Such a realism would take as its first principle with respect to issues of relative cost that policies aimed at adapting to gradual climate change make more sense than impossible efforts to stop all anthropogenic climate change in its tracks. Put somewhat crudely, it makes more economic and moral sense to build dikes to prevent coastal flooding, to relocate especially vulnerable human habitats, to adjust irrigation schemes for variant rainfall patterns, and to accelerate efforts to replace fossil fuel burning to meet energy requirements than it does to drive world GNP [gross national product] backwards several percentage points per year for half a century or more.

Even such an effort, undertaken over the better part of a century, will be no stroll in the park. It will require, first of all, accelerated research aimed at obtaining improved and unbiased scientific assessments of change, and the most sensible ways to adapt to it. But if one takes a factually based view of the problem, it is clear that the costs for adjustment spread out over time will be vastly lower than any serious effort to meet the Rio targets.

Lost in the Ozone

Now that it is obvious that there is no way to meet the main objective of the Framework Convention on Climate Change, is there any indication of a shift in thinking from a noble but impossible approach to a less dramatic but more rational one? Will we see more sober deliberations in Kyoto? From the evidence of the Conference of Parties to the FCCC convened in April 1995 in Berlin, of a second conference in July 1996 in Geneva, and of the UN/WMO conference in New York in June of [1997], the answer has to be "maybe."

The Berlin meeting was designed to provide a forum for countries to compare and assess their programs to formulate, implement, publish, and regularly update emission reduction measures to mitigate climate change. As expected, representatives of environmental movements also sought to increase and strengthen reduction targets for industrialized countries. A similar line was taken by many poor countries (a more realistic term for what used to be called developing countries), who refused to accept any reduction target applying to themselves.

The impossibility of attaining the 1992 Rio targets was not acknowledged at Berlin, let alone the lunacy of setting still more stringent ones. Little more was decided than to launch a new round of negotiations, termed the Berlin Mandate, aimed at delivering a legally binding instrument on which all delegates could agree at a December 1997 Kyoto conference. Indeed, most participants at Berlin seemed more concerned with making new commitments than with meeting old ones—it was, after all, easier. The real trade-offs were not mentioned, and many strains of hypocrisy were in evidence. Bureaucratic opportunists, having pushed policy formulation well ahead of scientific justification, now saw emerging career prospects from continuing rounds of expensive international negotiation. Environmental opportunists, grasping at any information no matter how selective or exaggerated to foment alarm, appeared completely oblivious to the downstream effects of their extravagant demands. Rich nation opportunists, because their current economic circumstances involve a temporary stabilization of their own gas emissions, saw a means of imposing economic restrictions on competitors not so favorably placed. Poor nation opportunists, while rejecting emission reduction targets for themselves, sought restrictions on rich nations on the grounds that their extravagance caused the problem in the first place.

And so it goes. In Geneva in July 1996, a 1995 scientific update of our understanding of the greenhouse gas-climate change connection, prepared by the Inter-governmental Panel on Climate Change, was received. Its most important component was the report of its Scientific Working Group, because in any logical progression its other two components (estimating impacts and devising strategies to cope) must be based on climate change predictions, which in turn are based on an understanding of how greenhouse gases get into the atmosphere and what happens once they do. The treatment accorded this report was as illuminating as it was discouraging.

Background information and the first draft of documentation were provided by hundreds of scientists who had met to coordinate and articulate the results of their research. An executive group edited the detailed material, prepared summary findings, and published both—which were then sharply criticized from within the ranks of both science and industry. Bias and exaggeration were apparent in the final policymakers' summaries. For example, while there is an implied increase in the frequency of severe droughts and floods in the final wording, there is no "on balance" evidence in the research results to justify this. Also, where there are clear results showing that, for example, tropical cyclone occurrence will remain unchanged, this is interpreted weakly as there not yet being sufficient evidence to show an increase. Careful study of the report by "IPCC watchers" associated with major world industry associations has revealed many examples of last minute changes to the earlier wording, the effect being to "scientifically cleanse" the final report of equivocations and caveats in the background documentation. The World Energy Council has also cited evidence of scientific bias, technical weakness, and political influence in the policymakers' summaries provided by other IPCC working groups.

Whether due to naivete or bias, the credibility of the IPCC has been damaged by these shortcomings. Those responsible for the final wording of the summaries appear to have been unaware that any selected passage that could advance alarmist prejudices would be seized upon by the environmental lobby and widely quoted, whether in context or not. These experiences, in turn, have made prospects for Kyoto even dimmer than they might otherwise be, because the credibility of the core scientific work has now been compromised.

Not all the news is bad, however. From the national reports presented at Geneva, and later in New York, it was evident that few countries would get near their existing and modest target of stabilizing emissions by the year 2000. Developing countries, meanwhile, are still excluded from such targets. Not surprisingly, then, much of the preparatory negotiations for Kyoto involve squabbling over whether any targets should involve "differentiation", that is, considerations of social and economic differences between countries. The United States, currently allied with part of the European Union, opposes differentiation; most other industrialized countries support it. Nevertheless, no country regards such "burden sharing" as other than a means of reducing its own share, while developing countries show little sign of any willingness to make sacrifices.

Still, reading between the lines of these discussions one can detect an increasing recognition of the unrealistic nature of worldwide emission reduction targets, of the still major scientific uncertainties at hand, and of the need to assess the full consequences of a policy before embarking upon it. A small group of countries, including Australia, Iceland, Japan, and Norway, refuses to conform to the pretense of being bound to even more unrealistic emission reduction commitments beyond 2000. Other countries, most notably the United States, while supporting the principle of binding targets, have demanded that they be realistic and verifiable, not compromise national prosperity, and include targets for developing countries.

That is good, of course, but not good enough. It remains politically incorrect, and hence so far impossible, to discuss the issues rationally, with all the attendant assumptions openly scrutinized, and with all the competing values acknowledged and analyzed. From what has been said, it should be clear that the global warming scare is based on four related assumptions: (1) that the greenhouse gas-climate change scientific theory is valid; (2) that any such climate change will necessarily be detrimental to human well-being; (3) that realistically we can achieve a sufficient reduction in greenhouse gas emissions to effect a worldwide stabilization of gas concentrations in the atmosphere; and (4) that the cost to society of such a reduction is less than the cost of adapting to the climate change. It follows that if even one of these assumptions is untrue, then the argument behind a policy of rapid and extensive reduction of greenhouse gas emissions is undermined. As we have seen, the basic scientific theory of global warming is sound, but predicts substantially more moderate effects than those that have captured the popular imagination. Imprecise and uncertain climate change estimates and the complexity of climatic impact assessments make the second assumption indeterminate; while the foregoing arguments have shown the third and fourth to be essentially false. Unless the Kyoto summit acknowledges these basic truths, it looks to be a dreadful affair that will needlessly worsen political tensions between rich and poor, mislead millions of scientific innocents, and misdirect government policies that must deal with the less severe but still real challenge before us.

POSTSCRIPT

Is the Threat of Global Warming Real?

Gelbspan's piece is from the introduction to his book on global warming. Nowhere is his position clearer than in his explanation of escalating climate extremes: "They are nature's expressions of the early stages of the heating of the atmosphere." His introduction also lays the foundation for the second major theme of the book, an examination of "the campaign of deception by big coal and big oil that is keeping the [global warming] issue off the public agenda." Because the excerpt included in this issue serves as a preliminary discussion to elaborations that follow, it is more difficult to buy into the two main arguments that he outlines. Gelbspan includes an appendix in the book that offers a "scientific critique of greenhouse skeptics." Here he cites the arguments put forth by such critics and offers a rebuttal for each one.

Tucker's main thesis is that science "does not support the conclusion that calamitous effects from global warming are nigh upon us." He continues, "There is no scientific justification for such a view." Tucker raises the stakes by asserting that the global warming controversy is much more than a debate about the causes and extent of the phenomenon. It is also about global development, power, and morality in the struggle between the rich and poor countries, with population "control" a central issue.

It is difficult for social scientists to assess the scientific merits of the arguments. Both Gelbspan and Tucker seem to be presenting reasonable arguments in defense of their positions. One has to look elsewhere for some help in assessing the relative merits of their cases. The good news is that perhaps no global issue takes up more space on the shelves of American libraries than that of global warming.

Three studies make valuable reading, each of which takes a different position (one at each extreme of the debate and a third one that suggests moderate climate change). S. Fred Singer's *Hot Talk, Cold Science: Global Warming's Unfinished Debate* (Independent Institute, 1998) enhances the author's reputation as one of the leading opponents of global warming's adverse consequences. At the other extreme, John Houghton, in *Global Warming: The Complete Briefing,* 2d ed. (Cambridge University Press, 1997), accepts global warming as a significant concern and describes how it can be reversed in the future. Finally, S. George Philander, in *Is the Temperature Rising? The Uncertain Science of Global Warming* (Princeton University Press, 1998), concludes that the global temperatures will rise 2°C over several decades, creating the prospect of some regional climate changes. For him, consequences may include an increase in severe storms and floods or prolonged droughts, with adverse effects on agriculture and other activities, and the spread of certain diseases into new locations.

Finally, the UN-sponsored Intergovernmental Panel on Climate Change has released a study revealing stronger evidence that there is "a discernable human influence" on the Earth's climate and that man-made greenhouse gases "have contributed substantially to the observed global warming over the last 50 years."

On the Internet . . .

Worldwide Refugee Information

The Worldwide Refugee Information Web site provides information on the status of refugees and internally displaced persons in 120 countries. Experts from around the world have submitted articles for publication on this site. Search by country or by issue and topic for information.

http://www.refugees.org/world/worldmain.htm

Center for Immigration Studies

The Center for Immigration Studies (CIS) is a nonpartisan, nonprofit organization that focuses on research and policy analysis of the impacts of immigration on the United States. This site is designed to expand the base of public knowledge concerning immigration. Included on this site are current articles, statistics, and a brief history of immigration in the United States.

http://www.cis.org

The Times of India

This Web site from *The Times of India* News Service contains an article on the countermigration of scientists and engineers back to India. This trend is attributed to expanding opportunities in India as well as the effects of the Internet on the global marketplace, which causes physical location to be less important to the success of careers.

http://www.timesofindia.com/100400/10busi1.htm

PART 3

The Movement of Peoples

*O*ur ability to travel from one part of the globe to another in a short amount of time has expanded dramatically since the Wright brothers first lifted an airplane off the sand dunes of North Carolina's Outer Banks. As a consequence, the movement of peoples both within and across national boundaries has grown at unprecedented levels.

Some of this movement is voluntary, as individuals willingly leave their homeland in search of a better life. Others are forced to abandon their familiar surroundings in the face of civil war, ethnic cleansing, and the physical deterioration of their land. This section discusses issues related to both voluntary and involuntary human migration.

- Is the Global Community Responding Well to the Plight of Refugees and Displaced Persons?

- Should Immigration to the United States and Other Developed Countries Be Curtailed?

- Is There a Global Brain Drain?

Is the Global Community Responding Well to the Plight of Refugees and Displaced Persons?

YES: Roberta Cohen and Francis M. Deng, from "Exodus Within Borders: The Uprooted Who Never Left Home," *Foreign Affairs* (July/August 1998)

NO: David Masci, from "Assisting Refugees," *CQ Researcher* (February 7, 1997)

ISSUE SUMMARY

YES: Roberta Cohen and Francis M. Deng, scholars at the Brookings Institution, contend that the international community should be ready to assist the millions of people who are fleeing persecution and war within their own countries when states fail to protect their own.

NO: David Masci, a staff writer for *CQ Researcher,* argues that there needs to be a reassessment among refugee-aid groups, national governments, the United Nations, and others about whether or not past humanitarian efforts have been appropriate.

One characteristic of the emerging global agenda of the twenty-first century is the host of issues associated with the movement of people, goods, information, ideas, and finances across national boundaries. Some of these issues are solely a product of the global information age, while others have been part of global affairs for some time. Many of the problems in the latter category, although in existence for awhile, have taken on a different meaning and urgency in the new millennium.

One set of issues relates to the forced movement of people, called *displaced persons* (within their homeland) or *refugees* (across national borders). On numerous occasions during the twentieth century, the international community attempted to assist individuals who were trying to flee situations that they deemed intolerable. For example, as early as 1921 the League of Nations, the forerunner to the United Nations, tried to help those who were fleeing the Russian Revolution. Also, during the latter part of World War II, an international relief agency was created to assist people who were displaced by the Western allies as they pushed the Germans eastward away from territory that they had occupied earlier in the war.

It was in the early 1950s, though, with the creation of the United Nations High Commissioner for Refugees (UNHCR), that the UN formally involved itself in the plight of displaced persons. During the cold war, the UN was called upon on several occasions to deal with refugee crises, such as those following U.S. withdrawal from Vietnam and the Soviet invasion of Afghanistan.

With the ending of the cold war in the early 1990s and the subsequent loosening of national borders in the former Soviet bloc of nations and elsewhere, more and more refugee problems emerged—the Kurds in Iraq, Bosnian Muslims in Bosnia and Herzegovina, and Rwandan Hutus in Zaire and Tanzania. Moreover, more people are being displaced within their own countries today because ethnic conflicts have escalated in both number and intensity in the past decade.

With the dramatic increase in the number of crises producing refugees and displaced persons as well as the number of refugees and displaced persons themselves, particularly those remaining within their own recognized homelands, a reassessment is beginning to take place within the international community. Should the power structure respond in all cases, no cases, or selected cases? What form should this response take? How can it be more effective than prior efforts? Is the plight of refugees beyond the scope of present-day world organizations?

The two selections for this issue address different aspects of the refugee problem. Roberta Cohen and Francis M. Deng assert that the international community should be ready to act whenever countries are unable to protect their own citizens, no matter what the circumstance. David Masci, on the other hand, argues for a comprehensive review regarding the appropriateness of past efforts by a wide range of international groups and world leaders. He questions whether or not situations have been made worse in the past by international intervention, including the use of soldiers.

Roberta Cohen and Francis M. Deng **YES**

Exodus Within Borders:
The Uprooted Who Never Left Home

Tens of millions of people have been forced from their homes during the past decade by armed conflict, internal strife, and systematic violations of human rights, all the while remaining within the borders of their own countries. No continent has been spared. Africa today counts about 10 million internally displaced persons, Europe and Asia some 5 million each, and Latin America up to 2 million. These masses in flight—who, unlike refugees, have not crossed a border—constitute the newest global crisis.

Internal displacement always has severe humanitarian implications. These displaced persons are at the greatest risk of starvation, have the highest rates of preventable disease, and are the most vulnerable to human rights abuses. Internal displacement is a symptom of state dysfunction that poses a threat to political and economic stability at the national and international levels. Both the communities left behind and the towns and villages in which the displaced find refuge are often ravaged. In some cases, so many people flee that whole societies are uprooted. Violence and instability can spread through entire regions, forcing neighboring states to bear the brunt of massive refugee flows. Even countries continents away may have to contend with a wave of desperate refugees.

Today's crisis of internal displacement is no less acute than the refugee crisis that confronted Europe after World War II. Then, humanitarian needs coupled with practical political and economic interests brought about a system of international protection and assistance for those displaced outside their native countries. In 1951, the position of United Nations High Commissioner for Refugees [UNHCR] was created and a U.N. refugee convention adopted. Today, UNHCR has a staff of 5,000, an annual budget of more than $1 billion, and 13.2 million refugees in its care.

But those forced from their homes who remain under their government's jurisdiction are not covered by any international arrangements. Although their numbers now exceed those of refugees, no international institution is specifically charged with their protection or assistance. The absurdity is that if these people had crossed a border, they would fall under U.N. protection.

From Roberta Cohen and Francis M. Deng, "Exodus Within Borders: The Uprooted Who Never Left Home," *Foreign Affairs*, vol. 77, no. 4 (July/August 1998). Copyright © 1998 by The Council on Foreign Relations, Inc. Reprinted by permission of *Foreign Affairs*.

A Cold War Legacy

Internal displacement became a subject of international concern in the late 1980s. When the numbers were first compiled in 1982, 1.2 million people were estimated to be displaced in 11 countries. Four years later the total had grown to 14 million. Since the early 1990s, the numbers have fluctuated between 20 million and 25 million in 35 to 40 countries.

The major reason for this dramatic increase was the rise in internal conflicts as the Cold War came to a close. The proxy wars the superpowers fought in the 1980s displaced millions of people who came into full view only as Cold War tensions eased in Angola, Mozambique, Ethiopia, Afghanistan, Cambodia, and El Salvador. The arms the United States and the Soviet Union had supplied to regimes or opposition movements furnished the weaponry for the ethnic and clan warfare that broke out once the superpowers departed. Liberia and Somalia, two countries that plunged into civil war, were among the largest recipients of U.S. military assistance in sub-Saharan Africa during the 1980s. In Europe and Central Asia, the collapse of the Soviet Union lifted the lid on nationalist aspirations and ethnic rivalries that displaced millions more.

Elsewhere, vast disparities in wealth, land ownership, and power have been at the root of conflict. In Rwanda and Burundi, high population density and limited fertile land exacerbated tensions between Hutus and Tutsis. In Colombia, conflict over land has forced hundreds of thousands from their homes. In other cases, struggles between governments and minorities have produced mass displacement. In Sudan, which has the world's largest internally displaced population, the efforts of successive northern governments to impose Islam on the black African south have made four million people homeless. In Turkey, which has the second-largest displaced population, government repression against the Kurdish minority has sent two million people fleeing for their lives.

The 1990s have seen greater willingness on the part of the international community to intervene in these situations, even without the consent of the government concerned. A major motivation has been the desire to forestall international flows of refugees. As the number of refugees has grown, Western governments as well as those in Africa and elsewhere have become less welcoming to those in flight. Their focus has shifted to keeping people in their homelands. The U.N. Security Council justified the international community's precedent-setting intervention on behalf of the Kurds in Iraq in 1991 on the grounds that massive flows of refugees threatened international peace and security. Subsequent Security Council resolutions on Somalia, Bosnia, and Rwanda have also authorized the use of force to facilitate the delivery of relief and, in the latter two cases, to protect internally displaced populations.

Nonetheless, the principles of sovereignty, territorial integrity, and non-interference in the internal affairs of states present formidable obstacles to intervention by international organizations. While some governments, such as Sri Lanka, invite international assistance, others deliberately bar humanitarian aid, seeing it as strengthening their opponents and undermining their authority. Sudan, for example, has obstructed humanitarian aid, while Turkey has blocked all international assistance to its displaced citizens. Some countries have deliberately starved the displaced while invoking their sovereignty to keep the international community at bay.

Redefining Terms

A response to such conduct requires a broadly recognized standards and arrangements to guide the actions of governments and international humanitarian agencies. The definition of sovereignty should be broadened to include responsibility: a state can claim the prerogatives of sovereignty only so long as it carries out its internationally recognized responsibilities to provide protection and assistance to its citizens. Failure to do so should legitimize the involvement of the international community. States that refuse access to populations at risk could expect calibrated actions ranging from diplomacy to political pressure, sanctions, and, as a last resort, military intervention.

Earlier [in 1998], the representative of the U.N. secretary-general on internally displaced persons outlined guiding principles for the rights of the displaced and the duties and obligations of states and insurgent groups. These principles include a right not to be arbitrarily displaced, access to humanitarian assistance and protection while in flight, and guarantees of reparations upon returning home. While the principles lack legal force, they set standards that should put both governments and insurgent groups on notice and give international and nongovernmental organizations (NGOs) a basis for legitimate action. The United Nations' acknowledgment of these principles and call for their observance would be an important step forward.

A Pick-and-Choose Policy?

During the last ten years, an array of humanitarian, human rights, and development organizations have come forward to provide protection, assistance, and reintegration and development aid to the internally displaced. The efforts of international agencies and the NGOs that work alongside them are being coordinated by the U.N. Office for the Coordination of Humanitarian Affairs. Nonetheless, many internally displaced persons remain neglected because the international response is largely ad hoc. Various agencies pick and choose the situations in which they wish to become involved; no organization has a global or comprehensive mandate to protect the displaced. The result is that the needs of the displaced are met to varying degrees in some countries and not at all in others.

The United Nations' best option is a more targeted approach that takes advantage of existing mandates and capacities. The U.N. emergency relief coordinator could assign principal responsibility in each emergency to one international agency, assisted by a U.N. coordinating mechanism. When a single agency has been made responsible for a group of internally displaced people, greater attention has been paid to their needs.

Since 1992 a representative of the secretary-general has been authorized to monitor displacement worldwide, undertake fact-finding missions, open dialogue with governments, and make proposals for strengthening legal and institutional protection for the internally displaced. He has raised international awareness and mobilized support from governments, foundations, academia, and the legal and NGO communities. The position's effectiveness, however, is limited because it is voluntary and part-time. It has no operational authority and minimal human and material resources at its disposal. The capacity of the representative to act in crises can be strengthened only if the United Nations provides staff and resources commensurate with the task.

To date, the international community has focused on providing food, shelter, and medical supplies. Yet displaced persons have regularly pointed out that security is as great a priority as food. Providing relief to uprooted people while ignoring the fact they are being beaten or raped has led some to call the victims the "well-fed dead." U.N. human rights activities are slowly being integrated into humanitarian programs. A next step would be for the newly appointed High Commissioner for Human Rights, Mary Robinson, to deploy field staff during internal displacement crises to monitor security problems, serve in safe areas and camps, and promote safety during their return home.

Humanitarian assistance and development agencies of all stripes will also have to become more responsible for protecting the people they assist. Many have silently witnessed abuses because of exaggerated fears that confronting a host government will result in expulsion of their personnel and termination of their programs. The effort would be strengthened if governments and insurgent groups were made aware that they were dealing with a united front bound by common human rights and humanitarian standards.

Muscle and Money

In recent years, military interventions have been more successful in preventing starvation than in physically defending people at risk. This failure underscores the need for strategies to prevent genocide and other crimes against humanity that lead to displacement. Early action must be encouraged when there are warning signs, as there were in Rwanda, and forces charged with protecting the displaced must have the equipment, training, and mandates needed to accomplish their task, which was not the case in Bosnia.

Unless accompanied by steps to address the causes of crises, military solutions are only temporary. Humanitarian assistance alone can prolong conflicts. Conflict and internal displacement can be resolved only through a broader commitment to the peaceful management and mediation of disputes.

Since today's conflicts take place mainly within developing countries and may go on for decades, international development and financial institutions cannot afford to wait until they burn themselves out. By getting involved early on, these organizations stand a better chance of influencing the outcome and helping lay a foundation for a transition to peace. Even when societies are still in conflict, they can help stabilize the situation and make reintegration more likely.

In countries devastated by civil wars, up to half the population can be uprooted. Whether in Mozambique, Angola, Afghanistan, Cambodia, or El Salvador, the rehabilitation of areas affected by conflict requires the reintegration of uprooted populations. An expanded role for international development and financial institutions in post-conflict reconstruction could influence the way these societies reintegrate displaced populations. A global reconstruction fund would be an important step toward assuring such transitions. Efforts by international development programs and financial institutions to redress economic inequities could also help prevent future strife.

Conflicts that are allowed to fester can produce mass displacement and leave political and economic scars that damage the economic well-being and political security of neighboring states, regions, and the international system as a whole. The world community cannot let this newest challenge go unchecked.

NO

David Masci

Assisting Refugees

The Issues

On the dusty road to Gisenyi, just inside Rwanda, 200,000 bedraggled people were at last nearing home.

"You could see this river of humanity, with all of their belongings on their heads and their kids straggling along," recalls Samantha Bolton, an aid worker. "Most of them were barefoot and exhausted."

The next day, says Bolton, communications director for Doctors Without Borders USA, another 150,000 people made the trek.

The people returning to Rwanda [November 1996] were Hutus. In 1994, by the hundreds of thousands, they had been chased out of Rwanda by an army of rebel Tutsis, a rival ethnic group. Now the Tutsis were pushing the Hutus back into Rwanda by forcibly closing the refugee camps in Zaire.

Thousands of refugees who had fled to Zaire would never come home. Many children and older people had died of starvation or cholera during the exodus from Rwanda. Others had been killed in the camps by thugs and extremists from their own tribe. Tens of thousands more had died in Hutu-Tutsi fighting that flared up [in 1996] in Zaire.[1]

Throughout the crisis, the United Nations High Commissioner for Refugees (UNHCR) and other aid groups scrambled, often with questionable success, to help. Many of the world's most powerful nations seemed in a quandary about whether to get involved at all, fearful of becoming too entangled in the horrific chaos.

As shocking and tragic as it has been, the situation in Rwanda and Zaire represents nothing more than the planet's latest refugee crisis, sandwiched between the festering upheavals in Bosnia and the next catastrophe yet to appear on the evening news.

Actually, many international experts say, the world is experiencing a level of conflict and population displacement rarely seen in human history. And, they warn, crises are becoming so commonplace that the world community can ignore them only at its own peril. Georgetown University Professor Charles Keeley predicts that multiethnic strife will force many states to collapse in coming decades, leading to still greater chaos.

From David Masci, "Assisting Refugees," *CQ Researcher*, vol. 7, no. 5 (February 7, 1997). Copyright © 1997 by Congressional Quarterly, Inc. Reprinted by permission of *CQ Researcher*, permission conveyed through Copyright Clearance Center, Inc. Some notes omitted.

The last decade has been especially volatile. While the United States, China, Germany and other global powers have been at peace through most of the post-World War II era, the developing world has seen a steady rise in war and civil strife. With the Cold War coming to an end, human misery and displacement became increasingly common in poorer countries, such as Somalia, Liberia and Burma. Since 1980, the estimated number of refugees in the world has roughly tripled, rising from 5.7 million to 15.3 million in 1996. The number of people displaced within their own countries is even higher, topping 20 million by most estimates.

The refugee increases generally have not been tied to one cause. In the past, a cataclysm on the scale of World War II or the partitioning of India would create millions of refugees for a relatively short period of time. But today, refugee crises are a series of small, constant blips on the world's radar screen, with many crises being precipitated by old ethnic conflicts that flare up periodically.

The growing plight of refugees has generated an unprecedented increase in the size and number of aid groups. The UNHCR, once a small agency that provided legal assistance to refugees seeking asylum in post-World War II Europe, aided more than 27 million people in 1995. In addition, there are now hundreds of non-governmental relief organizations (NGOs)—including CARE, the Red Cross and Doctors Without Borders.

Besides trying to produce food and shelter, UNHCR and other organizations are searching for new and innovative ways to prevent or at least mitigate the number of refugees. They also are focusing more attention on aiding displaced peoples after they have been repatriated, to decrease the chance that they will leave their homes again.

But some observers find fault with the aid efforts, and even question the motives of the aid groups themselves. A number of refugee experts argue that UNHCR may have done more harm than good in Rwanda and Zaire by blindly providing assistance to all Hutus who crossed into Zaire in 1994. The problem, they say, is that among the refugees was a large group of militants who were responsible for the genocidal slaughtering—often by machete—of more than 500,000 Tutsis and moderate Hutus. The Hutu extremists used the refugee camps as de facto military bases and treated the refugees as hostages.

Some cynics among the critics even say that UNHCR and the NGOs see it in their interest to create and perpetuate refugee crises. More starving children with bloated bellies on the evening news means more donations and government funding.

Aid groups call such views ridiculous. But they admit to owing their increased visibility, in no small part, to the news media, even as they fault the media for their short attention span and for ignoring many countries in turmoil. In the final analysis, they acknowledge, the media play the key role in making the global community aware of humanitarian needs.

Citizen awareness is crucial, aid experts say, and not just because it leads to charitable donations. Governments are more inclined to address a problem halfway around the world, they say, if their citizens call for action. Even then, nations in a position to help are often loath to do more than offer money.

Many U.S. lawmakers, among others, are apprehensive about sending soldiers into harm's way to aid refugees or others in need, unless a key American interest is threatened. For example, they say, the Persian Gulf War was really about protecting U.S. access to Saudi Arabian oil, not saving Kuwait from Saddam Hussein's plundering troops.

Aid officials argue that affluent world powers like the United States should, in the interests of humanity and global peace, send troops to protect refugees and aid workers. UNHCR officials say they were rebuffed when they asked the major powers to send soldiers to the refugee camps in Zaire to separate the Hutu extremists from the legitimate refugees. UNHCR officials also say the international community's refusal to help left the agency with no choice but to assist everyone, good and bad, in the camps, in order to prevent innocent refugees from starving.

"If we had not started feeding them immediately, many people would have starved to death," says Soren Jessen-Petersen, director of UNHCR's New York City office.

As refugee advocates, politicians and others debate how to best respond to crises like the one in Zaire, these are some of the questions being asked:

Do the methods used by UNHCR and private relief organizations to help refugees actually make matters worse?

The crisis in the great lakes region of Eastern Africa has rocked the UNHCR to its foundations. Never before has the agency faced such a difficult and chaotic situation on such a vast scale.

In the second half of 1994, an estimated 2 million Rwandans, mainly from the Hutu tribe, fled into Zaire and Tanzania. The flight was triggered by a rebel army of Tutsis, which unseated the country's Hutu-led government.

The coup by the Rwandan Patriotic Front (RPF) was triggered, in turn, by the massacre earlier in 1994 of Tutsis and some moderate Hutus by Hutu extremists. The death toll in what has come to be known as the "Rwandan genocide" is estimated at about 800,000.

When the RPF took control of Rwanda, the Hutus involved in the killings fled. Hundred of thousands of innocent Hutus followed the extremists into exile after being told that they would be targets of Tutsi retribution despite their innocence.

Critics of UNHCR say that it made egregious strategic mistakes at almost every step during the crisis in Zaire, revealing the organization's outmoded, institutional mindset. In particular, they say, UNHCR and the NGOs that support its work immediately moved to feed and care for all the Rwandan refugees streaming across the border, without considering the consequences.

Michael Maren, the author of a recent book highly critical of international aid efforts, contends that UNHCR, however unintentionally, provided aid and comfort to the perpetrators of the genocide when it set up camps for the Hutus. "The Hutu leaders ran the camps and essentially controlled the distribution of aid," he says. In addition, says Maren, a former field worker for the

U.S. Agency for International Development, the legitimate refugees were completely controlled by the Hutu killers, giving them enormous leverage with the international community. "The aid groups weren't feeding refugees," he says, "they were feeding hostages."

Instead of setting up camps, Maren says, the UNHCR and the NGOs should have provided services to Hutus in Rwanda. "The agencies should have told them: 'You cross the border, you're on your own,'" he says.

Stephen Stedman, a professor of African Studies at Johns Hopkins University's School of Advanced International Studies, agrees. He argues that if UNHCR had not assisted the Hutu refugees, they ultimately would have returned to Rwanda. This in turn would have denied the Hutu extremists the benefits they derived from the refugee camps.

Stedman also criticizes UNHCR and the NGOs for ignoring their own guidelines. "There are international conventions on what a refugee is, and it is very clear that they cannot be fleeing a country because they committed crimes; cannot be armed; and cannot use their refugee status to reconstruct an armed force," he says.

But others say that the UNHCR made the best of a bad situation. They argue the Hutus so feared for their lives that they would not have returned to Rwanda. If they had stayed, and UNHCR had remained aloof, mass starvation and disease would have resulted.

"What could we have done?" asks Harlan Hale, assistant director for food and logistics at Atlanta-based CARE. "Our humanitarian imperative is to minister to people who are at risk." Those who think that it would have been better in the long run to let some Hutus starve wouldn't feel that way "if it was one of their kids out there," Hale adds.

It is easy to ponder better strategies after the fact, when you don't have to make snap decisions, says Jessen-Petersen. "More than 1 million people fled, and we had to provide life-saving assistance within 72 hours, something that is not very easy when you're in the African bush," he says.

Jessen-Petersen says that it took UNHCR four to six weeks just to stabilize the situation to the point where his agency could begin considering issues beyond providing basic assistance. "Once we got our head above water, we understood that we had a monster on our hands," he says.

UNHCR decided that the only way to tame the monster—the Hutu militants—was to disarm them or drive them from the camps. "The UNHCR knew that the camps contained a lot of killers, and they advocated a police force to separate out the killers from the refugees," says Jeff Drumtra, a policy analyst at the U.S. Committee for Refugees, an advocacy group in Washington. But the appeal fell on deaf ears, according to Drumtra and others. "There was simply no interest in doing this."

UNHCR supporters say that the unwillingness of the United States and other donor nations to commit the forces necessary to separate the extremists left the agency with limited options. "It was a horrible situation, and we faced it alone," says Marie Okabe, a senior UNHCR liaison officer in New York.

Others say that the donor countries' inaction allowed them to blame the UNHCR for anything that went wrong. Instead of taking action, Drumtra says, donor nations assuaged their consciences by pouring money into UNHCR to run the refugee camps in Zaire and Tanzania. UNHCR became "a fig leaf for their own lack of political will," he says.

After it became apparent that no military help was forthcoming, UNHCR officials say they tried to exert more control over the camps by breaking them down into smaller, more manageable units and by distributing food directly to those deemed to be legitimate refugees. But these efforts were stymied by the Hutu militants, who retained a firm hold on the populations in the camps.

Finally, UNHCR hired 1,500 members of the notoriously corrupt Zairian military to provide security in the camps. The intention, Jessen-Peterson says, was to create "a minimum of security" for legitimate refugees inside the camps. But the tiny force proved ineffective against the estimated 50,000–60,000 members of the Hutu militia. "In the end," Jessen-Peterson says, "nothing worked."

Bolton at Doctors Without Borders agrees that UNHCR was in a difficult situation after the refugee camps in Zaire had been established. But she also says the agency made other, big mistakes before the refugee crisis even occurred. "We had two weeks' notice before the refugees crossed the border," she says, but "when they arrived no camps had been set up yet."

Bolton says UNHCR should have used the two-week window to set up many small camps, making it harder for militant Hutus to organize and control the refugees. "They had camps with 250,000 people, which you never do," she says, "because you're always going to have militarization."

But Jessen-Petersen and others say that with so many refugees crossing into Zaire at the same time, it was not logistically possible to break them into small groups while providing food and medical assistance.

Some critics also charge that many of the aid groups that responded to the crisis in Zaire can be criticized for more than shortsightedness. For instance, Maren says, UNHCR and other aid groups perpetuated this and other crises largely out of institutional self-interest. "NGOs don't want to shut down camps because they have a bureaucratic structure built up around these projects," he charges, adding that "there is very little accountability in the aid business, and that leaves lots of room for fat."

This is not true, Hale says. While he admits that groups like his receive more money—in the form of outside donations and UNHCR payments—during well-publicized crises, NGOs do not try to perpetuate disasters in order to improve their balance sheets, nor do they focus only on those situations that catch the public's eye. "It's not a question of helping some refugees and not others," he says, referring to those disasters that receive media attention and those that do not. "We distribute assistance based solely on need."

Should American military personnel be sent overseas to help refugees if it exposes them to danger?

The use of American troops to provide food and other aid to displaced people has become relatively common. In the last few years, U.S. soldiers have been sent to help people in Somalia, Haiti and Bosnia. In November, President

Clinton said he would send American troops to Zaire and only reversed that decision after he determined that the situation had improved.

Still, Americans and their leaders are generally wary of committing troops to humanitarian missions in far-off lands. As chairman of the Joint Chiefs of Staff, Gen. Colin L. Powell was an influential advocate for sending American forces rarely, and only when the mission's goals were clear and the use of overwhelming force made the chances of success high.

Much of the reluctance about using force stems from the nation's painful experience in Vietnam, where a small number of American military advisers grew to a half-million combat troops in a matter of years. More recently, Americans watched in horror in 1993 as news reports showed a dead American serviceman in Somalia being dragged through the streets of Mogadishu.

The incident produced what has been dubbed the "Somalia Syndrome," or lawmakers' and the military's fear of sending troops overseas if the possibility exists for even a few casualties. "They really got burned in Somalia, and they don't want to see any more body bags coming home," Bolton says.

Still, many refugee advocates argue that there are times when troops simply must be sent, particularly to protect refugees and aid workers. For instance, it is widely thought that the international community should have sent soldiers to drive Hutus who had participated in the Rwandan genocide out of the refugee camps.

"We had situations where Hutu soldiers just came into hospitals in the camps and shot patients dead," Bolton says. And, Bolton points out, refugees are not the only victims of such violence. Over the last five years, scores of aid workers have been killed in Somalia, Burundi and other hot spots. As recently as Feb. 4, five U.N. workers investigating human rights abuses in Rwanda were ambushed on a country road and shot to death. And in December, six International Red Cross workers in Chechnya were murdered in their beds.

While refugee advocates generally favor multiethnic forces, they argue that some situations demand a U.S. military presence if the intervention is to be effective. CARE's Hale notes that the U.S. has more heavy-lifting capacity, access to intelligence and sheer firepower than any other nation on Earth. Steven Hansch, a senior program officer at the Refugee Policy Group, agrees: "In certain circumstances, our armed forces are the only ones who can do the job."

But, Hansch says, the Somalia syndrome has set "such a conservative threshold of pain" that the nation won't send soldiers anywhere unless the missions is risk free. "We are chickens about this," Hansch says.

According to many refugee advocates, this attitude has soured other nations on working with the U.S. to resolve international problems. "We need to show that we are willing to be a player, that we stand for something," Hale says.

But others argue that the United States military has done more than its share in humanitarian crises, pointing to the developments in Haiti in 1994 and in Bosnia the following year. "We're doing this too routinely, and it's starting to become the norm," says Eugene B. McDaniel, president of the American Defense Institute, a Washington think tank.

Others question sending American soldiers under any circumstances. "Why should it always be the United States that answers the global 911 call?" asks Lionel Rosenblatt, executive director for Refugees International. Rosenblatt and others say that military leaders should be especially wary of sending troops into countries where warring factions are still fighting and civil society has broken down.

In addition, McDaniel says, "Our troops are for defending our country and its national interests," not feeding refugees in a country halfway around the world. This means defending the industrial world's access to oil—as was done during the 1991 Persian Gulf War—but not protecting combatants in Bosnia from each other, McDaniel says. "It's degrading to send our soldiers to those places on those missions," he says.

But Michael Clough, a research associate at the Institute of International Studies at the University of California-Berkeley, calls the argument put forward by McDaniel and others "nonsense." Clough says the United States and other industrialized countries have a clear interest in solving humanitarian and refugee crises around the world. "First, we have an interest in ensuring that places like Africa don't collapse," he says, adding that "by 2025, 30 percent of the world's population will live in Africa, and you just can't write off a part of the world that big."

Another reason rich countries cannot ignore poorer states, Clough says, stems from the fact that large numbers of refugees will eventually reach the shores of European nations and the United States. In addition, he argues, there needs to be stability in the developing world if the global economy is to continue to expand.

But there may be a way to satisfy both McDaniel and Clough. Rosenblatt is among those who propose the establishment of a permanent United Nations rapid deployment force to intervene in humanitarian crises. While the proposal has received some tepid support from the United States and other powers, no action has been taken on the idea, and its prospects are uncertain, at best.

Note

1. By early December [1996] more than 1 million of the 1.5 million Hutu refugees in Zaire had returned to Rwanda. Many of the half-million Hutus who had sought refuge in Tanzania also returned.

POSTSCRIPT

Is the Global Community Responding Well to the Plight of Refugees and Displaced Persons?

Cohen and Deng focus on people who are forced from their homes but who remain within their own countries. Since these displaced people have not crossed national boundaries, no international agreements cover their situation. The authors stress that despite the lack of such arrangements, the international community has been more willing during the past decade to intervene. These actions have been undertaken in the face of such longstanding international principles as sovereignty, territorial integrity, and noninterference in the internal affairs of states. Nevertheless, the authors advocate UN action because these principles do not free countries from the obligation to treat their citizens humanely.

Masci examines the situation of both refugees and displaced persons. He suggests that some observers have been critical of aid efforts, both of nongovernmental relief organizations and of UN agencies. The most damaging attacks suggest that some aid groups find it in their own interest to "create and perpetuate" refugee crises.

Anyone who values human dignity can identify with the plea outlined by Cohen and Deng. Newsmagazines have been replete with vivid accounts of the suffering of those who have been forced to leave their homes. In addition to the obvious kinds of misery that can be captured by a camera, there are more hidden and even insidious negative consequences of such displacement. Entire communities disappear, and ways of life known for centuries die quickly.

Masci goes into greater detail in describing the events surrounding displacement, including what he argues are mistakes made by international interveners. His is a story of episodic events, rather than a description of the broader picture. His examples, however, give one pause as the question of to what extent, if any, the international community has an obligation to assist all who are affected by physical upheaval is addressed.

The United Nations High Commissioner for Refugees publishes a periodic report on its recent accomplishments. See, for example, *The State of the World's Refugees: In Search of Solutions* (Oxford University Press, 1995). In addition to the big picture, the report includes case studies. A critical account of humanitarian aid in this area is Michael Maren's *The Road to Hell: The Ravaging Effects of Foreign Aid and International Charity* (Free Press, 1996). A more balanced account is Gil Loescher's *Beyond Charity: International Cooperation and the Global Refugees Crisis* (Oxford University Press, 1993). Finally, the U.S. Committee for Refugees, a refugee advocacy group, has published *World Refugee Survey 1996,* which assesses the refugee situation throughout the world.

ISSUE 11

Should Immigration to the United States and Other Developed Countries Be Curtailed?

YES: Mark W. Nowak, from *Immigration and U.S. Population Growth: An Environmental Perspective*, Negative Population Growth Special Report (December 19, 1997)

NO: John Isbister, from "Are Immigration Controls Ethical?" in Susanne Jonas and Suzie Dod Thomas, eds., *Immigration: A Civil Rights Issue for the Americas* (Scholarly Resources, 1999)

ISSUE SUMMARY

YES: Mark W. Nowak, an environmental writer and a resident fellow of Negative Population Growth, attacks six basic arguments favoring the loosening of U.S. immigration laws, including the argument that immigration contributes little to U.S. population growth.

NO: Professor of economics John Isbister attacks six basic arguments for population controls, among them the contention that open immigration would destroy important American values.

Open a major American newspaper on any given day and you are likely to find an article addressing some perceived problem relating to immigration, whether the referenced parties are in the United States legally or illegally. This is not surprising; the topic has become one of the most volatile issues of the day, a pattern that has escalated since the law basing immigration on country of origin (and favoring Caucasians) was replaced in 1965 by one that was deemed far less racist. The end result has been a vast opening of American borders to legal and illegal aliens alike, whose countries of origin are typically non-European.

The debate, unlike many within America today, does not fit neatly along conservative and liberal lines. Both groups are somewhat torn on the issue. Conservatives applaud the economic benefits that free-market entrepreneurs receive as a consequence of a larger supply of blue-collar and no-collar workers who will take jobs that are shunned by citizens of longer standing. However, they oppose the increased burden on the American taxpayer, whether an immigrant is participating in the tax system or not. Liberals view anti-immigration policies as racist or nativist and welcome the increased diversity that wider openings at the border bring, particularly for those of non-European origin. But they worry about the adverse effects such influxes have on Americans at the bottom of the socioeconomic ladder, particularly when economic times turn rocky.

John Isbister, in the first chapter of his book *The Immigration Debate: Remaking America* (Kumarian Press, 1996), outlines the various specific components of the debate along three lines—demographic, economic, and cultural. A summary of these components will help to set the background for this issue. To Isbister, two questions are at the heart of the demographic debate on immigration: Is the current wave of immigration unusually large, and will it change the ethnic composition of the country? Opponents of immigration believe that the numbers of outsiders entering the United States are unmatched in history and that, if controls were lifted, the resultant influx would be overwhelming. Supporters contend that current levels are actually lower, when measured as a percentage of the resident population, than they were at earlier heights of immigration in American history. Opponents also believe that America's ethnic mix is moving away from its predominant European origin. But proponents counter that the numbers will ease before the mix is drastically changed.

Isbister's economic debate centers around 11 specific questions: Is the quality of the immigrant labor force deteriorating? Are immigrants unusually enterprising? Is immigration desirable because it helps to alleviate labor shortages? Does it reduce American wages? Does it lead to a more unequal distribution of income? Does it increase unemployment? Do immigrants impose a fiscal burden on the rest of Americans? Why do they come? Do they generate enough economic growth to improve the living standards of those before them? Will immigration reduce America's international competitiveness? Will it harm the natural environment and deplete natural resources? For each of these questions, Americans hold one of three positions. One group argues that immigrants contribute in a positive manner to the economic vitality of the country. Another group sees no harm of any consequence. A third group believes that a substantial economic burden is placed on the country's citizens by immigrants.

Isbister's cultural debate addresses six issues: Is America of one culture or many cultures? Has the melting pot stopped melting? Can the United States increase its cultural diversity without causing more conflict? How should immigrant applications be prioritized? Could the education and skills of immigrants be upgraded? Has the United States lost control of its borders? The general view of opponents on the cultural dimension is that the typical immigrant of today is so different from that of yesterday that the dominant culture is harmed. Supporters of increased immigration counter that America is not diverse enough and that Anglos dominate too much as a consequence.

The two selections for this issue present opposing viewpoints on the basic question of loosening America's borders. Mark W. Nowak attacks six widely accepted reasons for widening U.S. borders put forth by immigration supporters. Isbister argues for more open immigration by countering six fundamental arguments for increasing immigration controls.

Mark W. Nowak

 YES

Immigration and U.S. Population Growth: An Environmental Perspective

Controversy over U.S. immigration policy is by no means new to the political landscape. Since 1819, when Congress passed the first significant law regulating immigration into the United States, successive debates over immigration have stirred emotions and polarized perceptions. It is not surprising, then, to find that environmentalists, confronted by the issue with increasing frequency, are by no means in agreement about the relationship between immigration and the environment.

On the one hand are those who argue that immigration, notwithstanding the benefits it provides, is fundamentally a form of population growth. Therefore, say supporters of this position, levels of immigration must be reduced (and fertility held at replacement-level or below) if we are to move toward environmental sustainability in the United States.

Others argue that treating immigration as an environmental issue is a wrong-headed approach to environmental protection. Rather than focusing on immigration, say these proponents, the environment would be better served by addressing issues such as Americans' hyper-consuming lifestyle, which are more to blame for our environmental ills.

It's true that numerous factors—including the high consumption rates of Americans—contribute substantially to environmental degradation, but diminishing or discounting the real role that immigration plays makes little sense. All other factors being equal, the environmental consequences of human activity increase with the growth of the population. This essential relationship is nearly universally recognized—particularly among environmental and population groups—as one of the fundamental bases for providing international population stabilization funding.

If immigration, then, serves as a contributor to U.S. population growth, what is the basis for excluding immigration from any comprehensive analysis of the consequences of U.S. population growth? It's time to look at and evaluate the arguments that are used against viewing immigration as a domestic population issue.

From Mark W. Nowak, *Immigration and U.S. Population Growth: An Environmental Perspective,* Negative Population Growth Special Report (December 19, 1997). Copyright © 1997 by Negative Population Growth, Inc. Reprinted by permission. Notes omitted.

Argument: Immigration Contributes Little to U.S. Population Growth

A common assertion about U.S. immigration is that its demographic effect is (and will continue to be) small, implying that any environmental consequence of immigration will be minimal. In reality, the demographic consequences of our current immigration policy will be considerable, as revealed by the population projections prepared by the Census Bureau.

In building its projections, the Census Bureau analyzes four factors—birth rates, death rates, immigration and emigration. Each time the Bureau prepares a substantial update to their projections, they vary their assumptions about each of these components to present a range of possible demographic outcomes.

The Bureau's latest projection, which assumes, essentially, that current demographic trends will continue, projects that the United States will grow from its current 268 million people to 393 million people in 2050, an increase of 125 million people.

Immigration emerges as a prominent component in the calculation: 60% of the population increase in the United States between 1994 and 2050 will be attributable to immigration and the descendants of immigrants.

What this means is that immigration will not be a marginal contributor to future U.S. population growth, but, in fact, the primary one. Further, the absolute numbers in the Census Bureau projection are large: adding 125 million people to the current U.S. population is the equivalent of adding 48 more cities, each the size of Chicago.

Argument: Historic Levels of Immigration Are Higher Than the Current Level

Regardless of immigration's demographic effect, immigration should not be considered solely a demographic issue, say some. It is equally important that we honor our past as an immigrant-receiving nation, and reducing immigration to stabilize the population flies in the face of this tradition. Furthermore, say proponents of this position, the percentage of the U.S. population that is foreign-born is far lower today than it was at the turn of the century, implying that we actually ought to consider increasing immigration levels so that our current policy might be consistent with tradition.

Pointing to the percentage of the population that is foreign-born as a measure of annual immigration makes little sense, however, since each is, at best, an indirect measure of the other. If we are interested in determining the traditional level of immigration into the United States, it makes much more sense to look at annual immigration flows. When we do, we see some surprising facts emerge.

[Figure 1] details legal immigration to the United States between 1821 and 1990, a period that saw more than 61 million people make this country their home. (Annual statistics prior to 1821 are not available since the Federal government didn't begin recording immigration until that year. For the period 1776–1819, however, immigration is estimated at only about 300,000 total.) This chart conveys two extremely important facts about immigration. The first is that no decade appears on the chart that we can point to as "typical." Immigration levels range from a ten-year low of 143,000 (1821–1830) to a ten-year high of 8.8 million (1901–1910). Immigration during the current decade will likely set a new record high. When we observe individual years, the range is even greater: 1823 saw only 6,300 people arrive, while 1.8 million people became legal immigrants in 1991.

Figure 1

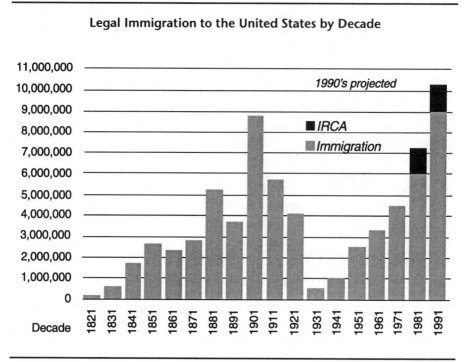

Legal Immigration to the United States by Decade

Note: IRCA = Illegal immigrants legalized under Immigration Reform and Control Act

Sources: US Census Bureau and 1995 Statistical Yearbook of INS (March 97)

In other words, while it is true that the United States has enjoyed a long tradition as an immigrant-receiving nation, there is no such thing as a traditional level of immigration to the United States. A proposal to set a net immigration level of 100,000 annually has as much historical authority as a proposal to cap immigration at 500,000 a year. Consequently, while the simple reminder that we are a nation of immigrants reveals a historic truth, it tells us precious little about what, specifically, our immigration policy should be.

The second fact is that, while the level of immigration into the United States has varied considerably, for the last 65 years absolute levels of immigration have risen steadily and appreciably from one decade to the next. This general trend of rising immigration levels, combined with a relatively steady annual rate of natural increase (births minus deaths), has meant that immigration's share of annual U.S. population growth has been growing larger and larger.

[Figure 2] shows that in 1970, first-generation legal immigrants (annual new arrivals) accounted for 16% of the increase in the U.S. population. By 1996, that figure more than doubled to 36%. These figures represent just the increase contributed by first-generation immigrants. In addition, the Census Bureau has found that first-generation immigrants tend to have higher fertility rates than the native-born. When the demographic contribution of immigrants and their descendants is combined, we find that immigration will account for about two-thirds of future U.S. population growth.

Figure 2

First-Generation Legal Immigrants as a Percentage of U.S. Population Growth

Sources: US Census Bureau and 1995 Statistical Yearbook of INS (March 97)

It's true that the percentage of foreign born in the United States is lower now than it was at the turn of the century, but that is because the U.S. population is so much larger now. The absolute size of the population of foreign born is actually larger today than it was at the turn of the century, even though it represents a smaller percentage of the total population.

In 1910, the United States had 92 million residents. At that time, the nation's 13.5 million first-generation immigrants accounted for a rather significant share of the total population—about 15%. In 1990, when the population had grown to 248 million, the nation's 19.5 million first-generation immigrants constituted a far smaller share—about 8%. But the percentage of the U.S. population that is foreign born has little bearing on the environmental risks of maintaining our current rate of population growth, which as we have seen, will be driven primarily by immigration in the future.

Argument: High Consumption Levels Are More to Blame Than Population Growth

Environmental degradation is a function of more than just sheer population size. The level at which a particular population consumes energy, natural resources and other materials plays a large role in determining total environmental impact, as well. Per capita consumption and waste production rates in the United States are among the highest in the world, leading some to argue that far more benefit would accrue to the environment if we focused our efforts on reducing consumption, rather than working to reduce population growth (and, by extension, immigration). Consumption and population growth, however, are not mutually exclusive issues. Both have a significant consequence, so both must be addressed.

Consider, for example, car and truck ownership by U.S. residents (which includes both the native-born and immigrant population). In 1970, there was one car or truck on the road for every two U.S. residents. Since then, vehicle ownership has increased. By 1994, there was one car or truck on the road for every 1.5 residents. While much of the increase in the number of vehicles on the road stems from higher per capita ownership, population growth accounted for 27% of the rise—not an insignificant figure. This means that had there been no change in the per capita consumption of vehicles at all, the number of cars on the road would still have increased by nearly 26 million—due entirely to the increased size of the population.

The impact of population growth on total energy consumption between 1970 and 1990 is especially dramatic. During this period, numerous conservation and efficiency measures were enacted and, as a result, per capita energy consumption barely increased over the two decades. But, because the U.S. population continued to grow during this period, total energy consumption increased by 36%, with more than 90% of this increase in energy consumption due entirely to population growth.

We can—and should—reduce consumption, but unless we address population growth our net gains will be reduced (or even reversed) by the demands imposed by our growing population.

Argument: Environmental Gains Can Be Made Despite Population Growth

Immigration's strong showing as a contributor to U.S. population growth provides a fundamental basis for including immigration in environmental policy discussions. Some, however, have argued that linking immigration to environmental policy is not necessary because, they say, population stabilization is not a necessary condition for environmental improvement. The basis for this argument is that every environmental advance of the last two decades—including improvements in air quality, water quality and habitat restoration, has been made while both immigration rates and total population size were increasing.

The introduction of environmental regulations and the adoption of more efficient technologies have certainly led to some recent gains in environmental quality, but environmental gains are only half the story. Consider some of our environmental losses:

- Annual energy consumption, despite the introduction of efficient technologies, has increased 36% since 1970.
- The United States continues to lose more than a million acres of farmland every year to urban sprawl and erosion.
- More than 90% of all old growth forests in the United States have been cut down.
- About 50% of all wetlands in the United States have been lost. Wetland loss is highest in areas with higher growth rates (and therefore more rapid development): in California, 93% of all wetlands have been destroyed.
- Scientists estimate that since the Declaration of Independence was signed, more than five hundred species in the United States have gone extinct. Nearly 1,100 species are currently listed as threatened or endangered.
- In many parts of the United States, demand for water exceeds supply so that we are now overdrafting our surface waters and "mining" our aquifers. By consuming water faster than the recharge rate, we are destroying an otherwise renewable resource.
- Over the past thirty years, nutrient loads in Chesapeake Bay (including nitrogen and phosphorus from agriculture) have increased as much as 250-fold, while areas of the bay that are oxygen depleted have increased 15-fold. The bay's famous oyster harvest has been decimated and harvests of other species, including crabs, are seriously threatened.
- Emissions of sulfur dioxide, nitrogen oxides and volatile organic compounds have fallen very slowly or not at all since 1980.

The significance of any environmental gains can only truly be measured in the long term. If the population increases, as projected, to 393 million by 2050, will our current environmental victories survive?

Argument: We Should Focus on International Development, Not Immigration Policy

Finally, some contend that immigration is simply too complex to be treated fundamentally as a demographic issue: instead of reducing immigration, which unfairly blames immigrants for problems in the United States, the U.S. should work internationally to reduce the push factors (such as poverty, overpopulation and war) that compel people to leave their own countries and move here. This argument, which essentially characterizes immigration as an inevitable economic process, identifies incorrectly the basis for most legal immigration. It also fails to recognize that immigration policy and foreign policy goals can be complementary.

"Push" factors explain primarily illegal, not legal, immigration into the United States. Legal immigration, in fact, is driven in part by the desire for economic gain, but a variety of other factors play a role. In 1994, 65% of immigrants arrived solely on the basis of family affiliation—a spouse, parent, child, brother or sister was already living in the United States. About 15% arrived as refugees or asylees (refugees and asylees are able to demonstrate that they would be persecuted if they remained at home), and about 8% arrived on the basis of possessing an identifiable skill. The remaining 12% arrived under one or more of several temporary programs.

In other words, poverty may explain the reason some potential immigrants come to the United States, but no legal immigrant arrives explicitly because he or she is poor—the current immigration law offers no provision to do so. Consequently, dramatically increased foreign assistance might help reduce the flow of illegal immigration (and flight by refugees and asylees), but its consequence for most legal immigration is less certain.

Second, the argument above suggests that trade and foreign aid should serve as a substitute for immigration policy—that rather than setting immigration levels directly, "immigration demand" should be allowed to evolve indirectly as a natural economic consequence of foreign assistance. A far more effective and reasonable strategy is to recognize the value (both environmental and economic) in regulating immigration levels while simultaneously pursuing our foreign aid and trade goals.

Argument: Immigrants Are Being Unfairly Blamed

Some have argued that by identifying immigration's contribution to population growth and advocating a reduction in that contribution, we are unfairly blaming immigrants for America's environmental problems. This argument makes little sense on the face of it. If such an argument were necessarily true, then demographers would be unfairly blaming couples—or their newborn children—for environmental degradation in the United States simply by acknowledging fertility's contribution to population growth. The blame game yields no profit, but does serve to sidetrack a critical policy issue with an unproductive and highly emotional debate.

Our Past—and Possible Futures

Over the past 25 years, the link between population growth and environmental degradation has been so well established that it is hard to find an environmental advocate who does not acknowledge it. Numerous governments have recognized the need for population stabilization, as well, and several international agencies now exist to address population growth directly. In the United States, officials at the highest levels of office have considered whether the United States should adopt a national population policy. In 1972, the recommendations of the Commission on Population Growth and the American Future (also known as the Rockefeller Commission) demonstrated what such a policy might look like: in part, the Commission recommended freezing immigration at its then-current level of about 400,000 a year as part of a national population policy. More recently, the President's Council on Sustainable Development (PCSD) advocated the goal of voluntary population stabilization in the United States, but fell short of recommending a specific immigration level.

Consider, also, the overwhelming national and international consensus on the relationship between population growth and environmental degradation. As recently as 1994 at the International Conference on Population and the Environment, the United States (with the endorsement of numerous U.S. environmental organizations) and dozens of other countries, reaffirmed the goal of stopping population growth as a key element in any environmental protection plan.

Immigration is a highly emotional issue so any debate over immigration policy is likely to be heated. Unfortunately, much of the population and environment community is reluctant even to acknowledge that immigration has a demographic impact, an issue that was long ago resolved by the demographers. Once this first step has been taken, then the environmental debate over immigration can truly begin.

John Isbister **NO**

Are Immigration Controls Ethical?

Americans typically express their opinions about immigration with certainty and moral outrage. This article argues that many of us are in an ethically fraught position with respect to immigration, however. We have deeply held convictions about the equality of all people. At the same time, though, we use immigration policy to perpetuate a privileged lifestyle at the expense of foreigners. We are not prepared to abandon either this use of immigration policy or the ideology of equality. At the very least, therefore, our moral stance should be one of humility, not outrage.

The moral muddle in which we find ourselves arises in part because of a tendency to confuse our interests with ethics; we persuade ourselves that what is best for us is best, period. It is not.

Most of the current debate about immigration has to do with the national interest or with the interests of various groups inside the U.S. Elsewhere I have explored the interests of Americans with respect to immigration (Isbister, 1996). Briefly, I think that from an economic point of view, some Americans are helped and others are hurt by immigration. On the whole, the former tend to be at the top of the income ladder, the latter at the bottom. Economics is not everything, however, Bill Clinton's 1992 presidential campaign to the contrary notwithstanding. Immigration is transforming the social structure of the U.S., changing it from a white country with several minority groups into a genuinely multicultural country in which no ethnic group will prevail, all ethnic groups will be able to meet each other on a basis of relative equality and the possibilities for mutual enrichment rather than suspicion, and exploitation and racism will be enhanced. Since this social transformation is so important to the U.S., I think that the interest of the country lies in welcoming relatively large numbers of immigrants. The numbers cannot be unlimited, however, since the maintenance of one of the world's highest standards of living requires some restrictions on the inflow of newcomers.

Interests of Americans are central; the national political system responds, it can be argued, to nothing else. Interests are not synonymous with morality, however. By definition, the national interest excludes the interests of foreigners. It would be a curious ethical system that denied moral standing to some people simply because of the accident of their nationality. The ethics of immigration controls require investigation, therefore, separate from the interests that Americans have in immigration. In the end, of course, interests will count more than ethics in the formulation of national immigration policy. We would do well, however, to keep in mind the conflict between the two perspectives.

Equal Moral Worth

The equal moral worth of all people is the principle on which the ethical arguments in this article are grounded. Philosophers have made many attempts to demonstrate equal worth. For the most part, however, those of us who believe in equality treat it as an assumption, an axiom, not something to be proven. The axiom of equal worth is at the core of the two most important statements of political philosophy in U.S. history, the Declaration of Independence and the Gettysburg Address.

In the Declaration of Independence, Thomas Jefferson wrote, "We hold these Truths to be self-evident, that all Men are created equal." He did not argue the point; it was "self-evident." The importance of equality was that equal rights accrue to all people: "They are endowed by their Creator with certain unalienable Rights, that among these are Life, Liberty, and the Pursuit of Happiness."

Neither Jefferson nor his Virginian compatriots conducted their lives in accordance with these "Truths," for they were slave holders. Similarly today, most people do not base their actions on a commitment to the equality of all people. Nevertheless, many of us believe in equality, not because we have reasoned it out and considered the arguments pro and con, but because it is "self-evident."

The radical equality of the Declaration of Independence was restricted sharply by the more conservative Constitution of 1789, a document that among other things protected slavery. As Gary Wills has argued, however, Abraham Lincoln's Gettysburg Address of 1863 had the effect of subverting the Constitution by restoring equality as the central American value (Wills, 1992). It began, in words now as familiar to Americans as those of the Declaration, and more familiar than any in the Constitution, "Fourscore and seven years ago, our fathers brought forth upon this continent a new nation, conceived in liberty and dedicated to the proposition that all men are created equal."

Neither document says "all Americans are created equal." Jefferson and Lincoln may or may not have implied "people" by their use of the word "men," but in our current reading, we do. These most formative of American documents assume the equality of all human beings.

People are equally valuable and therefore have equal rights. It does not follow from this that they have unlimited rights. Rights often conflict one with another; when they do, the liberal state (that is, the state based on the presumption of equal worth) is justified in restricting some rights, in order to protect others. Whenever it restricts rights, however, the state must be able to give morally justifiable reasons why it has done so—else it forfeits its claim to liberalism and descends into despotism.

An Argument for Open Borders

Immigration controls restrict free movement by establishing groups that have unequal rights. Among the people who wish to live in the U.S., some favored ones are allowed to, while others are not. Can one successfully argue that, while immigration controls infringe on some people's liberties, they are justified because they protect more important rights and liberties? Or does their allocation of unequal rights to people who are of equal worth make them morally impermissible?

Freedom of movement is a facet of the "Liberty" that the Declaration of Independence takes to be an inherent right of equal human beings. Countries that systematically restricted the movement of their people are rightly criticized. In recent years, the clearest example of the morally unjustified restriction of internal movement was in South Africa, which enforced its apartheid system with pass laws.

As a mental exercise, one could ask how a law passed by the residents of the city of New York, restricting the permanent entry of Americans who were not city residents, would be judged. Leaving aside the fact that it would be unconstitutional, would it be morally justified? The people of New York could offer some good reasons for the law. New York is already crowded and cannot tolerate further population growth, they might argue. The sanitation system is close to breaking down, the schools are crowded, the welfare system is bankrupt, the homeless shelters are inadequate, and the unemployment rate is rising.

These sorts of arguments would not prove convincing to most Americans, who would find the restriction on personal freedom too onerous. Every day, people migrate into (and out of) New York for compelling reasons. They move in order to accept a job or to look for a job or because their job has been relocated to New York. They could not have the same job in Boston or Chicago because New York is unique (as also Boston and Chicago are). They move to New York to be with their family or to care for a friend or for one of any number of other reasons. The decision to migrate to New York is seldom taken lightly; people have good reasons. The interests that New Yorkers may have in restricting entry, while perhaps meritorious, are not of sufficient weight to permit such massive violations of the rights and interests of outsiders. Morally, New York could not justify an immigration policy of its own.

If this argument is accepted, how can one accept immigration restrictions in the U.S.? What makes the U.S. fundamentally different from New York? Nothing much, except sovereign power.

Reasoning by analogy, it is difficult to find an ethical justification for the United States to restrict entry across its borders. In fact, it is more difficult, since the people of the U.S. are privileged, *vis-à-vis* the rest of the world, in a way that the residents of New York are not, in comparison to other Americans. New Yorkers could argue plausibly that among U.S. cities, their city is not so special, that people denied entry into it could find comparable amenities in other cities. The U.S. occupies a unique position in the world, however, or at least the long lines of potential immigrants would so indicate. The great majority of immigrants and potential immigrants hope to enjoy a significantly higher standard of living in the U.S. than they experienced in their home countries. Immigration controls on the U.S. border therefore restrict access to privilege.

It is the protection of privilege that is so damaging, ethically, to the country's immigration laws. It makes U.S. border controls even less justifiable than New York's would be. The purpose and effect of U.S. immigration controls are to maintain a state of inequality in the world between the haves (the Americans) and the have-nots (the foreigners, especially the potential immigrants). Americans maintain immigration laws because they fear that unrestricted entry would lead to a major influx of people, that the newcomers would compete for scarce resources and jobs in the U.S. and that they would drive down the standard of living of residents. No doubt it is in the interest of the privileged to protect their privileges, but it cannot be ethical if that protection has the effect of further disadvantaging the unprivileged.

The ethical case against immigration controls is based, therefore, not just on the fact that they convey unequal rights to morally equal people, but that they do so in a particularly damaging way, so as to protect advantage and deepen disadvantage. To understand the importance of this, one can consider the argument that some types of unequal treatment are morally justified. For example, a system of preferential hiring in which race is taken into account treats different groups of people unequally, but it may be fair if it is designed to benefit people who have been exploited or to dismantle a system of racial injustice (Wasserstrom, 1986). Unequal treatment is clearly unjust, however, when it is used to perpetuate rather than break down a system of privilege and disadvantage. This is just what U.S. immigration controls do. They violate the equal worth and equal rights of people in an egregious way, by sheltering already advantaged Americans at the expense of relatively disadvantaged potential immigrants.

Arguments for Immigration Controls

This section considers six ethical arguments that are made in favor of immigration controls, in ascending order of persuasiveness. They are not the only arguments made in the academic literature and the political discourse, but they seem to me to be the strongest. In the end, I find that the first five are rationalizations used to perpetuate a structure of advantage and disadvantage in the world while allowing Americans to avoid this truth, and that their moral logic fails. The sixth argument, however, has merit and leaves us with a conflict of rights.

> *1. "Immigration is theft." It is argued that the U.S., with all its wealth, is the property of Americans, to treat as they wish. Immigrants want to share in the country's wealth, but they have no right to it unless Americans willingly offer it to them. People have the legal and moral right to protect their property against theft. They are under no obligation to give it away.*

Is the country the private property of Americans? Can one say that Americans own the U.S., just as an individual owns a house? Or would a better analogy be to a public beach? Whoever arrives first on a secluded beach would perhaps like to claim title and keep others from access to it, but the first-comer has no right to do so, because the beach is common property. International law gives Americans the legal right to treat the country as their private house, but I think that morally the U.S. has more of the characteristics of a public beach.

The U.S. is both a land area and the society that has been built on it. As to the land itself, Americans are in a weak position to claim exclusive ownership of it, since they are such recent arrivals themselves. Most Americans are only a few generations removed from immigration. If they were to take seriously the claim of prior ownership, they would have to return the land to the descendants of the Native Americans, whom their forbears pushed aside and slaughtered. They are not prepared to do this. They cannot successfully claim, therefore, that a new wave of entrants has fewer rights of access to the land than their immigrant predecessors did.

The U.S. is more than the land, however; it is the improvements as well. Today the U.S. is far different from the place the settlers wrested from the Natives. It is now a rich country—and it is because of its standard of living, not its land mass, that it is a Mecca for immigrants. Can Americans claim that they created the wealth they enjoy and that they therefore have the sole right to decide whether and which foreigners have access to it? I think not.

For the most part, Americans now living did not create the wealth; they inherited it. At the time they were born, the U.S. was already one of the world's richest countries and its wealth was growing rapidly. If anything, the collective actions of Americans over the last quarter century have diminished their inheritance. By living beyond their means, both personally and publicly, Americans have actually lowered the standard of living of a good many people. They are living off their inheritance.

In other words, Americans now living found a lovely beach; they did not build or buy a new house. Since they are not responsible for their good fortune, they do not have the moral right to deny other people the opportunity to share in it.

Not so, Americans might reply. We have a right to our inheritance. Our ancestors built this country not just for their own pleasure, but for the well-being of their children. If one could ask them who has a claim to the riches they built up, they would reply that it is we, their descendants.

This argument is not silly, but it is not transparently valid either. Inheritance presents ethical difficulties. Ordinary, small inheritances are certainly morally justifiable, since they represent a simple expression of family love. Just as a mother cares for her baby, so does she want to pass some of her gains on to her children after her death. To want to do so is not wrong; indeed, to fail to do so would be thought by most people to mark a lack of parental love. It is when inheritance is so substantial that it perpetuates a system of privilege and disadvantage that it lacks moral justification, since it violates the norms of equal access, equal opportunity, and equal treatment, the norms that follow from the axiom of equal worth. Americans would reject as immoral the rigid class system of medieval Europe or the caste system of India, in which one's prospects in life were completely determined by the accident of birth. That sort of inheritance is immoral. It is just the sort of inheritance that Americans as a whole have received from their ancestors, an inheritance that gives them enormously greater privilege than most of the rest of humankind. It does not give them the right to exclude others from their country.

One cannot, therefore, defend immigration restrictions as protection against theft. Immigrants are not burglars.

2. "Open immigration would destroy important American values." *The second argument for border controls is that unrestricted immigration might destroy institutions or values in the U.S. that are of transcendent importance. Open immigration might destroy something that is vital not only to Americans, but also to foreigners and potential immigrants.*

What might such institutions or values be? Political scientist Frederick Whelan argues that liberal values—equal moral worth, democracy, equal access, etc.— are scarce and precious in the world and need protection. It is a mistake to use liberal principles to argue for open access if open access would diminish liberal values and institutions in the world (Whelan, 1988).

The concern is one of absorptive capacity and the assimilative powers of the U.S. A massive influx of foreigners who were unfamiliar with and uncommitted to American political values might use the democratic procedures of the country to destroy the institutions that support those procedures. This might happen before they had the opportunity to adopt as their own the principles of freedom and self-government. Under such circumstances, Whelan and others have argued that the state is morally justified in restricting immigration.

A closely related argument is that members of a community have the right to protect their values and culture by excluding outsiders if necessary (Walzer, 1983).

This argument perhaps has theoretical merit. However, no evidence exists that it relates to a real danger in the U.S. Native groups have often opposed the political positions taken by immigrants, regarding them as inimical to their interests, but this is simply evidence that the immigrants have adapted to the political norms of the country and have used the political process to their own benefit. Disagreement over political goals is not the same as rejection of basic political philosophy. During the entire period before the 20th century, when the U.S. maintained open borders, the principal threat to a liberal political system came not from recent immigrants, but from the slave holders who were descendants of the first white settlers.

3. "We have better ways of helping the world's disadvantaged." *The third argument in favor of immigration controls is that while Americans may be morally obliged to redress the imbalance of privilege in the world, they can do so more effectively through policies to improve standards of living in poor countries than they can by allowing a few residents of those countries to immigrate. Immigration focuses the benefits of U.S. resources upon just a few people. Better to take action to improve the entire economies of poor countries, actions that will affect far more people. The policy tools available to the U.S.*

government are innumerable, including foreign aid, loans and technical as-
sistance, and trade, investment, and fiscal and monetary policies designed to
benefit poor countries. In addition, individuals can contribute best to world
justice by making personal charitable contributions.

An effective rejoinder to this argument is that while rich countries and
their citizens may have a duty to assist in the economic development of poor
countries, fulfillment of this duty does not relieve them of the obligation to
allow immigration. The two policies are not alternatives; they can be thought
of rather as complements with different sorts of effects. Foreign economic aid,
while never enough and often ineffective, is normally designed to effect small
improvements in the lives of large numbers of people. Immigration enables a
relatively small number of people, the immigrants, to make a radical change in
their living situation. One would like to find a policy that combines the merits
of both, that in a short period of time lifts the economic disadvantage of a large
fraction of the world's people. No such policy exists. In its absence, therefore,
the residents of the world's richer countries have a duty to do what they can on
all fronts. The case for open borders is not refuted just because other ways exist
for Americans to redress injustice.

4. "Americans have a special obligation to their fellow citizens." *The fourth*
argument for immigration controls is that Americans have greater obligations
to their fellow citizens than to foreigners. If there is a reasonable possibility that
immigration may hurt some U.S. citizens, therefore, Americans are justified in
restricting entry, even though restrictions may violate the rights of foreigners.

Consider a parallel case that is clearer. A middle-class couple has enough
savings to provide either a basic education for a poor orphan or supplementary
educational enrichment for their own child. The orphan has the greater disadvantage and the greater need, but few would criticize the parents for deciding
that their priority was to provide the best possible education for their own child.
Can Americans not make a similar case relating to their fellow citizens?

Perhaps they can. Perhaps one can posit a series of widening circles, outside each of which our obligations diminish. Our greatest obligation is to our
family, then perhaps to our friends, then to our neighbors, then perhaps to our
ethnic group, then to our fellow citizens, and finally to all people. No doubt a
great many people think this way. To test oneself, one might think back to the
spring and summer of 1994 when hundreds of thousands of innocent Rwandans
were murdered and ask whether that event occasioned as much moral anger in
oneself as did a smaller, more local violation of rights, such as the burglary of
one's home. Most Americans had some sympathy for the Rwandans, but not as
much as they would have, had they been neighbors.

People think this way, but that does not mean that this kind of thinking
is morally justified. Before accepting this view as the proper basis for national
immigration policy, one should understand how devastating it is to the proposition with which this inquiry began: that all people are morally equal and as
a consequence have equal rights. The fourth argument denies this "Truth" of

the Declaration of Independence. If the argument is accepted, Americans have greater moral standing than foreigners and more rights, at least as seen through the eyes of Americans.

I think we must concede that kin have greater standing than nonrelatives in the moral considerations of most people and that this is natural and good. In all likelihood, it is an evolutionary necessity. Further departures from the norm of equal moral worth seem to me, however, to be unjustified. The failure to recognize the full humanity of people who are different from oneself—people who have different ethnic backgrounds, languages, religions, citizenships, and so forth—is at the root of much of the warfare and suffering in the word today. We may feel a more natural connection to people who are like us in some ways, but if we act on that feeling, we are in danger of creating terribly unjust situations as, for example, in Rwanda and Bosnia.

I do not mean to disparage patriotism. Love of one's country can be an affirming, healthy sentiment. Yet an ethical patriot recognizes that his or her patriotism does not diminish the rights of others. It is critical that patriotism and other kinds of group identity be grounded in the understanding that everyone else has equal rights and that one's own group is not justified in reducing the rights of other groups in any way.

Although it is tempting, therefore, the fourth argument for immigration controls fails. If we develop public policy on the presumption of unequal worth, we are heading down a path toward conflict and selfishness, not moral clarity.

5. *"Americans are not obliged to be heroic." The fifth argument for immigration controls is that although people may have an obligation to come to the aid of other people in distress, that obligation holds only if it can be done without undue sacrifice. The idea is sometimes called the "the principle of mutual aid" or "the cutoff for heroism." To incur or risk great sacrifice on behalf of someone else is commendable because it is heroic, but because it is heroic it is not required. Ordinary people have an obligation to take ordinary care for their fellow humans, but not to be saints (Wolf, 1982). Andrew Shacknove describes the principle this way:*

"In its classic form, the principle of mutual aid envisions a passer-by who encounters a drowning child. If the passer-by can easily save the child, she is morally obligated to do so, even if the child is a complete stranger. Failure to save the child under such conditions would be universally condemned as callousness. If, to the contrary, the passer-by could hope to rescue the child only at great personal risk, no one would chastise her for not acting. The passer-by is not expected to sacrifice life or limb because of a chance encounter with a stranger. Doing so is heroic, but heroism by its nature is voluntary; it exceeds the limits of obligation" (Shacknove, 1988).

The analogy to immigration policy is obvious. If the cutoff for heroism is a valid principle and if it takes precedence over other moral principles, if we are required to help our fellow human beings only when doing so is not very difficult or dangerous, then we may be rescued from the obligation to open our borders to all comers. For in the long run at least, open borders would probably entail a real sacrifice for many Americans. Immigrants come to the U.S. partly because of its high standard of living; they would likely continue to come until they had driven down wages and driven up unemployment to such an extent that immigration was no longer so attractive.

Perhaps we can say, then, that morality does not require such a heroic sacrifice. Americans are obliged to do what they can to alleviate suffering in the world, as long as they do not have to pay a significant price.

The argument is respectable, but it is too comforting to the rich and privileged to stand unmodified. It is a justification for continued injustice. If it is applicable to Americans, why is it not equally applicable to anyone in a position of privilege? Could it not be used by any reactionary to justify keeping his status and income: by the King of France before the Revolution, by southern slave holders before the Civil War, by South African whites before the transfer of power? Any readjustment of a privilege-disadvantage relationship calls for sacrifice on the part of the privileged. If the principle of the cutoff for heroism is dominant, if it holds greater weight than the principle of the equal moral worth of all people, then the privileged are morally justified in maintaining their privilege.

Attractive though the fifth objection is, therefore, it fails as an ethical justification for immigration controls. The cutoff for heroism may be a valid principle when a passer-by is considering saving a drowning child, because in that case the two people are not connected by a relationship of privilege and subordination. When it is used as an argument for protecting privilege, however, it does not have greater moral weight than the principle of equal worth or even the Golden Rule.

6. "Immigration controls protect the disadvantaged." The sixth and strongest argument against open borders is that immigration controls may not protect the privileged at all, but rather the unprivileged. The discussion so far has tacitly assumed that all Americans are the same, but they are not. Some are privileged while some are severely disadvantaged: the poor, the unskilled, and many members of non-Anglo ethnic groups.

It must be conceded that the research conducted so far on the impact of immigration on the prospects of disadvantaged Americans is not definitive. Nevertheless, it is likely that an increased and unending supply of low-wage labor from Third World countries would keep the earnings of unskilled workers low and profits high, thereby increasing the gap between the poor and the rich in the U.S. If so, it is argued, immigration should be curtailed.

Sometimes this argument is mixed with either the fourth or the fifth argument. It should not be, because those arguments can be refuted, as we have seen. The sixth argument should not depend on the assertion that Americans are more worthy than foreigners; they are not. Neither should it depend on the assertion that immigration should require no sacrifice from Americans; sacrifice may be morally required.

Can the sixth argument be refuted successfully? One way of attempting to do so would be to say that immigration policy need not bear the burden of reducing the inequities among Americans. Many other policy tools are available, one might argue, among them welfare, education, social insurance programs, the minimum wage, job training, etc. In the conservative political atmosphere of the mid-1990s, these policies are being de-emphasized—but if the country had a commitment to reducing poverty, it could reverse those trends. If it did, it could promote social justice at home while still allowing increased immigration. Put differently, the obligation to rectify the imbalances of privilege in the world rests on the shoulders of the privileged in the rich countries, not on everyone in those countries. Morality requires them to transfer resources to their less fortunate brethren at home *and* to allow immigrants from the Third World to enter their country.

This refutation is valid, but only up to a point. Certainly rich and middle-class Americans cannot ethically argue that the welfare of their poor fellow citizens requires them to discriminate against poor foreigners when they are actually reducing their help to their own people. Still, it is likely that, even if the U.S. made a massive good-faith effort to reduce domestic poverty, it could never be successful if completely open immigration were permitted. Whatever advances were made in the welfare of the U.S. poor would just be swallowed up by new immigrants from poor countries who were seeking to take advantage of American generosity.

A second possible refutation is to assert that the needs of foreigners are more pressing than the needs of even disadvantaged Americans. The relative gap between the rich and the poor in the U.S. is substantial and shameful, but it is far from the largest in the world; the gap in many Third World countries, including the largest senders of immigrants to the U.S., is greater. The standard of living of most poor Americans is higher than the *average* standard of living in most poor countries and certainly higher than the standard of living of most immigrants. Many Mexicans, for example, enter the U.S. to earn wages that, while low by American standards, are several multiples of what they could earn at home. In the hierarchy of advantage, therefore, poor Americans occupy an intermediate position, much worse off than other Americans, but still better off than many immigrants. Therefore, one might maintain, it is morally permissible to harm poor Americans, if this is the price that must be paid to improve the lot of poor immigrants.

This refutation is not persuasive. Poor Americans are genuinely needy and unfairly impoverished. It simply cannot be right to take conscious, public action to worsen their plight. Morality obliges us to protect the welfare not just of the most disadvantaged people in the world, but of all who suffer disadvantage.

The sixth argument in favor of border controls is therefore valid. So, however, is the argument in the previous section for open borders. We are left with an ethical conflict. Disadvantaged foreigners have a moral right to enter the world's most privileged country, in an attempt to improve their position. On the other hand, poor Americans have the right of protection against so much competition from low-income newcomers that their own circumstances deteriorate. The conflict cannot be resolved completely; in the end, the best solution may be a compromise.

Although the conflict of rights cannot be resolved completely, it can be resolved partially. Recall the point made above that as long as the U.S. is a rich country, with a majority of its people very well off or at least comfortable, it is not ethical to depend upon immigration restrictions alone to improve the position of poor Americans. Such a policy would put the burden of sacrifice on even poorer foreigners, rather than on comfortable Americans, the truly privileged among equally worthy human beings.

The sixth argument is therefore a valid justification for immigration restrictions only (1) if the restrictions are accompanied by a major national commitment to improve the quality of life of the U.S. poor and (2) if, in the absence of restrictions, the flow of immigrants would be too great to allow that program to be successful.

Conclusion

An ethically defensible immigration policy, based on the principle of equal moral worth, would be just one component of an integrated program in which rich and middle-class Americans fulfilled their obligations to those less fortunate. The policy would harm no one who was in an already disadvantaged position, would help as many disadvantaged people as possible, and would require sacrifice on the part of the privileged.

The program would consist of at least the following elements. First, privileged Americans (the majority in the U.S.) would greatly increase their commitment to improving the well-being of the American poor, by transferring such a significant portion of their resources to them that they bore a real sacrifice. Second, the U.S. would increase its commitment to foreign aid and other ways of improving the standard of living in poor countries.

Third, the U.S. would raise the flow of immigrants, in order to increase the number of foreigners who had a chance of participating in the advantages of American life. Two reasons exist for thinking that immigration could be increased substantially without hurting the domestic poor: (1) the fact that empirical research can detect little effect of current immigration upon the welfare of the U.S. poor and (2) the increased commitment to the poor postulated in the previous paragraph.

Fourth, the U.S. would maintain some quantitative limit on immigration, or at least the stand-by authority to impose a limit if the flow of immigration became too great to be absorbed without sacrifice by the U.S. poor.

Fifth, if the U.S. had to restrict the number of immigrants, and therefore had to choose among applicants, it would give first priority to the neediest, the refugees who are increasing in number around the world and who have no secure place to live, even if this meant cutting back on immigrants who were admitted for reasons of employment or family reunification.

In the end, the case for completely open borders can probably not be sustained; some limits on immigration may be required. Note, however, how different this argument is from the usual discourse. The usual view is that American immigration policy should maximize the interests of American residents. The argument I am making is that privileged Americans have a moral obligation to redress the balance of privilege in the world, through immigration policies and other policies. How exactly to do this is complex, because the structure of privilege and disadvantage in the world is not straightforward. Any adjustment of that relationship in the direction of greater equity, however, will require sacrifice by those who currently have the advantage, not the enhancement of their own self-interest.

This conclusion is troubling because it is so completely at variance not only with U.S. immigration policy, but also with every country's policy and with the opinions of almost every American. Faced with such overwhelming rejection of one's reasoning, a prudent person should consider the possibility of being in error. Of course, I may be. I think, however, that what has been uncovered is a fundamental dilemma. Americans are not about to admit so many immigrants that they bear a significant cost. For those who are comfortable simply with the pursuit of self-interest, this will not cause any sleepless nights. Those Americans who are genuinely altruistic, however, those who try to think out their positions from an ethical perspective and who believe in the equal worth of all people, those most admirable of Americans need to come to terms with the fact that they are among the world's privileged (their differential location on that scale in the U.S. notwithstanding), that immigration controls protect their privilege, and that they are not going to abandon that protection.

It is a dilemma familiar to thoughtful people, if not necessarily in the context of immigration. Who has not, at least momentarily, compared his or her life to Mother Teresa's and concluded that it is wanting in courage and ethics? Can those of us who are not willing to abandon our worldly goods and devote our lives completely to the service of the poor claim to live moral lives?

This investigation into the ethics of immigration policy has concluded that, if completely open borders are not required, Americans should still welcome immigrants to their country in such large numbers that they sacrifice and that their position of privilege in the world is reduced. We can be certain that this conclusion is not going to be translated into policy. Almost no American would stand for it. We are up against the uncomfortable realization, therefore, that our actions to maintain our standard of living through our immigration policy are inherently immoral. If this understanding does not change our behavior, it may at least clarify where we stand.

POSTSCRIPT

Should Immigration to the United States and Other Developed Countries Be Curtailed?

Nowak attacks six basic arguments in favor of immigration: (1) immigration contributes little to U.S. population growth; (2) historic levels of immigration are higher than the current level; (3) high consumption levels are more to blame for environmental degradation than population growth; (4) environmental gains can be made despite population growth; (5) the United States should focus on international development, not immigration policy; and (6) immigrants are being unfairly blamed for America's environmental problems.

With respect to population projections, Nowak asserts that the government's own figures reveal that 60 percent, or 75 million, of the projected population growth of 125 million in the United States between now and 2050 will be attributed to immigration, making it more than simply a marginal factor. The second argument really has no bearing, says Nowak, for many reasons. With respect to the third argument about consumption, Nowak argues that reducing per capita consumption will mean little if population numbers are allowed to rise dramatically. The fourth argument cannot be answered in the short run because America has witnessed environmental losses as well. The argument that the United States should focus on international development, asserts Nowak, ignores the fact that immigration policy and foreign policy goals can be complementary. Finally, Nowak simply dismisses the last argument about unfair treatment.

Isbister's arguments flow from the concept of "equal moral worth of all people," the core of the Declaration of Independence and the Gettysburg Address. Thus, he attacks what he terms "six ethical arguments" in favor of immigration controls, made in ascending order of importance. The bottom line is that he finds the first five to be "rationalizations used to perpetuate a structure of advantage and disadvantage in the world while allowing Americans to avoid this truth ... [thus] their moral logic fails." Isbister admits that the sixth argument has some validity, leaving him with a conflict of rights. The five arguments that Isbister deems without merit are the following: (1) "immigration is theft" because U.S. wealth "is the property of Americans, to treat as they wish"; (2) "open immigration would destroy important American values"; (3) "we have better ways of handling the world's disadvantaged"; (4) "Americans have a special obligation to their fellow citizens"; and (5) "Americans are not obliged to be heroic."

Isbister finds the first argument untenable for one basic reason: Americans found "a lovely beach" through no good deeds of their own, so they have no right to deny it to others. The author counters the second argument about the threat to values by asserting that there is no real evidence of such danger. In response to the third argument, Isbister maintains that fulfillment of the duty to assist in economic development "does not relieve [Americans] of the obligation to allow immigration." For the fourth argument, the author suggests that "if we develop public policy on the presumption of unequal worth, we are heading down a path toward conflict and selfishness, not moral clarity." To the fifth argument, Isbister says, "It fails as an ethical justification for immigration controls." To the sixth, the author counters that disadvantaged non-Americans "have a moral right to enter the world's most privileged country... [while] poor Americans have the right of protection against so much competition from low-income newcomers that their own circumstances deteriorate."

Nowak provides a succinct alternative view to each of the pro-immigration positions that he outlines. In short, if one views America's role in the global arena as one of simply advancing the interests of its own citizens, then Nowak's viewpoint makes sense. Isbister sets up his own set of arguments to attack. For him, humanitarian obligations do not stop at a nation's shores. The key question in both cases is whether America's own interests and the interests of the larger global society are one and the same, somewhat similar, or rather different. If one believes that America has an obligation primarily to its own citizens only, then Nowak's assessment makes sense. If one holds that America's humanitarian obligations go far beyond its own borders, then Isbister provides sufficient intellectual justification for open borders.

Isbister develops his arguments further in *The Immigration Debate: Remaking America* (Kumarian Press, 1996). Kenneth K. Lee, in *Huddled Masses, Muddled Laws: Why Contemporary Immigration Policy Fails to Reflect Public Opinion* (Praeger, 1998), examines immigration policy making from a historical perspective. Two books that examine immigration beyond the American case are W. T. S. Gould and A. M. Findlay, eds., *Population Migration and the Changing World Order* (John Wiley, 1994) and Christian Joppke's *Immigration and the Nation-State: The United States, Germany, and Great Britain* (Oxford University Press, 1999).

ISSUE 12

Is There a Global Brain Drain?

YES: William J. Carrington, from "International Migration and the 'Brain Drain,' " *The Journal of Social, Political, and Economic Studies* (Summer 1999)

NO: Jean M. Johnson and Mark C. Regets, from "International Mobility of Scientists and Engineers to the United States—Brain Drain or Brain Circulation?" National Science Foundation, Division of Science Resources Studies Issue Brief (November 10, 1998)

ISSUE SUMMARY

YES: William J. Carrington, an economist at the Bureau of Labor Statistics, details what he considers an extensive global brain drain, or the migration of the more qualified citizens of the developing world to the richer countries.

NO: Jean M. Johnson and Mark C. Regets, senior analysts in the Division of Science Resources Studies at the National Science Foundation, contend that roughly half of all foreign doctoral recipients leave the United States immediately upon completion of their studies, while others leave some years later, creating a brain circulation rather than a total drain.

One characteristic of globalization is the ease with which individuals can move from one country to another. The visit may be a short one, lasting a month or so. Or it may involve studying abroad, where the length of time is a function of the period needed to complete educational requirements. Finally, it may be an even longer move, approaching permanency, designed to find better employment opportunities. The current issue focuses on this last type of international movement.

The term *brain drain* does not imply the movement of less fortunate individuals within poor societies to wealthier countries in search of jobs, no matter how meager. Developing nations are far less concerned about their unemployable or underemployable residents emigrating to places that offer a potentially better life. To these countries, each emigrant means one less job to find, one less mouth to feed, one less potential health care recipient to provide for, and one less fertile individual to contribute to future population growth. This less fortunate group is viewed as net consumers in their societies rather than effective producers who will make important contributions on a daily basis.

One can acquire a better sense of the nature of the issue by examining the problem from an intracountry perspective. That is, consider the problem of brain drain *within* the United States itself. America is replete with examples of communities that are dying because their young people, particularly those with greater education or sophisticated employment skills, are leaving for greener pastures. The local area is typically a blue-collar town, the industrial base of which is primarily associated with the earlier industrial era but which now faces competition from abroad or from some more modern and, thus, more desirable location in the Sun Belt. Without employment opportunities, the young go off to college and rarely return home, opting instead for jobs in more alluring locations. The latter might be a big city close to the hometown, or it might be in another section of the country. The result is that the community where the individuals grew up never benefits from the initial investment of nurturing these people from birth to adulthood. In short, it never receives a return on its initial investment. It does not benefit from the assistance that its "best and brightest" could give in helping to solve local community problems by staying home or returning there after completing the final stages of their education.

Many scholars suggest that this situation also exists at the international level. Developing countries invest heavily in preparing their citizens for productive lives within their homelands, the argument goes, only to witness their more qualified people leaving for the developed world, where they can pursue careers or the education that will give them a career in their newly adopted home. There is wide agreement among scholars and policymakers about the number and places of origin of individuals who travel to countries of the developed world in pursuit of education and training. There is also agreement that the original country suffers in proportion to the number of individuals who do not return home.

The basic issue, therefore, is twofold. First, to what extent is the brain drain—in the words of Jean M. Johnson and Mark C. Regets—really simply a "brain circulation," where citizens *do* return home after a short period of time to take their place as contributors to their society? And second, what, if anything, should be done by the developed world to slow or stop one-way movement?

The two selections for this issue focus on the first question. William J. Carrington explores the nature and extent of the brain drain to the wealthy sector of the globe. Johnson and Regets, on the other hand, conclude that society is witnessing a movement away from permanent emigration (brain drain) toward a more temporary visit (brain circulation).

William J. Carrington

 YES

International Migration and the "Brain Drain"

Perhaps the oldest question in economics is why some countries are rich while others are poor. Economic theory has emphasized that differences in the educational levels of the population are an important part of the answer and that improved schooling opportunities should raise incomes in developing countries. Yet, while there is little doubt that highly educated workers in many developing countries are scarce, it is also true that many scientists, engineers, physicians, and other professionals from developing countries work in Canada, the United States, and Western Europe. This phenomenon, often referred to as the "brain drain," was noticed as early as the 1960s and has been a contentious issue in the North-South debate ever since. One important implication of the brain drain is that investment in education in a developing country may not lead to faster economic growth if a large number of its highly educated people leave the country. Also, efforts to reduce specific skill shortages through improved educational opportunities may be largely futile unless measures are taken to offset existing incentives for highly educated people to emigrate.

But how extensive is the brain drain? Which countries and regions are especially affected? Do highly educated professionals from developing countries living abroad represent a sizable proportion of the pool of skilled workers in their countries of origin or too small a number to worry about? Unfortunately, attempts to answer these important questions quickly come up against a formidable barrier: there is no uniform system of statistics on the number and characteristics of international migrants. Also, source countries typically do not keep track of emigrants' characteristics; and, although some receiving countries do, their definitions of immigration differ. Thus, it is difficult to measure precisely the flow and levels of education of immigrants. Further, it has only recently become possible to measure the stock of educated workers in each source country—the pool from which brainpower is drained.

The Brain Drain From the OECD to the U.S.A.

Despite the lack of systematic data about international migrants, estimates of the stock of migrants by educational level in member countries of the Organi-

From William J. Carrington, "International Migration and the 'Brain Drain,'" *The Journal of Social, Political, and Economic Studies*, vol. 24, no. 2 (Summer 1999). Copyright © 1999 by The Council for Social and Economic Studies. Reprinted by permission. Notes omitted.

zation for Economic Cooperation and Development (OECD) can be constructed using a variety of data sources. The resulting estimates are less than perfect in many respects, but they significantly improve our knowledge of the magnitude of the brain drain. The study on which we based this article (Carrington and Detragiache, 1998) covers migration from sixty-one developing countries accounting for about 70 percent of the total population of developing countries. Because of the lack of data, we have not attempted to estimate the extent of either the brain drain from the former Soviet Union and Eastern Europe, even though casual evidence suggests that it is substantial, or migratory flows among developing countries.

In our study we followed a two-step procedure: first, estimates of the brain drain to the United States were constructed using 1990 U.S. census data and other sources of information. Then, these estimates were used—together with data on migrants to OECD countries other than the United States drawn from the OECD's Continuous Reporting System on Migration—to estimate the extent of the brain drain to all OECD countries. While the resulting estimates should be reasonably precise for migration to the United States (which accounts for 54.3 percent of the total migration from the developing countries in our sample to all OECD countries), they are much more tentative for the brain drain to all OECD countries.

The U.S. census reports whether individuals polled are foreign born and, if they are, their country of origin and the number of years of schooling received is also reported for each individual. After individuals under 25 years of age are eliminated to ensure compatibility with the data on educational attainment described below, all foreign-born individuals in the census are put into one of three broad educational categories: primary (0 to 8 years of schooling), secondary (9 to 12 years of schooling), and tertiary (more than 12 years of schooling). A further adjustment involves subtracting from the group of foreign-born individuals with a tertiary education all graduate students in U.S. universities, using data from the Institute of International Education. This procedure yields, for each developing country in the sample, the number of migrants in the United States in each of the three educational categories. To assess the extent of the brain drain from each country considered, these estimates must be compared with the number of individuals in each educational group who remain in their home country. Doing this requires a breakdown by educational category of the population of each developing country in the sample, for which we rely on a data set recently assembled by Robert Barro and Jong-Wha Lee (Barro and Lee, 1993), which provides the best estimates available to date of educational attainment for individuals more than 25 years of age in a large sample of countries.

Source Countries

The first striking feature of the U.S. migration data is that immigration flows of individuals with no more than a primary education are quite small, both in absolute terms and relative to other educational groupings (about 500,000 individuals out of a total of 7 million immigrants). Foreign-born individuals with little or no education, however, may be undercounted by the census if they are in the country illegally or do not speak English. The largest group of immigrants into the United States (about 3.7 million) consists of individuals with secondary education from other North American countries (understood here to include Central American and Caribbean countries), primarily Mexico. Perhaps surprisingly, the second largest group (almost 1.5 million individuals) consists of highly educated migrants from Asia and the Pacific. Total immigration from South America and, especially, Africa is quite small. It is noteworthy, however, that immigrants from Africa consist primarily of highly educated individuals (about 95,000 of the 128,000 African migrants).

Among the countries in Asia and the Pacific, the biggest source is the Philippines, with 730,000 migrants. Of these, the great majority have a tertiary education. The second largest stock of migrants is from China (400,000), which is split almost equally between the secondary and tertiary educational groups. Both India and Korea have seen more than 300,000 people migrate to the United States. It is striking that more than 75 percent of Indian immigrants have a tertiary education, compared with only 53 percent of Korean immigrants.

The biggest migratory flows from Africa to the United States are from Egypt, Ghana, and South Africa, with more than 60 percent of immigrants from those three countries having a tertiary education. Migration of Africans with only a primary education is almost nil. The picture is quite different for the migratory flows from the Western Hemisphere: Mexico is by far the largest sending country (2.7 million), with the large majority of its migrants (2.0 million) having a secondary education and fewer than 13 percent having a tertiary education. This pattern is also observed for the smaller countries of Central America, but not for the two Caribbean countries for which we have information, for which migrants with a tertiary education are a more substantial percentage of the total (42 percent for Jamaica and 46 percent for Trinidad and Tobago). Finally, migration from South America to the United States is relatively small in absolute numbers, with immigrants split almost equally between the secondary and the tertiary educational groups.

In each sending country, how do the numbers of emigrants compare with the size of the population with a given educational attainment? For most countries, people with a tertiary education have the highest migration rate, with the exceptions of the Central American countries, Ecuador, and Thailand (in Thailand, people with a secondary education and those with a tertiary one have approximately the same migration rates). Thus, migrants to the United States tend to be better educated than the average person in their home (that is, the sending) country, and the proportion of very highly educated people who migrate is particularly high. Also, migration from Central America seems to follow a somewhat different pattern than migration from other developing countries, in that the highest migration rate is for persons with a secondary education, rather than those with a tertiary education. The brain drain to the United States from many Central American and Caribbean countries is substantial: for persons with a tertiary education, immigration rates for virtually all these countries are above 10 percent, and some appear to be 50 percent or even higher. In South

America, the country with by far the largest brain drain is Guyana, from which more than 70 percent of individuals with a tertiary education have moved to the United States; for the rest of the region, the immigration rates for this educational group are much lower. The Islamic Republic of Iran has had a substantial drain of highly educated individuals (more than 15 percent) and so has Taiwan Province of China (8–9 percent).

Problems of Methodology

To construct estimates of the brain drain from developing countries to OECD countries, we have relied on the OECD Continuous Reporting System on Migration. Unfortunately, unlike the U.S. census, this data source does not report the years of schooling that migrants have received. For lack of any practical alternatives, we have assumed that the distribution of immigrants by educational category from each source country is the same for the United States as for other OECD countries. Although this is the only feasible approach, which often produces numbers that are consistent with anecdotal evidence, there are some instances in which it yields implausible results, particularly for countries with low rates of immigration to the United States but high rates to one or more of the other OECD countries. Immigrants to the United States from such countries are likely to be better educated than immigrants to other OECD countries, who thus may be more representative of the source country's population.

A second problem with the data for OECD countries other than the United States lies in the different criteria for classifying individuals as immigrants. Although Australia, Canada, and the United States define an immigrant as a person who was born abroad to noncitizens, most European countries define immigrant status based on the ethnicity or immigration status of the parent. A third difficulty with the OECD data is that they did not permit us to exclude immigrants under the age of 25. Finally, the OECD records immigrants from only the top 5 or 10 countries from which they come to each OECD country. Thus, for example, the OECD figures for Canada would include specific information on the numbers of immigrants from China and Mexico, but not those from Jamaica and El Salvador. This is a problem when emigration flows are significant for the source country but small for the receiving country. Thus, particularly for small countries, our estimates of immigration to OECD countries other than the United States may be seriously understated.

If, as a rule of thumb, we consider estimates to be unreliable when migrants to the United States account for less than one-third of the total of immigrants to all OECD member countries, then all estimates for immigration from the Asian and Pacific countries are reliable with the exceptions of those for Malaysia and Sri Lanka. Turkey is also an exception. Among the remaining countries, the extent of the brain drain to all OECD members is substantial—and it increases significantly compared with the U.S. data for the Islamic Republic of Iran, Korea, and, to a lesser extent, the Philippines. For the Islamic Republic of Iran, the fraction of the population with a tertiary education living in OECD countries is around 25 percent; for Korea, 15 percent; and for the Philippines, about 10 percent. For Pakistan, the migration rate of individuals with a tertiary education is more than 7 percent, while for India it is about 2.7 percent; these figures, however, fail to take into account the sizable flow of professionals from the Indian subcontinent to Bahrain, Kuwait, Oman, Qatar, and the United Arab Emirates and therefore neglect an important component of the brain drain from the relevant source countries. The migration rate of highly educated individuals from China is about 3 percent.

For Africa, the estimates are unreliable for Algeria, Senegal, and Tunisia, from which migrants go mainly to France. For most other countries in the sample, however, migration to OECD countries other than the United States is quite small, so the results derived for the United States remain essentially valid. There are, however, some exceptions: for Ghana, the migration rate of highly educated individuals is a dramatic 26 percent; for South Africa, it is more than 8 percent; for Egypt, the brain drain includes 2.5 percent of such individuals emigrating to the United States and another 5 percent emigrating to other OECD countries. For countries in the Western Hemisphere, the bulk of migration is to the United States, and inclusion of flows to the rest of the OECD makes little difference. The only exception is Jamaica, which has a considerable stock of migrants living in the United Kingdom. The drain from Jamaica's population with secondary education is 33 percent, while that from its population with tertiary education is more than 77 percent.

Our estimates show that there is an overall tendency for migration rates to be higher for highly educated individuals. With the important exceptions of Central America and Mexico, the highest migration rates are for individuals with a tertiary education. A number of countries especially small countries in Africa, the Caribbean, and Central America lost more than 30 percent of this group to migration. We have also found sizable brain drain from Iran, Korea, the Philippines, and Taiwan Province of China. These numbers suggest that in several developing countries the outflow of highly educated individuals is a phenomenon that policymakers cannot ignore.

Why the Brain Drain?

More research, especially empirical studies, is needed to evaluate the impact of the brain drain on source economies and on worldwide welfare, as well as the reasons for such migration. In regard to the latter subject, immigration policies in OECD countries tend to favor better educated people, which may explain why the educational composition of total migration is skewed toward the better educated but cannot explain why so many skilled workers are willing to leave developing countries.

Wage differentials may be part of the explanation, but this raises the question of what accounts for such differentials. Differences in the quality of life, educational opportunities for children, and job security may also play a role, as may the desire to interact with a broader group of similarly skilled colleagues. Another important issue is the extent to which the benefits of education acquired by citizens of developing countries are externalities that individuals cannot be expected to take into account when making their private decisions. If such externalities are substantial, as is emphasized by the "new growth theory," then policies to curb the brain drain may be warranted.

Our research also indicates several ways in which estimates of the brain drain could be improved using existing data. The first would be to use census information for other large immigrant-receiving countries, such as Australia, Canada, France, and Germany. Together with the United States, these four countries account for about 93 percent of total migratory flows to OECD countries, so the resulting figures would be a very good approximation of the total. Another promising direction for future research would be to try to obtain, from census data or other sources, more detailed information about the occupational categories of highly skilled migrants, in order to assess whether the brain drain from a given country is especially marked for particular professional groups. This type of analysis could be useful for evaluating the problems that policy programs—such as health sector reform, financial liberalization, or civil service reform—may encounter in developing countries.

Jean M. Johnson and Mark C. Regets **NO**

Brain Drain or Brain Circulation?

Foreign-born scientists and engineers (S&Es) contribute significantly to the brain power of the United States. Considering the U.S. labor force with doctoral degrees in S&E fields, immigrants are 29 percent of those conducting R&D.

Several decades ago, the emigration of such highly skilled personnel to the United States was considered one-way mobility, a permanent brain drain depriving the countries of origin of the "best and the brightest." More recently, however, the mobility of highly talented workers is referred to as "brain circulation," since a cycle of study and work abroad may be followed by a return to the home country to take advantage of high-level opportunities. What do the data tell us about foreign-born S&E personnel in the United States? Are we seeing brain drain or brain circulation? This issue brief discusses student flows into U.S. higher education, the stay rates of foreign doctoral recipients, and their short- and long-term employment in U.S. industry, universities, and Government.

U.S. Higher Education and Foreign S&E Graduate Students

The large foreign component of U.S. human intellectual capital is linked to the ability of U.S. higher education to attract, support, and retain foreign S&E graduate students. Foreign students, particularly those from Asia, represent a large fraction of enrollment and degrees in S&E fields in U.S. graduate institutions. In 1995, of the 420,000 graduate students in S&E programs, roughly 100,000 were foreign students, mainly from a dozen countries of origin. In 1995, at the doctoral level, foreign students (including those with permanent and temporary visas) earned 39 percent of the natural science degrees, 50 percent of the mathematics and computer sciences degrees, and 58 percent of the engineering degrees. Students from China, India, South Korea, and Taiwan accounted for over half of these S&E doctorates.

Financial support available from academic research activities appears to be a major factor associated with attracting foreign students to U.S. doctoral programs. More than 75 percent of the 10,000 foreign doctoral recipients at U.S. universities in 1996 reported their universities as the primary source of

From Jean M. Johnson and Mark C. Regets, "International Mobility of Scientists and Engineers to the United States—Brain Drain or Brain Circulation?" National Science Foundation, Division of Science Resources Studies Issue Brief (November 10, 1998). Washington, DC: U.S. Government Printing Office, 1998. Notes omitted.

support for their graduate training. Of those who did so, the majority reported that their primary support came in the form of research assistantships. Financial resources for research assistantships are provided to universities by Federal Government agencies, industry, and other non-Federal sources in the form of research grants. At the same time that academic research expenditures have been growing, the number of foreign doctoral students supported by university S&E departments has also been increasing. From 1985–96, academic research expenditures increased from $13 to $21 billion in constant (1992) dollars. During the same period, the number of foreign doctoral students primarily supported as research assistants more than tripled—from 2,000 in 1985 to 7,600 in 1996.

Between 1988 and 1996, foreign students from major Asian and European countries, Canada, and Mexico earned over 55,000 U.S. S&E doctoral degrees.

During this period, about 63 percent of these doctoral recipients planned to remain in the United States after completion of their studies, and about 39 percent had firm plans to do so. The proportion of foreign students who remain in the United States, referred to as the "stay rate," differs widely by country. In the last decade, approximately half of the foreign doctoral recipients from China and India have sought and received firm opportunities for further study and employment in the United States. In contrast, only 23 percent of the doctoral recipients from South Korea and 28 percent from Taiwan accepted firm offers to remain in the United States.

What Do Foreign S&E Doctoral Recipients Who Stay in the United States Do?

Foreign S&E doctoral recipients remaining in the United States do so mainly by entering postdoctoral study. Of the 55,000 foreign students from these major countries of origin who earned S&E doctoral degrees between 1988 and 1996, about 22 percent (12,000) stayed on for postdoctoral study, and 17 percent (9,000) accepted employment in the United States.

Firm employment offers to foreign doctoral recipients are strongly geared toward research and development, mainly within business or industry. The decision to remain for a postdoctoral appointment is, not surprisingly, greatest in fields where post-doctorates are a common career path. Over 50 percent of all foreign students earning doctoral degrees in the biological sciences remained in the United States for postdoctoral experiences; only 5 percent were offered jobs at universities or in industry. In contrast, in computer sciences, only 7 percent remained for postdoctoral experiences, while over 38 percent accepted employment.

Do Foreign S&E Doctoral Recipients Who Plan to Stay Actually Join the U.S. Labor Force?

A recent study of foreign doctoral recipients working and earning wages in the United States (Finn, 1997) shows that about 47 percent of the foreign students on temporary student visas who earned doctorates in 1990 and 1991 were working in the United States in 1995. The majority of the 1990–91 foreign doctoral recipients from India (79 percent) and China (88 percent) were still working in the United States in 1995. In contrast, only 11 percent of South Koreans who completed S&E doctorates from U.S. universities in 1990–91 were working in the United States in 1995.

Do Foreign S&E Doctorates Stay in the United States in the Long Term?

The same study looked at foreign doctoral recipients from 1970–72. Finn estimated that 47 percent were working in the United States in 1995, and that the stay rate for that group was around 50 percent during the 25 years leading up to 1995. There is no evidence of significant net return migration of these scientists and engineers after 10 or 20 years of work experience in the United States. The fairly constant stay rates indicate that any tendency of the 1970–72 cohorts to leave the United States after gaining work experience here has been largely offset by others from the same cohort returning to the United States after going abroad. Remaining in the United States does not represent a complete brain drain on their home country. Choi has shown extensive networking by Asian-born faculty and researchers working in the United States to advise, disseminate information, and assist in building their home-country S&T infrastructure. This is particularly true for the foreign-born faculty in S&E departments. In 1993, foreign-born faculty in U.S. higher education represented 37 percent of the engineering professors and over a quarter of the mathematics and computer science teachers.

Conclusions

Data on mobility and stay rates of foreign-born S&Es working in the United States support the notion of brain circulation for some countries (Taiwan and South Korea) and somewhat more brain drain for other countries (China and India). In the aggregate, roughly half of all foreign doctoral recipients leave the United States immediately after completing their graduate education, and others leave after some years of teaching or industrial experience in the United States. In addition, some of those who remain in the United States network with home-country scientists. More research is needed, however, on the activities of foreign doctoral recipients who return to their home countries. For example, we need to know more about their contributions to their home countries' S&T infrastructure, including research, teaching, and science administration. Also, we need to be able to identify patterns of circulation and lengths of stay that are beneficial to the United States, the countries of origin, and the diffusion of S&E knowledge in the world. Information presented in this issue brief on foreign doctoral recipients and their planned stay rates comes mainly from the forthcoming NSF report: *Statistical Profiles of Foreign Doctoral Recipients in Science and Engineering: Plans to Locate in the United States.* Data for this report were collected in the Survey of Earned Doctorates (SED) conducted by the National Opinion Research Center (NORC) for NSF and four other Federal agencies. Information on foreign-born scientists and engineers in the U.S. labor force is from the NSF Division of Science Resources Studies (SRS), SESTAT data system, available on the SRS World Wide Web site (http://www.nsf.gov/sbe/srs/).

POSTSCRIPT

Is There a Global Brain Drain?

The perceived brain drain from one country to another is typically, although not exclusively, from developing countries to developed countries. In the minority of cases in which the flow is from one developed country to another, it is likely to be the consequence of the immigrant's inability to maximize his or her employment potential in the home country.

Carrington's article is based on his earlier analysis of migration from 61 developing countries to the United States. His conclusion is that education of the immigrant plays an important role in the immigration decision. The largest group of immigrants in his study came with a secondary education from other North American countries; the second-largest group consisted of highly educated immigrants from Asia and the Pacific. Among this latter group, the number of immigrants from the Philippines is the largest, with a majority having a tertiary education. The same can be said of a majority of immigrants from Africa. Carrington's basic conclusion is that many countries are experiencing a sizable brain drain.

Carrington is quick to point out a number of methodological problems (not of his making) associated with the study. The principal limitation is the large number of unreliable estimates or missing data. Much work needs to be done before definitive statements about the brain drain in the author's sample can be made with confidence.

Johnson and Regets's report begins with the observation that "foreign-born scientists and engineers . . . contribute significantly to the brain power of the United States." The authors caution, however, that one ought not to conclude that the situation qualifies as a brain drain or a one-way ticket from the countries of origin, as was the case several decades ago. Rather, they have coined the phrase "brain circulation" to characterize the current situation, which they suggest features many foreign-born scientists and engineers' returning home after finishing their education or engaging in a cycle of work abroad. Their general conclusion is that about half of all foreign doctoral students leave the United States after obtaining their degrees. The percentage is not uniform among the countries of origin, however. And some of those who stay in the United States network with their counterparts back home, although the exact percentage is unknown.

The National Science Foundation continues to study the issue, releasing its findings periodically. One such analysis is *Statistical Profiles of Foreign Doctoral Recipients in Science and Engineering: Plans to Stay in the United States* authored by Jean M. Johnson (November 1998). Hyaeweol Choi examines America's Asian scientific community in *An International Scientific Community: Asian Scholars in the United States* (Praeger, 1995). Xiaonan Cao presents a thoughtful article about the subject in "Debating 'Brain Drain' in the Context of Globalisation," *Compare* (vol. 26, no. 3, 1996). Finally, W. T. Gould and Anne M. Findlay, eds., *Population Migration and the Changing World Order* (John Wiley, 1994) cites several examples of brain drain, with special emphasis on that from Ireland.

On the Internet . . .

Globalization: Threat or Opportunity?

This Web site contains the article, "Globalization: Threat or Opportunity?" and was created by the International Monetary Fund. This article discusses aspects of globalization such as current trends, positive and negative outcomes, and the role of institutions and organizations. Also included on this site is an article entitled, "The Challenge of Globalization in Africa."

http://www.imf.org/external/np/exr/ib/2000/041200.htm

Center for Democracy and Technology

The Center for Democracy and Technology (CDT) works to preserve and enhance free expression on the Internet as well as protecting privacy. Democratic values are promoted through public policy advocacy, online grassroots organizing, and public education campaigns. Explore this site to gain knowledge on the CDT's proposals for achieving its goals, as well as its thoughts on other Internet issues such as digital authentication, bandwidth, terrorism, and access to government information.

http://www.cdt.org

Popular Culture Association: American Culture Association

The Popular Culture Association: American Culture Association Web site fosters intellectual discussion of popular culture. View the discussion logs by month or by specific topic. Also included on this site is a list of links to sites on specific aspects of American culture.

http://www2.h-net.msu.edu/~pcaaca/

PART 4

The Flow of Information and Ideas

*T*he global information network and the technology that drives it are creating a global communication village. Fiber optic lines carry information, products, ideas, values, and cultures across the globe. As a result, millions are affected by what they encounter as they affect what is produced. The impact has yet to be calculated, but we know that it is both uplifting and unsettling.

This section examines the impact on people around the globe of international communication networks and the actors who manage them.

- Is Globalization a Positive Development for the International Community?

- Will the Digital/Computer World Lead to Greater Individual Freedom?

- Is the Globalization of American Culture a Positive Development?

ISSUE 13

Is Globalization a Positive Development for the International Community?

YES: Thomas L. Friedman, from "DOScapital," *Foreign Policy* (Fall 1999)

NO: Peter L. Berger, from "Four Faces of Global Culture," *The National Interest* (Fall 1997)

ISSUE SUMMARY

YES: Journalist Thomas L. Friedman argues that globalization is built around three balances, each of which makes the system more individualized and democratic by empowering individuals on the world stage.

NO: Peter L. Berger, a professor of sociology and theology, argues that globalization is a complex process that could be positive but more likely will lead to the "vulgar homogenization" of indigenous cultures and people.

Globalization is a phenomenon and a revolution. It is sweeping the world with increasing speed and changing the global landscape into something new and different. Yet, like all such trends, its meaning, development, and impact puzzle many. We talk about globalization and experience its positive and negative effects, but few of us really understand the forces that are at work in the global political economy.

When people use their cell phones, log onto the Internet, view events from around the world on live television, and experience varying cultures in their own backyards, they begin to believe that this process of globalization is a good thing that will bring a variety of new and sophisticated changes to people's lives. Many aspects of this technological revolution provide fun, ease, and sophistication to people's daily lives. Yet the recent anti–World Trade Organization (WTO) riots in Seattle, Washington, and Washington, D.C., are graphic illustrations of the fact that not everyone believes that globalization is a good thing. Many Americans who have felt left out of the global economic boom as well as Latin Americans, Africans, and Asians who feel that their job skills and abilities are being exploited by multinational corporations (MNCs) in a global division of labor believe that this system does not meet their needs. Local cultures that understand that Walmart and McDonald's bring cultural change and harm rather than cheap products and convenience criticize the process. In this way, globalization, like all revolutionary forces, polarizes people, alters the fabric of their lives, and creates rifts within and between people.

Many in the West along with the prominent and elite—among MNCs, educators, and policymakers—seem to have embraced globalization. They argue that it helps to streamline economic systems, disciplines labor and management, brings forth new technologies and ideas, and fuels economic growth. They point to the relative prosperity of many Western countries and argue that this is proof of globalization's positive effects. They see little of the problems that critics identify. In fact, those who recognize some structural problems in the system argue that despite these issues, globalization is like an inevitable tide of history, unfortunate for some but unyielding and impossible to change. Any problems that are created by this trend, they say, can be solved.

Many poor and middle-class workers, as well as hundreds of millions across the developing world, view globalization as an economic and cultural wave that tears at the fabric of centuries-old societies. They see jobs emerging and disappearing in a matter of months, people moving across the landscape in record numbers, elites amassing huge fortunes while local cultures and traditions are swept away, and local youth being seduced by promises of American material wealth and distanced from their own cultural roots. These critics look past the allure of globalization and focus on the disquieting impact of rapid and system-wide change.

The irony of such a far-ranging and rapid historical process such as globalization is that both proponents and critics may be right. The realities of globalization are both intriguing and alarming. As technology and the global infrastructure expands, ideas, methods, and services are developed and disseminated to greater and greater numbers of people. As a result, societies and values are altered, some for the better and others for the worse.

In the selections that follow, the authors explore the positive and negative impacts of globalization and come to different conclusions. Thomas L. Friedman argues that globalization has an empowering effect. He surmises that individuals will gain greater control over their own destinies and that life will become more democratic, with greater freedom of choice as a result. Peter L. Berger argues that globalization is sweeping away diversity and differences, promoting one culture based largely on Western consumerism. This, he argues, is inherently negative and destabilizing for hundreds of millions across the rest of the world.

Thomas L. Friedman **YES**

DOScapital

If there can be a statute of limitations on crimes, then surely there must be a statute of limitations on foreign-policy cliches. With that in mind, I hereby declare the "post-Cold War world" over.

For the last ten years, we have talked about this "post-Cold War world." That is, we have defined the world by what it wasn't because we didn't know what it was. But a new international system has now clearly replaced the Cold War: globalization. That's right, globalization—the integration of markets, finance, and technologies in a way that is shrinking the world from a size medium to a size small and enabling each of us to reach around the world farther, faster, and cheaper than ever before. It's not just an economic trend, and it's not just some fad. Like all previous international systems, it is directly or indirectly shaping the domestic politics, economic policies, and foreign relations of virtually every country.

As an international system, the Cold War had its own structure of power: the balance between the United States and the USSR, including their respective allies. The Cold War had its own rules: In foreign affairs, neither superpower would encroach on the other's core sphere of influence, while in economics, underdeveloped countries would focus on nurturing their own national industries, developing countries on export-led growth, communist countries on autarky [economic self-sufficiency], and Western economies on regulated trade. The Cold War had its own dominant ideas: the clash between communism and capitalism, as well as detente, nonalignment, and perestroika. The Cold War had its own demographic trends: The movement of peoples from East to West was largely frozen by the Iron Curtain; the movement from South to North was a more steady flow. The Cold War had its own defining technologies: Nuclear weapons and the Second Industrial Revolution were dominant, but for many developing countries, the hammer and sickle were still relevant tools. Finally, the Cold War had its own defining anxiety: nuclear annihilation. When taken all together, this Cold War system didn't shape everything, but it shaped many things.

Today's globalization system has some very different attributes, rules, incentives, and characteristics, but it is equally influential. The Cold War system was characterized by one overarching feature: division. The world was chopped

From Thomas L. Friedman, "DOScapital," *Foreign Policy*, no. 116 (Fall 1999). Copyright © 1999 by The Carnegie Endowment for International Peace. Reprinted by permission of *Foreign Policy*.

up, and both threats and opportunities tended to grow out of whom you were divided from. Appropriately, that Cold War system was symbolized by a single image: the Wall. The globalization system also has one overarching characteristic: integration. Today, both the threats and opportunities facing a country increasingly grow from whom it is connected to. This system is also captured by a single symbol: the World Wide Web. So in the broadest sense, we have gone from a system built around walls to a system increasingly built around networks.

Once a country makes the leap into the system of globalization, its elite begin to internalize this perspective of integration and try to locate themselves within a global context. I was visiting Amman, Jordan, in the summer of 1998 when I met my friend, Rami Khouri, the country's leading political columnist, for coffee at the Hotel Inter-Continental. We sat down, and I asked him what was new. The first thing he said to me was "Jordan was just added to CNN's worldwide weather highlights." What Rami was saying was that it is important for Jordan to know that those institutions that think globally believe it is now worth knowing what the weather is like in Amman. It makes Jordanians feel more important and holds out the hope that they will profit by having more tourists or global investors visiting. The day after seeing Rami I happened to interview Jacob Frenkel, governor of the Bank of Israel and a University of Chicago-trained economist. He remarked to me: "Before, when we talked about macroeconomics, we started by looking at the local markets, local financial system, and the interrelationship between them, and then, as an afterthought, we looked at the international economy. There was a feeling that what we do is primarily our own business and then there are some outlets where we will sell abroad. Now, we reverse the perspective. Let's not ask what markets we should export to after having decided what to produce; rather, let's first study the global framework within which we operate and then decide what to produce. It changes your whole perspective."

Integration has been driven in large part by globalization's defining technologies: computerization, miniaturization, digitization, satellite communications, fiber optics, and the Internet. And that integration, in turn, has led to many other differences between the Cold War and globalization systems.

Unlike the Cold War system, globalization has its own dominant culture, which is why integration tends to be homogenizing. In previous eras, cultural homogenization happened on a regional scale—the Romanization of Western Europe and the Mediterranean world, the Islamization of Central Asia, the Middle East, North Africa, and Spain by the Arabs, or the Russification of Eastern and Central Europe, and parts of Eurasia, under the Soviets. Culturally speaking, globalization is largely the spread (for better and for worse) of Americanization from Big Macs and iMacs to Mickey Mouse.

Whereas the defining measurement of the Cold War was weight, particularly the throw-weight of missiles, the defining measurement of the globalization system is speed—the speed of commerce, travel, communication, and innovation. The Cold War was about Einstein's mass-energy equation, $e = mc^2$. Globalization is about Moore's Law, which states that the performance power of microprocessors will double every 18 months. The defining document of the

Cold War system was "the treaty." The defining document of the globalization system is "the deal." If the defining anxiety of the Cold War was fear of annihilation from an enemy you knew all too well in a world struggle that was fixed and stable, the defining anxiety in globalization is fear of rapid change from an enemy you cannot see, touch, or feel—a sense that your job, community, or workplace can be changed at any moment by anonymous economic and technological forces that are anything but stable.

If the defining economists of the Cold War system were Karl Marx and John Maynard Keynes, each of whom wanted to tame capitalism, the defining economists of the globalization system are Joseph Schumpeter and Intel chairman Andy Grove, who prefer to unleash capitalism. Schumpeter, a former Austrian minister of finance and Harvard University professor, expressed the view in his classic work *Capitalism, Socialism, and Democracy* (1942) that the essence of capitalism is the process of "creative destruction"—the perpetual cycle of destroying old and less efficient products or services and replacing them with new, more efficient ones. Grove took Schumpeter's insight that only the paranoid survive for the title of his book about life in Silicon Valley and made it in many ways the business model of globalization capitalism. Grove helped popularize the view that dramatic, industry-transforming innovations are taking place today faster and faster. Thanks to these technological breakthroughs, the speed at which your latest invention can be made obsolete or turned into a commodity is now lightning quick. Therefore, only the paranoid will survive —only those who constantly look over their shoulders to see who is creating something new that could destroy them and then do what they must to stay one step ahead. There will be fewer and fewer walls to protect us.

If the Cold War were a sport, it would be sumo wrestling, says Johns Hopkins University professor Michael Mandelbaum. "It would be two big fat guys in a ring, with all sorts of posturing and rituals and stomping of feet, but actually very little contact until the end of the match, when there is a brief moment of shoving and the loser gets pushed out of the ring, but nobody gets killed." By contrast, if globalization were a sport, it would be the 100-meter dash, over and over and over. No matter how many times you win, you have to race again the next day. And if you lose by just one one-hundredth of a second, it can be as if you lost by an hour.

Last, and most important, globalization has its own defining structure of power, which is much more complex than the Cold War structure. The Cold War system was built exclusively around nation-states, and it was balanced at the center by two superpowers. The globalization system, by contrast, is built around three balances, which overlap and affect one another.

The first is the traditional balance between nation-states. In the globalization system, this balance still matters. It can still explain a lot of the news you read on the front page of the paper, be it the containment of Iraq in the Middle East or the expansion of NATO against Russia in Central Europe.

The second critical balance is between nation-states and global markets. These global markets are made up of millions of investors moving money around the world with the click of a mouse. I call them the "Electronic herd." They gather in key global financial centers, such as Frankfurt, Hong Kong,

London, and New York—the "supermarkets." The United States can destroy you by dropping bombs and the supermarkets can destroy you by downgrading your bonds. Who ousted President Suharto in Indonesia? It was not another superpower, it was the supermarkets.

The third balance in the globalization system—the one that is really the newest of all—is the balance between individuals and nation-states. Because globalization has brought down many of the walls that limited the movement and reach of people, and because it has simultaneously wired the world into networks, it gives more direct power to individuals than at any time in history. So we have today not only a superpower, not only supermarkets, but also super-empowered individuals. Some of these super-empowered individuals are quite angry, some of them quite constructive but all are now able to act directly on the world stage without the traditional mediation of governments or even corporations.

Jody Williams won the Nobel Peace Prize in 1997 for her contribution to the International Campaign to Ban Landmines. She managed to build an international coalition in favor of a landmine ban without much government help and in the face of opposition from the major powers. What did she say was her secret weapon for organizing 1,000 different human rights and arms control groups on six continents? "E-mail."

By contrast, Ramzi Ahmed Yousef, the mastermind of the February 26, 1993, World Trade Center bombing in New York, is the quintessential "super-empowered angry man." Think about him for a minute. What was his program? What was his ideology? After all, he tried to blow up two of the tallest buildings in America. Did he want an Islamic state in Brooklyn? Did he want a Palestinian state in New Jersey? No. He just wanted to blow up two of the tallest buildings in America. He told the Federal District Court in Manhattan that his goal was to set off an explosion that would cause one World Trade Center tower to fall onto the other and kill 250,000 civilians. Yousef's message was that he had no message, other than to rip up the message coming from the all-powerful America to his society. Globalization (and Americanization) had gotten in his face and, at the same time, had empowered him as an individual to do something about it. A big part of the U.S. government's conspiracy case against Yousef (besides trying to blow up the World Trade Center in 1993, he planned to blow up a dozen American airliners in Asia in January 1995) relied on files found in the off-white Toshiba laptop computer that Philippine police say Yousef abandoned as he fled his Manila apartment in January 1995, shortly before his arrest. When investigators got hold of Yousef's laptop and broke into its files, they found flight schedules, projected detonation times, and sample identification documents bearing photographs of some of his co-conspirators. I loved that—Ramzi Yousef kept all his plots on the C drive of his Toshiba laptop! One should have no illusions, though. The super-empowered angry men are out there, and they present the most immediate threat today to the United States and the stability of the new globalization system. It's not because Ramzi Yousef can ever be a superpower. It's because in today's world, so many people can be Ramzi Yousef.

So, we are no longer in some messy, incoherent "post-Cold War world." We are in a new international system, defined by globalization, with its own moving parts and characteristics. We are still a long way from fully understanding how this system is going to work. Indeed, if this were the Cold War, the year would be about 1946. That is, we understand as much about how this new system is going to work as we understood about how the Cold War would work in the year Churchill gave his "Iron Curtain" speech.

Nevertheless, it's time we recognize that there is a new system emerging, start trying to analyze events within it, and give it its own name. I will start the bidding. I propose that we call it "DOScapital."

NO

Peter L. Berger

Four Faces of Global Culture

The term "globalization" has become somewhat of a cliche. It serves to explain everything from the woes of the German coal industry to the sexual habits of Japanese teenagers. Most cliches have a degree of factual validity; so does this one. There can be no doubt about the fact of an ever more interconnected global economy, with vast social and political implications, and there is no shortage of thoughtful, if inconclusive, reflection about this great transformation. It has also been noted that there is a cultural dimension, the obvious result of an immense increase in worldwide communication. If there is economic globalization, there is also cultural globalization. To say this, however, is only to raise the question of what such a phenomenon amounts to.

Again, there can be no doubt about some of the facts. One can watch CNN in an African safari lodge. German investors converse in English with Chinese apparatchiks. Peruvian social workers spout the rhetoric of American feminism. Protestant preachers are active in India, while missionaries of the Hare Krishna movement return the compliment in Middle America. Both hope and fear attach to these facts.

The hope is that a putative global culture will help to create a more peaceful world. If a global culture is in the making, then perhaps a global civil society might come into being. Ever since John Locke re-emerged from Eastern Europe speaking with a Polish accent, a great amount of hope has been invested in the notion of civil society, that agglomerate of intermediate institutions that Tocqueville saw as the foundation of a vital democracy. Civil society depends on a consensus on civic virtues, and that, after all, is what a culture is supposed to supply. The French sociologist Daniele Hervieu-Leger (in her contribution to the forthcoming volume *The Limits of Social Cohesion,* edited by me) speaks of an "ecumenism of human rights." The same idea is conveyed in a much cruder form by the advertisements of the Benetton company. Whether the idea is couched in sophisticated or crude terms, it too has an evident factual basis. It is also reasonable to hope that a world in which there would be a greater consensus on human rights would also be a more peaceful world.

But there is also fear attached to the prospect of cultural globalization, fear of a worldwide "airport culture" in which the rich diversity of human civilizations will be homogenized and vulgarized. This fear has been vocalized in

From Peter L. Berger, "Four Faces of Global Culture," *The National Interest,* no. 49 (Fall 1997). Copyright © 1997 by National Affairs, Inc. Reprinted by permission of *The National Interest.*

the rhetoric of "Asian values" that has attained a certain political significance in recent years, as well as in the rhetoric of the various movements of Islamic resurgence. Similar fear, in less virulent form, can be observed elsewhere, for example in the worries about cultural homogenization among Euroskeptics. One of the arguments made by those who opposed Austria's joining the European Union was that Austrians would no longer be able to refer to potatoes as Erdapfel, a homey word that was suddenly imbued with the genius of Austrian identity, but would have to use the High German word Kartoffeln. Of course this was silly. But the desire to preserve distinct cultural traditions and a distinct cultural identity in the intense economic and political pressure cooker of the new Europe is not silly at all. The fear, like the hope, is not without foundation.

A more nuanced understanding of cultural globalization will have to take account of both the homogenizing forces and the resistances to them. Benjamin Barber made a move toward such an understanding in his book *Jihad vs. McWorld* (1995). Most recently, and in a more subtle way, Samuel Huntington has discussed the same issues in his *Clash of Civilizations and the Remaking of World Order* (1996), a book to which the present observations are greatly indebted. Huntington, whose view of the contemporary world cannot be accused of being overly optimistic, ends his book with a call to search for commonalities between the contending civilizations, a dialogue of cultures. One need not agree with every aspect of his analysis to agree with his conclusion. A dialogue between cultures, however, presupposes a clearer understanding of all the processes at work, both those of cultural globalization and of resistance to it. It is proposed here that there are at least four distinct processes of cultural globalization going on simultaneously, relating in complex ways both to each other and to the many indigenous cultures on which they impinge.

Davos: From Boardroom to Bedroom

First is what Huntington nicely calls the "Davos culture" (after the annual World Economic Summit that meets in that Swiss luxury resort). This culture is globalized as a direct accompaniment of global economic processes. Its carrier is international business. It has obvious behavioral aspects that are directly functional in economic terms, behavior dictated by the accoutrements of contemporary business. Participants in this culture know how to deal with computers, cellular phones, airline schedules, currency exchange, and the like. But they also dress alike, exhibit the same amicable informality, relieve tensions by similar attempts at humor, and of course most of them interact in English. Since most of these cultural traits are of Western (and mostly American) provenance, individuals coming from different backgrounds must go through a process of socialization that will allow them to engage in this behavior with seemingly effortless spontaneity. This is not always easy. A growing number of consultants in "diversity management" are making a good living advising corporations on how to affect this sort of socialization as smoothly as possible.

But it would be a mistake to think that the "Davos culture" operates only in the offices, boardrooms, and hotel suites in which international business is transacted. It carries over into the lifestyles and presumably also the values of those who participate in it. Thus, for example, the frenetic pace of contemporary business is carried over into the leisure activities and the family life of business people. There is a yuppie style in the corporation, but also in the bodybuilding studio and in the bedroom. And notions of costs, benefits, and maximization spill over from work into private life.

The "Davos culture" is a culture of the elite and (by way of what sociologists call "anticipatory socialization") of those aspiring to join the elite. Its principal social location is in the business world, but since elites intermingle, it also affects at least the political elites. There is, as it were, a yuppie internationale. Some years ago, while the apartheid regime was still in power in South Africa, a friend of mine had lunch with a representative of the African National Congress [ANC] at the United Nations. To my friend's surprise, this individual spent most of the lunch talking about apartment costs in Manhattan. While this yuppification of a representative of what then still understood itself as an anti-capitalist revolutionary movement might have had an ironic aspect, it was a cultural trait that turned out to be very useful a few years later. A number of people from both sides have reported how, when they first met, young ANC exiles and young Afrikaners were surprised by their similar lifestyle preferences and personal values. These were certainly not derived from their respective historical traditions; rather, they were, precisely, commonalities rooted in the "Davos culture." There have been similar reports about the first meetings between young Israelis and Palestinians leading up to the Oslo agreements. Whether one is edified by this spectacle or not, it may be that commonalities in taste make it easier to find common ground politically.

While cultural globalization facilitates interaction between elites, it creates difficulties between these elites and the non-elite populations with whom they must deal. Many moral and ideological conflicts in contemporary societies pit an elite culture against a resentful mass of culturally accredited and economically underprivileged people. As Huntington points out, these resentments may lead to the emergence of a nationalist or religious counter-elite. Also, individuals who participate in the "Davos culture" with reasonable success vary in their ability to balance this participation with other parts of their lives. While some, as previously pointed out, may allow yuppie behavior and values to inundate their private lives, others seek more complicated compromises. On my last visit to Hong Kong I happened to stray into a Buddhist temple and came upon a truly graphic vignette: In front of an altar, facing a large statue of the Buddha, stood a middle-aged man wearing a dark business suit over stocking feet. He was burning incense and at the same time talking on his cellular phone.

Faculty Club International

Both critics and advocates of contemporary global capitalism mainly think in terms of the "Davos culture" and its ramifications in popular culture ("Davos" in interaction with "McWorld"). Yet there are at least two other quite different types of cultural globalization going on. One of these is what one might call the "faculty club culture." Essentially, this is the internationalization of the Western intelligentsia, its values and ideologies. To put it graphically, if the "Davos culture" tries to sell computer systems in India, the "faculty club culture" tries to promote feminism or environmentalism there—a rather different agenda.

While this culture has also penetrated the business world (and in turn has been penetrated by it), its principal carrier is not business. Rather, it is carried by foundations, academic networks, non-governmental organizations, and some governmental and multinational agencies (such as development agencies with social and cultural missions). It too is primarily an elite culture, though here again there are those who aspire to it from the lower echelons of cultural enterprises (say, schoolteachers or social workers who read the books and periodicals that reflect the views emanating from the great cultural centers).

More importantly, the "faculty club culture" spreads its beliefs and values through the educational system, the legal system, various therapeutic institutions, think tanks, and at least some of the media of mass communication. If this culture internationalizes the Western intelligentsia, it also internationalizes the conflicts in which this intelligentsia has been engaged on its home territories. James Hunter has written very insightfully about the American "culture wars" (first in his 1991 book with that title). These conflicts can now be observed worldwide, though always of course subject to local modifications.

A good example of this second process of cultural globalization is the anti-smoking movement, arguably one of the most successful movements in developed societies over the last twenty years or so. Before then it was a small, marginal sect, hardly noticed in public discourse; today, especially in North America and Western Europe, it has largely achieved the goal proclaimed early on by one of its spokesmen—to make smoking an activity engaged in privately by consenting adults. The reasons for this stunning success need not concern us here. The point is that this movement, clearly a product of Western intellectuals, was disseminated worldwide by an alliance of governmental and nongovernmental organizations. In a series of conferences, the World Health Organization propagated the anti-smoking cause internationally. At one of the early conferences the travel expenses of all participants from developing societies were paid by the Scandinavian development agencies (the conference was held in Stockholm). These participants, mostly from health and education ministries, came from countries with horrendous health problems and the campaign against smoking was not high on their list of priorities. As was to be expected, they re-ordered their priorities given the incentives to do so. Ironically, the concepts of neo-Marxist dependency theory, which have not been very good at interpreting the transformations of advanced capitalism, fit rather well in the globalization of the "faculty club culture." Here there is overwhelming "dependency", with an indigenous "comprador class" carrying out the agendas devised in the cultural centers of the "metropolis."

There are obvious tensions between the first and second processes of cultural globalization. Clearly, the anti-smoking movement collides with the interests of the tobacco industry. More generally, both feminism and environmentalism collide with notions of economic efficiency held by the international economic elite. At this time, the most visible conflict is between the "ecumenism of human rights", carried out by a multitude of nongovernmental organizations, and the belief of the "Davos culture" that all good things, including human rights, will eventually result from the global establishment of successful market economies. And of course there are also tensions between the "faculty club culture" and various indigenous movements of cultural revitalization. The recent women's conference in Beijing pitted mostly Western feminists against an odd alliance of Islamists and the Vatican. Most significant politically, the Western-centered human rights community is meeting with strong opposition in a sizable number of non-Western countries.

The McWorld Culture

Third, of course, is popular culture. Here Barber's term "McWorld" fits best. And it is this culture that is most credibly subsumed under the category of Westernization, since virtually all of it is of Western, and more specifically American, provenance. Young people throughout the world dance to American music, wiggling their behinds in American jeans and wearing T-shirts with messages (often misspelled) about American universities and other consumer items. Older people watch American sitcoms on television and go to American movies. Everyone, young and old, grows taller and fatter on American fast foods. Here indeed is a case of cultural hegemony, and it is not surprising that others, such as French ministers of culture and Iranian mullahs (not to mention the now defunct Soviet Komsomol functionaries), greatly resent the fact.

These critics of "cultural imperialism" also understand that the diffusion of popular culture is not just a matter of outward behavior. It carries a significant freight of beliefs and values. Take the case of rock music. Its attraction is not just due to a particular preference for loud, rhythmic sound and dangerously athletic dancing. Rock music also symbolizes a whole cluster of cultural values—concerning self-expression, spontaneity, released sexuality, and, perhaps most importantly, defiance of the alleged stodginess of tradition. The consumption of American popular culture has, as it were, sacramental character. Paraphrasing the *Book of Common Prayer,* these items of consumption are visible signs of an invisible grace—or curse. The hegemony becomes clear by the asymmetry of consumption. Mexicans eat hamburguesas, Americans eat tacos. But the Mexicans are consuming whole chunks of American values "in, with, and under" the American hamburgers; the Americans are certainly not absorbing non-culinary aspects of Mexican culture by eating tacos.

A couple of years ago, I met a representative of Hallmark greeting cards for the Chinese province of Guandong (a market of some sixty million people). He was happy to report that his product was selling very well. When asked which greeting cards were most popular, he said Valentine cards. "You see, young Chinese men are quite shy with members of the opposite sex. It is difficult for them to express their feelings. It is much easier to send a Valentine card." I did not know what to say to this and mumbled something about how there must be a lot of work translating the texts into Chinese. "Oh no", he said, "they want the cards to be in English."

The people in charge of the globalization of popular culture are, of course, members or aspiring members of the "Davos" elite. The aforementioned Hallmark representative evinced all the characteristics of a successful, with-it yuppie. But the consumers of these cultural exports are a vastly broader population. The indigenous reactions once again vary from complete acceptance to complete rejection, with many degrees of compromise in between. Complete acceptance generally leads to a conflict between the generations, and presumably an important motive for such acceptance among young people is to outrage one's parents. Complete rejection is difficult, even under repressive regimes (the Komsomol functionaries, after trying repression, finally had to compromise by inventing something they would call "Soviet rock"). There are many and complex degrees of compromise, some of them puzzling to the outsider.

A few years ago I visited the Meiji Grand Shrine in Tokyo. I was in the company of my hosts, who were pious adherents of Shinto. When inviting me to go to the Shrine with them, they asked me solicitously whether my religious feelings would be offended by their venerating the Meiji Emperor; I replied courteously (and perhaps rashly) that this would be quite all right. I then stood with them, holding incense sticks in my hands and bowing to the deafening accompaniment of drums being beaten by a row of Shinto priests lined up behind us. I re-emerged from the Shrine somewhat dazed, reflecting that I had just been praying to a dead Japanese potentate. Outside the Shrine was a large park filled with hundreds of young people, fervently dancing to rock music blaring from numerous portable radios. I had noticed some young people inside the Shrine and wondered whether they were now joining the crowd in the park. I asked my hosts whether they saw any contradiction between what was going on inside and outside the Shrine. They were actually puzzled by my question. Certainly not, they replied after a moment of reflection, "Japanese culture has always been successful in integrating elements coming from abroad." One of the most interesting questions about contemporary Japan is whether my hosts were correct in their sanguine view about the absorptive capacity of Japanese culture.

Evangelical Protestantism

Fourthly (though perhaps not finally), a distinctive process of globalization is provided by Evangelical Protestantism, especially in its Pentecostal version (which accounts for something like 80 percent of its worldwide growth). Its globalizing force is best seen by comparing it with the other dynamic religious phenomenon of our time, that of the Islamic resurgence. While the latter has been limited to countries that have always been Muslim and to Muslim diaspora communities, Evangelical Protestantism has been exploding in parts of the world to which this religious tradition has always been alien, indeed, mostly unknown. The most dramatic explosion has occurred in Latin America (it was magisterially described in David Martin's 1990 book, *Tongues of Fire*). But the same variety of Protestantism has been rapidly growing in East Asia (with the notable exception of Japan), in all the Chinese societies (including, despite repression, the People's Republic), in the Philippines, the South Pacific, and throughout sub-Saharan Africa. There are recent, as yet vague, accounts of an incipient growth in Eastern Europe. And while the origins of this religion are in the United States (the "metropolis"), its new incarnations are thoroughly indigenized and independent of foreign missionaries or financial support.

Evangelical Protestantism brings about a cultural revolution in its new territories (in that respect it is very different from its social function on its American homeground). It brings about radical changes in the relations between men and women, in the upbringing and education of children, in the attitudes toward traditional hierarchies. Most importantly, it inculcates precisely that "Protestant ethic" that Max Weber analyzed as an important ingredient in the genesis of modern capitalism—a disciplined, frugal, and rationally oriented approach to work. Thus, despite its indigenization (converts in Mexico and Guatemala sing American gospel songs in Mayan translation), Evangelical Protestantism is the carrier of a pluralistic and modernizing culture whose original location is in the North Atlantic societies.

It is not clear at this point how this startlingly new phenomenon relates to the previously enumerated processes of cultural globalization. It certainly enters into conflicts with indigenous cultures. Most of the persecution of Christians recently publicized by human rights organizations—notably in China, in the Islamic world, and (sporadically) in Latin America—has been directed against Evangelical Protestants. What is clear is that this type of Protestantism is creating a new international culture, increasingly self-conscious as such (here the relation to American Evangelicals is relevant), with vast social, economic, and political ramifications. While the new Protestantism should not be misunderstood as a movement of social protest or reform (its motives are overwhelmingly personal and religious), it has large and unintended consequences. These are decidedly favorable to pluralism, to the market economy, and to democracy. It should be observed here that there may be other globalizing popular movements, but Evangelicalism is clearly the most dynamic.

Four faces of globalization: each is distinctive, each relates to the other three in complex ways. Yet they have important common features. The two perhaps most important features have already been mentioned—their Western, principally American, provenance, and related to this, their relation to the English language.

The Western provenance of these processes has given credibility to the frequent charge that they are part and parcel of Western imperialism, with the United States being the core of this malevolent phenomenon. The charge will not hold up. The "Davos culture" is today fully internationalized. It is centered as much in Tokyo and Singapore as it is in New York and London. One could more plausibly speak of an imperialism of the global capitalist system, but that is simply to attach a pejorative term to the fact of an immensely powerful global reality. The concepts of neo-Marxist theory simply do not fit it. As already mentioned, those concepts are somewhat more apt in describing the globalization of the "faculty club culture." Feminist or environmentalist agitators in Bangladesh can indeed be described as agents of a Western-based "cultural imperialism", but it is difficult to see how their activity benefits global capitalism. Multinational corporations do indeed make large profits from the distribution of popular culture, but there is no coercion involved in their success. No one is forcing Japanese teenagers to enjoy rock music or young men in China to express their emotions in terms derived from American romanticism.

Claudio Veliz (in his 1994 book *The New World of the Gothic Fox*) has made this point very tellingly in his description of the collapse of Latin American tradition before the onslaught of "Anglo-Saxon" values and lifestyles, notably those connected with a pluralistic society. He has used a good metaphor to denote this process, proposing that "Anglo-Saxon" culture is now in its "Hellenistic" phase. That is, it is no longer diffused by means of imperial power, British or American; rather, it has become a cultural force in itself, with large numbers of people clamoring to share it. As to Evangelical Protestantism, both leftist intellectuals and Roman Catholic bishops have portrayed it as a gigantic CIA plot, especially in Latin America, but a look at the empirical evidence presents a very different picture, one of a vital, autonomous movement no longer dependent on support from the outside.

If cultural globalization today represents the "Hellenistic" phase of a civilization originating in the northern parts of Europe and America, the English language is its koine (the "basic Greek" that served as the lingua franca of late classical antiquity and that, among other things, became the language of the New Testament). We live, as Veliz puts it, in "a world made in English", and he points out that no other language appears to be a viable successor to English in the foreseeable future. By now there are very straightforward practical reasons for this hegemony of the English language. However much this may enrage intellectuals in certain places (France, for example, or Quebec), English has become the medium of international economic, technological, and scientific communication. The millions of people learning English all over the world do so in order to participate in this global communication, not (with few exceptions) because they want to read Shakespeare or Melville in the original. However, one does not use a language innocently. Every language carries a freight of values, of sensibilities, of approaches to reality, all of which insinuate themselves into the consciousness of those who speak it. It makes sense to assume that the attractiveness of English, especially in its American form, is due at least in part to its capacity to express the sensibilities of a dynamic, pluralistic, and rationally innovative world. This is even true of Evangelical Protestantism, which mostly expresses itself in languages other than English, but whose leaders and young people learn English in order to be in touch with the Evangelical centers in the United States. In doing so, they may get more than they bargained for. The road from the Christian Broadcasting Network to Oprah Winfrey is disturbingly straight.

The picture I have sketched is huge and exceedingly complex. There are many aspects of it that are not yet fully understood. There is a very large research agenda here. But one conclusion can be ventured: If one is to heed Huntington's call for a dialogue between cultures, one must pay as much attention to the manner in which the different processes of cultural globalization relate to each other as to their relation with many indigenous cultures. This then will not just be a dialogue between "the West and the rest", but a considerably more complicated enterprise.

POSTSCRIPT

Is Globalization a Positive Development for the International Community?

It is hard to argue that this kind of revolution is all positive or all negative. Many will find the allure of technological growth and expansion too much to resist. They will adopt values and ethics that seem compatible with a materialistic Western culture. And they will embrace speed over substance, technical expertise over knowledge, and wealth over fulfillment.

Others will reject this revolution. They will find its promotion of materialism and Western cultural values abhorrent and against their own sense of humanity and being. They will seek enrichment in tradition and values rooted in their cultural pasts. This resistance will take many forms. It will be political and social, and it will involve actions ranging from protests and voting to division and violence.

Trying to determine whether a force as dominant and all encompassing as globalization is positive or negative is like determining whether the environment is harsh or beautiful. It is both. One can say that in the short term, globalization will be destabilizing for many millions of people because the changes that it brings will cause some fundamental shifts in beliefs, values, and ideas. Once that period is past, it is conceivable that a more stable environment will result as people come to grips with globalization and either learn to embrace it, cope with it, or keep it at bay.

The literature on globalization is growing rapidly, much of it centering on defining its parameters and evaluating its impact. One important work that presents a deeper understanding of globalization is Thomas L. Friedman's best-seller *The Lexus and the Olive Tree* (Farrar, Straus & Giroux, 1999), which provides a positive view of the globalization movement. Two counterperspectives are William Greider's *One World Ready or Not: The Manic Logic of Global Capitalism* (Simon & Schuster, 1997) and David Korten's *When Corporations Rule the World* (Kumarian Press, 1996).

The literature that will help us to understand the full scope of globalization has not yet been written. Also, the determination of globalization's positive or negative impact on the international system has yet to be decided. For certain, globalization will bring profound changes that will cause people from the United States to Zimbabwe to rethink assumptions and beliefs about how the world works. And equally certain is the realization that globalization will empower some people but that it will also leave others out, helping to maintain and perhaps exacerbate the divisions that already exist in global society.

ISSUE 14

Will the Digital/Computer World Lead to Greater Individual Freedom?

YES: Paul Starr, from "Cyberpower and Freedom," *The American Prospect* (July/August 1997)

NO: Jerry Kang, from "Cyberspace Privacy: A Primer and Proposal," *Human Rights* (Winter 1999)

ISSUE SUMMARY

YES: Professor of sociology Paul Starr argues that the information revolution will help to create a period of individual freedom empowered by computer technology.

NO: Professor of law Jerry Kang argues that privacy, which is fundamental to the concept of freedom, is severely threatened by the current love of cyberspace. He suggests that the U.S. Congress and, by extension, individual states should take action to ensure individual privacy in cyberspace.

Scanning the Internet for products, services, friends, lovers, and information has become an obsession for some people, a necessity for others, and a desire for still others. Forty-six percent of all U.S. households have a computer. Most of these have Internet access. Experts estimate that by the end of the decade, over 80 percent of U.S. households will have a computer and Internet access. In an increasingly wireless world, these numbers will explode in the years to come. New technologies, such as the all-in-one device (computer, television, and telephone), will solidify the presence of the computer in the Western home. In economic terms, the largest growth businesses are Web-based, with estimates running from a conservative $25 billion to an astounding $1 trillion in financial impact over the next decade.

The ease with which people can find information, purchase products, and seek out communication and companionship makes the computer and cyberspace appealing. From information storage and retrieval to communicating around the globe, the computer is fast becoming a necessary tool for many. Educators and students with computer access can search and retrieve information, explore new and heretofore inaccessible data, and make rare the age-old complaint heard by many professors that "I can't write on this topic because there is not enough information on the subject."

Yet not all people have access to Internet services, and those that do often do not know how to utilize the technology to empower themselves. In fact, most of the world does not have widespread access to this technology and are therefore left out of its potential benefits. Many who do have access become caught in a growing web of information, making their personal needs common knowledge and, indeed, public record. As people surf around the Internet, they leave trails of information about their money, buying habits, personal tastes, and thoughts. In essence, people leave volumes of personal material that can be collected, stored, and used to market, investigate, or monitor those on the information superhighway.

The digital/computer age brings with it a variety of interesting and conflicting experiences. One can scan the Internet for products and items not found elsewhere. A person can obtain valuable information, research his or her ancestry, and experience virtual tours of faraway places. A computer-active person can speak with people in far-off lands, talk to his or her leaders, and solicit information from a growing variety of sources. One can also have one's bank accounts searched and drained, personal information collected and distributed, private messages recorded and read, and rights as an individual violated without one's knowledge. In some ways, logging on and being wired in have become a form of gambling with information, privacy, and freedom.

Privacy, which is fundamental to the conduct of political, economic, and social relations, is at risk in a cyberworld with little law and numerous technological ways of peeping into others' lives. The incredible speed of the growth of this technology has outstripped laws and ethics about its use and misuse. As a result, cyberspace is like a Wild West of information, ideas, and activities, where one can make a fortune or have one's life torn asunder with a few keystrokes. People's conception of individual freedom and expression will be severely tested in this new world.

In the following selections, Paul Starr argues that the digital computer world will empower people. It will give them more choices, greater freedom of access and action, more knowledge, and greater control over their lives. He concludes that people will ultimately benefit in a host of ways as a consequence. Jerry Kang contends that the nature of cyberspace makes it a dangerous highway where millions of people are capable of peering into others' bank accounts, journals, and files; compiling information; and making people hostage to unseen forces. Kang maintains that these forces can manipulate individuals' buying habits, examine their political views, and track their whereabouts, thus inhibiting privacy and freedom.

Paul Starr **YES**

Cyberpower and Freedom

In politics and the public imagination, computers have gone from symbolizing our vulnerability to embodying our possibilities. In their early days during the 1950s and 1960s, computers seemed destined to increase the power of government and big corporations, and the great worry was how to protect privacy and individual freedom. Then the advent of the personal computer and other low-cost electronics suggested that information technology might be the ultimate tool of decentralization and individual empowerment, and the rise of global telecommunications and the Internet promised to annihilate national borders. Now many of us sit at keyboards easily connecting to computers all over the world, and to some people the thought suggests itself: "Why do we need national government at all?" Things have swung around so completely that influential analysts, especially on the right, see the information revolution as a great historical reversal of power, ushering in a new age of individualism on the digital frontier.

This high-tech libertarianism can be found in *Wired* magazine, the writings of George Gilder, the publications of Newt Gingrich's Progress and Freedom Foundation, and countless sites on the Net itself. Optimistic and forward-looking, high-tech libertarianism is more appealing than the older variety that looked back to the devil-take-the-hindmost individualism of the nineteenth century. But the new version shares the same old misunderstanding of the bases of freedom—that liberty will prosper the more government is diminished. To this it adds a new illusion—that technology is now freedom's reliable shield.

Advanced communications networks offer "the ultimate shopping experience: shopping for better government," writes one exponent of these ideas, the communications lawyer Peter Huber, in an article on "cyberpower" in *Forbes* last December [1996]. By "better" government, he chiefly means lower taxes and less stringent regulation. Now it's not just corporations that can shop around and buy, say, a legal home in Delaware; "ordinary investors," Huber observes, can shop on the Net for the tax environment, monetary policy, or regulations of their choice. If you think that your government's economic policies are wrong, you too can put your money into another currency. If the Food and Drug Administration (FDA) bars sale of a drug, you can buy it from an on-line pharmacy in another country and have it delivered by Federal Express. The American consumer who buys shoes made abroad will soon "shop for life insurance in London and health insurance in Geneva, and the offshore actuaries will discriminate fiercely in favor of the healthy."

To Huber, this is all to the good. Here is his happy vision: "As managers, workers and consumers," he writes, "we buy government in much the same way we buy shoes" and when one government is too costly or inconvenient, we can just switch to another. In thinking about the relations of people and governments, he has thus nicely dispensed with the old-fashioned concept of a citizen encumbered with obligations and loyalties, along with the idea of a people collectively addressing their problems through democratic institutions—all this was just a "political carnival" that is thankfully over. Governments in the new global market will be disciplined by money moving offshore, not by voters and public deliberation, and public policies will be improved because politicians will be impotent to do anything except what markets allow them to do.

Huber conceives of this system as a superior version of democracy, as if we all had equal "votes" in the global government market. But, of course, not all of us "buy government" with equal facility or effect. Managers can move plants abroad, and consumers can buy tradable foreign goods; but except for the limited class of professionals who can sell their services to foreign clients, workers need to uproot themselves to make use of foreign labor markets. As savers and investors, we also have unequal offshore opportunities since the principal asset of most families is their home. In other words, inasmuch as we are limited by our physical existence, social connections, and political loyalties, we cannot simply search and switch among global markets. The issue here is not simply income inequality, but also an imbalance of human interests. Why feel any obligation to people or places, community or nation, if you're just shopping?

Membership in a democratic state has historically implied a "bundle" of relationships. We enjoy the security and other services a state provides us and, if we fulfill our part of the bargain, we obey its rules, pay its taxes, and have our say in elections. Huber is saying technology makes it easier and cheaper to unbundle that package. The difficulty is that many people would like to enjoy the services of effective government but not pay the costs. They might like to live under one government, do business under another, and park their assets under a third. But in a world of unlimited opportunism, the government would lack the effective authority and resources to provide collective benefits that the majority of us want from it—including... the very rights we prize.

There is no denying that the combined force of advanced technology and global markets has undermined the regulatory capacity of government. But it is important to distinguish what technology has changed and what it hasn't. Corporations can now more easily organize production on a global basis, and investors can more readily move financial assets across national borders. Where products and services consist of bits rather than atoms, the Net may make their origins, literally, immaterial. But economic activities that require local knowledge and trust as well as physical presence are not so easily moved. And governments still have effective means of enforcing laws and regulations even when one of the parties to a transaction is offshore.

Consider two of the examples mentioned by Huber: pharmaceuticals and health insurance. His offshore alternatives confront a minor difficulty—they're illegal and for good reason. Anyone in the United States ordering drugs banned by the FDA from an offshore pharmacy would be importing them in violation of federal law. No matter where domiciled, any insurer doing business with people residing in a state needs to be licensed to do so and must comply with federal requirements under the recent Kennedy-Kassebaum legislation—technology doesn't change that. If there is any justification for pharmaceutical regulation (some minimum standard of safety) or insurance regulation (some minimum standard of solvency), the laws cannot simply be nullified by the ruse of an offshore location. As a practical matter, few people are likely to use online pharmacies located abroad because of delivery costs; and if the drugs have not received FDA approval, insurers won't reimburse them. Foreign health insurers, lacking contracts with providers, would be in a poor position to compete with domestic insurers in the age of managed care. If a market in the U.S. for offshore pharmacies and insurers existed, they could long ago have done business by snail mail and telephone, but they haven't, and the new technology doesn't affect the sources of hesitation among both sellers and buyers—the illegality of the transactions and lack of detailed knowledge about the other party and relevant market conditions.

Huber assumes that people can evaluate regulatory protections in other countries and that they will knowingly opt for more lax regulations. In some cases, that may be so. But here he underestimates the importance of trust in economic as well as social relationships and the role of government in promoting trust by assuring common ground rules and effective recourse in the event of fraud and negligence. Without a state strong enough to enforce rules and assure confidence, people are reluctant to come into the market and do business with strangers.

And so it is with global electronic commerce. The economic development of cyberspace is lagging because governments have not yet established laws and regulations that promote trust and confidence. Consumers continue to be "wary" of the Internet, a recent White House paper on the Internet and global commerce points out, "because of the lack of a predictable legal environment governing transactions.... This is particularly true for international commercial activity where concerns about enforcement of contracts, liability, intellectual property protection, privacy, security, taxation and other matters have caused businesses and consumers to be cautious."

In other words, what we have today on the Net is not so much individuals shopping for governments as both individuals and firms fearing to do business globally for lack of consistent laws and regulations that their governments need to agree upon. The libertarians see government as always restricting markets; they miss the positive role government plays in creating the foundations of social trust that markets (and nonmarket institutions) require.

Far from taking trust for granted in the information age, we are going to face especially serious problems sustaining it because of the growing use of the new technology for deception. I am not only referring to the difficulty of authenticating electronic exchanges—for example, determining whether e-mail is actually from the ostensible sender, whether a Web site originates from the group or person listed as responsible for it, or whether e-cash is genuine. New technology is also undermining the integrity of older forms of communication and exchange by generating improved techniques and lower costs for altering photographs, counterfeiting documents, and stealing identities (reproducing forms of identification, often for credit card fraud). Recently a company was reported to have figured out how to recombine an individual's recorded speech into new sentences that sound exactly as if the original person spoke them—a kind of audio counterfeiting that may soon, in effect, make us say anything. Information technology alone cannot provide us an absolute shield against its evil twin—disinformation technology. Our only protection is law, and that protection is available to us only if legitimate governments have the power to govern.

Another problem with high-tech libertarianism is the belief that the development of information technology and electronic markets on their own will promote maximum choice. In its current form, the Internet clearly does expand the ability of people with minimal resources to originate communication as well as to receive it. In this sense, the Web is the best rejoinder to A.J. Liebling's old complaint that "freedom of the press belongs to the man who owns one." More generally, the new era of digital communications has the potential to end the old scarcity of bandwidth in the radio spectrum that limited the number of broadcast channels. But there are also powerful forces favoring concentrated power in the new era of communications, and it would be a mistake just to rely on technology and the marketplace to curb abuses of that power.

One source of concentrated power is developing around control of the "interface"—the menu of alternatives that first pops up on the screen. Interfaces like the current browsers for navigating the Web are relatively open (they connect to nearly all sites), but more closed interfaces, like the menu of options on television sets in hotel rooms, suggest how a more closed regime might be reestablished. An interface is a choke point and potentially of enormous economic value. Why should choke points emerge? Because under the current, open regime on the Web, hardly anyone providing "content" is making money; and because of the demand for simplicity of use as the Web (or some alternative) turns into a more universal system of communication and entertainment. Companies are already creating more limited interfaces to sort out options for consumers, deliver audiences to advertisers, and assure originators of content a dependable stream of income. "Webcasting" and "push" media—which simplify the complexity of the Web by automatically downloading preselected information to the user—exemplify this shift. But to simplify is to exclude. Think of such a system not as censorship but rather as control of the means of marginalization.

The information revolution also tends to concentrate power in the firms that control dominant "architectures," such as IBM in the mainframe era and Microsoft and Intel today. Architectural dominance is endemic in industries that have rapidly evolving proprietary technical standards vital to every firm.

As Charles H. Ferguson and Charles R. Morris write in their book *Computer Wars*, struggles over architectural control are a powerful stimulus to technological progress. But as Microsoft's victims can testify, the firm in control of the dominant architecture has extraordinary leverage over any potential competitor in its core or related businesses. Without government restraint in the form of antitrust, markets of these kinds easily end in monopoly.

The rapid improvement in price-performance ratios of computers, software, and other technology today seems to validate the faith in free markets. But to say that the information revolution proves the inevitable superiority of markets requires a monumental failure of short-term historical memory. After all, not just the Internet, but the computer sciences and computer industry represent a spectacular success of public investment. As late as the 1970s and early 1980s, according to Kenneth Flamm's 1987 study *Targeting the Computer*, the federal government was paying for 40 percent of all computer-related research and probably 60 to 75 percent of basic research. The motivation was national security, but the result has been the creation of comparative advantage in information technology for the United States that private firms have happily exploited and extended. When the returns were uncertain and difficult to capture, private firms were unwilling to invest, and government played the decisive role. But when the market expanded and the returns were more definite, the government receded, which is exactly the path it should have followed.

The view of government favored by the high-tech libertarians would make it impossible for us ever to repeat the success of the United States with the computers and the Net (or more generally to respond to many other examples of market failure). One of the ironies of the information revolution is that government's hand has apparently become the invisible one. There we sit at our computers, and we feel like Masters of the Universe. We press the keys and command distant computers, and we think everyone else should be able to manage their affairs as we do. But, of all spaces, cyberspace is most singularly the product of political invention and social agreement, and only law will give us the security to use it freely.

NO

Jerry Kang

Cyberspace Privacy:
A Primer and Proposal

Human ingenuity has provided us a great gift, cyberspace. This blooming network of computing-communication technologies is quickly changing the world and our behavior in it. Already, it has become cliche to catalog cyberspace's striking benefits, its endless possibilities. But great gifts often come with a great price. Congress thinks that the price will be sexual purity due to easy access to pornography. Industry thinks it will be our economy due to easy copying of Hollywood's and Silicon Valley's programs. I worry that it will be our privacy.

When I mention "privacy," lawyers naturally think of privacy as used in the historic case, *Roe v. Wade*. Others think of the privacy of their own homes and backyards, largely in territorial terms. I use "privacy" differently. Instead of emphasizing privacy in a decisional or spatial sense, I mean it in an information sense. Information privacy is an individual's claim to control the terms under which personal information is acquired, disclosed, and used.

My thesis is that cyberspace threatens information privacy in extraordinary ways, and without much thought or collective deliberation, we may be in the process of surrendering our privacy permanently as we enter the next century.

Why Care About Privacy?

Some people do not understand what the big deal is about privacy. They assume that privacy is important only for those who have something to hide. This view is misguided. Let me articulate why individuals should enjoy meaningful control over the acquisition, disclosure, and use of their personal information.

Use of personal data. Personal data are often misused. For example, personal data can be used to commit identity theft, in which an impostor creates fake financial accounts, runs up enormous bills, and disappears leaving only a wrecked credit report behind. Personal data, such as home addresses and telephone numbers, can be used to harass and stalk. Personal data, such as one's sexual orientation, can be used to deny employment because of unwarranted prejudice.

Disclosure of personal data.   Sometimes, even if such data will not be "used" against us, its mere disclosure may lead to embarrassment. In any culture, certain conditions are embarrassing even when they are not blameworthy. Take impotency for example. In most cases, impotency will not affect whether one receives a job, a loan, or a promotion. In this sense, the data will not be misused in the allocation of rewards and opportunities. However, the mere disclosure of this medical condition would cause intense embarrassment for most men.

In addition to causing embarrassment, the inability to control the disclosure of personal data can hamper the building of intimate relationships. We construct many intimacies not only by sharing experiences but also by sharing secrets about ourselves, details not broadcast to a mass audience. If we have information privacy, we can regulate the outflow of such private information to others. By reducing this flow to a trickle (for example, to your boss), we maintain aloofness; by releasing a more telling stream (for example, to your former college roommate living afar) we invite and affirm intimacy. If anyone could find out anything about us, secrets would lose their ability to help construct intimacy.

Acquisition of personal data.   Finally, consider the fact that personal information is acquired by observing who we are and what we do. When such observation is nonconsensual and extensive, we have what amounts to surveillance, which is in tension with human dignity. Human beings have dignity because they are moral persons—beings capable of self-determination, with the capacity to reflect upon and choose personal and political projects. Extensive, undesired observation interferes with this exercise of choice because we act differently when we are being watched. Simply put, surveillance leads to self-censorship. When we do not want to be surveilled, it disrespects our dignity to surveil us nonetheless, unless some important social justification exists. This insult to individual dignity has social ramifications. It chills out-of-the-mainstream behavior. It corrodes private experimentation and reflection. It threatens to leave us with a bland, unoriginal polity, characterized by excessive conformity.

The Difference That Cyberspace Makes

So now that we know why privacy matters, we must ask what difference does cyberspace make? My claim is that cyberspace makes broad societal surveillance possible and, if we do nothing, likely. To see the greater threat that cyberspace poses, imagine the following two visits to a mall—one in real space, the other in cyberspace.

In real space, you drive to a mall, walk its corridors, peer into numerous shops, and stroll through the aisles of inviting stores. You walk into a bookstore and flip through a few magazines. Finally, you stop at a clothing store and buy a friend a scarf with a credit card. In this narrative, numerous persons interact with you and collect information along the way. For instance, while walking through the mall, fellow visitors visually collect information about you, if for no other reason than to avoid bumping into you. But such information is general, e.g., it does not pinpoint the geographical location and time of the sighting, is not in a format that can be processed by a computer, is not indexed to your name or any unique identifier, and is impermanent, residing in shortterm human memory. You remain a barely noticed stranger. One important exception is the credit card purchase.

By contrast, in cyberspace, the exception becomes the norm: Every interaction may soon be like the credit card purchase. The best way to grasp this point is to take seriously, if only for a moment, the metaphor that cyberspace is an actual place, a virtual reality. In this alternate universe, you are invisibly stamped with a bar code as soon as you venture outside your home. There are entities called "road providers" (your Internet Service Provider), who supply the streets and ground you walk on, who track precisely where, when, and how fast you traverse the lands, in order to charge you for your wear on the infrastructure. As soon as you enter the cyber-mall's domain, the mall tracks you through invisible scanners focused on your bar code. It automatically records which stores you visit, which windows you browse, in which order, and for how long. The specific stores collect even more detailed data when you enter their domain. For example, the cyberbookstore notes which magazines you skimmed, recording which pages you have seen and for how long, and notes the pattern, if any, of your browsing. It notes that you picked up a health magazine featuring an article on Viagra, read for seven minutes a newsweekly detailing a politician's sex scandal, and flipped ever-so-quickly through a tabloid claiming that Elvis lives. Of course, whenever any item is actually purchased, the store, as well as the credit, debit, or virtual cash company that provides payment through cyberspace, takes careful notes of what you bought—in this case, a silk scarf, red, expensive, a week before Valentine's Day.

All these data generated in cyberspace are detailed, computer-processable, indexed to the individual, and permanent. While the mall example may not concern data that appear especially sensitive, the same extensive data collection can take place as we travel through other cyberspace domains—for instance, to research health issues and politics; to communicate to friends, businesses, and the government; and to pay our bills and manage our finances. Moreover, the data collected in these various domains can be aggregated to produce telling profiles of who we are, as revealed by what we do and with whom we associate. The very technology that makes cyberspace possible also makes detailed, cumulative, invisible observation of ourselves possible. One need only sift through the click streams generated by our cyber-activity.

It turns out that few laws limit what can be done with this data collected in cyberspace. Unlike Europe, the United States has no omnibus privacy law covering the private sector's processing of personal information. Instead, U.S. law features a legal patchwork that regulates different types of personal information in different ways, depending on how it is acquired, by whom, and how it will be used. To be sure, there are numerous statutes that govern specific sectors, such as consumer credit, education, cable programming, electronic communications, videotape rentals, motor vehicle records, and the recently enacted Children's Online Privacy Protection Act. But it turns out that in toto, information collectors can largely do what they want.

The Market Solution

Let me restate the problem. All cyberactivity, even simply browsing a Webpage, involves a "transaction" between an individual and potential information collectors. These collectors not only include the counterparty to the transaction but also intermediaries (transaction facilitators) that support the electronic communications (telephone company, cable company, Internet service provider) and sometimes payment (credit card company, electronic cash company). In these transactions, personal information is inevitably generated as either necessary or incidental by-products. Privacy enthusiasts insist that the individual owns this data; information collectors vigorously disagree. What shall be done?

Perhaps the market might solve the problem. One might reasonably view personal information as a commodity, whose pricing and consumption can and should be governed by the laws of supply and demand. Through offers and counteroffers between individual and information collector, the market will move the correctly priced personal data to the party that values it most. Economists love this approach because it appears to be economically efficient. The private sector loves this approach because it staves off regulation. Regulators love this approach for the same reason in the current antiregulatory environment.

The problem is that in practice, individuals and information collectors do not negotiate express privacy contracts before engaging in each transaction. Although privacy notices have become more frequent on Webpages, it is a stretch to say that there is a "meeting of the minds" on privacy terms each time an individual browses a Webpage. What is necessary, then, is a clear articulation of the default rules governing personal data collected in a cyberspace transaction, when parties have not agreed explicitly otherwise.

There are two default rules that society might realistically adopt. First, there is the status quo's "plenary" default rule: Unless the parties agree otherwise, the information collector may process the personal data anyway it likes. Second, there is the "functionally necessary" default rule: Unless the parties agree otherwise, the information collector may process the personal data only in functionally necessary ways. This rule allows the information collector to process personal data on a need-only basis to complete the transaction in which the information was originally collected.

A one-size-fits-all default rule is efficient for some transactions but inefficient for others. Those parties for whom the default is inefficient will either contract around the rule—"flip"—or they will "stick" with the rule and accept the inefficiencies. Thus, the social cost of a default rule equals the sum of the transaction costs of contracting around the rule—the "flip cost"—plus the inefficiency cost of not contracting around the rule even when it would be more efficient to do so—the "stick cost." We seek the rule that minimizes social costs.

If we implement the plenary rule, most parties will stick because it is hard for a consumer to flip out of the default rule. First, she would face substantial research costs to determine what information is being collected and how it is used. That is because individuals today are largely clueless about how personal information is processed through cyberspace. Sometimes, they are deceived by the information collectors themselves, as the Federal Trade Commission recently charged against the Internet Service Provider, Geocities. Second, the individual would run into a collective action problem. Realistically, the information collector would not entertain one person's idiosyncratic request to purchase back personal information because the costs of administering such an individually tailored program would be prohibitive. Therefore, to make it worth the firm's while, the individual would have to band together with other like-minded individuals to renegotiate the privacy terms of the underlying transaction. These individuals would suffer the collective action costs of locating each other, then coming to a mutually acceptable proposal to deliver to the information collector—all the while discouraging free riders.

By contrast, the "functionally necessary" rule would not be sticky at all. With this default, if the firm valued personal data more than the individual, then the firm would have to buy permission to process the data in functionally unnecessary ways. Note, however, two critical differences in contracting around this default. First, unlike the individual who has to find out how information is processed, the collector need not bear such research costs since it already knows what its information practices are. Second, the collector does not confront collective action problems. It need not seek out other like-minded firms and reach consensus before coming to the individual with a request. This is because an individual would gladly entertain an individualized, even idiosyncratic, offer to purchase personal information.

Now, the task is to compare the costs of the equilibrium generated by each default rule. For the "plenary" equilibrium, the cost of the default rule is approximately the stick cost because few parties will flip. By contrast, for the "functionally necessary" equilibrium, the cost of the default rule is approximately the flip cost; almost all parties who care to flip will flip. Which cost is higher? We lack the data to be confident in our answer. However, we do know that given how seriously many individuals feel about their privacy, the stick cost of the plenary rule will not be trivial. Many individuals who care deeply about their privacy will not be able to get it. By contrast, the flip cost of the functionally necessary rule will be small because cyberspace makes communications cheap. The information collector can ask in a simple dialog box whether the individual will allow some unnecessary use of personal data, in exchange for some benefit. What is more, this inequality will increase over time. As information processing becomes more sophisticated, people will feel less in control of their personal information; accordingly they will value control more (making the cost of "sticking" greater). Simultaneously, the cost of communication will decrease as cyberspace improves (making the cost of "flipping" less).

In conclusion, I think it is more likely than not that a functionally necessary rule will be less costly to society than the plenary rule we currently have. Putting economic efficiency aside, the functionally necessary rule also better respects human dignity by respecting an individual's desire not to be surveilled.

A Modest Proposal

Congress should adopt a Cyberspace Privacy Act (the "Act"), that implements the "functionally necessary" default rule for all personal information collected in cyberspace. This rule is more efficient and more respectful of human dignity. Parties are, of course, free to contract around the default rule. The full proposed statute is available online at http://www.law.ucla.edu/faculty/kang/scholars, but here is a quick summary:

- First, a person who acquires personal data in the course of a cyberspace transaction must provide clear notice about what will be done with that information.
- Second, a person will not process personal information in a manner functionally unnecessary to the transaction without the prior consent of the individual.
- Third, an individual will have reasonable access to and rights of correction of personal data.
- Fourth, personal data that is no longer functionally necessary to the cyberspace transaction will be generally destroyed unless there is some legitimate pending request or the individual has given consent otherwise.
- Fifth, if compelled by court order or a dire emergency to the individual's own welfare, personal data may be disclosed as necessary.
- Finally, a person who violates this Act may be sued in federal court for civil damages. Moreover, the Federal Trade Commission will have administrative authority to enforce the Act.

Politically moderate, the proposed legislation should enjoy broad appeal. The private sector should not oppose the Act because it does not choke off electronic commerce in cyberspace.

Although the Act constrains certain forms of advertising based on detailed data collection, and the sharing of data with third parties, these constraints can be lifted simply by obtaining the customer's consent. Moreover, the Cyberspace Privacy Act would promote consumer confidence in—and thereby encourage —electronic commerce. Multinational corporations working in Europe might have an independent reason to accept the Act. By applying the Act to data received from the European Union, these corporations could credibly assert that they have begun to adopt adequate privacy protections necessary to maintain transborder flows under the recent European Union Data Protection Directive. Finally, the Act does not violate the First Amendment. In structure, the proposed Act does not differ materially from the privacy provisions of the Cable Act or the Video Privacy Protection Act. Neither act has been successfully challenged on First Amendment grounds.

Conclusion

A vision protective of information privacy in cyberspace will be singularly hard to maintain. Cyberspace's essence is the processing of information in ways and at speeds unimaginable just years ago. To retard this information processing juggernaut in the name of privacy seems antitechnology, even antiprogress. It cuts against the hackneyed cyber-proclamation that information wants to be free. Nevertheless, this intentional application of friction to personal information flows is warranted. If profit-seeking organizations are instituting such friction in the name of intellectual property, individuals should not be chastised for doing the same in the name of privacy.

Historically, privacy issues have been an afterthought. Technology propels us forward, and we react to the social consequences only after the fact. But the amount of privacy we retain is—to use a decidedly low-tech metaphor—a oneway ratchet. Once we ratchet privacy down, it will be extraordinarily difficult to get it back. More disturbingly, after a while, we might not mind so much. It may dawn on us too late that privacy should have been saved along the way.

POSTSCRIPT

Will the Digital/Computer World Lead to Greater Individual Freedom?

The computer, like the television, telephone, and automobile before it, provides millions with access to a larger world around them. They can access information, ideas, people, places, and cultures beyond their own physical and economic limitations. The computer is a tool that can empower and inform beyond the tools of any previous generation. The digital/computer world is the next great technological revolution, and it may turn out to be the greatest in many respects. Information storage, retrieval, and access will be greater than at any other time in human history. Theoretically, billions will have the collected human experience at their fingertips and will be able to educate themselves about almost any subject or issue. The impact for education, economics, politics, and society is phenomenal.

However, the digital/computer world is also a commercial world. The technology and infrastructure that support this world is privately owned and run for profit. Therefore, the technology must serve the interests of those who own it in order for it to be implemented and mass-produced. To understand the full impact of this technology on individual freedom, one must understand the goals of those who control it. For example, the phone allows people to call out as well as others to call in. This means that external access demands internal access. Likewise, the digital/computer world allows for the cataloging of information—commercial, personal, private, and political. People's tastes, buying habits, desires, and beliefs are cataloged and stored so that more and more products can be marketed to individuals based on their tastes and so that more and more actors can know who those individuals are. Anonymity will die, and with it a degree of freedom.

Is it convenient that The Gap can know your tastes in clothes, buying habits, and even your friends' and family members' birthdays so that they can send you e-mail ads at key times offering products for you to buy? Or is that kind of knowledge intrusive? Is it good that the government can track your buying habits, private communications, and travel patterns down to the minute? Or is that potentially threatening to your freedom?

Three works of note that will help you to explore this issue in greater depth are Benjamin Barber, "Three Scenarios for the Future of Technology and a Strong Democracy," *Political Science Quarterly* (Winter 1998–1999); Michael Mehta and Eric Darier, "Virtual Control and Disciplining on the Internet: Electronic Governmentality in the New Wired World," *Information Society* (April/June 1998); and Albert H. Teich, *Technology and the Future* (St. Martin's Press, 1997).

ISSUE 15

Is the Globalization of American Culture a Positive Development?

YES: David Rothkopf, from "In Praise of Cultural Imperialism?" *Foreign Policy* (Summer 1997)

NO: Jeffrey E. Garten, from " 'Cultural Imperialism' Is No Joke," *Business Week* (November 30, 1998)

ISSUE SUMMARY

YES: David Rothkopf, an adjunct professor of international and public affairs, discusses the creation of a global culture and argues that the Americanization of the world along a U.S. value system is good and should be encouraged in the interests of the United States.

NO: Jeffrey E. Garten, dean of Yale University's School of Management, argues that people around the world see globalization as a form of American imperialism. He contends that such fears have a strong basis in reality and cannot be ignored.

In 1989 the Berlin Wall collapsed. Two years later the Soviet Union ceased to exist. With this relatively peaceful and monumental series of events, the cold war ended, and with it one of the most contentious and conflict-ridden periods in global history. It is easy to argue that in the wake of those events the United States is in ascendancy. The United States and its Western allies won the cold war, defeating communism politically and philosophically. Since 1990 democracies have emerged and largely flourished as never before across the world stage. According to a recent study, over 120 of the world's 190 nations now have a functioning form of democracy. Western companies, values, and ideas now sweep across the globe via airwaves, computer networks, and fiber-optic cables that bring symbols of U.S. culture and values (such as Michael Jordan and McDonald's) into villages and schools and cities around the world.

If American culture is embodied in the products sold by many multinational corporations (MNCs), such as McDonald's, Ford, IBM, The Gap, and others, then the American cultural values and ideas that are embedded in these products are being bought and sold in record numbers around the world. Globalization largely driven by MNCs and their control of technology brings with it values and ideas that are largely American in origin and expression. Values such as speed and ease of use, a strong emphasis on leisure time over work time, and a desire for increasing material wealth and comfort dominate the advertising practices of these companies. For citizens of the United States, this seems a natural part of the landscape. They do not question it; in fact, many Americans enjoy seeing signs of "home" on street corners abroad: a McDonald's in Tokyo, a Sylvester Stallone movie in Djakarta, or a Gap shirt on a student in Nairobi, for example.

While comforting to Westerners, this trend is disquieting to the hundreds of millions of people around the world who wish to partake of the globalizing system without abandoning their own cultural values. Many people around the globe wish to engage in economic exchange and develop politically but do not want to abandon their own cultures amidst the wave of values embedded in Western products. This tension is most pronounced in its effect on the youth around the world. Millions of impressionable young people in the cities and villages of the developing world wish to emulate the American icons that they see on soft drink cans, for example, or in movie theaters. They attempt to adopt U.S. manners, language, and modes of dress, often in opposition to their parents and local culture. These young people are becoming Americanized and, in the process, creating huge generational rifts within their own societies.

David Rothkopf and Jeffrey E. Garten explore this process in the following selections, with each coming at it from very different positions. Rothkopf argues that the promotion of American culture across the globe is a good thing. Americanization, he says, will help to homogenize the world and to bring it closer together, and the United States will solidify itself as the political, economic, and cultural leader of the globe. Garten sees real problems with this process and contends that charges of American imperialism and cultural genocide cannot be ignored, lest America find itself facing a severe anti-U.S. backlash that takes a variety of nonviolent and violent forms.

David Rothkopf **YES**

In Praise of Cultural Imperialism?

The gates of the world are groaning shut. From marble balconies and over the airwaves, demagogues decry new risks to ancient cultures and traditional values. Satellites, the Internet, and jumbo jets carry the contagion. To many people, "foreign" has become a synonym for "danger."

Of course, now is not the first time in history that chants and anthems of nationalism have been heard. But the tide of nationalism sweeping the world today is unique. For it comes in reaction to a countervailing global alternative that—for the first time in history—is clearly something more than the crackpot dream of visionaries. It is also the first time in history that virtually every individual at every level of society can sense the impact of international changes. They can see and hear it in their media, taste it in their food, and sense it in the products that they buy. Even more visceral and threatening to those who fear these changes is the growth of a global labor pool that during the next decade will absorb nearly 2 billion workers from emerging markets, a pool that currently includes close to 1 billion unemployed and underemployed workers in those markets alone. These people will be working for a fraction of what their counterparts in developed nations earn and will be only marginally less productive. You are either someone who is threatened by this change or someone who will profit from it, but it is almost impossible to conceive of a significant group that will remain untouched by it.

Globalization has economic roots and political consequences, but it also has brought into focus the power of culture in this global environment—the power to bind and to divide in a time when the tensions between integration and separation tug at every issue that is relevant to international relations.

The impact of globalization on culture and the impact of culture on globalization merit discussion. The homogenizing influences of globalization that are most often condemned by the new nationalists and by cultural romanticists are actually positive; globalization promotes integration and the removal not only of cultural barriers but of many of the negative dimensions of culture. Globalization is a vital step toward both a more stable world and better lives for the people in it.

Furthermore, these issues have serious implications for American foreign policy. For the United States, a central objective of an Information Age foreign

From David Rothkopf, "In Praise of Cultural Imperialism?" *Foreign Policy* (Summer 1997). Copyright © 1997 by The Carnegie Endowment for International Peace. Reprinted by permission of *Foreign Policy*.

policy must be to win the battle of the world's information flows, dominating the airwaves as Great Britain once ruled the seas.

Culture and Conflict

Culture is not static; it grows out of a systematically encouraged reverence for selected customs and habits. Indeed, *Webster's Third New International Dictionary* defines culture as the "total pattern of human behavior and its products embodied in speech, action, and artifacts and dependent upon man's capacity for learning and transmitting knowledge to succeeding generations." Language, religion, political and legal systems, and social customs are the legacies of victors and marketers and reflect the judgment of the marketplace of ideas throughout popular history. They might also rightly be seen as living artifacts, bits and pieces carried forward through the years on currents of indoctrination, popular acceptance, and unthinking adherence to old ways. Culture is used by the organizers of society—politicians, theologians, academics, and families—to impose and ensure order, the rudiments of which change over time as need dictates. It is less often acknowledged as the means of justifying inhumanity and warfare. Nonetheless, even a casual examination of the history of conflict explains well why Samuel Huntington, in his *The Clash of Civilizations*, expects conflict along cultural fault lines, which is precisely where conflict so often erupts. Even worse is that cultural differences are often sanctified by their links to the mystical roots of culture, be they spiritual or historical. Consequently, a threat to one's culture becomes a threat to one's God or one's ancestors and, therefore, to one's core identity. This inflammatory formula has been used to justify many of humanity's worst acts.

Cultural conflicts can be placed into three broad categories: religious warfare, ethnic conflict, and conflict between "cultural cousins," which amounts to historical animosity between cultures that may be similar in some respects but still have significant differences that have been used to justify conflict over issues of proximity, such as resource demands or simple greed.

Religion-based conflicts occur between Christians and Muslims, Christians and Jews, Muslims and Jews, Hindus and Muslims, Sufis and Sunis, Protestants and Catholics, and so forth. Cultural conflicts that spring from ethnic (and in some cases religious) differences include those between Chinese and Vietnamese, Chinese and Japanese, Chinese and Malays, Normans and Saxons, Slavs and Turks, Armenians and Azerbaijanis, Armenians and Turks, Turks and Greeks, Russians and Chechens, Serbs and Bosnians, Hutus and Tutsis, blacks and Afrikaners, blacks and whites, and Persians and Arabs. Conflicts between "cultural cousins" over resources or territory have occurred between Britain and France, France and Germany, Libya and Egypt, and many others.

Another category that might be included in our taxonomy is quasi-cultural conflict. This conflict is primarily ideological and is not deeply enough rooted in tradition to fit within standard definitions of culture, yet it still exhibits most if not all of the characteristics of other cultural clashes. The best example here is the Cold War itself, a conflict between political cultures that was portrayed by its combatants in broader cultural terms: "godless communists" versus "corrupt capitalists." During this conflict, differences regarding the role of the individual within the state and over the distribution of income produced a "clash of civilizations" that had a relatively recent origin.

Finally, as a reminder of the toll that such conflicts take, one need only look at the 20th century's genocides. In each one, leaders used culture to fuel the passions of their armies and other minions and to justify their actions among their people. One million Armenians; tens of millions of Russians; 10 million Jews, Gypsies, and homosexuals; 3 million Cambodians; and hundreds of thousands of Bosnians, Rwandans, and Timorese all were the victims of "culture"—whether it was ethnic, religious, ideological, tribal, or nationalistic in its origins. To be sure, they fell victim to other agendas as well. But the provocative elements of culture were to these accompanying agendas as Joseph Goebbels was to Adolf Hitler—an enabler and perhaps the most insidious accomplice. Historians can, of course, find examples from across the ages of "superior" cultures eradicating "inferior" opponents—in the American West, among the native tribes of the Americas and Africa, during the Inquisition, and during the expansion of virtually every empire.

Satellites as Cultural Death Stars

Critics of globalization argue that the process will lead to a stripping away of identity and a blandly uniform, Orwellian world. On a planet of 6 billion people, this is, of course, an impossibility. More importantly, the decline of cultural distinctions may be a measure of the progress of civilization, a tangible sign of enhanced communications and understanding. Successful multicultural societies, be they nations, federations, or other conglomerations of closely interrelated states, discern those aspects of culture that do not threaten union, stability, or prosperity (such as food, holidays, rituals, and music) and allow them to flourish. But they counteract or eradicate the more subversive elements of culture (exclusionary aspects of religion, language, and political/ideological beliefs). History shows that bridging cultural gaps successfully and serving as a home to diverse peoples requires certain social structures, laws, and institutions that transcend culture. Furthermore, the history of a number of ongoing experiments in multiculturalism, such as in the European Union, India, South Africa, and the United States, suggests that workable, if not perfected, integrative models exist. Each is built on the idea that tolerance is crucial to social well-being, and each at times has been threatened by both intolerance and a heightened emphasis on cultural distinctions. The greater public good warrants eliminating those cultural characteristics that promote conflict or prevent harmony, even as less-divisive, more personally observed cultural distinctions are celebrated and preserved.

The realization of such integrative models on a global scale is impossible in the near term. It will take centuries. Nor can it be achieved purely through rational decisions geared toward implementing carefully considered policies and programs. Rather, current trends that fall under the broad definitional umbrella of "globalization" are accelerating a process that has taken place throughout history as discrete groups have become familiar with one another, allied, and commingled—ultimately becoming more alike. Inevitably, the United States has taken the lead in this transformation; it is the "indispensable nation" in the management of global affairs and the leading producer of information products and services in these, the early years of the Information Age.

The drivers of today's rapid globalization are improving methods and systems of international transportation, devising revolutionary and innovative information technologies and services, and dominating the international commerce in services and ideas. Their impact affects lifestyles, religion, language, and every other component of culture.

Much has been written about the role of information technologies and services in this process. Today, 15 major U.S. telecommunications companies, including giants like Motorola, Loral Space & Communications, and Teledesic (a joint project of Microsoft's Bill Gates and cellular pioneer Craig McCaw), offer competing plans that will encircle the globe with a constellation of satellites and will enable anyone anywhere to communicate instantly with anyone elsewhere without an established telecommunications infrastructure on the ground near either the sender or the recipient. (Loral puts the cost of such a call at around $3 per minute.)

Technology is not only transforming the world; it is creating its own metaphors as well. Satellites carrying television signals now enable people on opposite sides of the globe to be exposed regularly to a wide range of cultural stimuli. Russian viewers are hooked on Latin soap operas, and Middle Eastern leaders have cited CNN as a prime source for even local news. The Internet is an increasingly global phenomenon with active development under way on every continent.

The United States dominates this global traffic in information and ideas. American music, American movies, American television, and American software are so dominant, so sought after, and so visible that they are now available literally everywhere on the Earth. They influence the tastes, lives, and aspirations of virtually every nation. In some, they are viewed as corrupting.

France and Canada have both passed laws to prohibit the satellite dissemination of foreign—meaning American—content across their borders and into the homes of their citizens. Not surprisingly, in many other countries—fundamentalist Iran, communist China, and the closely managed society of Singapore—central governments have aggressively sought to restrict the software and programming that reach their citizens. Their explicit objective is to keep out American and other alien political views, mores, and, as it is called in some parts of the Middle East, "news pollution." In these countries, the control of new media that give previously closed or controlled societies virtually unlimited access to the outside world is a high priority. Singapore has sought to filter out certain things that are available over the Internet—essentially processing all information to eliminate pornography. China has set up a "Central Leading Group" under the State Planning Commission and the direct supervision of a vice premier to establish a similar system that will exclude more than just what might be considered obscene.

These governments are the heirs of King Canute, the infamous monarch who set his throne at the sea's edge and commanded the waves to go backward. The Soviet Union fell in part because a closed society cannot compete in the Information Age. These countries will fare no better. They need look no further than their own élites to know this. In China, while satellite dishes are technically against the law, approximately one in five citizens of Beijing has access to television programming via a dish, and almost half of the people of Guangzhou have access to satellite-delivered programming. Singapore, the leading entrepôt of Southeast Asia, is a hub in a global network of business centers in which the lives of the élites are virtually identical. Business leaders in Buenos Aires, Frankfurt, Hong Kong, Johannesburg, Istanbul, Los Angeles, Mexico City, Moscow, New Delhi, New York, Paris, Rome, Santiago, Seoul, Singapore, Tel Aviv, and Tokyo all read the same newspapers, wear the same suits, drive the same cars, eat the same food, fly the same airlines, stay in the same hotels, and listen to the same music. While the people of their countries remain divided by culture, they have realized that to compete in the global marketplace they must conform to the culture of that marketplace.

The global marketplace is being institutionalized through the creation of a series of multilateral entities that establish common rules for international commerce. If capital is to flow freely, disclosure rules must be the same, settlement procedures consistent, and redress transparent. If goods are also to move unimpeded, tariff laws must be consistent, customs standards harmonized, and product safety and labeling standards brought into line. And if people are to move easily from deal to deal, air transport agreements need to be established, immigration controls standardized, and commercial laws harmonized. In many ways, business is the primary engine driving globalization, but it would be a mistake to conclude that the implications of globalization will be limited primarily to the commercial arena.

In politics, for example, as international organizations arise to coordinate policy among many nations on global issues such as trade, the environment, health, development, and crisis management, a community of international bureaucrats is emerging. These players are as comfortable operating in the international environment as they would be at home, and the organizations that they represent in effect establish global standards and expectations—facilitating the progress of globalization.

The community of nations increasingly accepts that such supranational entities are demanded by the exigencies of the times; with that acceptance also comes a recognition that the principal symbol of national identity—namely sovereignty—must be partially ceded to those entities. The United States in particular seems to have problems with this trend. For example, the United States was involved in creating the World Trade Organization and now undermines its effectiveness by arbitrarily withdrawing from its efforts to blunt the effects of the Helms-Burton act. Still, the recognition that sometimes there are interests greater than national interests is a crucial step on the path to a more peaceful, prosperous world.

Toward a Global Culture

It is in the general interest of the United States to encourage the development of a world in which the fault lines separating nations are bridged by shared interests. And it is in the economic and political interests of the United States to ensure that if the world is moving toward a common language, it be English; that if the world is moving toward common telecommunications, safety, and quality standards, they be American; that if the world is becoming linked by television, radio, and music, the programming be American; and that if common values are being developed, they be values with which Americans are comfortable.

These are not simply idle aspirations. English is linking the world. American information technologies and services are at the cutting edge of those that are enabling globalization. Access to the largest economy in the world—America's—is the primary carrot leading other nations to open their markets.

Indeed, just as the United States is the world's sole remaining military superpower, so is it the world's only information superpower. While Japan has become quite competitive in the manufacture of components integral to information systems, it has had a negligible impact as a manufacturer of software or as a force behind the technological revolution. Europe has failed on both fronts. Consequently, the United States holds a position of advantage at the moment and for the foreseeable future.

Some find the idea that Americans would systematically seek to promote their culture to be unattractive. They are concerned that it implies a sense of superiority on Americans' part or that it makes an uncomfortable value judgment. But the realpolitik of the Information Age is that setting technological standards, defining software standards, producing the most popular information products, and leading in the related development of the global trade in services are as essential to the well-being of any would-be leader as once were the resources needed to support empire or industry.

The economic stakes are immense considering the enormous investments that will be made over the next 10 years in the world's information infrastructure. The U.S. government estimates that telecommunications investment in Latin America alone during this period will top $150 billion. China will spend a similar amount, as will the member states of the Association of South East Asian Nations. In fact, the market for telecommunications services is expected to top $1 trillion by the turn of the century.

During the decade ahead, not only will enormous sums be directed toward the establishment of the global network of networks that the Clinton administration has dubbed the "Global Information Infrastructure," but those sums will pay for the foundations of a system that will dictate decades of future choices about upgrades, systems standards, software purchases, and services. At the same time, new national and international laws will be written, and they will determine how smoothly information products and services may flow from one market to another. Will steps be taken to ensure that Internet commerce remains truly free? What decisions will be made about the encryption of data that will impact not only the security of information markets but the free flow of ideas and the rights of individuals in the Information Age? Will governments allow the democratizing promise of the Internet to enable virtually anyone with a computer to contact anyone else?

The establishment of the Global Information Infrastructure is not just an enormous commercial opportunity for the world's information leader. The development of the rules governing that infrastructure will shape the nature of global politics decisively, either enhancing or undermining freedoms, thereby either speeding or slowing the pace of integration, understanding, and tolerance worldwide. The nature of individual and national relations will be transformed. Those wires and constellations of satellites and invisible beams of electronic signals crisscrossing the globe will literally form the fabric of future civilization.

Consequently, it could not be more strategically crucial that the United States do whatever is in its power to shape the development of that infrastructure, the rules governing it, and the information traversing it. Moreover, even if much of this process of developing what we might call the "infosphere" is left to the marketplace (as it should be), governments will control crucial elements of it. Governments will award many of the biggest infrastructure development contracts offered in the next decade: Some will assist their national companies in trying to win those contracts, and state officials will meet to decide the trade rules that will govern international traffic in the world's telecommunications markets, the global regulatory environment, encryption standards, privacy standards, intellectual property protections, and basic equipment standards. Governments will determine whether these are open or closed markets and what portion of development dollars will be targeted at bringing the benefits of these technologies to the poor to help counteract information inequities. Already some government intercessions into this marketplace have failed. Notably, Japan's efforts to shape the development of high-definition television standards sent that nation down an analog path in what turned out to be a digital race. Yet there are many places where there is an important role for governments and where the United States should have a carefully considered overarching policy and an aggressive stance to match.

Exporting the American Model

Many observers contend that it is distasteful to use the opportunities created by the global information revolution to promote American culture over others, but that kind of relativism is as dangerous as it is wrong. American culture is fundamentally different from indigenous cultures in so many other locales. American culture is an amalgam of influences and approaches from around the world. It is melded—consciously in many cases—into a social medium that allows individual freedoms and cultures to thrive. Recognizing this, Americans should not shy away from doing that which is so clearly in their economic, political, and security interests—and so clearly in the interests of the world at large. The United States should not hesitate to promote its values. In an effort to be polite or politic, Americans should not deny the fact that of all the nations in the history of the world, theirs is the most just, the most tolerant, the most willing to constantly reassess and improve itself, and the best model for the future.

At the same time, Americans should not fall under the spell of those like Singapore's Lee Kuan Yew and Malaysia's Mahathir bin-Mohamad, who argue that there is "an Asian way," one that non-Asians should not judge and that should be allowed to dictate the course of events for all those operating in that corner of the world. This argument amounts to self-interested political rhetoric. Good and evil, better and worse coexist in this world. There are absolutes, and there are political, economic, and moral costs associated with failing to recognize this fact.

Repression is not defensible whether the tradition from which it springs is Confucian, Judeo-Christian, or Zoroastrian. The repressed individual still suffers, as does society, and there are consequences for the global community. Real costs accrue in terms of constrained human creativity, delayed market development, the diversion of assets to enforce repression, the failure of repressive societies to adapt well to the rapidly changing global environment, and the dislocations, struggles, and instability that result from these and other factors. Americans should promote their vision for the world, because failing to do so or taking a "live and let live" stance is ceding the process to the not-always-beneficial actions of others. Using the tools of the Information Age to do so is perhaps the most peaceful and powerful means of advancing American interests.

If Americans now live in a world in which ideas can be effectively exported and media delivery systems are powerful, they must recognize that the nature of those ideas and the control of those systems are matters with which they should be deeply concerned. Is it a threat to U.S. interests, to regional peace, to American markets, and to the United States's ability to lead if foreign leaders adopt models that promote separatism and the cultural fault lines that threaten stability? It certainly is. Relativism is a veil behind which those who shun scrutiny can hide. Whether Americans accept all the arguments of Huntington or not, they must recognize that the greater the cultural value gaps in the world, the more likely it is that conflict will ensue. The critical prerequisite for gaining the optimum benefits of global integration is to understand which cultural attributes can and should be tolerated—and, indeed, promoted—and which are the fissures that will become fault lines.

It is also crucial that the United States recognize its limitations. Americans can have more influence than others, but they cannot assure every outcome. Rather, the concerted effort to shape the development of the Global Information Infrastructure and the ideas that flow within it should be seen merely as a single component of a well-rounded foreign and security policy. (And since it is not likely to be an initiative that is widely liked or admired or enhanced through explicit promotion, it is not an approach that should be part of American public diplomacy efforts.)

Of course, implementing such an approach is not going to be easy in an America that is wracked by the reaction to and the backlash against globalization. Today, the extreme left and right wings of both major political parties are united in a new isolationist alliance. This alliance has put the brakes on 60 years of expanding free trade, has focused on the threats rather than the promise posed by such critical new relationships as those with China and other key emerging markets, and has seized on every available opportunity to disengage from the world or to undermine U.S. abilities to engage or lead effectively. It will take a committed effort by the president and cooperation from leaders on Capitol Hill to overcome the political opposition of the economic nationalists and neoisolationists. It will not happen if those in leadership positions aim simply to take the path of least political resistance or to rest on the accomplishments of the recent past. In a time of partisan bickering, when the emphasis of top officials has shifted from governing to politicking, there is a risk that America will fail to rise to these challenges. While the Clinton administration has broken important ground in developing a Global Information Infrastructure initiative and in dealing with the future of the Internet, encryption issues, and intellectual property concerns, these efforts are underfunded, sometimes managed to suit political rather than strategic objectives, shortsighted (particularly the steps concerning encryption, in which rapid changes and the demands of the marketplace are being overlooked), and poorly coordinated. At the same time, some of America's most powerful tools of engagement—which come in the form of new trade initiatives—seemingly have been shelved. This problem is most clearly manifested in the fact that fast-track negotiating-authority approval has not yet been granted and in the real possibility that Congress will refuse to grant such approval before the turn of the century.

The Clinton administration and its successors must carefully consider the long-term implications of globalization, such as the impact of the rise of new markets on America's economic influence and how America can maintain its leadership role. Aspects of American culture will play a critical role in helping to ensure the continuation of that leadership. American cultural diversity gives the United States resources and potential links with virtually every market and every major power in the world. America's emphasis on the individual ensures that American innovation will continue to outstrip that of other nations. Working in its favor is the fact that the "Pax Americana" is a phenomenon of the early years of globalization and that the U.S. ascendancy to undisputed leadership came at the same time as the establishment of international institutions such as the United Nations, the World Bank, and the International Monetary Fund; thus, for all the challenges of adjustment, the United States has more leadership experience than any other nation in this new global environment. Also, though some may decry Americans' emphasis on "newness" and suggest that it is a result of their lack of an extensive history, it also represents a healthy lack of cultural "baggage": It is this emphasis on newness that puts the United States in the best position to deal with a world in which the rapidity of change is perhaps the greatest strategic challenge of all.

Identity Without Culture

The opportunity lies before us as Americans. The United States is in a position not only to lead in the 21st century as the dominant power of the Information Age but to do so by breaking down the barriers that divide nations—and groups within nations—and by building ties that create an ever greater reservoir of shared interests among an ever larger community of peoples. Those who look at the post–Cold War era and see the "clash of civilizations" see only one possibility. They overlook the great strides in integration that have united the world's billions. They discount the factors that have led to global consolidation and the reality that those factors grow in power with each new day of the global era—integration is a trend that builds upon itself. They argue that America should prepare for the conflicts that may come in this interim period without arguing that it should accelerate the arrival of a new era with every means at its disposal.

Certainly, it is naive to expect broad success in avoiding future conflicts among cultures. But we now have tools at our disposal to diminish the disparities that will fuel some of those conflicts. While we should prepare for conflict, we should also remember that it is not mere idealism that demands that we work for integration and in support of a unifying global culture ensuring individual rights and enhancing international stability: It is also the ultimate realpolitik, the ultimate act of healthy self-interest.

Allowing ourselves to be swept up in the backlash against globalization would undermine America's ability to advance its self-interests. Americans must recognize that those interests and the issues pertaining to them reach across the disciplines of economics, politics, science, and culture. An interdisciplinary approach to international policymaking is thus required. We must also fully understand the new tools at our disposal. We must understand the profound importance and nature of the emerging infosphere—and its potential as a giant organic culture processor, democratic empowerer, universal connector, and ultimate communicator. Moreover, it is not enough to create and implement the right policies using the new tools at our disposal. Policymakers must better communicate the promise of this new world and make clear America's stake in that promise and the role Americans must play to achieve success. The United States does not face a simple choice between integration or separation, engagement or withdrawal. Rather, the choice is between leading a more peaceful world or being held hostage to events in a more volatile and violent one.

Jeffrey E. Garten

 NO

"Cultural Imperialism" Is No Joke

Washington's crusade for free trade is often seen abroad as a Trojan horse for companies, such as Walt Disney Co. and Cable News Network, that would dominate foreign lifestyles and values. Most Americans react to these fears with a shrug. That's a big mistake.

The entertainment industry, including movies, music, software, and broadcasting, is America's second-largest exporter after aircraft and has penetrated all global markets. Films such as *Lethal Weapon* are hits on every continent. *Reader's Digest* publishes in 19 languages. Windows computer programs and MTV can be found in remote corners of China.

The transmission of our culture goes beyond the arts or the media. When Washington exalts free enterprise, it promotes the notion that individual freedom has a higher value than government authority. When it advocates the rule of law overseas, it pushes a U.S.-style legal system.

Rebellion From the Roman to the Soviet empires, superpowers have aimed to spread their cultures, and from Lorenzo de' Medici to Michael Eisner, there has always been a link between commerce and culture. Still, while America's lifestyle and ideas can be liberating and uplifting, they are also often destabilizing abroad. Movies and music frequently glorify violence and rebellion. Darwinian capitalism requires societies to uproot traditional structures without adequate regulation, safety nets, or education. The U.S. legal system encourages confrontation, not conciliation.

Americans should not have difficulty empathizing with foreign fears of cultural invasion. Recall U.S. anxieties a decade ago when Sony Corp. bought Columbia Pictures and Mitsubishi Corp. purchased New York's Rockefeller Center. Now reaction against American "cultural imperialism" is building. Just a few years ago, France almost torpedoed the Uruguay Round of global trade negotiations because it wanted to limit the activities of U.S. entertainment companies. Last spring, a multilateral treaty on investment rules was derailed in part because of a spat between Brussels and Washington over protection of Europe's cultural industries. In August, Canada called together 19 other governments to plot ways to ensure their cultural independence from America. Mexico is considering legislation requiring that a certain percentage of its media programming remain in the hands of its citizens. U.N.-sponsored conferences on preserving national cultures are proliferating. In contrast to the American preference for financial liberalization, capital controls are becoming respectable in Asia.

The U.S. should do more than heed these warnings; it should recognize that strong cultures abroad are in America's self-interest. Amid the disorientation that comes with globalization, countries need cohesive national communities grounded in history and tradition. Only with these in place can they unite in the tough decisions necessary to building modern societies. If societies feel under assault, insecurities will be magnified, leading to policy paralysis, strident nationalism, and anti-Americanism.

With satellites and the Internet, the spread of American culture cannot be stopped—nor should it. But Corporate America and Washington could lessen U.S. dominance by encouraging cultural diversity around the globe. Companies such as Time Warner Inc. and PepsiCo Inc. could fund native entrepreneurs wishing to create local cultural industries. They could showcase regional film and theatrical productions and finance university research and teaching in the region's history, art, and literature.

The Clinton Administration could reverse current trade policy and permit temporary quotas and subsidies abroad to preserve certain local cultural industries, such as film and TV. It could encourage the World Bank to build up foreign countries' tourism infrastructure. It could expand assistance to U.N. efforts to restore national monuments that have been neglected or destroyed.

At a time when so many nations that have recently embraced Adam Smith are in deep recession, the Treasury and State Depts. could lower the volume on their rhetoric about the magic of the free marketplace. And when so much of U.S. society is fed up with inordinate litigation, officials could be more modest about the glories of America's legal system.

Protecting national cultures could soon become a defensive rallying point for societies buffeted by globalization and undergoing tumultuous change. Being more sensitive to foreign concerns would ease the prospect of backlash and even bolster America's ability to export its ideas and ideals for the long haul. The U.S. should at least try.

POSTSCRIPT

Is the Globalization of American Culture a Positive Development?

Globalization is a process of technological change and economic expansion under largely capitalist principles. The key actors driving the globalization process are multinational corporations like McDonald's, Coca-Cola, Nike, and Exxon Mobil. These companies are rooted in the American-Western cultural experience, and their premise is based on a materialistic world culture that is striving for greater and greater wealth. That value system is Western and American in origin and evolution. It is therefore logical to assume that as globalization goes, so goes American culture.

Evidence of "American" culture can be seen across the planet: kids in Djakarta or Lagos wearing Michael Jordan jerseys and Nike shoes, for example, and millions of young men and women from Cairo to Lima listening to Michael Jackson records. Symbols of American culture abound in almost every corner of the world, and most of that is associated with economics and the presence of multinational corporations.

As the youth of the world are seduced into an American cultural form and way of life, other cultures are often eclipsed. They lose traction and fade with generational change. Many would argue that this loss is unfortunate, but others would counter that it is part of the historical sweep of life. Social historians suggest that the cultures of Rome, Carthage, Phoenicia, and the Aztecs, while still influential, were eclipsed by a variety of forces that were dominant and historically rooted. While tragic, it was inevitable in the eyes of some social historians.

Regardless of whether this eclipse is positive or negative, the issue of cultural imperialism remains. Larger and more intrusive networks of communication, trade, and economic exchange bring values. In this world of value collision comes choices and change. Unfortunately, millions will find themselves drawn toward a lifestyle of materialism that carries with it a host of value choices. The losers in this clash are local cultures and traditions that, as so often is the case among the young, are easily jettisoned and discarded. It remains to be seen whether or not they will survive the onslaught.

Works on this subject include Benjamin Barber, "Democracy at Risk: American Culture in a Global Culture," *World Policy Journal* (Summer 1998); Seymore Martin Lipset, *American Exceptionalism: A Double-Edged Sword* (W. W. Norton, 1996); and Richard Barnet and John Cavanagh, *Global Dreams: Imperial Corporations and the New World Order* (Simon & Schuster, 1995).

On the Internet . . .

Chemical and Biological Weapons Resource Page

The Chemical and Biological Weapons Resource Page was created by the Center for Nonproliferation Studies and provides a list of documents concerning threat assessment, response, counterterrorism, domestic preparedness, and funding to combat terrorism.

http://cns.miis.edu/research/cbw/cbterror.htm

The Comprehensive Test Ban Treaty

This site on the Comprehensive Test Ban Treaty provides information on the treaty as well as quotations about the treaty from around the world. Also included are press releases and the text of the treaty itself.

http://www.basicint.org/ctbtmain.htm

International Criminal Court: Resources in Print and Electronic Format

The International Criminal Court: Resources in Print and Electronic Format Web site contains a comprehensive list of links. Included are texts of conferences, courses, symposia, and other events as well as a bibliography of books, journals, and other resources.

http://www.lib.uchicago.edu/~llou/icc.html

Exploring Global Conflict: An Internet Guide to the Study of Conflict

Exploring Global Conflict: An Internet Guide to the Study of Conflict is an Internet resource designed to provide understanding of global conflict. Information related to specific conflicts in areas such as Northern Ireland, the Middle East, the Great Lakes region in Africa, and the former Yugoslavia is included on this site. Current news and educational resource sites are listed as well.

http://www.uwm.edu/Dept/CIS/conflict/congeneral.html

PART 5

The New Global Security Agenda

*W**ith the end of the cold war, the concept of security has been freed from its bipolar constraints. Security is now the purview of all peoples and, as such, our concept of security in a postmodern age has broadened considerably. Issues that were once on the back burner of geopolitics are now front page news. Stories about chemical and biological terrorism, genocide, and ethnic conflicts are covered daily.*

This section examines some of the key issues shaping the security dilemma of the twenty-first century.

- Is Biological and Chemical Terrorism the Next Grave Threat to the World Community?

- Should the International Community Intervene in Other States to Prevent Ethnic Cleansing and Genocide?

- Will the Comprehensive Test Ban Treaty Reduce the Risk of Nuclear War?

- Is the Establishment of a Permanent International Criminal Court a Positive Development for Global Security?

- Are Cultural Rivalries and Ethnic Conflicts the Next Great Threats to International Security?

ISSUE 16

Is Biological and Chemical Terrorism the Next Grave Threat to the World Community?

YES: Al J. Venter, from "Keeping the Lid on Germ Warfare," *International Defense Review* (May 1, 1998)

NO: Ehud Sprinzak, from "The Great Superterrorism Scare," *Foreign Policy* (Fall 1998)

ISSUE SUMMARY

YES: Journalist Al J. Venter examines newly emerging biological germs and asserts that they will expand the threat of germ warfare in the coming years.

NO: Professor of political science Ehud Sprinzak argues that a biological or chemical terrorist attack is highly unlikely and that governments, in justifying expanding defense spending and other measures, are exploiting people's fears of such an occurrence.

Ever since the advent of nuclear and, later, biological and chemical weapons, the specter of their use on a widespread scale against military and civilian targets has hung over the globe. The realities of chemical weaponry have been with us since the crude gas bombs of World War I. Subsequent advances in chemical weaponry have been utilized on relatively small scales (although with tremendously tragic consequences) in places like Iraq, Afghanistan, and Vietnam. Such agents as sarin, cyanogen chloride, anthrax, ricin, and Ebola virus can render individuals dead or dying with little chance of survival—some within hours of contact. These and others now head the list of chemical and biological agents that can inflict great death in relatively small amounts.

Our worst fears—which are often dramatized in books and movies—is that clever terrorists will obtain chemical or biological weapons and use them against mass populations in cities like New York, London, Tokyo, and Paris. The events surrounding the Aum Shinrikyo cult's release of sarin nerve gas into the Tokyo subway system in 1995 took this threat from Hollywood fodder to stark reality. Examination of the widespread use of chemical weapons by Saddam

Hussein against his own Kurdish population underscores the potential use of such weapons against defenseless civilian populations.

With the demise of the superpower conflict and the apparent lessening of the threat of country-to-country nuclear war, chemical and biological terrorism has become one of the top defense concerns. There are many reasons for this. First, such weapons are relatively cheap to develop and manufacture when compared to their nuclear counterparts. They are also easy to conceal and deliver. Modest amounts of certain chemical agents injected into air or water supplies can kill thousands, perhaps even millions, in concentrated urban areas. Second, laws and treaties governing the production, sale, and use of such weapons have been spotty. Different governments (including that of the United States) are reluctant to ban such weapons because others already have them. Also, nations have yet to agree on the proper wording of treaties to ban chemical weapons. Third, these weapons are increasingly alluring to groups with political goals who feel impotent in the fight against larger, more powerful enemies. They believe that by striking a dramatic blow at civilian targets, they can realize their aims without the sure suicide of using conventional military or political means.

Many experts believe that these chemical and biological weapons will become more prevalent as modern science produces new chemical compounds and biological elements that lead to greater risk of toxicity. They point to increased governmental concerns over such agents, as evidenced by growing intelligence activity designed to thwart these very occurrences.

Yet others suggest that the fears raised by these agents are overblown and melodramatic. They argue that raising this fear in the aftermath of the cold war is dubious and probably indicates a desire to maintain threat levels in order to increase military and defense spending in various states. Some contend that national security structures and agencies around the world are looking for new justifications for their presence and, thus, have raised the specter of chemical and biological warfare without due cause or real threat.

The following selections debate this issue from opposite ends of the spectrum. Al J. Venter argues that the threat of biological and chemical terrorism is real and pronounced. He contends that keeping the lid on germ warfare is our greatest challenge and that it demands increased knowledge, awareness, and spending to prevent such threats from becoming catastrophic realities. Ehud Sprinzak maintains that warnings about germ warfare are part of a big scare tactic designed to allow for greater military spending and surveillance. He argues that the nature of biological and chemical weapons and potential adversaries is such that the threat is limited and not particularly credible.

Al J. Venter

 YES

Keeping the Lid on Germ Warfare

The 21st century will be the age of the gene just as the 20th century was the age of the atom.

Molecular bio-technology will transform agriculture, energy production, health care, and microelectronics, however, it will also pose significant military and strategic challenges. Whereas recombinant DNA technology offers great benefits to humankind, it also has a darker side—the genetic engineering of microbial pathogens, toxins, and even natural brain chemicals, to create more deadly and persistent weapons of war.

Although Iraq's biological weapons (BW) program is under the microscope of those seeking to halt BW proliferation, the *Wall Street Journal* wrote that this "diverts Western attention away from the broader problems of chemical and biological weapons worldwide—and especially in Russia".

During the Cold War a consensus existed that the Soviet Union was using recombinant DNA technology for military purposes. It was also attempting the recombination of the venom-producing genes from cobras and scorpions (and even bees) with the DNA of normally harmless bacteria. Such an organism would infect the body and surreptitiously produce paralytic cobra toxin. If delivered as a respirable aerosol, such an engineered agent could infect tens of thousands of people.

Former Soviet scientists have described a jointly-operated gene warfare program between the military and the Soviet Academy of Sciences which enjoyed the full support of the Kremlin leadership. The United States, meanwhile, had unilaterally stopped military research into offensive biological and toxin warfare capability in 1972.

Some observers are worried that work in this field is continuing. However, Prof. Matthew Meselson, professor of biochemistry at Harvard University and former chairman of the Federation of American Scientists, has spent a great deal of time investigating what the Soviets, and now the Russians, are doing in the area of biological warfare. He maintains that Moscow's biological research programs are now minimal, pointing to the fact that at every one of the known BW installations, recent satellite imaging has not revealed any ultraviolet emissions.

However, biological issues continue to feature in the media. UK and US troops were inoculated against anthrax during their recent deployment in the

From Al J. Venter, "Keeping the Lid on Germ Warfare," *International Defense Review*, vol. 31, no. 5 (May 1, 1998). Copyright © 1998 by Jane's Information Group Limited. Reprinted by permission.

Persian Gulf, and the UK government issued an all-ports alert following intelligence reports of an attempted smuggling of an anthrax toxin into the country concealed in duty-free merchandise.

The Greatest Threat

Iraq's research into anthrax, botulinum toxin, gas gangrene bacteria, and various chemical poisons such as VX gas, is regarded as the greatest threat. Mustard gas and nerve agents were used in combat against Iran during the 1980–88 Gulf War, and nerve agents were deployed against a Kurdish village in 1988 with casualty figures in the thousands. Moreover, a little-publicized CIA report from 1996—*Intelligence Related to Gulf War Illness*—said that: "There are no indications that any biological agent was destroyed by Coalition bombing."

Understanding the potential of biological warfare remains something of a gray area. Eric Croddy in his book *Chemical and Biological Warfare, An Annotated Bibliography* makes a persuasive case that it is actually quite difficult to kill huge numbers of people using chemical or biological warfare (CBW) agents. "In fact," says Croddy, "it is a considerable challenge to use microbes and biological toxins as weapons of any scale."

Most bacteria and protein toxins are fragile. They are thermolabile (unstable when heated), and are sensitive to acidic solutions and ultraviolet radiation from the sun. Not only must a biological agent 'jump' a number of environmental hurdles, it must also face the antibody/antigen response once inside human tissue.

"The Russians, as with ourselves in the West," says Croddy, "discovered a long time ago that the human body is remarkably resilient. The largest organ, the skin, is a selectively permeable shield against common bacteria, rickettsia and parasites that are ubiquitous in our atmosphere. Even if ingested in food or water, most microbes that would otherwise be remarkably virulent, usually die —their protein toxins denatured by acidic and enzymic action in the gut. And if they find their way in through a cut in the skin, likely as not almost all bacteria will be engulfed by the phagocytic guardians of our immune systems."

Overcoming these defensive mechanisms requires unique features: because the most 'hospitable' and vulnerable sites of entry are the lungs, any biological warfare microbes have to be delivered in some form of respirable aerosol to cause mass casualties. Consequently, microencapsulation is a possible future technology for delivery of some of the more fragile viruses.

Only the most hardy microbes survive the necessary processing in today's biological weapons, and one pathogen—anthrax—fits most criteria as an effective BW. In addition to its ability to form an aerosol, this bacterium on infection attacks the body's own defenses. Significantly, Russia has experimented with an anthrax strain that shows resistance to antibiotic treatment.

Found in domestic livestock, anthrax (Bacillus anthracis) is most commonly encountered among sheep. Shearing of these animals allows the bacteria to become airborne and is the causative agent in woolsorter's disease (a form of pneumonia).

As a spore-forming bacterium, anthrax can survive for decades in soil. This makes it ideal for freeze-drying into an exceptionally fine powder. Once ensconced in the lungs, the capsule surface of the spore resists the body's immunological response. One of three toxins released by the anthrax bacteria further reduces the body's ability to react protectively.

For decades, scientists believed that anthrax killed its victims by forming 'logjams' in the blood stream. Research has since determined that Anthrax toxin III (in combination with other factors) is arguably the most intrusive culprit. Multiplying in the lungs and then in the bloodstream, anthrax reproduces in ever greater numbers by geometric progression. Anecdotal reports of patients succumbing suddenly to anthrax following two or three days of symptoms are consistent with the release of lethal toxin.

Further investigations into anthrax reveal more unsettling discoveries, not least that some strains appear to be resistant to penicillin. This presents another dilemma: in the event of a terrorist anthrax attack, sufficient antibiotics for large population concentrations might not be immediately available. It takes time to manufacture antibiotics. If the threat is real, tens of millions of people would need to be immediately inoculated. Then there is the question of time and whether a therapeutic course could be given quickly enough.

The potential for genetic engineering of this bacterium also presents some horrific consequences: a bacteriological weapon, already well-suited to killing thousands of people within days, could be modified (as Russia has done) to make it resistant to antibiotics. It is, as one observer noted, the perfect weapon and there is every indication that Iraq possesses it in abundance. During the 1990–91 Gulf War, Iraq had large quantities of anthrax, with the intention of dispersing the bacteria over Coalition lines and across Israel.

An outbreak of anthrax in humans occurred in 1979 at Sverdlovsk (now Ekaterinburg) in the former Soviet Union. The original release of spores came from a biological warfare research laboratory in the southern suburbs of the city of 1.2 million people on the eastern slopes of the Urals. It was freeze-dried and the amount released into the atmosphere, according to Meselson, was anything from 4mg to 1g. (It is impossible to see 4mg with the naked eye.)

The resultant epidemic—96 people were infected and 64 died—provoked intense international debate. The Russians never revealed how much anthrax was involved, and it took years to get to the point where they were prepared even to admit that it was an accident.

Speculation continues as to whether the accidental release resulted from activities prohibited by the Biological and Toxin Weapons Convention of 1972. Subsequent research has shown that under such circumstances, the fatality rate—without aggressive medical treatment—would have been more than 95 per cent.

Anthrax particles are most effective when they are within a certain micron range; the accepted wisdom indicates anything between 1–10m. Extensive research that has been carried out at the United States Army Medical Research Institute of Infectious Diseases (USAMRIID), Fort Detrick, Maryland, has indicated that between 8,000 and 10,000 spores constitute an LD50 (lethal dose that will kill half of those infected) for humans. If anthrax is disseminated in sufficiently fine particles, it quickly gets into the bloodstream through the lungs.

Significantly, capsulating bacteria like Bacillus anthracis tend to defeat the body's immune system in two ways: first they resist being engulfed by white blood cells; second, they produce toxins that actually vitiate the human immune response. Then the bacteria start multiplying at a rapid rate, producing a most lethal toxin. Fortunately this symptom can be treated if caught early enough.

Sudden Death

However, if the strain is the latest Russian development and proves to be impervious to antibiotics, any such treatment is rendered ineffective. The progression in such a case is simple; as the bacteria multiply, the level of toxin dramatically increases. Death can be sudden, following a few days of incubation. At Sverdlovsk the first victim was dead in days, and the last case died six weeks after infection.

The consensus is that anyone exposed to at least 20 anthrax spores per cubic liter of air for about 30min will probably receive close to an LD50 dose. If enough infected air is inhaled in that time, sufficient spores will enter the victim's lungs to make for an infectious dose.

Iraq carried out research in this field in laboratories at Al Hakam and Salman Pak, both on the outskirts of Baghdad. Although Coalition bombing in 1991 destroyed much of this, intelligence sources indicate that a significant measure of this BW program has survived intact. United Nations inspectors with the UN Special Commission (UNSCOM) are now searching for these assets. There is no doubt that the weapons exist—the problem is finding them.

Those countries with advanced research BW programs—such as Iraq, Iran, Libya, North Korea, and Syria—have anthrax occurring naturally, usually in such places as stockyards, wool shearing depots and the like. Governments are consequently able to seek scientific aid regarding treatment from humanitarian organizations as part of their ongoing research, because anthrax is a viable threat to livestock.

Mail-Order 'Anthrax'

In 1986, before the breakdown of relations between Iraq and the US, the latter country supplied seed cultures of anthrax from the American Type Culture Collection, a laboratory in Rockville, Maryland. Spore samples were ordered by telephone and were sent, as a matter of course, by normal mail. Iraq and other renegade states working on BWs were then able to ask the relevant bodies for anthrax, claiming it was needed for research on antibiotic regimens.

This supply channel has since been blocked. According to the US Department of Defense (DoD), this is the most common method of creating a national BW program; as such, anthrax will continue to be the prime experimental pathogen, which is why it is regarded as such a serious threat.

Similarly, botulinum toxin—another 'pathogen of choice' for some developing countries—presents a different type of threat. In humans the toxin interrupts conduction between our peripheral nervous system and muscle receptors. Botox, as it is commonly called, is prescribed by doctors to treat Strabismus dystonius and other neurological disorders. It is also in everyday cosmetic use (to counter the onset of facial or other bodily wrinkles); botox makes the muscles flaccid or paralyzes them and they take months to recover.

If this occurred on a larger scale in the human body—where the majority of functions are determined by the way muscles behave—it would be fatal. It takes only an extremely small dose of botulinum to kill by respiratory paralysis. One such example is that of a woman who was poisoned by botulinum from eating just half of a green bean (which became infected during the canning process); there are not many microbes in half a green bean, but it contained sufficient toxin for it to kill. In the case of botulinism, the LD50 is about 0.001g/kg of body weight.

It is difficult to establish which of the two—anthrax or botulinum—is the more toxic. Certainly, botulinum acts considerably faster than anthrax which takes some days to get into the system before a septicaemic reaction is manifested. It can be preceded by flu-like symptoms. Although scientists are aware of the end result, not enough is known about botulinum to describe the sequence of events in detail.

For all this, neither anthrax nor botulinum has been tested on any scale in modern warfare. The Japanese Aum Shinrikyo cult [the cult responsible for the 1995 nerve gas attack on a crowded Tokyo subway station] made an unsuccessful attempt to rig a fan in a Tokyo building in order to spray anthrax spores over the city, but errors were made either in production or delivery. Militarily, the consensus is that these biological and toxin agents, while devastating to those who are unprepared, will not make or break wars. These pathogens remain unproven entities, but that does not make them any less potent as killers.

Cult Chemists

Aum Shinrikyo had access to a considerable amount of money (estimated at between US$300 million and US$1 billion) with which it hired chemists and biologists. Members of the cult were also reported to have arrived in Kikwit in the former Zaire (now the Republic of Congo) at the time of an outbreak of the Ebola epidemic, to obtain samples for BW purposes.

Dr Jane Alexander, of the US Defense Advanced Research Projects Agency (DARPA), has studied the Japanese sect. She discovered that Aum had also undertaken research into the 0157:H7 variant of E.coli, which produces a toxin. Although E.coli is difficult to manipulate as an aerosol for BW use, such bugs can cause serious problems (in Osaka, Japan, 10,000 people were infected with a deviant form of E.coli 0157:H7).

What Aum was working on entailed the insertion of botulinum toxin inside E.coli bacteria in an attempt to manufacture a lethal carrier of this toxin. It is likely that Aum was investigating plasmids (small rings of DNA material that carry genetic information) to implant material into bacteria as well. In fact, pharmaceutical companies use E.coli plasmids to produce Vitamin C which is cheaper than trying to synthesize it—for these purposes E.coli is relatively innocuous and exists as a normal and healthy bacteria in human intestines.

In this way, says Croddy, the processing of E.coli as a weapon is an attempt to 'sneak' an E.coli strain into the body, which does not (or cannot) react immediately. This virulent new strain would then start to multiply. (It is much more serious if a toxin-generating gene has been inserted into a bacterial DNA.)

The ramifications of such genetic engineering are endless: in the case of the E.coli 0157:H7 strain, a toxin would be produced that can result in serious problems in children and the elderly, including renal failure. This strain of E.coli was responsible for an outbreak of food poisoning in Scotland during 1996, when more than a dozen people died and hundreds were taken ill.

Such effects can be taken one step further by inserting other genes to produce more virulent toxins, which is what the former Soviet Union was researching. Western intelligence agencies are aware that some work into biological warfare programs continued in the Commonwealth of Independent States until at least 1992 (the Sverdlovsk-17 BW plant was shut down in the same year).

The UK and US have monitored these developments carefully. They are in the process of determining the long-term implications, largely to ensure that the West has adequate defenses should the deployment of germ weapons become a reality.

One of the issues raised—particularly in the light of revelations about Iraq's BW program—is whether the US will ever again acquire a real offensive CBW capability. The consensus is 'absolutely not'. There are, however, numerous institutions—the military (USAMRIID [U.S. Army Medical Research Institute of Infectious Diseases] in particular), universities, and so on—that spend a great deal of money in establishing how and which microbial pathogens might be manipulated, in order to anticipate what potentially hostile states or subversive groups might be working on.

DARPA is making a serious effort to look closely at E.coli in terms of biological defense. Here, too, Russia has been working to transfer segments of genetic material from one bacterium to another, which is relevant in terms of antibiotic resistance. The upshot is whether or not a new germ manufactured by a hostile power can be effectively countered.

This has caused scientists to speculate how E.coli 0157:H7 originally came into existence, and how it became a toxin-generating microbe. There are some scientists who argue that the strain emerged naturally and mutated from bacteria exchanging genetic information. According to others, it could have been bio-engineered in a laboratory and spread from there. Most scientific favor rests with the first argument. In terms of research into E.coli, Croddy's view is that: "All the major European powers are tinkering about with it defensively. Personally, I would say that USAMRIID is further ahead than just about anybody else."

In the area of biological warfare defense, money—and a lot of it—is being spent. In the US, DARPA is co-ordinating most of the purse strings, channeling much of the money through the Biological Defense Program Office. Significant funds are also being diverted to educational institutions such as Johns Hopkins University and others in the academic research field.

Real-Time Detection

Research into a small mass-spectrometer that will fit into a standard-sized briefcase which could conceivably be used under battlefield conditions is also under way. This will be capable of identifying in real-time if a friendly force is deployed in a 'hot' (contaminated) zone. Although this development is better suited for the characterization of chemical agents, it is hoped that highly accurate readings of the primary eight BW threats will also be available.

"Then," says Croddy, "if you detect any sort of biological presence, you may not know immediately what it is and whether it is a potential threat. But you will have a pretty good idea. You will probably want to 'suit-up' anyway."

The DoD concluded recently that the biological warfare threat was one area in which the United States has found itself to be the most vulnerable. This was said repeatedly at a symposium on the subject held in Atlanta, Georgia, in March [1998]. More than 2,000 delegates from 70 countries were present, many of them military officers. This indicates the significant level of interest in a menace which could, if ever released from the confines of a laboratory, herald a global epidemic.

NO

Ehud Sprinzak

The Great Superterrorism Scare

Last March [1998], representatives from more than a dozen U.S. federal agencies gathered at the White House for a secret simulation to test their readiness to confront a new kind of terrorism. Details of the scenario unfolded a month later on the front page of the *New York Times*: Without warning, thousands across the American Southwest fall deathly ill. Hospitals struggle to rush trained and immunized medical personnel into crisis areas. Panic spreads as vaccines and antibiotics run short—and then run out. The killer is a hybrid of smallpox and the deadly Marburg virus, genetically engineered and let loose by terrorists to infect hundreds of thousands along the Mexican-American border.

This apocalyptic tale represents Washington's newest nightmare: the threat of a massive terrorist attack with chemical, biological, or nuclear weapons. Three recent events seem to have convinced the policymaking elite and the general public that a disaster is imminent: the 1995 nerve gas attack on a crowded Tokyo subway station by the Japanese millenarian cult Aum Shinrikyo; the disclosure of alarming new information about the former Soviet Union's massive biowarfare program; and disturbing discoveries about the extent of Iraqi president Saddam Hussein's hidden chemical and biological arsenals. Defense Secretary William Cohen summed up well the prevailing mood surrounding mass-destruction terrorism: "The question is no longer if this will happen, but when."

Such dire forecasts may make for gripping press briefings, movies, and bestsellers, but they do not necessarily make for good policy. As an unprecedented fear of mass-destruction terrorism spreads throughout the American security establishment, governments worldwide are devoting more attention to the threat. But as horrifying as this prospect may be, the relatively low risks of such an event do not justify the high costs now being contemplated to defend against it. Not only are many of the countermeasures likely to be ineffective, but the level of rhetoric and funding devoted to fighting superterrorism may actually advance a potential superterrorist's broader goals: sapping the resources of the state and creating a climate of panic and fear that can amplify the impact of any terrorist act.

From Ehud Sprinzak, "The Great Superterrorism Scare," *Foreign Policy* (Fall 1998). Copyright © 1998 by The Carnegie Endowment for International Peace. Reprinted by permission of *Foreign Policy*.

Capabilities and Chaos

Since the Clinton administration issued its Presidential Decision Directive on terrorism in June 1995, U.S. federal, state, and local governments have heightened their efforts to prevent or respond to a terrorist attack involving weapons of mass destruction. A report issued in December 1997 by the National Defense Panel, a commission of experts created by congressional mandate, calls upon the army to shift its priorities and prepare to confront dire domestic threats. The National Guard and the U.S. Army Reserve must be ready, for example, to "train local authorities in chemical—and biological—weapons detection, defense, and decontamination; assist in casualty treatment and evacuation; quarantine, if necessary, affected areas and people; and assist in restoration of infrastructure and services." In May, the Department of Defense announced plans to train National Guard and reserve elements in every region of the country to carry out these directives.

In his 1998 State of the Union address, President Bill Clinton promised to address the dangers of biological weapons obtained by "outlaw states, terrorists, and organized criminals." Indeed, the president's budget for 1999, pending congressional approval, devotes hundreds of millions of dollars to superterrorism response and recovery programs, including large decontamination units, stockpiles of vaccines and antibiotics, improved means of detecting chemical and biological agents and analyzing disease outbreaks, and training for special intervention forces. The FBI, Pentagon, State Department, and U.S. Health and Human Services Department will benefit from these funds, as will a plethora of new interagency bodies established to coordinate these efforts. Local governments are also joining in the campaign. Last April [1998], New York City officials began monitoring emergency room care in search of illness patterns that might indicate a biological or chemical attack had occurred. The city also brokered deals with drug companies and hospitals to ensure an adequate supply of medicine in the event of such an attack. Atlanta, Denver, Los Angeles, San Francisco, and Washington are developing similar programs with state and local funds. If the proliferation of counterterrorism programs continues at its present pace, and if the U.S. army is indeed redeployed to the home front, as suggested by the National Defense Panel, the bill for these preparations could add up to tens of billions of dollars in the coming decades.

Why have terrorism specialists and top government officials become so obsessed with the prospect that terrorists, foreign or homegrown, will soon attempt to bring about an unprecedented disaster in the United States? A close examination of their rhetoric reveals two underlying assumptions:

- **The Capabilities Proposition.** According to this logic, anyone with access to modern biochemical technology and a college science education could produce enough chemical or biological agents in his or her basement to devastate the population of London, Tokyo, or Washington. The raw materials are readily available from medical suppliers, germ banks, university labs, chemical-fertilizer stores, and even ordinary pharmacies. Most policy today proceeds from this assumption.

- **The Chaos Proposition.** The post-Cold War world swarms with shadowy extremist groups, religious fanatics, and assorted crazies eager to launch a major attack on the civilized world—preferably on U.S. territory. Walter Laqueur, terrorism's leading historian, recently wrote that "scanning the contemporary scene, one encounters a bewildering multiplicity of terrorist and potentially terrorist groups and sects." Senator Richard Lugar agrees: "fanatics, small disaffected groups and subnational factions who hold various grievances against governments, or against society, all have increasing access to, and knowledge about the construction of, weapons of mass destruction. . . . Such individuals are not likely to be deterred . . . by the classical threat of overwhelming retaliation."

There is, however, a problem with this two-part logic. Although the capabilities proposition is largely valid—albeit for the limited number of terrorists who can overcome production and handling risks and develop an efficient means of dispersal—the chaos proposition is utterly false. Despite the lurid rhetoric, a massive terrorist attack with nuclear, chemical, or biological weapons is hardly inevitable. It is not even likely. Thirty years of field research have taught observers of terrorism a most important lesson: Terrorists wish to convince us that they are capable of striking from anywhere at anytime, but there really is no chaos. In fact, terrorism involves predictable behavior, and the vast majority of terrorist organizations can be identified well in advance.

Most terrorists possess political objectives, whether Basque independence, Kashmiri separatism, or Palestinian Marxism. Neither crazy nor stupid, they strive to gain sympathy from a large audience and wish to live after carrying out any terrorist act to benefit from it politically. As terrorism expert Brian Jenkins has remarked, terrorists want lots of people watching, not lots of people dead. Furthermore, no terrorist becomes a terrorist overnight. A lengthy trajectory of radicalization and low-level violence precedes the killing of civilians. A terrorist becomes mentally ready to use lethal weapons against civilians only over time and only after he or she has managed to dehumanize the enemy. From the Baader-Meinhoff group in Germany and the Tamil Tigers in Sri Lanka to Hamas and Hizballah in the Middle East, these features are universal.

Finally, with rare exceptions—such as the Unabomber—terrorism is a group phenomenon. Radical organizations are vulnerable to early detection through their disseminated ideologies, lesser illegal activities, and public statements of intent. Some even publish their own World Wide Web sites. Since the 1960s, the vast majority of terrorist groups have made clear their aggressive intentions long before following through with violence.

We can draw three broad conclusions from these findings. First, terrorists who threaten to kill thousands of civilians are aware that their chances for political and physical survival are exceedingly slim. Their prospects for winning public sympathy are even slimmer. Second, terrorists take time to become dangerous, particularly to harden themselves sufficiently to use weapons of mass destruction. Third, the number of potential suspects is significantly less than doomsayers would have us believe. Ample early warning signs should make effective interdiction of potential superterrorists easier than today's overheated rhetoric suggests.

The World's Most Wanted

Who, then, is most likely to attempt a superterrorist attack? Historical evidence and today's best field research suggest three potential profiles:

- Religious millenarian cults, such as Japan's Aum Shinrikyo, that possess a sense of immense persecution and messianic frenzy and hold faith in salvation via Armageddon. Most known religious cults do not belong here. Millenarian cults generally seclude themselves and wait for salvation; they do not strike out against others. Those groups that do take action more often fit the mold of California's Heaven's Gate, or France's Order of the Solar Temple, seeking salvation through group suicide rather than massive violence against outsiders.
- Brutalized groups that either burn with revenge following a genocide against their nation or face the prospect of imminent destruction without any hope for collective recovery. The combination of unrestrained anger and total powerlessness may lead such groups to believe that their only option is to exact a horrendous price for their loss. "The Avengers," a group of 50 young Jews who fought the Nazis as partisans during World War II, exemplifies the case. Organized in Poland in 1945, the small organization planned to poison the water supply of four German cities to avenge the Holocaust. Technical problems foiled their plan, but a small contingent still succeeded in poisoning the food of more than 2,000 former SS storm troopers held in prison near Nuremberg.
- Small terrorist cells or socially deranged groups whose alienated members despise society, lack realistic political goals, and may miscalculate the consequences of developing and using chemical or biological agents. Although such groups, or even individual "loners," cannot be totally dismissed, it is doubtful that they will possess the technical capabilities to produce mass destruction.

Groups such as Hamas, Hizballah, and Islamic Jihad, which so many Americans love to revile—and fear—do not make the list of potential superterrorists. These organizations and their state sponsors may loathe the Great Satan, but they also wish to survive and prosper politically. Their leaders, most of whom are smarter than the Western media implies, understand that a Hiroshima-like disaster would effectively mean the end of their movements.

Only two groups have come close to producing a superterrorism catastrophe: Aum Shinrikyo and the white supremacist and millenarian American Covenant, the Sword and the Arm of the Lord, whose chemical-weapons stockpile was seized by the FBI in 1985 as they prepared to hasten the coming of the Messiah by poisoning the water supplies of several U.S. cities. Only Aum Shinrikyo fully developed both the capabilities and the intent to take tens of thousands of lives. However, this case is significant not only because the group epitomizes the kind of organizations that may resort to superterrorism in the future, but also because Aum's fate illustrates how groups of this nature can be identified and their efforts preempted.

Although it comes as no comfort to the 12 people who died in Aum Shinrikyo's attack, the cult's act of notoriety represents first and foremost a colossal Japanese security blunder. Until Japanese police arrested its leaders in May 1995, Aum Shinrikyo had neither gone underground nor concealed its intentions. Cult leader Shoko Asahara had written since the mid-1980s of an impending cosmic cataclysm. By 1995, when Russian authorities curtailed the cult's activities in that country, Aum Shinrikyo had established a significant presence in the former Soviet Union, accessed the vibrant Russian black market to obtain various materials, and procured the formulae for chemical agents. In Japan, Asahara methodically recruited chemical engineers, physicists, and biologists who conducted extensive chemical and biological experiments in their lab and on the Japanese public. Between 1990 and 1994, the cult tried six times—unsuccessfully—to execute biological-weapons attacks, first with botulism and then with anthrax. In June 1994, still a year before the subway gas attack that brought them world recognition, two sect members released sarin gas near the judicial building in the city of Matsumoto, killing seven people and injuring 150, including three judges.

In the years preceding the Tokyo attack, at least one major news source provided indications of Aum Shinrikyo's proclivity toward violence. In October 1989, the *Sunday Mainichi* magazine began a seven-part series on the cult that showed it regularly practiced a severe form of coercion on members and recruits. Following the November 1989 disappearance of a lawyer, along with his family, who was pursuing criminal action against the cult on behalf of former members, the magazine published a follow-up article. Because of Japan's hypersensitivity to religious freedom, lack of chemical—and biological—terrorism precedents, and low-quality domestic intelligence, the authorities failed to prevent the Tokyo attack despite these ample warning signs.

Anatomy of an Obsession

If a close examination reveals that the chances of a successful superterrorist attack are minimal, why are so many people so worried? There are three major explanations:

Sloppy Thinking

Most people fail to distinguish among the four different types of terrorism: mass-casualty terrorism, state-sponsored chemical- or biological-weapons (CBW) terrorism, small-scale chemical or biological terrorist attacks, and superterrorism. Pan Am 103, Oklahoma City, and the World Trade Center are all examples of conventional terrorism designed to kill a large number of civilians. The threat that a "rogue state," a country hostile to the West, will provide terrorist groups with the funds and expertise to launch a chemical or biological attack falls into another category: state-sponsored CBW terrorism. The use of chemical or biological weapons for a small-scale terrorist attack is a third distinct category. Superterrorism—the strategic use of chemical or biological agents to bring about a major disaster with death tolls ranging in the tens or hundreds of thousands must be distinguished from all of these as a separate threat.

Today's prophets of doom blur the lines between these four distinct categories of terrorism. The world, according to their logic, is increasingly saturated with weapons of mass destruction and with terrorists seeking to use them, a volatile combination that will inevitably let the superterrorism genie out of the bottle. Never mind that the only place where these different types of terrorism are lumped together is on television talk shows and in sensationalist headlines.

In truth, the four types of terrorism are causally unrelated. Neither Saddam Hussein's hidden bombs nor Russia's massive stockpiles of pathogens necessarily bring a superterrorist attack on the West any closer. Nor do the mass-casualty crimes of Timothy McVeigh in Oklahoma City or the World Trade Center bombing. The issue is not CBW quantities or capabilities but rather group mentality and psychological motivations. In the final analysis, only a rare, extremist mindset completely devoid of political and moral considerations will consider launching such an attack.

Vested Interests

The threat of superterrorism is likely to make a few defense contractors very rich and a larger number of specialists moderately rich as well as famous. Last year, Canadian-based Dycor Industrial Research Ltd. unveiled the CB Sentry, a commercially available monitoring system designed to detect contaminants in the air, including poison gas. Dycor announced plans to market the system for environmental and antiterrorist applications. As founder and president Hank Mottl explained in a press conference, "Dycor is sitting on the threshold of a multi-billion dollar world market." In August, a *New York Times* story on the Clinton administration's plans to stockpile vaccines around the country for civilian protection noted that two members of a scientific advisory panel that endorsed the plan potentially stood to gain financially from its implementation. William Crowe, former chair of the joint chiefs of staff, is also bullish on the counterterrorism market. He is on the board of an investment firm that recently purchased Michigan Biologic Products Institute, the sole maker of an anthrax vaccine. The lab has already secured a Pentagon contract and expects buyers from around the world to follow suit. As for the expected bonanza for terrorism specialists, consultant Larry Johnson remarked last year to *U.S. News & World Report*, "It's the latest gravy train."

Within the U.S. government, National Security Council experts, newly created army and police intervention forces, an assortment of energy and public-health units and officials, and a significant number of new Department of Defense agencies specializing in unconventional terrorism will benefit from the counterterrorism obsession and megabudgets in the years ahead. According to a September 1997 report by the General Accounting Office, more than 40 federal agencies have been involved already in combating terrorism. It may yet be premature to announce the rise of a new "military-scientific-industrial complex," but some promoters of the superterrorism scare seem to present themselves as part of a coordinated effort to save civilization from the greatest threat of the twenty-first century.

SETTING THE FBI FREE

When members of the Japanese cult Aum Shinrikyo went shopping in the United States, they were not looking for cheap jeans or compact discs. They were out to secure key ingredients for a budding chemical-weapons program —and they went unnoticed. Today, more FBI agents than ever are working the counterterrorism beat: double the number that would-be superterrorists had to contend with just a few years ago. But is the FBI really better equipped now than it was then to discover and preempt such terrorist activity in its earliest stages?

FBI counterterrorism policy is predicated on guidelines issued in 1983 by then-U.S. attorney general William French Smith: The FBI can open a full investigation into a potential act of terrorism only "when facts or circumstances reasonably indicate that two or more persons are engaged in activities that involve force or violence and a violation of the criminal laws of the United States." Short of launching a full investigation, the FBI may open a preliminary inquiry if it learns from any source that a crime might be committed and determines that the allegation "requires some further scrutiny." This ambiguous phrasing allows the FBI a reasonable degree of latitude in investigating potential terrorist activity.

However, without a lead—whether an anonymous tip or a public news report—FBI agents can do little to gather intelligence on known or potential terrorists. Agents cannot even download information from World Wide Web sites or clip newspapers to track fringe elements. The FBI responds to leads; it does not ferret out potential threats. Indeed, in an interview with the Center for National Security Studies, one former FBI official griped, "You have to wait until you have blood on the street before the Bureau can act."

CIA analysts in charge of investigating foreign terrorist threats comb extensive databanks on individuals and groups hostile to the United States. American citizens are constitutionally protected against this sort of intrusion. A 1995 presidential initiative intended to increase the FBI's authority to plant wiretaps, deport illegal aliens suspected of terrorism, and expand the role of the military in certain kinds of cases was blocked by Congress. Critics have argued that the costs of such constraints on law enforcement may be dangerously high—reconsidering them would be one of the most effective (and perhaps least expensive) remedies against superterrorism.

Morbid Fascination

Suspense writers, publishers, television networks, and sensationalist journalists have already cashed in on the superterrorism craze. Clinton aides told the *New York Times* that the president was so alarmed by journalist Richard Preston's depiction of a superterrorist attack in his novel *The Cobra Event* that he passed the book to intelligence analysts and House Speaker Newt Gingrich for review.

But even as media outlets spin the new frenzy out of personal and financial interests, they also respond to the deep psychological needs of a huge audience. People love to be horrified. In the end, however, the tax-paying public is likely to be the biggest loser of the present scare campaign. All terrorists—even those who would never consider a CBW attack—benefit from such heightened attention and fear.

Counterterrorism on a Shoestring

There is, in fact, a growing interest in chemical and biological weapons among terrorist and insurgent organizations worldwide for small-scale, tactical attacks. As far back as 1975, the Symbionese Liberation Army obtained instructions on the development of germ warfare agents to enhance their "guerrilla" actions. More recently, in 1995, four members of the Minnesota Patriots Council, an antitax group that rejected all forms of authority higher than the state level, were convicted of possession of a biological agent for use as a weapon. Prosecutors contended that the men conspired to murder various federal and county officials with a supply of the lethal toxin ricin they had developed with the aid of an instruction kit purchased through a right-wing publication. The flourishing mystique of chemical and biological weapons suggests that angry and alienated groups are likely to manipulate them for conventional political purposes. And indeed, the number of CBW threats investigated by the FBI is increasing steadily. But the use of such weapons merely to enhance conventional terrorism should not prove excessively costly to counter.

The debate boils down to money. If the probability of a large-scale attack is extremely small, fewer financial resources should be committed to recovering from it. Money should be allocated instead to early warning systems and preemption of tactical chemical and biological terrorism. The security package below stresses low-cost intelligence, consequence management and research, and a no-cost, prudent counterterrorism policy. Although tailored to the United States, this program could form the basis for policy in other countries as well:

- **International deterrence.** The potential use of chemical and biological weapons for enhanced conventional terrorism, and the limited risk of escalation to superterrorism, call for a reexamination of the existing U.S. deterrence doctrine—especially of the evidence required for retaliation against states that sponsor terrorism. The United States must relay a stern, yet discreet message to states that continue to support terrorist organizations or that disregard the presence of loosely affiliated terrorists within their territory: They bear direct and full responsibility for any future CBW attack on American targets by the organizations they sponsor or shelter. They must know that any use of weapons of mass destruction by their clients against the United States will constitute just cause for massive retaliation against their countries, whether or not evidence proves for certain that they ordered the attack.

- **Domestic deterrence.** There is no question that the potential use of chemical and biological weapons for low-level domestic terrorism adds a new and dangerous dimension to conventional terrorism. There is consequently an urgent need to create a culture of domestic deterrence against the nonscientific use of chemical and biological agents. The most important task must be accomplished through legislation. Congress should tighten existing legislation against domestic production and distribution of biological, chemical, and radiological agents and devices.

The Anti-Terrorism Act of 1996 enlarged the federal criminal code to include within its scope a prohibition on any attempts, threats, and conspiracies to acquire or use biological agents, chemical agents, and toxins. It also further redefined the terms "biological agent" and "toxin" to cover a number of products that may be bioengineered into threatening agents. However, the legislation still includes the onerous burden of proving that these agents were developed for use as weapons. Take the case of Larry Wayne Harris, an Ohio man arrested in January [1998] by the FBI for procuring anthrax cultures from an unknown source. Harris successfully defended his innocence by insisting that he obtained the anthrax spores merely to experiment with vaccines. He required no special permit or license to procure toxins that could be developed into deadly agents. The FBI and local law enforcement agencies should be given the requisite authority to enforce existing laws as well as to act in cases of clear and present CBW danger, even if the groups involved have not yet shown criminal intent. The regulations regarding who is allowed to purchase potentially threatening agents should also be strengthened.

A campaign of public education detailing the dangers and illegality of nonscientific experimentation in chemical and biological agents would also be productive. This effort should include, for example, clear and stringent university policies regulating the use of school laboratories and a responsible public ad campaign explaining the serious nature of this crime. A clear presentation of the new threat as another type of conventional terrorism would alert the public to groups and individuals who experiment illegitimately with chemical and biological substances and would reduce CBW terrorism hysteria.

- **Better Intelligence.** As is currently the case, the intelligence community should naturally assume the most significant role in any productive campaign to stop chemical and biological terrorism. However, new early warning CBW indicators that focus on radical group behavior are urgently needed. Analysts should be able to reduce substantially the risk of a CBW attack if they monitor group radicalization as expressed in its rhetoric, extralegal operations, low-level violence, growing sense of collective paranoia, and early experimentation with chemical or biological substances. Proper CBW intelligence must be freed from the burden of proving criminal intent.
- **Smart and compact consequence management teams.** The threat of conventional CBW terrorism requires neither massive preparations

nor large intervention forces. It calls for neither costly new technologies nor a growing number of interagency coordinating bodies. The decision to form and train joint-response teams in major U.S. cities, prompted by the 1995 Presidential Decision Directive on terrorism, will be productive if the teams are kept within proper proportions. The ideal team would be streamlined so as to minimize the interagency rivalry that has tended to make these teams grow in size and complexity. In addition to FBI agents, specially trained local police, detection and decontamination experts, and public-health specialists, these compact units should include psychologists and public-relations experts trained in reducing public hysteria.

- **Psychopolitical research.** The most neglected means of countering CBW terrorism is psychopolitical research. Terrorism scholars and U.S. intelligence agencies have thus far failed to discern the psychological mechanisms that may compel terrorists to contemplate seriously the use of weapons of mass destruction. Systematic group and individual profiling for predictive purposes is almost unknown. Whether in Europe, Latin America, the Middle East, or the United States, numerous former terrorists and members of radical organizations are believed to have considered and rejected the use of weapons of mass destruction. To help us understand better the considerations involved in the use or nonuse of chemical and biological weapons, well-trained psychologists and terrorism researchers should conduct a three-year, low-cost, comprehensive project of interviewing these former radicals.

- **Reducing unnecessary superterrorism rhetoric.** Although there is no way to censor the discussion of mass-destruction terrorism, President Clinton, his secretaries, elected politicians at all levels, responsible government officials, writers, and journalists must tone down the rhetoric feeding today's superterrorism frenzy.

There is neither empirical evidence nor logical support for the growing belief that a new "postmodern" age of terrorism is about to dawn, an era afflicted by a large number of anonymous mass murderers toting chemical and biological weapons. The true threat of superterrorism will not likely come in the form of a Hiroshima-like disaster but rather as a widespread panic caused by a relatively small CBW incident involving a few dozen fatalities. Terrorism, we must remember, is not about killing. It is a form of psychological warfare in which the killing of a small number of people convinces the rest of us that we are next in line. Rumors, anxiety, and hysteria created by such inevitable incidents may lead to panic-stricken evacuations of entire neighborhoods, even cities, and may produce many indirect fatalities. It may also lead to irresistible demands to fortify the entire United States against future chemical and biological attacks, however absurd the cost.

Americans should remember the calls made in the 1950s to build shelters, conduct country-wide drills, and alert the entire nation for a first-strike nuclear attack. A return to the duck-and-cover absurdities of that time is likely to be as ineffective and debilitating now as it was then. Although the threat of chemical and biological terrorism should be taken seriously, the public must know that the risk of a major catastrophe is extremely minimal. The fear of CBW terrorism is contagious: Other countries are already showing increased interest in protecting themselves against superterrorism. A restrained and measured American response to the new threat may have a sobering effect on CBW mania worldwide.

POSTSCRIPT

Is Biological and Chemical Terrorism the Next Grave Threat to the World Community?

It is easy to predict that terrorist organizations will strike at their enemies. It is their stated goal and part of their tactical approach to achieving political aims. However, it is hard to predict how and when terrorist organizations will act. Weapons choice is a highly idiosyncratic issue fraught with many variables, including available cash, training, expertise, understanding, and determination. It is reasonable to speculate that certain weapons will be tempting to groups that want to exercise maximum effect. For example, the bomb that Timothy McVeigh detonated outside an Oklahoma City federal building in April 1995 was simple and easy to develop, reflecting a lack of resources coupled with a desire to have maximum effect. The explosive used in the World Trade Center bombing in February 1993 was more sophisticated but also a function of resources and training.

It is important to note that the line between wanting to employ more sophisticated weapons and actual action is difficult to establish. Many states have pursued the development of nuclear weapons, for example, but few (Libya, North Korea, Syria, and Iraq) have achieved such capability. Still others with the capability (such as Germany, Sweden, Italy, Brazil, and Spain) have decided not to develop such weapons. The assumption that all terrorist groups would use such weapons if they were available is not necessarily true unless one subscribes to the view that all terrorists are irrational, which is not supported by the facts.

Most terrorist organizations engage in their methods of conflict for political goals: self-determination of a people, removal of a particular regime, or ideological objectives. As a recent study by the RAND Corporation shows, terrorists do have goals, and the consequences of their actions are calculated. Potential impacts, world opinion, media coverage, and retaliation are factored into the decision-making process. Therefore, it is not logical to assume that with new weapons comes the likelihood of their use. What may be more likely is that different types of organizations may push toward or away from certain weapons based on their stated political goals and also on the quality of their leadership.

Literature on this subject includes *The Next War* by Caspar Weinberger and Peter Schweizer (Regnery, 1996) and John F. Sopko, "The Changing Proliferation Threat," *Foreign Policy* (Winter 1996–1997). In both publications, the authors argue that the United States is ignoring the threat of chemical and biological warfare at its own peril. John Mueller and Karl Mueller counter this argument in "Sanctions of Mass Destruction," *Foreign Affairs* (May/June 1999).

ISSUE 17

Should the International Community Intervene in Other States to Prevent Ethnic Cleansing and Genocide?

YES: Robert C. Johansen, from "Will We Do Nothing?" *Christian Century* (March 20–27, 1996)

NO: Edward N. Luttwak, from "Give War a Chance," *Foreign Affairs* (July/August 1999)

ISSUE SUMMARY

YES: Robert C. Johansen, a professor of government and international studies, argues that the international community, operating via the United Nations, needs to establish a permanent force to intervene in situations of ethnic cleansing and genocide.

NO: Edward N. Luttwak, a senior fellow of the Center for Strategic and International Studies, contends that some conflicts among ethnic groups need to take place as a means of settling political disputes and that intervention by the United Nations and other groups is often counterproductive and should be discouraged.

Ethnic cleansing and genocide are not new phenomena. People across the globe have engaged in these activities for centuries. From the hordes of Genghis Khan sweeping across Asia to the Spanish conquest of the Incas and Aztecs, to the American subjugation of the Native American, to the European colonialization of Africa, such events have soiled global history. In this past century, the Turkish genocide of the Armenians, the Holocaust against the Jews by the Nazis, and the recent mass killings in Rwanda and the former Yugoslavia underscore the horrors of such extreme forms of conflict. These events tear at the very core of global society in moral and ethical terms.

Several important elements of ethnic cleansing and genocide in today's international arena are vital to understanding of the current issue. First is the reasons why they have become such major issues today, considering that they apparently did not demand great interest or outrage in past centuries. Today atrocities are beamed to television screens around the world, touching millions of lives with horrors that are seldom seen. The technology of this globalizing age allows millions of people to witness firsthand such events and to feel the human suffering and tragedy. It thus challenges our sense of morality and righteousness and consequently calls us to act to prevent such events.

Second, since genocide and ethnic cleansing can be identified as they happen, citizens of the world are quickly challenged to act, and the policy question of international intervention becomes an immediate imperative. When one learns of atrocities after they have been perpetrated, one can only condemn and perhaps help in the search for justice. But since these events can now be seen in real time, there is a more immediate moral imperative to act.

Although most people and governments around the world share in the revulsion toward genocide and ethnic cleansing, debate rages as to what to do about it. Many cling to the traditional notion that intervention in another state's affairs is wrong and also dangerous, lest your own state face possible intervention by others in other circumstances. Other nations, including the United States, are reluctant to argue for blanket intervention powers because of the precedent that it would set. Americans prefer to invoke national interest as the prerequisite and, thus, to intervene in places where it is advantageous for the United States to do so (such as Kosovo) but not in others (such as Liberia and Rwanda). Still other nations cannot afford the expense of intervention nor do they possess the air or sealift capability to even contemplate such action in places like Rwanda, Liberia, and Kosovo.

Some critics argue that international organizations like the United Nations and military power like that possessed by the United States mean nothing if they cannot be used to stop such hideous events as ethnic cleansing and genocide. They contend that it is a moral responsibility to act in ways that will prevent these events from happening and to bring those responsible to justice in international forums like the World Court. These critics argue that had states taken action against Adolf Hitler, the horrors of the Holocaust may never have occurred. They take a decidedly moral position like that of the Wilsonian idealists of the early twentieth century, who advocated collective security to prevent these and other acts of aggression by rogue states or regimes.

This debate, while not entirely crucial to the role of international organizations, is necessary insofar as it informs our understanding of the use of military power and the role of foreign policy in several states, including the sole remaining superpower, the United States. Your position on this issue may determine your philosophy of military force and global responsibility in the coming century.

In the following selection, Robert C. Johansen argues that the United States and the international community must intervene in ethnic conflicts in other nations. He maintains that the UN should have a permanent force designed to intervene in such circumstances because individual nation-states are too reliant on political considerations to be consistently reliable in such instances. Edward N. Luttwak's argument in the second selection centers on the notion that conflicts of all types, including ethnic ones, have the effect of solving political conflicts. He contends that the international community needs to refrain from intervening in most instances.

Robert C. Johansen **YES**

Will We Do Nothing?

D espite sharp disagreements among people in the United States, Europe and elsewhere over what went wrong in the former Yugoslavia and Rwanda, everyone agrees that when tragedies engulfed these lands the international community was sadly unprepared to halt "ethnic cleansing" and mass killings. Because these conclusions seem so familiar and unexceptional, we overlook their profound significance for the future of world peace, and for our own moral integrity.

It is too late to erase the disasters suffered by people in Yugoslavia and Rwanda; it is not too late to prevent future Rwandas and Yugoslavias. Communal conflict is smoldering from Sri Lanka to Chechnya, from Georgia to Mexico, from Sudan to the Philippines, from India to Burundi, and from Iraq and Turkey to Kossovo, Macedonia and Moldova. Unless we act now to discourage conditions that will give rise to violent bigotry and genocidal slaughters, we cannot claim to be morally responsible.

Many people do nothing to prevent future genocides because they believe nothing can be done: they argue that the people of the Balkans can be expected to inflict cruelty on one another from time to time, as can Hutus and Tutsis, and that the international community can provide no antidote at an acceptable cost. These are false assumptions. It is not difficult to imagine practical measures that could be taken to prevent genocide. Five deficiencies, clearly identified in the Rwandan and Yugoslavian cases, come to mind:

- The United Nations does not have highly developed early warning and conflict prevention systems.
- The United Nations does not possess constabulary forces of sufficient size, appropriate training, preparedness and financial backing to discourage "ethnic cleansing" and genocidal killings.
- The Security Council has not been able to act decisively or with sufficient legitimacy and political support to prevent genocide.
- The world community lacks adequate international institutions for holding individuals accountable to the internationally established rules designed to prohibit genocide and crimes against the peace.

From Robert C. Johansen, "Will We Do Nothing?" *Christian Century*, vol. 113 (March 20-27, 1996). Copyright © 1996 by The Christian Century Foundation. Reprinted by permission.

- The financial resources available for protecting succeeding generations from the scourges of genocide and war are grossly inadequate.

With these problems in mind, citizens and governments should cooperate with the UN secretary-general in developing a long-term plan to guide the UN Secretariat, the Security Council, the General Assembly and other relevant organs of the UN in addressing these deficiencies.

の

The plan should include the creation of a UN Dispute Settlement Service that would provide the timely dispatch of trained and experienced UN fact-finders, conciliators and mediators when a conflict threatens to turn violent. When disputes prove to be intractable, these representatives would have the authority to recommend legally binding arbitration or advisory opinions from the International Court of Justice.

Preventing genocide or war almost always entails lower costs than paying for the consequences of violence. Because the UN could provide professional services in early stages of conflicts, its permanent dispute settlement machinery would have many advantages over ad hoc diplomatic initiatives.

The plan would entail the establishment of a permanent UN constabulary force of from 10,000 to 100,000 personnel, carefully selected and trained by the UN from among men and women of all nations who volunteer to aid in policing, peacekeeping and enforcement. A well-trained, highly motivated and sophisticated force cannot result from ad hoc arrangements such as those used in past peacekeeping forces. The UN was unwilling to send ad hoc forces to Rwanda in 1994, in part because no member wanted to place its forces immediately under UN command and send them into high-risk environments. UN members expressed similar reservations about sending their forces to protect Bosnian areas designated as "safe" by the Security Council. Because governments may not feel that their own national interests are sufficiently at stake to send their forces into high-risk operations, it is essential to have a permanent UN force that can respond quickly and skillfully.

Moreover, if a sufficient number of UN personnel are sent into a conflict early enough, they can often take actions more characteristic of police upholding order than of soldiers embarking on major military combat. During debate on Rwanda, a high-ranking UN official said that one brigade "deployed in Kigali within seven to 14 days might have stabilized the situation." These early, strong measures are essential in preventing a spiral toward genocide.

With a moderate expansion of council membership and democratization of procedures, the Security Council could more fairly represent all peoples of the world and make decisions that would not be subject to veto by any one member. The council's legitimacy is dwindling because it does not fairly represent the world's people. It gives disproportionate weight to those who dominated diplomacy at the time the United Nations was founded at the end of World War II. The societies that were defeated in World War II and the regions that were underrepresented now deserve equitable representation. This could be achieved by giving permanent seats to Japan, Germany, India, Brazil, and South Africa or Nigeria.

In addition, no country should exercise a veto power that allows it to be judge in its own case. No nation can safely demilitarize its own society or rely on the council to act impartially on behalf of its security if some council members can immobilize the council when they, their allies or their friends are guilty of aggression. The veto should be gradually phased out.

Of course, the Permanent Five object strongly to qualifying the veto, even though their size and strength give them ample means with which to protect their interests. Yet because they will obstruct any plan to remove the veto altogether, the veto must be qualified in a more modest and palatable way.

❧

Without any Charter revision, the council could decide that the proposed International Criminal Court should function automatically, without any further council votes, to investigate and prosecute alleged war crimes and crimes against humanity wherever convincing allegations arise. The council could also agree that the secretary-general could automatically send his emissaries and conflict resolution teams to any trouble spot in the world when he deems their services essential to prevent genocide. The secretary-general could even be empowered to deploy the proposed UN Peace Force whenever a straw vote showed that two-thirds of the council members, and four-fifths of the permanent members, favored sending the Peace Force to emergencies in which genocide threatens, but in a police rather than a military mode of operations. These cautious innovations would protect the legitimate interests of UN members large and small; they also would enable the UN to respond more quickly and effectively.

To enforce norms against genocide and aggression effectively and at a politically acceptable cost, the Security Council needs to move as quickly as possible toward holding individuals accountable to the law. Laws must be enforced on the individuals who commit misdeeds rather than on entire societies in which many people are innocent of any wrongdoing. Enforcement must be strictly impartial. Once established, a permanent International Criminal Court and a mechanism for prosecution would systematically gather information about alleged crimes, prepare indictments, issue international warrants for arrest and hold impartial trials under due-process procedures. The temporary nature of the existing ad hoc tribunals inevitably gives the impression that the law against genocide will be applied in some cases but not in others. The international community can no longer tolerate this practice. The proposed court should act automatically; it should not be required to wait for special authorization from the Security Council, as the United States now insists, or be subject to political decisions by the council.

The presence of a court and indictment procedure would help deter crimes against the peace, war crimes and crimes against humanity. To reinforce this deterrent, the Security Council should request that all members include in their military training a clear exposition of the precedents set in the Nuremberg and Tokyo war crimes tribunals, whose standards and purposes have been overwhelmingly endorsed by the UN membership. A government's refusal to do so should be considered a threat to international peace and grounds for Security Council sanctions against the delinquent government. These legal precedents stipulate that no commander or officer may use as a justifiable defense the claim that he or she was acting under orders from superiors while committing war crimes. In its November 1994 report the International Law Commission drew up draft articles that can serve as a basis for establishing the court.

ᵉᐧᗷᕀᵉ

To make enforcement effective and to protect UN personnel, UN forces engaged in upholding the peace must have the right to arrest anyone committing aggression or violent acts, including violence against UN personnel themselves. The Security Council should also impose sanctions or take other action to dissuade any society from shielding or refusing to extradite persons for whom an international arrest warrant has been issued by the court.

No threatened people or government will take seriously the existing international prohibitions of genocide and aggression unless a Peace Force and International Criminal Court have sufficient financial backing to make them effective in action. Perhaps the most equitable and practical way to generate revenue is to charge an extremely modest fee of, say, five-hundredths of 1 percent (0.05 percent) on the world's international currency exchanges. Such a small levy would not overburden anyone. In addition to discouraging currency speculations that can cause economic havoc, such a fee is a fair strategy. It would generate over $150 billion per year which could be divided among these essential functions: peace operations (preventive diplomacy, monitoring, peacekeeping and enforcement), establishment and operation of an International Criminal Court, preventive development and peace-building activities to promote social integration and eliminate conditions giving rise to violence, and programs for environmental sustainability that would alleviate disputes over water, food and land that might erupt into violence. Other approaches to generating revenue should also be considered, including fees imposed on arms production and transfers or on commercial and military uses of the global commons.

Most of the world's people stand united in opposing genocide, yet they have felt powerless to prevent mass killings in Cambodia, the former Yugoslavia, Rwanda and elsewhere. By mandating a plan to stop genocide, officials in Washington and other capitals can respond to the people's just demand for an end to the killing. The scourge of genocide and aggression can be lifted if the UN members are prompted to act forcefully in the UN's 50th anniversary year. Although some governments may feel that such a plan of action is too dramatic, nothing less can ensure that we will discharge our responsibility to protect innocent people against unjustifiable violence.

Edward N. Luttwak **NO**

Give War a Chance

Premature Peacemaking

An unpleasant truth often overlooked is that although war is a great evil, it does have a great virtue: it can resolve political conflicts and lead to peace. This can happen when all belligerents become exhausted or when one wins decisively. Either way the key is that the fighting must continue until a resolution is reached. War brings peace only after passing a culminating phase of violence. Hopes of military success must fade for accommodation to become more attractive than further combat.

Since the establishment of the United Nations and the enshrinement of great-power politics in its Security Council, however, wars among lesser powers have rarely been allowed to run their natural course. Instead, they have typically been interrupted early on, before they could burn themselves out and establish the preconditions for a lasting settlement. Cease-fires and armistices have frequently been imposed under the aegis of the Security Council in order to halt fighting. NATO's intervention in the Kosovo crisis follows this pattern.

But a cease-fire tends to arrest war-induced exhaustion and lets belligerents reconstitute and rearm their forces. It intensifies and prolongs the struggle once the cease-fire ends—and it does usually end. This was true of the Arab-Israeli war of 1948–49, which might have come to closure in a matter of weeks if two cease-fires ordained by the Security Council had not let the combatants recuperate. It has recently been true in the Balkans. Imposed cease-fires frequently interrupted the fighting between Serbs and Croats in Krajina, between the forces of the rump Yugoslav federation and the Croat army, and between the Serbs, Croats, and Muslims in Bosnia. Each time, the opponents used the pause to recruit, train, and equip additional forces for further combat, prolonging the war and widening the scope of its killing and destruction. Imposed armistices, meanwhile—again, unless followed by negotiated peace accords—artificially freeze conflict and perpetuate a state of war indefinitely by shielding the weaker side from the consequences of refusing to make concessions for peace.

The Cold War provided compelling justification for such behavior by the two superpowers, which sometimes collaborated in coercing less-powerful

From Edward N. Luttwak, "Give War a Chance," *Foreign Affairs*, vol. 78, no. 4 (July/August 1999). Copyright © 1999 by The Council on Foreign Relations, Inc. Reprinted by permission of *Foreign Affairs*.

belligerents to avoid being drawn into their conflicts and clashing directly. Although imposed cease-fires ultimately did increase the total quantity of warfare among the lesser powers, and armistices did perpetuate states of war, both outcomes were clearly lesser evils (from a global point of view) than the possibility of nuclear war. But today, neither Americans nor Russians are inclined to intervene *competitively* in the wars of lesser powers, so the unfortunate consequences of interrupting war persist while no greater danger is averted. It might be best for all parties to let minor wars burn themselves out.

The Problems of Peacekeepers

Today cease-fires and armistices are imposed on lesser powers by multilateral agreement—not to avoid great-power competition but for essentially disinterested and indeed frivolous motives, such as television audiences' revulsion at harrowing scenes of war. But this, perversely, can *systematically* prevent the transformation of war into peace. The Dayton accords are typical of the genre: they have condemned Bosnia to remain divided into three rival armed camps, with combat suspended momentarily but a state of hostility prolonged indefinitely. Since no side is threatened by defeat and loss, none has a sufficient incentive to negotiate a lasting settlement; because no path to peace is even visible, the dominant priority is to prepare for future war rather than to reconstruct devastated economies and ravaged societies. Uninterrupted war would certainly have caused further suffering and led to an unjust outcome from one perspective or another, but it would also have led to a more stable situation that would have let the postwar era truly begin. Peace takes hold only when war is truly over.

A variety of multilateral organizations now make it their business to intervene in other peoples' wars. The defining characteristic of these entities is that they insert themselves in war situations while refusing to engage in combat. In the long run this only adds to the damage. If the United Nations helped the strong defeat the weak faster and more decisively, it would actually enhance the peacemaking potential of war. But the first priority of U.N. peacekeeping contingents is to avoid casualties among their own personnel. Unit commanders therefore habitually appease the *locally* stronger force, accepting its dictates and tolerating its abuses. This appeasement is not strategically purposeful, as siding with the stronger power overall would be; rather, it merely reflects the determination of each U.N. unit to avoid confrontation. The final result is to prevent the emergence of a coherent outcome, which requires an imbalance of strength sufficient to end the fighting.

Peacekeepers chary of violence are also unable to effectively protect civilians who are caught up in the fighting or deliberately attacked. At best, U.N. peacekeeping forces have been passive spectators to outrages and massacres, as in Bosnia and Rwanda; at worst, they collaborate with it, as Dutch U.N. troops did in the fall of Srebenica by helping the Bosnian Serbs separate the men of military age from the rest of the population.

The very presence of U.N. forces, meanwhile, inhibits the normal remedy of endangered civilians, which is to escape from the combat zone. Deluded into thinking that they will be protected, civilians in danger remain in place until it is too late to flee. During the 1992–94 siege of Sarajevo, appeasement interacted with the pretense of protection in an especially perverse manner: U.N. personnel inspected outgoing flights to prevent the escape of Sarajevo civilians in obedience to a cease-fire agreement negotiated with the locally dominant Bosnian Serbs—who habitually violated that deal. The more sensible, realistic response to a raging war would have been for the Muslims to either flee the city or drive the Serbs out.

Institutions such as the European Union, the Western European Union, and the Organization for Security and Cooperation in Europe lack even the U.N.'s rudimentary command structure and personnel, yet they too now seek to intervene in warlike situations, with predictable consequences. Bereft of forces even theoretically capable of combat, they satisfy the interventionist urges of member states (or their own institutional ambitions) by sending unarmed or lightly armed "observer" missions, which have the same problems as U.N. peacekeeping missions, only more so.

Military organizations such as NATO or the West African Peacekeeping Force (ECOMOG, recently at work in Sierra Leone) are capable of stopping warfare. Their interventions still have the destructive consequence of prolonging the state of war, but they can at least protect civilians from its consequences. Even that often fails to happen, however, because multinational military commands engaged in disinterested interventions tend to avoid any risk of combat, thereby limiting their effectiveness. U.S. troops in Bosnia, for example, repeatedly failed to arrest known war criminals passing through their checkpoints lest this provoke confrontation.

Multinational commands, moreover, find it difficult to control the quality and conduct of member states' troops, which can reduce the performance of all forces involved to the lowest common denominator. This was true of otherwise fine British troops in Bosnia and of the Nigerian marines in Sierra Leone. The phenomenon of troop degradation can rarely be detected by external observers, although its consequences are abundantly visible in the litter of dead, mutilated, raped, and tortured victims that attends such interventions. The true state of affairs is illuminated by the rare exception, such as the vigorous Danish tank battalion in Bosnia that replied to any attack on it by firing back in full force, quickly stopping the fighting.

The First "Post-Heroic" War

All prior examples of disinterested warfare and its crippling limitations, however, have been cast into shadow by NATO's current intervention against Serbia for the sake of Kosovo. The alliance has relied on airpower alone to minimize the risk of NATO casualties, bombing targets in Serbia, Montenegro, and Kosovo for weeks without losing a single pilot. This seemingly miraculous immunity from Yugoslav anti-aircraft guns and missiles was achieved by multiple layers of precautions. First, for all the noise and imagery suggestive of a massive operation, very few strike sorties were actually flown during the first few weeks. That reduced the risks to pilots and aircraft but of course also limited the scope of the bombing to a mere fraction of NATO's potential. Second, the air campaign targeted air-defense systems first and foremost, minimizing present and future allied casualties, though at the price of very limited destruction and the loss of any shock effect. Third, NATO avoided most anti-aircraft weapons by releasing munitions not from optimal altitudes but from an ultra-safe 15,000 feet or more. Fourth, the alliance greatly restricted its operations in less-than-perfect weather conditions. NATO officials complained that dense clouds were impeding the bombing campaign, often limiting nightly operations to a few cruise-missile strikes against fixed targets of known location. In truth, what the cloud ceiling prohibited was not all bombing—low-altitude attacks could easily have taken place—but rather perfectly safe bombing. . . .

Make War to Make Peace

Too many wars nowadays become endemic conflicts that never end because the transformative effects of both decisive victory and exhaustion are blocked by outside intervention. Unlike the ancient problem of war, however, the compounding of its evils by disinterested interventions is a new malpractice that could be curtailed. Policy elites should actively resist the emotional impulse to intervene in other peoples' wars—not because they are indifferent to human suffering but precisely because they care about it and want to facilitate the advent of peace. The United States should dissuade multilateral interventions instead of leading them. New rules should be established for U.N. refugee relief activities to ensure that immediate succor is swiftly followed by repatriation, local absorption, or emigration, ruling out the establishment of permanent refugee camps. And although it may not be possible to constrain interventionist NGOs [nongovernmental organizations], they should at least be neither officially encouraged nor funded. Underlying these seemingly perverse measures would be a true appreciation of war's paradoxical logic and a commitment to let it serve its sole useful function: to bring peace.

POSTSCRIPT

Should the International Community Intervene in Other States to Prevent Ethnic Cleansing and Genocide?

With the growing global media and the power of live images to move us, more and more states will likely be called to intervene in the most hideous forms of conflict, including ethnic cleansing and genocide. This phenomenon has been building momentum since the advent of moving pictures and, of course, television and satellites.

Yet compassion for the victims and outrage at the crimes do not necessarily translate into action. Not all countries or actors have the capability to act nor do all actors have the resources or the will. Herein lies the key to the problem. While the forced removal of Albanians from Kosovo or the slaughter of Hutus in Rwanda may outrage the world community, only a few states have the airlift capacity, resources, and personnel to act. While outrage may be equally expressed and felt, intervention is not equally shared. Only those states that have the capability (the United States, Great Britain, and France, for example) share the burden of international intervention in such conflicts.

This raises the question of whether or not these states are able to intervene in every instance with equal speed, force, and effect. Also, does this mean that global outrage translates into a few states having to share the outrage, even when they do not perceive intervention to be in their national interests? If intervention is indeed proper, a system of intervention needs to be established before a blanket policy of intervention can be articulated. Johansen's argument of moral outrage means little without a concerted strategy to address it. And that strategy must not be ad hoc but rather systematic and equal.

If the world is moving into an era of greater interconnection and increased interdependency, as many argue, then ethnic cleansing and genocide have no place in that international landscape. Can a globalizing economy with communication networks that link people, companies, governments, and organizations ignore such events when they are current, fresh, and increasingly graphic?

Two important works on this subject are Michael Hirsch, "Calling All Regio-Cops: Peacekeeping's Hybrid Future," *Foreign Affairs* (November/ December 2000) and Kenneth Christie, *Ethnic Conflict, Tribal Politics: A Global Perspective* (Curzon Press, 1998).

ISSUE 18

Will the Comprehensive Test Ban Treaty Reduce the Risk of Nuclear War?

YES: Robert A. Jordan, from "World a Less Safe Place for GOP After Test Ban Treaty Rejection," *The Boston Globe* (October 17, 1999)

NO: Baker Spring, from "The Comprehensive Test Ban Treaty: In Arms Control's Worst Tradition," *The Heritage Foundation Backgrounder* (October 7, 1999)

ISSUE SUMMARY

YES: Robert A. Jordan, a columnist for the *Boston Globe*, argues in favor of the Comprehensive Test Ban Treaty and surmises that U.S. rejection of the treaty will prove disastrous for the future.

NO: Baker Spring, a research fellow of the Heritage Foundation, maintains that a test ban treaty, like other arms control efforts, will undermine U.S. and global security and should be avoided at all costs.

Since the explosion of the first atomic bomb in Los Alamos in 1945 and its use against the Japanese in Hiroshima and Nagasaki at the end of World War II, scholars, scientists, policymakers, and others have debated ways to control, regulate, and eliminate the presence and use of nuclear weapons. During the cold war (1947–1989) this issue was left to the superpowers and subsequent nuclear states (Great Britain, France, and China) to debate and discuss, but there was little resolution. During periods of great tension and conflict, the nuclear superpowers pursued arms control agreements that were designed to limit the growth of weapons and stabilize the nuclear balance between the United States and the USSR. In the 1960s, 1970s, and 1980s, arms control agreements were signed that limited above-ground testing, froze antiballistic missile defenses, and allowed for verification of intercontinental ballistic missiles (ICBMs), submarine-launched ballistic missiles (SLBMs), and other types of nuclear systems. All of these agreements reflected a desire to maintain a balance of power between the superpowers and also to maintain their edge over other nuclear states.

The Treaty on the Non-Proliferation of Nuclear Weapons (NPT, 1968) attempted to regulate the spread of such weapons. It has met with some success despite the fact that several states, including Israel, India, Pakistan, and South Africa, have acquired nuclear weapons since its signing.

One of the fundamental bedrocks of the arms control movement has been the focus on testing. Whenever weapons are developed, they need to be tested. Without such testing, one cannot be certain of their applicability; thus, they more than likely will never be deployed. Many have argued that by banning testing, the world can begin to limit and eventually reduce nuclear weapons development and production. The first such effort was the limited Test Ban Treaty of 1963, which prohibited atmospheric nuclear testing. This has been followed by periodic moratoriums on underground testing. Not all nations have adhered to these test ban treaties, but they have limited such actions significantly since the 1940s, 1950s, and 1960s.

In the post-cold war period, the United States and the USSR significantly reduced their nuclear stockpiles. Under the most recent agreement, they have pledged to reduce their stockpiles to below 5,000 from a high of over 34,000 per country. Critics of the Comprehensive Test Ban Treaty argue that banning testing will not reduce nuclear stockpiles and that with testing, reductions have taken place. They contend that threats to the United States and others from around the world remain and that nuclear powers like the United States need to continue to develop nuclear weapons and to test them for defensive purposes. Critics also argue that banning testing places the United States in a disadvantageous position vis-à-vis other nuclear states and potential nuclear states.

In the following selections, Robert A. Jordan argues that the current test ban treaty needs ratification by the U.S. Senate and that failure to do so will endanger the United States and the world. He contends that the United States must exercise moral leadership on this issue to force others to comply and, thus, to halt proliferation at its current levels. In the second selection, Baker Spring maintains that the United States needs to pursue its own unilateral policy on testing and to keep its options open in the area of weapons development and testing. He argues that U.S. national security interests, especially those against rogue states, would be ill-served by the advocation of a test ban.

Robert A. Jordan **YES**

World a Less Safe Place for GOP After Test Ban Treaty Rejection

When Senate Republicans stuck their heads in the sand . . . and rejected the global nuclear test ban treaty, they may have put more than only themselves at risk.

As President Clinton and Democratic senators warned, the GOP's self-serving vote—in which only four Republicans joined Democrats in voting for ratification—makes the United States and other nations more vulnerable than ever to nuclear terrorism.

The GOP-led rejection was primarily aimed at embarrassing Clinton, who made the test ban treaty a big goal of his administration. Most media reports called the vote a "major defeat" for the president. That's just how the Republicans hoped the vote would be portrayed.

But in reality, the Republican-led vote is a resounding defeat of a long, arduous effort of both Democratic and Republican presidents to bring an end to the nuclear arms race and make the world a safer place. Nations engaging in a nuclear arms race, such as India and Pakistan, can now continue their testing and implicit threats to each other, without any justifiable moral admonition from the United States. Other nations can also use the Senate rejection as an excuse to escalate their own nuclear arsenals.

In essence, Senate Republicans may have jeopardized the national security just to enhance their own political security. But in the end, the GOP may have made itself more vulnerable—to a Democratic takeover of the House and Senate in the 2000 election. The GOP's rejection of the test ban may, on its own, not be enough to oust the party's leadership. But consider it along with the other GOP actions over the past few years that were primarily aimed at embarrassing, if not destroying, President Clinton and his administration. It could prove to be the proverbial last straw that finally breaks the GOP's already shaky grip on the House and Senate.

Clinton and other Democrats have vowed to make the GOP's rejection of the test ban treaty a campaign issue in the next election. Apparently so have the Republicans, who are betting that voters will give them credit for keeping the

United States on top as the world's leading nuclear power. The test ban, some GOP members argue, would have weakened the nation's nuclear dominance.

Vice President Al Gore, hoping to succeed Clinton, said that if he is elected, he would resubmit the treaty for US ratification. Texas Governor George W. Bush and other Republican presidential hopefuls such as Elizabeth Dole and Arizona Senator John McCain oppose the treaty, signaling that it may become a definitive issue in the presidential campaign.

Trent Lott, majority leader in the Senate, voiced the GOP's view, labeling the treaty deeply flawed; he called it unverifiable, and said it would harm US efforts to maintain the strength and reliability of its nuclear arsenal. But that argument flies in the face of the United States' self-imposed moratorium on nuclear testing, which was done primarily to maintain and improve its nuclear strength. This moratorium has not met with Republican criticism.

Passage of the test ban treaty would have allowed the United States to retain its supremacy in nuclear weapons, as it is now doing under the moratorium —a fact that Senator Patty Murray, a Democrat from Washington, pointed out during debate.

If the treaty is ratified by all 44 nuclear powers, the treaty would have stopped all nuclear tests, established 300 monitoring stations and, as supporters argued, maintained US nuclear superiority. Thus far, the treaty was signed by 154 nations, including the United States, but has been ratified by only 51. Had we ratified the treaty, other nations probably would have followed suit.

China, for example, which has signed but not ratified the treaty, expressed, through its foreign ministry, "profound regret" over the rejection, adding that the United States "has great influence in bringing the treaty into effect."

The Japanese foreign ministry said the "adverse effects are inestimable, and it is of extreme concern." It said it had hoped for US leadership in nuclear disarmament and stopping proliferation.

The Russian foreign ministry said the rejection "deals a serious blow to the whole system of agreements in the field of nuclear disarmament and nonproliferation."

And US allies such as France and the European Union expressed "disappointment" in the Senate rejection.

Clinton, on the right side of this issue, said he would continue to work "to strengthen the worldwide consensus in favor of the treaty" while continuing to observe the moratorium on nuclear testing that has been in effect for seven years.

But that is not nearly as good as ratifying the treaty—something that the GOP has been angling to avoid for quite some time. Senator Jesse Helms, the North Carolina Republican who is chairman of the Senate Foreign Relations Committee, reportedly kept the treaty bottled up in committee for two years before suddenly bringing it before the committee [recently].

Helms and other conservative Republicans apparently knew that they had enough votes to reject the treaty and strategized to give Clinton and other Democrats little opportunity to lobby lawmakers, and the public, for support.

The conservative Republicans' strategy apparently worked, to the detriment of US leadership and world peace.

In Arms Control's Worst Tradition

T he United States Senate may soon vote on whether to ratify the 1996 Comprehensive Test Ban Treaty (CTBT). If it does, the CTBT will permanently bar the United States from conducting explosive tests of nuclear weapons. Before the Senate votes on this treaty, its members should pause and review the history of America's arms control agreements. History will reveal that ill-conceived and overly ambitious notions of arms control often encourage adverse, if not unintended, outcomes. Conversely, when arms control is pursued according to strict standards and with recognition of its inherent limitations, it can add to the nation's security.

The question for the Senate is what kind of an arms control agreement is the CTBT? Is it the utopian version, with adverse and unintended consequences? Or is it the latter, more realistic version that enhances U.S. security?

Unfortunately, the answer is that it is the former. The CTBT fails every single test of what makes a good arms control agreement. It promises sweeping nuclear disarmament that will not only exceed its means, but also undermine national security. Once the CTBT is in force, the United States will be unable to maintain a safe, reliable, and effective nuclear arsenal without testing. Furthermore, as a treaty of unlimited duration, the CTBT will over time undermine the global stability guaranteed by the U.S. nuclear deterrent. America's allies, unable to depend on this nuclear deterrent for their security, will grow more insecure, and some may build their own nuclear arsenals. Lastly, the CTBT fails the most important arms control test of all: It is neither effectively verifiable nor enforceable.

Arms control that fails to meet any or all of these standards represents a tradition of arms control policies at their worst. The most prominent of these policies are the 1928 Kellogg-Briand Pact, the 1972 Anti-Ballistic Missile (ABM) Treaty, the "Nuclear Freeze Resolution" of the early 1980s, the 1972 Biological Weapons Convention (BWC), and the 1922 Five Power Naval Treaty of Washington. These policies either failed to deliver as promised or inadvertently made matters worse by weakening American resolve, fostering a sense of complacency regarding the security environment, jeopardizing the security relationship of the United States with U.S. allies, and emboldening its adversaries.

The Comprehensive Test Ban Treaty falls within this tradition of failure. If enacted, it will, like the Kellogg-Briand Pact and the Nuclear Freeze Resolution, fail to deliver as promised or make matters far worse.

Five Lessons From the History of Arms Control

History teaches many valuable lessons on how arms-control efforts can go awry, despite the best intentions or, perhaps, because of them. These lessons are directly applicable to the Comprehensive Test Ban Treaty and, therefore, are worth analyzing in the context of the Senate's impending decision on CTBT ratification. The lessons can be seen in the failure of five important arms-control policies of the 20th century. Individually, and together, the lessons demonstrate why the CTBT will make the United States more vulnerable.

An End in Itself: The Kellogg-Briand Pact

The 1928 Kellogg-Briand Pact, formally known as the "Pact of Paris," embodied the principle that agreements are the culmination of the "peace process." Informally named after the former U.S. Secretary of State Frank Kellogg and the French Foreign Minister Aristide Briand, who backed the proposal and encouraged other nations to approve it, the Pact's purpose was ambitious and, ultimately, unachievable. It declared in utopian grandeur that war was henceforth outlawed and its use forbidden as "an instrument of national policy." At the outset, 15 nations signed the Pact. Virtually every nation in existence at that time later approved it.

The common, central flaw in both the Kellogg-Briand Pact and the CTBT is that they confuse the ends with the means. The Kellogg-Briand Pact followed a premise that war itself, distinct from the purposes for which it is waged, is evil and thus can and should be outlawed. But, paradoxically, if war were truly outlawed, the means ultimately needed to enforce such a provision would be war itself.

The CTBT likewise attempts to label nuclear weapons, as distinct from the purposes for which they are used, as evil. But war and nuclear weapons are also means through which to fulfill national policy goals, from maintaining national security to subjugating another state. Both war as an instrument and nuclear weapons as tools lack moral content. The question of morality arises only in the context of their purpose.

The failure to appreciate this distinction doomed the Kellogg-Briand Pact. By the 1930s, it became clear to many states that the Kellogg-Briand Pact was utopian. The Japanese determined that war was a useful instrument of national policy in subjugating Manchuria and ultimately creating a puppet state. In 1932, Japan attacked the city of Shanghai. Its actions were a prelude to a cycle of rearmament and conflict in Asia and Europe that culminated in World War II. The United States did not recover from its period of unfounded faith in the Kellogg-Briand Pact until Japan attacked U.S. naval forces at Pearl Harbor on December 7, 1941. Only then was the American public convinced that only its own will to defend itself, and not the negotiated terms of an unrealistic treaty, would fulfill its aspirations for security.

This same lesson should be applied to the CTBT. The preamble of the CTBT states that its prohibition on nuclear testing "constitutes an effective measure of nuclear disarmament and nonproliferation in all its aspects." The uninformed reader could easily assume that the purpose of the treaty is nuclear disarmament and that the United States will no longer need to field a nuclear deterrent because the treaty itself will expunge the nuclear threat. The CTBT thus promises the utopian goal of total nuclear disarmament in much the same way that the Kellogg-Briand Pact promised that war henceforth would no longer be "an instrument of national policy."

However, the CTBT will not result in universal nuclear disarmament because it will only disarm the states that honor it. Not all states will participate in the regime, and some of those that do will find ways to circumvent its requirements, just as Imperial Japan sidestepped the Kellogg-Briand Pact. The Clinton Administration, a strong proponent of the CTBT, denies that the treaty will result in U.S. nuclear disarmament. Nevertheless, nuclear disarmament is what the treaty promises—and nuclear disarmament of the United States will likely be the result. And a nuclear disarmed America would be a vulnerable and weak America.

Vulnerability as Delusional Deterrence: The ABM Treaty

The 1972 Anti-Ballistic Missile (ABM) Treaty barred the United States and the Soviet Union from fielding defenses to protect their national territories against missile attack. As such, it sought to limit, both qualitatively and quantitatively, the level of armaments in both countries. The problem is that the treaty, despite these limitations, undermined strategic stability and increased the likelihood of conflict. It provided an incentive for the Soviet Union to achieve a first strike capability against which the United States could not respond. U.S. negotiators of the treaty had stated that the United States would withdraw if a circumstance of vulnerability arose.

Yet by the early 1980s, when it became clear that the ABM Treaty had opened a window of vulnerability that was considered destabilizing and dangerous, the United States failed to withdraw from the treaty. Hence, the ABM Treaty experience offers a valuable lesson: Purposeful vulnerability does not promote arms control; rather, increasing stability and reducing the risk of conflict are far more important considerations than limiting the quantity and quality of arms.

Unfortunately, this lesson was not learned. This same scenario is being repeated in Washington regarding the CTBT. The Clinton Administration has stated that the United States would withdraw from the CTBT if it undermines the U.S. nuclear deterrent, which is vital to fostering international stability and peace. But, as is the case with the ABM Treaty, it appears unlikely that this Administration will fulfill its stated intention.

The mistakes made in the ABM Treaty are on the verge of being repeated in the CTBT process. The Clinton Administration in September 1997 announced a list of "safeguards" regarding CTBT implementation (assuming ratification and entry into force). These safeguards include a possible future withdrawal from the CTBT that echoes statements made during negotiations of the ABM Treaty in 1972. In this case, the Clinton Administration accepts and understands that there is a risk arising from the prohibition on nuclear testing imposed by the CTBT, in that the lack of testing could undermine confidence in the U.S. nuclear arsenal. The Administration also recognizes that such a loss of confidence could be profoundly destabilizing. Specifically, the Administration has stated that the United States will withdraw from the CTBT if the Secretaries of Defense and Energy cannot certify the safety and reliability of a nuclear weapon considered critical to the maintenance of the U.S. nuclear deterrent.

Members of the Senate should ask themselves whether the Clinton Administration and future administrations will remain steadfast in limiting the risk of conflict by withdrawing from the CTBT if necessary. Can this Administration be more steadfast than the Carter Administration was regarding the ABM Treaty? If the Senate cannot answer this question with certainty, the effects of the CTBT's qualitative limitations on nuclear arms could well eclipse the higher goal of reducing the risk of conflict.

Compromising U.S. Commitments: The Nuclear Freeze Resolution

In the early 1980s, a coalition of arms control advocacy groups proposed what came to be called the "Nuclear Freeze Resolution." The proposal before Congress would have established an arms control policy based on negotiating an agreement with the Soviet Union to bar the further testing, production, and deployment of nuclear weapons. Although the Nuclear Freeze Resolution had many critical shortcomings, perhaps its most serious was its incompatibility with U.S. security commitments to its NATO allies.

An effective U.S. nuclear deterrent had always been at the core of U.S. security commitments to NATO. In recognition of this fact, NATO members agreed in 1979 to deploy throughout Europe by 1983 two types of intermediate-range nuclear missiles: the Ground-Launched Cruise missile (GLCM) and the Pershing II missile. Militarily, the deployment was designed to counter the Soviet deployments of a similar missile, the SS-20 Saber. Politically, it was designed to counter Soviet attempts to intimidate and coerce Western Europeans into breaking their security relationship with the United States under the NATO alliance. The Nuclear Freeze Resolution, its supporters hoped, would at least slow and ultimately stop, NATO's deployment of those missiles. As such, the Resolution represented a threat to the viability of NATO against the Soviet Union's pressure tactics.

The Nuclear Freeze Resolution and CTBT share an important flaw. The Nuclear Freeze Resolution would have undermined U.S. commitments to its allies by preventing the implementation of the decision to deploy the GLCM and Pershing II missiles. U.S. ratification of the CTBT would have the same effect on the United States' commitments to its allies by undermining the nuclear deterrent on which the allies' security still depends.

The Senate should take stock of its October 31, 1983, decision to reject the Nuclear Freeze Resolution. That decision upheld the essential principle of arms control—the United States would not enter into any agreement that undermines its own security or security commitments to its allies. Following that decision, deployment of GLCMs and Pershing IIs commenced in December 1983.

Ratification of the CTBT, by comparison, would mean the Senate is backing away from the sound principle of the United States not allowing arms control to weaken or undermine its security or its commitment to it alliances.

Trust But Do Not Verify: The Biological Weapons Convention

President Richard M. Nixon renounced the U.S. biological warfare program on November 25, 1969, and the federal government agreed to dispose of its existing stocks of biological agents and weapons. A similar announcement was made regarding toxins on February 14, 1970. President Nixon signed the Biological Weapons Convention (BWC) banning the possession and stockpiling of biological weapons and weapons carrying toxins on April 10, 1972. The Ford Administration ratified the BWC on January 22, 1975. This treaty remains in force today.

The BWC contains a monumental flaw. It is unverifiable. It fails to provide a means to validate that participating states are complying with the prohibition on biological weapons. This omission in itself is an acknowledgment that it is relatively easy to build and maintain militarily significant stockpiles of biological weapons. There is no means to confirm that a participating state has destroyed its biological weapons stockpile or has not built one.

The CTBT, which bans nuclear test explosions no matter how small their yields, is also unverifiable. Low-yield underground tests are very difficult to detect with the seismic monitors used to verify compliance with the test ban. In past administrations, CTBT negotiations focused on fashioning an agreement that allowed explosions below a certain threshold because it is impossible to verify explosions below those levels. This was confirmed in recent articles in *The Washington Post* and *The Washington Times,* which reported on speculation in the intelligence community that Russia may have conducted a clandestine nuclear test on September 8, 1999. The inability of the intelligence community to make a determined judgment makes clear the impossibility of verifying adherence to the CTBT.

In understanding the implications of the CTBT's lack of verifiability, the Senate should consider the problems with verifying the BWC. Iraq, for example, not only built a biological arsenal in defiance of its BWC obligations, but years of intrusive inspections by the United Nations after Iraq's defeat in the Persian Gulf War failed to give a full accounting of Iraq's biological weapons programs. The lack of effective verification also allowed the Soviet Union to violate the BWC at will. Although Russian President Boris Yeltsin has renounced the biological weapons program Russia inherited from the Soviet Union in 1992, suspicions that Russia is continuing that program remain.

Even the Clinton Administration, a fervent supporter of the BWC, acknowledges that the BWC is flawed. The 1997 annual report of the Arms Control and Disarmament Agency noted, "Over the two decades since entry-into-force of the BWC, confidence in the effectiveness of the [BWC] has been undermined by instances of non-compliance, notably on the part of the former Soviet Union and Iraq."

The "zero-yield" feature of the CTBT will compound the verification problems found in the BWC. As wrongheaded as the BWC is in terms of ignoring the standard of verifiability, at least it leaves no illusion that other countries could cheat. But the CTBT represents an attempt to deceive the American people and the Senate concerning verification because it includes an elaborate "verification" regime. The inherent lack of true verifiability in the CTBT is all but certain to result in cheating, which will undermine U.S. security just as Soviet and Iraqi cheating under the BWC jeopardizes U.S. security. In the CTBT's case, however, the problem is made much more severe because its "verification" regime will create the illusion that no violations occur because cheaters will be caught. The "absence of evidence" that a clandestine test has occurred will be treated as "evidence of [the] absence" of cheating.

Illusion is a dangerous commodity in the area of national security. When it involves weapons as powerful as nuclear weapons, illusion can easily lead to widespread destruction.

Simply Unenforceable: The Five Power Naval Treaty of Washington

Following World War I, a spate of diplomatic activities sought to ensure that this war was "the war to end all wars." Some of these efforts included arms control. The 1922 Five Power Naval Treaty of Washington, for example, both capped and established a specific ratio for the number of ships (primarily battleships) that the major naval powers of the day could possess. This treaty failed because its terms were not honored and could not be enforced. The CTBT will suffer the same problems with enforcement, because the final enforcement powers will be left to the Security Council of the United Nations, in which China and Russia have an equal vote and can veto any enforcement efforts.

The Washington Naval Treaty offers Congress a lesson in bad arms control policies. In 1921, U.S. Secretary of State Charles E. Hughes invited eight select naval powers (Belgium, China, France, Great Britain, Italy, Japan, the Netherlands, and Portugal) to discuss security matters at a conference in Washington, D.C. In his opening remarks, Secretary Hughes outlined a proposed 10-year moratorium on the construction of capital ships and a ratio of 5-5-3 for ships already in the possession of the United States, Great Britain, and Japan, respectively. His proposal was popular in the United States. In negotiating the agreement, the United States made a concession to Japan that it would not fortify certain island possessions in the Pacific, including the Philippines, Guam, Wake Island, and the Aleutians. After France and Italy joined the agreement, the final ratio of ships was 5 for the United States, 5 for Great Britain, 3 for Japan, 1.7 for France, and 1.7 for Italy. The agreement was signed on February 22, 1922.

The relative naval strengths established in the treaty were never enforced. The other naval powers continued building ships not expressly limited by the treaty, such as cruisers, destroyers, and submarines. The U.S. government had naively assumed that the ratio governing capital ships would be applied to these other ships as well. By 1930, in terms of overall naval power, the United States lost parity with Great Britain and its naval superiority over Japan. The relationship that was designed to maintain a balance of naval power and peace, particularly in the Pacific, was shattered. But few in America seemed concerned during the complacent period following the adoption of the Kellogg-Briand Pact.

Not so with the increasingly aggressive Japanese. By 1934, the Japanese formally renounced the Washington Naval Treaty. The cycle of rearmament and suspicion intensified. The United States continued to lag in this new naval arms race. Not until President Franklin Roosevelt requested a $1 billion appropriation for the U.S. Navy did the United States begin a serious naval rearmament effort. But this was late in the game. Japanese naval forces attacked Pearl Harbor three years later.

Enforcement proved to be the critical ingredient missing from the Washington Naval Treaty. Unfortunately, the United States is likely to be just as complacent about enforcement of the CTBT as it was with the naval treaty in the late 1920s. Under Article V of the CTBT, the ultimate authority for enforcing the prohibition on nuclear test explosions will rest with the U.N. Security Council. This "enforcement" provision is, in reality, a dead end. If China or Russia were caught cheating, for example, they could exercise their right in the Security Council to veto any enforcement resolution aimed at curtailing their activity. This Administration, rather than introduce such a resolution, which could jeopardize the CTBT, is more likely to try to resolve the problem by ineffectual quiet diplomacy.

The lack of means to enforce the CTBT's provisions will prove to be its Achilles' heel, just as it proved to be the Achilles' heel of the Washington Naval Treaty. Both treaties engender an attitude of complacency. Any enforcement action that confronts complacency, short of a direct threat to the people of the United States—such as the attack on Pearl Harbor—will be unpopular. Supporters of the CTBT are likely to charge that the United States, by taking effective steps to enforce the treaty, will instigate another arms race. But the United States should never allow itself to fall again into the enforcement trap that undermined the Washington Naval Treaty and jeopardized U.S. security, which will be the case if the CTBT is ratified.

Conclusion

Arms control will be a counterproductive tool of national security policy as long as rigorous standards learned from past experiences are not observed. The CTBT fails to satisfy even one of the five important lessons that the history of arms control teaches. In fact, all of the shortcomings in five of the most discredited arms control policies and treaties of the 20th century are embodied in this single treaty. Historians of the future will likely view the CTBT, if it is ratified and enters into force, as a national security disaster for the United States. The question that remains is whether the Senate, understanding the harmful repercussions ratifying the CTBT will have on U.S. security and U.S. alliances, will abandon it altogether.

POSTSCRIPT

Will the Comprehensive Test Ban Treaty Reduce the Risk of Nuclear War?

Arms control agreements have always been subject to the political debate over security. Is security best obtained through unilateral arming or through agreements that reduce the risks of confrontation? Politicians around the world have long debated which strategy is best, and nations usually adopt a mixture of both views. The Comprehensive Test Ban Treaty does provide a measure of security in that without testing, new weapons development is significantly hindered.

However, there are many subissues within the larger question. Does a test ban treaty merely solidify the dominance of the United States in the nuclear regime? Is compliance verifiable, and can punishments be implemented if states violate the ban? Is such a ban in the best interests of global security, since testing leads to greater knowledge and presumably greater safeguards on weaponry?

Despite the fall of the Soviet Union, the United States' greatest nuclear threat during the cold war, the debate still rages over the test ban treaty and other arms control initiatives. This issue calls into question some basic assumptions regarding the role of security in a national and collective context. This issue also challenges us to deal with the issue of nuclear weaponry and its place in a post–cold war world. Whatever your views, it is clear that without testing, new developments in weaponry and advanced deployments are nearly impossible and, thus, the nuclear arms race is frozen at the current technological level. Whether that is a positive or a negative outcome is still open to debate.

Two articles that explore this issue from both sides are Robert Manning, "The Nuclear Age: The Next Chapter," *Foreign Policy* (Winter 1997/1998) and Jack Mendelsohn, "Arms Control: The Unfinished Agenda," *Current History* (April 1997). Also see the Web site for the International Atomic Energy Agency at http://www.iaea.org/worldatom/.

ISSUE 19

Is the Establishment of a Permanent International Criminal Court a Positive Development for Global Security?

YES: Joe Stork, from "In Focus: International Criminal Court," Foreign Policy *In Focus* Brief (April 1998)

NO: Lee A. Casey and David B. Rivkin, Jr., from "The International Criminal Court vs. the American People," *The Heritage Foundation Backgrounder* (February 5, 1999)

ISSUE SUMMARY

YES: Joe Stork, advocacy director of Human Rights Watch/Middle East, contends that an International Criminal Court (ICC) for war crimes is vital to U.S. and global security. He argues that the only way to prevent war crimes is to have the full weight of the international community, including the United States, behind such a court.

NO: Lee A. Casey and David B. Rivkin, Jr., who both practice law in Washington, D.C., contend that the International Criminal Court is against U.S. national interests and would be used as a political weapon by nations that are opposed to American policies. They argue that it should not be established or recognized by the United States.

Prussian military strategist Carl von Clausewitz once said, "War is politics by another means." This has become one of the most famous quotes in the study of conflict and global issues. It reflects a commonly held notion among policymakers and scholars that war, while tragic and sometimes devastating, is part of the global landscape of nations and actors competing for power and, as such, is a part of our common human condition. One result of this view is that war crimes—atrocities committed during the prosecution of war—have always been looked upon as tragic, often unstoppable consequences of war. This view was dominant, and in some ways, unquestioned until World War II. During the war, the unspeakable horrors of the Holocaust and the numerous atrocities committed by Nazi Germany under state sanction and orders raised global consciousness regarding war crimes and atrocities and sensitized millions to the fact that war did not excuse all acts. The Nuremberg Trials, which were held in the aftermath of the war, represent the first united attempt to prosecute leaders who are deemed war criminals. The verdicts set the precedent for future conflicts and forever placed certain acts committed during war outside the realm of excusable actions.

Since World War II the United Nations has attempted to codify international law in this area and to deem certain actions outside the bounds of state-sanctioned wartime activities. These include genocide, ethnic cleansing, mass rape, terrorizing civilians, and other such acts that are normally left to the discretion of local and regional authorities. During various conflicts the World Court in The Hague has attempted to oversee accusations of war crimes and adjudicate them. Yet without binding authority many such cases were merely rhetorical in their effect. The results of all these efforts were limited due to the veto authority of the superpowers during the cold war. Each time efforts were made to address these issues, the superpowers would scuttle the effects of these efforts in the UN and elsewhere because they did not want to be found on the "wrong" end of an accusation of war crimes and, thus, have their foreign policy interests inhibited.

Since the end of the cold war, a new push has begun to codify the war crimes into an International Criminal Court. Negotiations to create such a court and to give it jurisdiction over all crimes where a nation's own court systems fail to act have been under way for a decade. These negotiations have been stalled of late due to opposition by a few nations who have misgivings about "political justice" being handed out by the United Nations. Although the treaty to establish an ICC has widespread support and was adopted at the Rome Diplomatic Conference for an International Criminal Court in July 1998, these nations' misgivings mean a rough road ahead if it is ever to become functioning legal reality.

In the following selection, Joe Stork contends that the treaty to institute an International Criminal Court will help to establish credibility for international law and provide the legal framework for the prosecution of war criminals. He argues that the United States must give meaning to its leadership role in the post-cold war world by supporting legal frameworks that apply equally to all nations. Stork concludes that this will help to solidify American moral and ethical leadership in the new world order.

In the second selection, Lee A. Casey and David B. Rivkin, Jr., oppose this court, contending that it will be used as a political weapon to punish some but not all violators. They argue that the violations are too broadly defined and that the ICC prosecutor has too much power to initiate prosecution. They also argue that certain acts, while regrettable, do occur during wartime and that sovereign states should deal with their own soldiers and officials under their own codes of military and civilian justice.

Joe Stork

In Focus: International Criminal Court

On June 15, 1998, diplomats from around the world [assembled] in Rome to finalize a treaty [to] establish an International Criminal Court (ICC). A key issue is the role of the U.S. government in these negotiations and its apparent effort to ensure that actions of U.S. citizens, particularly U.S. military personnel, will always remain beyond the conceivable reach of such a court.

Suggestions for such a court—which could operate when national judicial systems collapse or when no national court prosecutes persons suspected of war crimes or genocide—emerged after World War II but were shelved during the cold war. Responding to a 1989 initiative by the government of Trinidad and Tobago, the United Nations General Assembly commissioned a draft statute for an ICC. Interest in the project grew in the aftermath of the slaughter of hundreds of thousands of people in Bosnia and Rwanda. Delegates from some 80 countries began Preparatory Committee (Prep Com) meetings in the spring of 1996 to negotiate and consolidate a final draft.

The impunity enjoyed by the architects and perpetrators of some of the worst massacres and atrocities of a bloody century underlies the drive to establish such a court. Complementing the International Court of Justice in The Hague, which hears disputes between governments, the ICC would investigate and try individuals accused of genocide, war crimes, and crimes against humanity. An ICC, if it had existed, could have been the venue for the work of the special tribunals now dealing with the atrocities committed in Rwanda and the former Yugoslavia.... [W]hen the Khmer Rouge appeared ready to hand over Pol Pot for prosecution, Cambodia was in no position to adjudicate and there was no existing international forum. An ICC could have fulfilled this role. A standing International Criminal Court, had it existed in 1988, would also have been the place to draw up an indictment against Iraqi President Saddam Hussein and his top cohorts for their genocidal campaign against that country's Kurds. Such a court should be crucial in addressing war crimes against women, including rape and sexual slavery, which are often ignored in national courts and have been minimally pursued by existing ad hoc tribunals.

The last of the six Prep Com sessions ended April 3, 1998, but still at issue is what kind of court will emerge. Will the ICC have the authority and independence to deliver justice, or will it be subject to veto control by the Security

From Joe Stork, "In Focus: International Criminal Court," Foreign Policy *In Focus* Brief, vol. 3, no. 4 (April 1998). Copyright © 1998 by The Institute for Policy Studies and The Interhemispheric Resource Center. Reprinted by permission.

Council and by the states implicated in any investigation, as U.S. negotiators suggest? A bloc of like-minded states—led by Canada and including Germany, South Africa, and Argentina—have worked closely with nongovernmental organizations to spearhead the effort for an effective and independent court. Supporters of an independent court have thwarted efforts by China, France, the U.S., and others to delay indefinitely the creation of an ICC, and they have insisted on treaty language extending automatic jurisdiction of the court to cover war crimes and crimes against humanity as well as genocide. Among the like-minded group are states that have undergone transitions from authoritarian rule and understand how impunity undermines political reform and the rule of law. Some of the larger global powers, however, advocate positions that would subordinate the court to the Security Council (where they have a veto) or would require that the state where the indicted citizen resides—Iraq, in the case of Saddam Hussein, for instance—consent to the ICC's jurisdiction on a case-by-case basis. At best, this would result in a permanent ad hoc tribunal, subject to political discretion rather than the imperatives of justice.

Some of the organizations and governments involved in the ICC campaign have cited the recently concluded international treaty banning the use of antipersonnel landmines to argue that the priority should be an effective and independent court, even if the U.S. declines to sign the treaty. The Clinton administration is eager not to be sidelined once again, as it was in the Ottawa landmines negotiations. Yet Washington contends that the two treaties are not comparable and that there could be no meaningful court without the participation and financial support of the United States. These are the stakes going into the final conference in June.

President Clinton, after initial hesitations, has endorsed the concept of an ICC, and U.S. experts have been constructive in many aspects of the negotiations, especially in drafting fair trial procedures and detailing the rights of defendants. But the U.S. has also put forward positions and reservations that, if they prevail, would give the U.S. (and other states) effective veto power over the cases the court investigates and prosecutes.

Problems With Current U.S. Policy

Key Problems

- The Pentagon insists that the U.S. only agree to a treaty that preserves the U.S. ability to reject ICC jurisdiction over cases in which U.S. military personnel might be prosecuted.
- This sort of treaty would appeal to the very states most likely to ignore their own war crimes, genocide, and crimes against humanity.
- If the final treaty adopts some of Washington's current positions, the result will be a permanent ad hoc tribunal, subject to political discretion rather than the imperatives of justice.

The U.S. position in ICC negotiations would compromise the court's independence and credibility by politicizing the most crucial decisions—namely, determining which cases the ICC will be able to consider.

The issue of the court's independence and credibility revolves around three areas of dispute. The first area concerns the role of the Security Council. The current draft denies the court jurisdiction in situations that the Security Council is "dealing with," unless the council expressly authorizes the court's involvement. Since the court's areas of jurisdiction—war crimes, genocide, and crimes against humanity—will necessarily involve it in situations likely to be under active Security Council scrutiny, this would give an effective veto to any of the permanent members. The possibility of an unfettered ICC prosecuting a political leader or military commander—one of the leaders responsible for the carnage in Bosnia, for instance—could seriously complicate negotiations to restore peace. Such concerns, though, could be addressed by less drastic means than vetoes. Singapore has proposed that the Security Council could initiate action to delay or forestall the ICC's involvement in such an instance. Under the current draft, one member of the council's permanent five could singlehandedly stop the court from moving forward on a case by vetoing approval. Under the Singapore proposal, a member of the Perm Five could stop the court from pursuing a case only by obtaining both the agreement of the other four permanent members and a majority vote of the entire Security Council.

Britain has endorsed the Singapore compromise, and there are indications that the U.S., finding itself relatively isolated on this question, will eventually support it as well. In dropping such hints, though, Washington has also signaled that it intends to secure U.S. veto power by other means—namely, by insisting on language that would require the ICC, before it could initiate an investigation, to secure the consent of any state with an "interest" in the case. According to some proposals, "interested states" could include the state with custody of the accused, the state where the alleged crime took place, and the state of the accused's nationality. One U.S. official involved in the negotiations privately characterized the consent issue as "our nuclear bomb" in the negotiations, referring to the intimidating and potentially destructive impact of this stance.

This issue leads to the second major area of contention: what authority will the ICC have to determine the cases it will investigate and prosecute? One aspect of authority involves defining the court's inherent jurisdiction. There is considerable support, even from the U.S., for enlarging the present language of the draft statute to give the court inherent jurisdiction over not only genocide but also war crimes and crimes against humanity, such as targeting noncombatants, mass rape, and torture. Because these are crimes considered to be covered by customary international law, all states would be subject to ICC jurisdiction over such matters whether or not they have signed a particular treaty or convention. But the U.S. is also threatening to insist that even here interested states would have to give express consent to the ICC to prosecute individual cases. A key aspect of the "state consent" question is complementarity—in other words, the relationship of the ICC to national criminal justice systems. The purpose of the ICC is not to replace or substitute for those systems but rather to operate where such systems do not exist or are ineffective. It is to make sure that those responsible for the most heinous crimes are investigated and prosecuted when political turmoil renders a national justice system ineffective or when the government itself is responsible for gross abuses. An effective ICC would spur governments to ensure that their judicial systems function effectively as the first line of accountability. By encouraging national governments to address crimes of sexual violence, mainly against women, the ICC could potentially make a huge difference, if the statute is drafted to specify the court's jurisdiction over such crimes.

The present draft statute language, however, fails to clarify where responsibility lies for determining the inability or unwillingness of a state to conduct a genuine investigation or prosecution. If the final statute's wording is weak, a state could decide unilaterally not to cooperate with the ICC by deeming its own actions sufficient. States should be able to challenge the ICC's jurisdiction in a given case, but it is important that the court have the final decision. The U.S. says that it is reserving its position on the issue of state consent until the relationship between the ICC and the Security Council is clarified. This suggests that Washington intends to emerge from the negotiations with its veto power preserved in one way or another. Of course, a high consent threshold would also have the support of numerous other states anxious to guarantee the same prerogative of immunity for themselves.

A third and related area of dispute concerns the role of the ICC prosecutor. The present language, endorsed by the U.S. in no uncertain terms, restricts the prosecutor to initiating an investigation only in situations referred by the Security Council or in response to a complaint by a state that has ratified the treaty. Such language would reduce the ICC to the role of an executor of decisions by the Security Council or by governments that have agreed to its jurisdiction—decisions that invariably embody political considerations that may well outweigh the demands of justice. Prosecutorial autonomy will clearly be important, also, if the court is to adequately address gender-based war crimes. It is important to expand the ICC's trigger mechanisms to allow the prosecutor to initiate an investigation based on his or her own findings or on information obtained from individuals or nongovernmental organizations. There exist provisions of judicial review in the treaty that safeguard against the prosecutor's taking up frivolous, spurious, or politically motivated complaints.

Toward a New Foreign Policy

Key Recommendations

- The Clinton administration needs to realize that it risks being sidelined once again, as it was in the landmine negotiations.
- The priority should be a treaty worth signing, establishing an effective, credible, and independent court, not a marginal and meaningless entity tailored to win the support of the most conservative U.S. Senators.

- The administration should tap into the currents of actual and potential citizen support for an effective ICC among church and civic groups, bar associations, and NGOs [nongovermental organizations].

Any treaty that emerges from the Rome conference will go into effect after the required number of governments ratify it. The creation of an effective and credible International Criminal Court is critical to fostering the rule of law—an often-proclaimed objective of the United States. If a strong treaty emerges from the Rome conference, and assuming that the U.S. is one of the signatories, it will be necessary to mount an effective grassroots campaign to secure Senate ratification. The immediate need, however, is to ensure that there will be a treaty worth signing and ratifying.

The very problematic U.S. positions on the key issues described above derive mainly from the insistence of the Pentagon on the ability to prevent the prosecution of U.S. military personnel for actions undertaken in the course of duty. The administration cites the global deployment of U.S. forces, particularly those assigned to peacekeeping and humanitarian intervention missions, to suggest that it ought to have some special dispensation when it comes to accountability. "No other country shoulders the burden of international security as does the United States," David Scheffer, chief U.S. negotiator for the ICC, said..., citing Security Council mandates, NATO commitments, humanitarian objectives, and counter-proliferation. "It is in our collective interests that the personnel of our militaries and civilian commands be able to fulfill their many legitimate responsibilities without unjustified exposure to criminal legal proceedings. The permanent court must not be manipulated for political purposes to handcuff governments taking risks to promote international peace and security and to save human lives," he added.

Leaving aside the disputable claim that the global deployment of U.S. military forces is primarily for humanitarian purposes, there are several reasons why Scheffer's scenario is farfetched. First, the court's jurisdiction will be limited to genocide, war crimes, and crimes against humanity—levels of atrocity unrelated to isolated and minor offenses committed during a peacekeeping or aid delivery mission. Second, if and when serious crimes and atrocities are committed, it will remain the paramount responsibility of a national judicial or military justice system—which certainly exists in the United States—to investigate and prosecute those alleged to be responsible. One of the desirable effects of a standing ICC will be to provide an inducement for individual countries to meet their responsibilities to investigate and prosecute such crimes. Third, the draft treaty contains checks and judicial review procedures that would prevent an ICC prosecutor from pursuing politically motivated and spurious allegations. Only if U.S. troops committed atrocities in the line of duty and were not investigated and prosecuted by U.S. authorities could such a case be addressed by the ICC. That is the point of justice for all.

The Clinton administration argues that a treaty establishing a strong court —one whose operations could not be restrained unilaterally by U.S. veto power —would stand no chance of being ratified by the Republican-controlled U.S.

Senate. Such an argument is premature, given that there has not yet been serious advocacy with the Congress or the general public. Even more to the point, it shortsightedly suggests that the quality and character of such a potentially critical international institution should be determined in the final instance by what Senator Jesse Helms and his colleagues might be willing to accept. Having the U.S. on board for this international undertaking is an important objective, but not worth the price of having to settle for a weak and politicized body with little autonomy and less credibility. What needs to happen now is for White House proponents of a strong and effective ICC to strategize within their ranks for a more forward-looking U.S. position. There is a vital role, also, for an educated and activist citizenry to ensure that the concerns of the Defense Department are balanced with the stated goal of a credible and effective court.

Though Washington often proclaims a commitment to multilateralism, it often fails to support multilateral initiatives that may compel a higher degree of accountability to the international community. The U.S. should support an effective ICC—one that will not be impossibly constrained by the political imperatives of the moment in particular capitals, including Washington. If the Clinton administration declines to take up this challenge, then it may find itself once again—as in the Ottawa landmines negotiations—sidelined by history.

Lee A. Casey and David B. Rivkin, Jr. **NO**

The International Criminal Court vs. the American People

On July 17, 1998, in Rome, a treaty was adopted creating a permanent International Criminal Court (ICC) under the auspices of the United Nations. If 60 countries ratify this treaty, a court in the Netherlands will have the power to try and punish individuals for violations of certain international humanitarian norms. Some of these offenses are so broadly defined that Americans—indeed, citizens of any nation—could be subject to penalties of up to life imprisonment for actions never before considered punishable on the international level.

The powers of the ICC outlined in the Rome treaty are an open invitation to abuse. Cases could be brought before the court based upon the complaint of any country that ratified the treaty (an "ICC States Party") or the initiative of the ICC's prosecutor—an international independent counsel. Once indicted, the defendant(s) would be tried by a bench of judges chosen by the States Parties. As an institution, the ICC would act as police, prosecutor, judge, jury, and jailer. These functions would all be performed by ICC staff, or under their supervision, with only bureaucratic divisions of authority. The ICC would be the sole judge of its own power, and there would be no process to appeal its decisions, however irrational or unjust those might be.

In Rome, the Clinton Administration rightly refused to sign the ICC treaty because it could not obtain even minimum safeguards to prevent this court from being used as a political tool against the United States. The Administration's decision, however, came late in the process and apparently was motivated by fears that prosecutions might be brought against U.S. peacekeepers overseas, not by the belief that a permanent ICC is fundamentally flawed.

In fact, the participation of the United States in this treaty regime runs counter to U.S. national interests. Moreover, U.S. participation would be unconstitutional because it would subject individual Americans to trial and punishment in an extra-constitutional court without affording them all of the rights and protections the U.S. Constitution guarantees.

Unfortunately, merely refusing to join the Rome treaty will not protect Americans from the ICC's reach. In an astonishing break with the accepted norms of international law, the Rome treaty would extend the ICC's jurisdiction to the nationals of countries that do not sign and ratify the treaty. Because of this unprecedented and unlawful attempt to assert power over the citizens of non-party states, it is not sufficient for the U.S. government merely to reject the treaty.

The existence of such a supranational court is a threat to the security of U.S. citizens both at home and overseas. The United States should use all of its considerable resources to prevent the ICC from being implemented. Specifically, Congress and the Administration should:

1. **Inform** other countries that ratifying the ICC treaty will negatively affect their relations with the United States.
2. **Condition** non-military assistance to a country on its rejection of the ICC treaty.
3. **Make plain** that a country's ratification of the ICC treaty will result in a reassessment of U.S. troop deployments in that country.
4. **Renegotiate** treaties and agreements governing the rights and responsibilities of U.S. military personnel stationed overseas so that no host state may surrender U.S. nationals to the ICC.
5. **Demand** that Americans serving in multilateral peacekeeping operations, if accused of criminal actions, be turned over to U.S. courts for trial and be exempt from ICC jurisdiction.
6. **Renegotiate** extradition treaties to specify that individuals extradited from the United States cannot, under any circumstances, be then extradited or otherwise transferred by the requesting state to the ICC for prosecution.
7. **Prevent** any U.S. funding from going to support the ICC.
8. **Prevent** cases from coming before the ICC that would establish precedents for investigation, trial, and conviction—if necessary, by vetoing any attempt by the U.N. Security Council to refer a matter to the ICC.

The purpose of these steps is twofold. First, they would provide American civilians and U.S. military personnel certain basic protections against the possibility that they would be brought for judgment before a court that does not meet the minimum due process standards guaranteed in the U.S. Constitution. Second, they would make it clear that, in the view of the United States, the ICC is an *illegal and illegitimate* institution that violates the principles of self-government and popular sovereignty, as well as the accepted norms of international law.

The fundamental rights secured by the Constitution—rights successfully defended by Americans on battlefields around the world—can be summed up as follows: The American people govern themselves, and they have a right to be tried in accordance with the laws enacted by their elected representatives and to be judged by their peers and none other. The Rome ICC treaty, in concept and execution, is utterly antithetical to these rights. It should be opposed by the United States with all the vigor it has mustered, throughout its history, to fight similar threats to the fundamental values of the Republic.

POSTSCRIPT

Is the Establishment of a Permanent International Criminal Court a Positive Development for Global Security?

The creation of an International Criminal Court seems on the surface to be a simple issue. When international laws are violated, it seems logical that a court would be established to prosecute such crimes. Yet issues of crime and punishment are at the heart of each country's notion of its own sovereignty. It is one of the traits of a nation-state that it has the power to determine law and to exact punishment in cases of its violation. Nations and governments are often reluctant to cede that authority unless they can be sure that their citizens and actions will not be unduly subjected to prosecution and punishment.

The ICC was under the signature and ratification phase until 2001. Nations could sign and ratify the treaty until that time. To date, well over 100 countries have signed the treaty, while many others, including China and Japan, are waiting or are refusing to sign it under its current form. The United States held off on signing the treaty until December 31, 2000, just under the deadline, and it has indicated that it still has important concerns about the treaty.

Whatever the outcome, the move toward a permanent ICC is gaining momentum. The desire to internationalize certain criminal behavior is a function of a growing complexity in global affairs combined with the realization that individual countries' mechanisms for crime and punishment may be inadequate to cope with the issues and crimes that are currently being perpetrated across the globe.

The literature against signing the treaty includes David Frum, "The International Criminal Court Must Die," *The Weekly Standard* (August 1998). Those who advocate signing the treaty include Jonathan Stanley, "Focus: International Criminal Court—A Court That Knows No Boundaries," *The Lawyer* (August 1998)

ISSUE 20

Are Cultural Rivalries and Ethnic Conflicts the Next Great Threats to International Security?

YES: Samuel P. Huntington, from "The Clash of Civilizations?" *Foreign Affairs* (Summer 1993)

NO: John R. Bowen, from "The Myth of Global Ethnic Conflict," *Journal of Democracy* (October 1996)

ISSUE SUMMARY

YES: Political scientist Samuel P. Huntington argues that the emerging conflicts of the twenty-first century will be cultural and not ideological. He identifies the key fault lines of conflict and discusses how these conflicts will reshape global policy.

NO: John R. Bowen, a professor of sociocultural anthropology, rejects the idea that ethnic and cultural conflicts are decisive. He argues that political choices made by governments and nations, not cultural divides and intercultural rivalry, dictate much of global international affairs.

Ethnic conflicts seem to be flaring up around the world with greater and greater frequency. The last few years have witnessed ethnic fighting in places such as Northern Ireland, the Middle East, Southeast Asia, and southern Africa. Ethnic clashes have also broken out in places like Bosnia, Kosovo, Rwanda, East Timor, and Chechnya. Certainly, such ethnic conflicts have flared up throughout the centuries in various places. Yet is it possible that ethnic conflict and clashes between cultures are on the rise and will dominate understanding of conflict in the twenty-first century?

For most of the twentieth century ideological battles between nations took center stage. From the growth of communism and fascism in the 1920s and 1930s came ideological battles centered on notions of governance, economics, race, and the role of people in relation to the state. In that major battle communism and capitalist democracy won out. In the subsequent years the ideological bipolar conflict dominated, as the United States, the USSR, and their surrogates fought on battlefields from Angola to El Salvador and from Vietnam to Afghanistan. At least in part, the battle centered over which system and method of governance would achieve preeminence. In the end the United States won, and capitalist democracy triumphed over communism.

Today scholars and policymakers grapple with the new dynamics of the global system and search for unifying elements that will help to explain why and how groups engage in conflict. Since ideology has lost its zest, and since no apparent philosophies stand ready to directly challenge capitalism, other rallying cries are being uttered and adopted. This period has witnessed the rise or reinvigoration of such philosophies as Islamic fundamentalism, environmentalism, national self-determination (omnipresent in global politics), and ethnic identity as movements and rallying cries for groups to challenge perceived or real oppressors.

Combined with this development is a technological revolution that has brought people in various parts of the world closer than ever before. Ethnic groups traditionally divided by closed borders or reduced contact are now increasingly thrust together by political, economic, and social factors. While this development is benign enough on the surface, many who feel that their cultures are threatened, their identities challenged, and their rights usurped have reacted with disdain and distrust for "the other." As a result, ethnic conflicts have flared in the Balkans, the Middle East, the former Soviet Union, the Great Lakes region of Africa, South America, and the Indian subcontinent.

With increased tensions, greater amounts of weaponry, and less restraint offered by a bipolar world, these conflicts have raged with devastating human consequences. Issues of ethnic cleansing, genocide, land mines, nuclear proliferation, and narcoterrorism have all sprung from or been fueled by these conflicts.

In the following selection, Samuel P. Huntington argues that cultural rivalries are the wave of the coming age. He contends that fault lines between civilizations (where dominant cultures meet) will be "the flash points for crisis and bloodshed" in the coming decades. He contends that cultures will predominate in the battle for hearts and minds and that groups will engage in conflict to defend and protect challenges to their cultures as they perceive them.

In the second selection, John R. Bowen argues that cultural conflict is borne of a myth about people and diversity in that, by definition, they cannot live with one another. He contends that political, economic, and social issues predominate in issues of conflict and that to focus on ethnicity as the central variable obscures that reality.

Samuel P. Huntington

The Clash of Civilizations?

The Next Pattern of Conflict

World politics is entering a new phase, and intellectuals have not hesitated to proliferate visions of what it will be—the end of history; the return of traditional rivalries between nation states, and the decline of the nation state from the conflicting pulls of tribalism and globalism, among others. Each of these visions catches aspects of the emerging reality. Yet they all miss a crucial, indeed a central, aspect of what global politics is likely to be in the coming years.

It is my hypothesis that the fundamental source of conflict in this new world will not be primarily ideological or primarily economic. The great divisions among humankind and the dominating source of conflict will be cultural. Nation states will remain the most powerful actors in world affairs, but the principal conflicts of global politics will occur between nations and groups of different civilizations. The clash of civilizations will dominate global politics. The fault lines between civilizations will be the battle lines of the future.

Conflict between civilizations will be the latest phase in the evolution of conflict in the modern world. For a century and a half after the emergence of the modern international system with the Peace of Westphalia [1648], the conflicts of the Western world were largely among princes—emperors, absolute monarchs and constitutional monarchs attempting to expand their bureaucracies, their armies, their mercantilist economic strength and, most important, the territory they ruled. In the process they created nation states, and beginning with the French Revolution the principal lines of conflict were between nations rather than princes. In 1973, as R. R. Palmer put it, "The wars of kings were over; the wars of peoples had begun." This nineteenth-century pattern lasted until the end of World War I. Then, as a result of the Russian Revolution and the reaction against it, the conflict of nations yielded to the conflict of ideologies, first among communism, fascism-Nazism and liberal democracy, and then between communism and liberal democracy. During the Cold War, this latter conflict became embodied in the struggle between the two superpowers, neither of which was a nation state in the classical European sense and each of which defined its identity in terms of its ideology.

From Samuel P. Huntington, "The Clash of Civilizations?" *Foreign Affairs*, vol. 72, no. 3 (Summer 1993). Copyright © 1993 by The Council on Foreign Relations, Inc. Reprinted by permission of *Foreign Affairs*.

These conflicts between princes, nation states and ideologies were primarily conflicts within Western civilization, "Western civil wars," as William Lind has labeled them. This was as true of the Cold War as it was of the world wars and the earlier wars of the seventeenth, eighteenth and nineteenth centuries. With the end of the Cold War, international politics moves out of its Western phase, and its centerpiece becomes the interaction between the West and non-Western civilizations and among non-Western civilizations. In the politics of civilizations, the peoples and governments of non-Western civilizations no longer remain the objects of history as targets of Western colonialism but join the West as movers and shapers of history.

The Nature of Civilizations

During the Cold War the world was divided into the First, Second and Third Worlds. Those divisions are no longer relevant. It it far more meaningful now to group countries not in terms of their political or economic systems or in terms of their level of economic development but rather in terms of their culture and civilization.

What do we mean when we talk of a civilization? A civilization is a cultural entity. Villages, regions, ethnic groups, nationalities, religious groups, all have distinct cultures at different levels of cultural heterogeneity. The culture of a village in southern Italy may be different from that of a village in northern Italy, but both will share in a common Italian culture that distinguishes them from German villages. European communities, in turn, will share cultural features that distinguish them from Arab or Chinese communities. Arabs, Chinese and Westerners, however, are not part of any broader cultural entity. They constitute civilizations. A civilization is thus the highest cultural grouping of people and the broadest level of cultural identity people have short of that which distinguishes humans from other species. It is defined both by common objective elements, such as language, history, religion, customs, institutions, and by the subjective self-identification of people. People have levels of identity: a resident of Rome may define himself with varying degrees of intensity as a Roman, an Italian, a Catholic, a Christian, a European, a Westerner. The civilization to which he belongs is the broadest level of identification with which he intensely identifies. People can and do redefine their identities and, as a result, the composition and boundaries of civilizations change.

Civilizations may involve a large number of people, as with China, ("a civilization pretending to be a state," as Lucian Pye put it), or a very small number of people, such as the Anglophone Caribbean. A civilization may include several nation states, as is the case with Western, Latin American and Arab civilizations, or only one, as is the case with Japanese civilization. Civilizations obviously blend and overlap, and may include subcivilizations. Western civilization has two major variants, European and North American, and Islam has its Arab, Turkic and Malay subdivisions. Civilizations are nonetheless meaningful entities, and while the lines between them are seldom sharp, they are real. Civilizations are dynamic; they rise and fall; they divide and merge. And, as any student of history knows, civilizations disappear and are buried in the sands of time.

Westerners tend to think of nation states as the principal actors in global affairs. They have been that, however, for only a few centuries. The broader reaches of human history have been the history of civilizations. In *A Study of History*, Arnold Toynbee identified 21 major civilizations; only six of them exist in the contemporary world.

Why Civilizations Will Clash

Civilization identity will be increasingly important in the future, and the world will be shaped in large measure by the interactions among seven or eight major civilizations. These include Western, Confucian, Japanese, Islamic, Hindu, Slavic-Orthodox, Latin American and possibly African civilization. The most important conflicts of the future will occur along the cultural fault lines separating these civilizations from one another.

Why will this be the case?

First, differences among civilizations are not only real; they are basic. Civilizations are differentiated from each other by history, language, culture, tradition and, most important, religion. The people of different civilizations have different views on the relations between God and man, the individual and the group, the citizen and the state, parents and children, husband and wife, as well as differing views of the relative importance of rights and responsibilities, liberty and authority, equality and hierarchy. These differences are the product of centuries. They will not soon disappear. They are far more fundamental than differences among political ideologies and political regimes. Differences do not necessarily mean conflict, and conflict does not necessarily mean violence. Over the centuries, however, differences among civilizations have generated the most prolonged and the most violent conflicts.

Second, the world is becoming a smaller place. The interactions between peoples of different civilizations are increasing; these increasing interactions intensify civilization consciousness and awareness of differences between civilizations and commonalities within civilizations. North African immigration to France generates hostility among Frenchmen and at the same time increased receptivity to immigration by "good" European Catholic Poles. Americans react far more negatively to Japanese investment than to larger investments from Canada and European countries. Similarly, as Donald Horowitz has pointed out, "An Ibo may be . . . an Owerri Ibo or an Onitsha Ibo in what was the Eastern region of Nigeria. In Lagos, he is simply an Ibo. In London, he is a Nigerian. In New York, he is an African." The interactions among peoples of different civilizations enhance the civilization-consciousness of people that, in turn, invigorates differences and animosities stretching or thought to stretch back deep into history.

Third, the processes of economic modernization and social change throughout the world are separating people from longstanding local identities. They also weaken the nation state as a source of identity. In much of the world religion has moved in to fill this gap, often in the form of movements that are labeled "fundamentalist." Such movements are found in Western Christianity, Judaism, Buddhism and Hinduism, as well as in Islam. In most countries and most religions the people active in fundamentalist movements are young, college-educated, middle-class technicians, professionals and business persons. The "unsecularization of the world," George Weigel has remarked, is one of the dominant social facts of life in the late twentieth century." The revival of religion, "la revanche de Dieu," as Gilles Kepel labeled it, provides a basis for identity and commitment that transcends national boundaries and unites civilizations.

Fourth, the growth of civilization-consciousness is enhanced by the dual role of the West. On the one hand, the West is at a peak of power. At the same time, however, and perhaps as a result, a return to the roots phenomenon is occurring among non-Western civilizations. Increasingly one hears references to trends toward a turning inward and "Asianization" in Japan, the end of the Nehru legacy and the "Hinduization" of India, the failure of Western ideas of socialism and nationalism and hence "re-Islamization" of the Middle East, and now a debate over Westernization versus Russianization in Boris Yeltsin's country. A West at the peak of its power confronts non-Wests that increasingly have the desire, the will and the resources to shape the world in non-Western ways.

In the past, the elites of non-Western societies were usually the people who were most involved with the West, had been educated at Oxford, the Sorbonne or Sandhurst, and had absorbed Western attitudes and values. At the same time, the populace in non-Western countries often remained deeply imbued with the indigenous culture. Now, however, these relationships are being reversed. A de-Westernization and indigenization of elites is occurring in many non-Western countries at the same time that Western, usually American, cultures, styles and habits become more popular among the mass of the people.

Fifth, cultural characteristics and differences are less mutable and hence less easily compromised and resolved than political and economic ones. In the former Soviet Union, communists can become democrats, the rich can become poor and the poor rich, but Russians cannot become Estonians and Azeris cannot become Armenians. In class and ideological conflicts, the key question was "Which side are you on?" and people could and did choose sides and change sides. In conflicts between civilizations, the question is "What are you?" That is a given that cannot be changed. And as we know, from Bosnia to the Caucasus to the Sudan, the wrong answer to that question can mean a bullet in the head. Even more than ethnicity, religion discriminates sharply and exclusively among people. A person can be half-French and half-Arab and simultaneously even a citizen of two countries. It is more difficult to be half-Catholic and half-Muslim.

Finally, economic regionalism is increasing. The proportions of total trade that were intraregional rose between 1980 and 1989 from 51 percent to 59 percent in Europe, 33 percent to 37 percent in East Asia, and 32 percent to 36 percent in North America. The importance of regional economic blocs is likely to continue to increase in the future. On the one hand, successful economic regionalism will reinforce civilization-consciousness. On the other hand, economic regionalism may succeed only when it is rooted in a common civilization. The European Community rests on the shared foundation of European culture and Western Christianity. The success of the North American Free Trade

Area depends on the convergence now underway of Mexican, Canadian and American cultures. Japan, in contrast, faces difficulties in creating a comparable economic entity in East Asia because Japan is a society and civilization unique to itself. However strong the trade and investment links Japan may develop with other East Asian countries, its cultural differences with those countries inhibit and perhaps preclude its promoting regional economic integration like that in Europe and North America.

Common culture, in contrast, is clearly facilitating the rapid expansion of the economic relations between the People's Republic of China and Hong Kong, Taiwan, Singapore and the overseas Chinese communities in other Asian countries. With the Cold War over, cultural commanalities increasingly overcome ideological differences, and mainland China and Taiwan move closer together. If cultural commonality is a prerequisite for economic integration, the principal East Asian economic bloc of the future is likely to be centered on China. This bloc is, in fact, already coming into existence. As Murray Weidenbaum has observed,

> Despite the current Japanese dominance of the region, the Chinese-based economy of Asia is rapidly emerging as a new epicenter for industry, commerce and finance. This strategic area contains substantial amounts of technology and manufacturing capability (Taiwan), outstanding entrepreneurial, marketing and services acumen (Hong Kong), a fine communications network (Singapore), a tremendous pool of financial capital (all three), and very large endowments of land, resources and labor (mainland China).... From Guangzhou to Singapore, from Kuala Lumpur to Manila, this influential network—often based on extensions of the tranditional clans —has been described as the beckbone of the East Asian economy.[1]

Culture and religion also form the basis of the Economic Cooperation Organization, which brings together ten non-Arab Muslim countries: Iran, Pakistan, Turkey, Azerbaijan, Kazakhstan, Kyrgyzstan, Turkmenistan, Tadjikistan, Uzbekistan and Afghanistan. One impetus to the revival and expansion of this organization, founded originally in the 1960s by Turkey, Pakistan and Iran, is the realization by the leaders of several of these countries that they had no chance of admission to the European Community. Similarly, Caricom, the Central American Common Market and Mercosur rest on common cultural foundations. Efforts to build a broader Caribbean-Central American economic entity bridging the Anglo-Latin divide, however, have to date failed.

As people define their identity in ethnic and religious terms, they are likely to see an "us" versus "them" relation existing between themselves and people of different ethnicity or religion. The end of ideologically defined states in Eastern Europe and the former Soviet Union permits traditional ethnic identities and animosities to come to the fore. Differences in culture and religion create differences over policy issues, ranging from human rights to immigration to trade and commerce to the environment. Geographical propinquity gives rise to conflicting territorial claims from Bosnia to Mindanao. Most important, the efforts of the West to promote its values of democracy and liberalism as universal values, to maintain its military predominance and to advance its economic interests engender countering responses from other civilizations.

Decreasingly able to mobilize support and form coalitions on the basis of ideology, governments and groups will increasingly attempt to mobilize support by appealing to common religion and civilization identity.

The clash of civilizations thus occurs at two levels. At the micro-level, adjacent groups along the fault lines between civilizations struggle, often violently, over the control of territory and each other. At the macro-level, states from different civilizations compete for relative military and economic power, struggle over the control of international institutions and third parties, and competitively promote their particular political and religious values.

The Fault Lines Between Civilizations

The fault lines between civilizations are replacing the political and ideological boundaries of the Cold War as the flash points for crisis and bloodshed. The Cold War began when the Iron Curtain divided Europe politically and ideologically. The Cold War ended with the end of the Iron Curtain. As the ideological division of Europe has disappeared, the cultural division of Europe between Western Christianity, on the one hand, and Orthodox Christianity and Islam, on the other, has reemerged. The most significant dividing line in Europe, as William Wallace has suggested, may well be the eastern boundary of Western Christianity in the year 1500. This line runs along what are now the boundaries between Finland and Russia and between the Baltic states and Russia, cuts through Belarus and Ukraine separating the more Catholic western Ukraine from Orthodox eastern Ukraine, swings westward separating Transylvania from the rest of Romania, and then goes through Yugoslavia almost exactly along the line now separating Croatia and Slovenia from the rest of Yugoslavia. In the Balkans this line, of course, coincides with the historic boundary between the Hapsburg and Ottoman empires. The peoples to the north and west of this line are Protestant or Catholic; they shared the common experiences of European history—feudalism, the Renaissance, the Reformation, the Enlightenment, the French Revolution, the Industrial Revolution; they are generally economically better off than the peoples to the east; and they may now look forward to increasing involvement in a common European economy and to the consolidation of democratic political systems. The peoples to the east and south of this line are Orthodox or Muslim; they historically belonged to the Ottoman or Tsarist empires and were only lightly touched by the shaping events in the rest of Europe; they are generally less advanced economically; they seem much less likely to develop stable democratic political systems. The Velvet Curtain of culture has replaced the Iron Curtain of ideology as the most significant dividing line in Europe. As the events in Yugoslavia show, it is not only a line of difference; it is also at times a line of bloody conflict.

Conflict along the fault line between Western and Islamic civilizations has been going on for 1,300 years. After the founding of Islam, the Arab and Moorish surge west and north only ended at Tours in 732. From the eleventh to the thirteenth century the Crusaders attempted with temporary success to bring Christianity and Christian rule to the Holy Land. From the fourteenth to the seventeenth century, the Ottoman Turks reversed the balance, extended their sway over the Middle East and the Balkans, captured Constantinople, and twice laid siege to Vienna. In the nineteenth and early twentieth centuries as Ottoman power declined Britain, France, and Italy established Western control over most of North Africa and the Middle East.

After World War II, the West, in turn, began to retreat; the colonial empires disappeared; first Arab nationalism and then Islamic fundamentalism manifested themselves; the West became heavily dependent on the Persian Gulf countries for its energy; the oil-rich Muslim countries became money-rich and, when they wished to, weapons-rich. Several wars occurred between Arabs and Israel (created by the West). France fought a bloody and ruthless war in Algeria for most of the 1950s; British and French forces invaded Egypt in 1956; American forces went into Lebanon in 1958; subsequently American forces returned to Lebanon, attacked Libya, and engaged in various military encounters with Iran; Arab and Islamic terrorists, supported by at least three Middle Eastern governments, employed the weapon of the weak and bombed Western planes and installations and seized Western hostages. This warfare between Arabs and the West culminated in 1990, when the United States sent a massive army to the Persian Gulf to defend some Arab countries against aggression by another. In its aftermath NATO planning is increasingly directed to potential threats and instability along its "southern tier."

This centuries-old military interaction between the West and Islam is unlikely to decline. It could become more virulent. The Gulf War left some Arabs feeling proud that Saddam Hussein had attacked Israel and stood up to the West. It also left many feeling humiliated and resentful of the West's military presence in the Persian Gulf, the West's overwhelming military dominance, and their apparent inability to shape their own destiny. Many Arab countries, in addition to the oil exporters, are reaching levels of economic and social development where autocratic forms of government become inappropriate and efforts to introduce democracy become stronger. Some openings in Arab political systems have already occurred. The principal beneficiaries of these openings have been Islamist movements. In the Arab world, in short, Western democracy strengthens anti-Western political forces. This may be a passing phenomenon, but it surely complicates relations between Islamic countries and the West.

Those relations are also complicated by demography. The spectacular population growth in Arab countries, particularly in North Africa, has led to increased migration to Western Europe. The movement within Western Europe toward minimizing internal boundaries has sharpened political sensitivities with respect to this development. In Italy, France and Germany, racism is increasingly open, and political reactions and violence against Arab and Turkish migrants have become more intense and more widespread since 1990.

On both sides the interaction between Islam and the West is seen as a clash of civilizations. The West's "next confrontation," observes M. J. Akbar, an Indian Muslim author, "is definitely going to come from the Muslim world. It is in the sweep of the Islamic nations from the Maghreb to Pakistan that the struggle for a new world order will begin." Bernard Lewis comes to a similar conclusion:

> We are facing a mood and a movement far transcending the level of issues and policies and the governments that pursue them. This is no less than a clash of civilizations—the perhaps irrational but surely historic reaction of an ancient rival against our Judeo-Christian heritage, our secular present, and the worldwide expansion of both.[2]

Historically, the other great antagonistic interaction of Arab Islamic civilization has been with the pagan, animist, and now increasingly Christian black peoples to the south. In the past, this antagonism was epitomized in the image of Arab slave dealers and black slaves. It has been reflected in the on-going civil war in the Sudan between Arabs and blacks, the fighting in Chad between Libyan-supported insurgents and the government, the tensions between Orthodox Christians and Muslims in the Horn of Africa, and the political conflicts, recurring riots and communal violence between Muslims and Christians in Nigeria. The modernization of Africa and the spread of Christianity are likely to enhance the probability of violence along this fault line. Symptomatic of the intensification of this conflict was the Pope John Paul II's speech in Khartoum in February 1993 attacking the actions of the Sudan's Islamist government against the Christian minority there.

On the northern border of Islam, conflict has increasingly erupted between Orthodox and Muslim peoples, including the carnage of Bosnia and Sarajevo, the simmering violence between Serb and Albanian, the tenuous relations between Bulgarians and their Turkish minority, the violence between Ossetians and Ingush, the unremitting slaughter of each other by Armenians and Azeris, the tense relations between Russians and Muslims in Central Asia, and the deployment of Russian troops to protect Russian interests in the Caucasus and Central Asia. Religion reinforces the revival of ethnic identities and restimulates Russian fears about the security of their southern borders. This concern is well captured by Archie Roosevelt:

> Much of Russian history concerns the struggle between the Slavs and the Turkic peoples on their borders, which dates back to the foundation of the Russian state more than a thousand years ago. In the Slavs' millennium-long confrontation with their eastern neighbors lies the key to an understanding not only of Russian history, but Russian character. To understand Russian realities today one has to have a concept of the great Turkic ethnic group that has preoccupied Russians through the centuries.[3]

The conflict of civilizations is deeply rooted elsewhere in Asia. The historic clash between Muslim and Hindu in the subcontinent manifests itself now not only in the rivalry between Pakistan and India but also in intensifying religious strife within India between increasingly militant Hindu groups and India's substantial Muslim minority. The destruction of the Ayodhya mosque in December 1992 brought to the fore the issue of whether India will remain a secular democratic state or become a Hindu one. In East Asia, China has outstanding territorial disputes with most of its neighbors. It has pursued a ruthless policy toward the Buddhist people of Tibet, and it is pursuing an increasingly ruthless policy toward its Turkic-Muslim minority. With the Cold War over, the underlying differences between China and the United States have reasserted themselves in areas such as human rights, trade and weapons proliferation. These differences are unlikely to moderate. A "new cold war," Deng Xiaoping reportedly asserted in 1991, is under way between China and America....

Civilization Rallying: The Kin-Country Syndrome

Groups or states belonging to one civilization that become involved in war with people from a different civilization naturally try to rally support from other members of their own civilization. As the post–Cold War world evolves, civilization commonality, what H. D. S. Greenway has termed the "kin-country" syndrome, is replacing political ideology and traditional balance of power considerations as the principal basis for cooperation and coalitions. It can be seen gradually emerging in the post–Cold War conflicts in the Persian Gulf, the Caucasus and Bosnia. None of these was a full-scale war between civilizations, but each involved some elements of civilizational rallying, which seemed to become more important as the conflict continued and which may provide a foretaste of the future.

First, in the Gulf War one Arab state invaded another and then fought a coalition of Arab, Western and other states. While only a few Muslim governments overtly supported Saddam Hussein, many Arab elites privately cheered him on, and he was highly popular among large sections of the Arab publics. Islamic fundamentalist movements universally supported Iraq rather than the Western-backed governments of Kuwait and Saudi Arabia. Forswearing Arab nationalism, Saddam Hussein explicitly invoked an Islamic appeal. He and his supporters attempted to define the war as a war between civilizations. "It is not the world against Iraq," as Safar Al-Hawali, dean of Islamic Studies at the Umm Al-Qura University in Mecca, put it in a widely circulated tape. "It is the West against Islam." Ignoring the rivalry between Iran and Iraq, the chief Iranian religious leader, Ayatollah Ali Khamenei, called for a holy war against the West: "The struggle against American aggression, greed, plans and policies will be counted as a jihad, and anybody who is killed on that path is a martyr." "This is a war," King Hussein of Jordan argued, "against all Arabs and all Muslims and not against Iraq alone."

The rallying of substantial sections of Arab elites and publics behind Saddam Hussein caused those Arab governments in the anti-Iraq coalition to moderate their activities and temper their public statements. Arab governments opposed or distanced themselves from subsequent Western efforts to apply pressure on Iraq, including enforcement of a no-fly zone in the summer of 1992 and the bombing of Iraq in January 1993. The Western-Soviet-Turkish-Arab anti-Iraq coalition of 1990 had by 1993 become a coalition of almost only the West and Kuwait against Iraq.

Muslims contrasted Western actions against Iraq with the West's failure to protect Bosnians against Serbs and to impose sanctions on Israel for violating

U.N. resolutions. The West, they alleged, was using a double standard. A world of clashing civilizations, however, is inevitably a world of double standards: people apply one standard to their kin-countries and a different standard to others.

Second, the kin-country syndrome also appeared in conflicts in the former Soviet Union. Armenian military successes in 1992 and 1993 stimulated Turkey to become increasingly supportive of its religious, ethnic and linguistic brethren in Azerbaijan. "We have a Turkish nation feeling the same sentiments as the Azerbaijanis," said one Turkish official in 1992. "We are under pressure. Our newspapers are full of the photos of atrocities and are asking us if we are still serious about pursuing our neutral policy. Maybe we should show Armenia that there's a big Turkey in the region." President Turgut Özal agreed, remarking that Turkey should at least "scare the Armenians a little bit." Turkey, Özal threatened again in 1993, would "show its fangs." Turkish Air Force jets flew reconnaissance flights along the Armenian border; Turkey suspended food shipments and air flights to Armenia; and Turkey and Iran announced they would not accept dismemberment of Azerbaijan. In the last years of its existence, the Soviet government supported Azerbaijan because its government was dominated by former communists. With the end of the Soviet Union, however, political considerations gave way to religious ones. Russian troops fought on the side of the Armenians, and Azerbaijan accused the "Russian government of turning 180 degrees" toward support for Christian Armenia.

Third, with respect to the fighting in the former Yugoslavia, Western publics manifested sympathy and support for the Bosnian Muslims and the horrors they suffered at the hands of the Serbs. Relatively little concern was expressed, however, over Croatian attacks on Muslims and participation of the dismemberment of Bosnia-Herzegovina. In the early stages of the Yugoslav breakup, Germany, in an unusual display of diplomatic initiative and muscle, induced the other 11 members of the European Community to follow its lead in recognizing Slovenia and Crotia. As a result of the pope's determination to provide strong backing to the two Catholic countries, the Vatican extended recognition even before the Community did. The United States followed the European lead. Thus the leading actors in Western civilization rallied behind their coreligionists. Subsequently Croatia was reported to be receiving substantial quantities of arms from Central European and other Western countries. Boris Yeltsin's government, on the other hand, attempted to pursue a middle course that would be sympathetic to the Orthodox Serbs but not alienate Russia from the West. Russian conservative and nationalist groups, however, including many legislators, attacked the government for not being more forthcoming in its support for the Serbs. By early 1993 several hundred Russians apparently were serving with the Serbian forces, and reports circulated of Russian arms being supplied to Serbia.

Islamic governments and groups, on the other hand, castigated the West for not coming to the defense of the Bosnians. Iranian leaders urged Muslims from all countries to provide help to Bosnia; in violation of the U.N. arms embargo, Iran supplied weapons and men for the Bosnians; Iranian-supported Lebanese groups sent guerrillas to train and organize the Bosnian forces. In 1993 up to 4,000 Muslims from over two dozen Islamic countries were reported to be fighting in Bosnia. The governments of Saudi Arabia and other countries felt under increasing pressure from fundamentalist groups in their own societies to provide more vigorous support for the Bosnians. By the end of 1992, Saudi Arabia had reportedly supplied substantial funding for weapons and supplies for the Bosnians, which significantly increased their military capabilities vis-à-vis the Serbs.

In the 1930s the Spanish Civil War provoked intervention from countries that politically were fascist, communist and democratic. In the 1990s the Yugoslav conflict is provoking intervention from countries that are Muslim, Orthodox and Western Christian. The parallel has not gone unnoticed. "The war in Bosnia-Herzegovina has become the emotional equivalent of the fight against fascism in the Spanish Civil War," one Saudi editor observed. "Those who died there are regarded as martyrs who tried to save their fellow Muslims."

Conflicts and violence will also occur between states and groups within the same civilization. Such conflicts, however, are likely to be less intense and less likely to expand than conflicts between civilizations. Common membership in a civilization reduces the probability of violence in situations where it might otherwise occur. In 1991 and 1992 many people were alarmed by the possibility of violent conflict between Russia and Ukraine over territory, particularly Crimea, the Black Sea fleet, nuclear weapons and economic issues. If civilization is what counts, however, the likelihood of violence between Ukrainians and Russians should be low. They are two Slavic, primarily Orthodox peoples who have had close relationships with each other for centuries. As of early 1993, despite all the reasons for conflict, the leaders of the two countries were effectively negotiating and defusing the issues between the two countries. While there has been serious fighting between Muslims and Christians elsewhere in the former Soviet Union and much tension and some fighting between Western and Orthodox Christians in the Baltic states, there has been virtually no violence between Russians and Ukrainians.

Civilization rallying to date has been limited, but it has been growing, and it clearly has the potential to spread much further. As the conflicts in the Persian Gulf, the Caucasus and Bosnia continued, the positions of nations and the cleavages between them increasingly were along civilizational lines. Populist politicians, religious leaders and the media have found it a potent means of arousing mass support and of pressuring hesitant governments. In the coming years, the local conflicts most likely to escalate into major wars will be those, as in Bosnia and the Caucasus, along the fault lines between civilizations. The next world war, if there is one, will be a war between civilizations.

The West Versus the Rest

The West is now at an extraordinary peak of power in relation to other civilizations. Its superpower opponent has disappeared from the map. Military conflict among Western states is unthinkable, and Western military power is unrivaled. Apart from Japan, the West faces no economic challenge. It dominates international political and security institutions and with Japan international economic institutions. Global political and security issues are effectively settled by a directorate of the United States, Britain and France, world economic issues by a directorate of the United States, Germany and Japan, all of which maintain extraordinarily close relations with each other to the exclusion of lesser and largely non-Western countries. Decisions made at the U.N. Security Council or in the International Monetary Fund [IMF] that reflect the interests of the West are presented to the world as reflecting the desires of the world community. The very phrase "the world community" has become the euphemistic collective noun (replacing "the Free World") to give global legitimacy to actions reflecting the interests of the United States and other Western powers.[4] Through the IMF and other international economic institutions, the West promotes its economic interests and imposes on other nations the economic policies it thinks appropriate. In any poll of non-Western peoples, the IMF undoubtedly would win the support of finance ministers and a few others, but get an overwhelmingly unfavorable rating from just about everyone else who would agree with Georgy Arbatov's characterization of IMF officials as "neo-Bolsheviks who love expropriating other people's money, imposing undemocratic and alien rules of economic and political conduct and stifling economic freedom."

Western domination of the U.N. Security Council and its decisions, tempered only by occasional abstention by China, produced U.N. legitimation of the West's use of force to drive Iraq out of Kuwait and its elimination of Iraq's sophisticated weapons and capacity to produce such weapons. It also produced the quite unprecedented action by the United States, Britain and France in getting the Security Council to demand that Libya hand over the Pan Am 103 bombing suspects and then to impose sanctions when Libya refused. After defeating the largest Arab army, the West did not hesitate to throw its weight around in the Arab world. The West in effect is using international institutions, military power and economic resources to run the world in ways that will maintain Western predominance, protect Western interests and promote Western political and economic values.

That at least is the way in which non-Westerners see the new world, and there is a significant element of truth in their view. Differences in power and struggles for military, economic and institutional power are thus one source of conflict between the West and other civilizations. Differences in culture, that is basic values and beliefs, are a second source of conflict. V. S. Naipaul has argued that Western civilization is the "universal civilization" that "fits all men." At a superficial level much of Western culture has indeed permeated the rest of the world. At a more basic level, however, Western concepts differ fundamentally from those prevalent in other civilizations. Western ideas of individualism, liberalism, constitutionalism, human rights, equality, liberty, the rule of law, democracy, free markets, the separation of church and state, often have little resonance in Islamic, Confucian, Japanese, Hindu, Buddhist or Orthodox cultures. Western efforts to propagate such ideas produce instead a reaction against "human rights imperialism" and a reaffirmation of indigenous values, as can be seen in the support for religious fundamentalism by the younger generation in non-Western cultures. The very notion that there could be a "universal civilization" is a Western idea, directly at odds with the particularism of most Asian societies and their emphasis on what distinguishes one people from another. Indeed, the author of a review of 100 comparative studies of values in different societies concluded that "the values that are most important in the West are least important worldwide."[5] In the political realm, of course, these differences are most manifest in the efforts of the United States and other Western powers to induce other peoples to adopt Western ideas concerning democracy and human rights. Modern democratic government originated in the West. When it has developed in non-Western societies it has usually been the product of Western colonialism or imposition.

The central axis of world politics in the future is likely to be, in Kishore Mahbubani's phrase, the conflict between "the West and the Rest" and the responses of non-Western civilizations to Western power and values.[6] Those responses generally take one or a combination of three forms. At one extreme, non-Western states can, like Burma and North Korea, attempt to pursue a course of isolation, to insulate their societies from penetration or "corruption" by the West, and, in effect, to opt out of participation in the Western-dominated global community. The costs of this course, however, are high, and few states have pursued it exclusively. A second alternative, the equivalent of "band-wagoning" in international relations theory, is to attempt to join the West and accept its values and institutions. The third alternative is to attempt to "balance" the West by developing economic and military power and cooperating with other non-Western societies against the West, while preserving indigenous values and institutions; in short, to modernize but not to Westernize....

The Confucian-Islamic Connection

The obstacles to non-Western countries joining the West vary considerably. They are least for Latin American and East European countries. They are greater for the Orthodox countries of the former Soviet Union. They are still greater for Muslim, Confucian, Hindu and Buddhist societies. Japan has established a unique position for itself as an associate member of the West: it is in the West in some respects but clearly not of the West in important dimensions. Those countries that for reason of culture and power do not wish to, or cannot, join the West compete with the West by developing their own economic, military and political power. They do this by promoting their internal development and by cooperating with other non-Western countries. The most prominent form of this cooperation is the Confucian-Islamic connection that has emerged to challenge Western interests, values and power.

Almost without exception, Western countries are reducing their military power; under Yeltsin's leadership so also is Russia. China, North Korea and several Middle Eastern states, however, are significantly expanding their military capabilities. They are doing this by the import of arms from Western and non-Western sources and by the development of indigenous arms industries. One result is the emergence of what Charles Krauthammer has called "Weapon States," and the Weapon States are not Western states. Another result is the redefinition of arms control, which is a Western concept and a Western goal. During the Cold War the primary purpose of arms control was to establish

a stable military balance between the United States and its allies and the Soviet Union and its allies. In the post–Cold War world the primary objective of
arms control is to prevent the development by non-Western societies of military capabilities that could threaten Western interests. The West attempts to do
this through international agreements, economic pressure and controls on the
transfer of arms and weapons technologies.

The conflict between the West and the Confucian-Islamic states focuses
largely, although not exclusively, on nuclear, chemical and biological weapons,
ballistic missiles and other sophisticated means for delivering them, and the
guidance, intelligence and other electronic capabilities for achieving that goal.
The West promotes non-proliferation as a universal norm and nonproliferation treaties and inspections as means of realizing that norm. It also threatens
a variety of sanctions against those who promote the spread of sophisticated
weapons and proposes some benefits for those who do not. The attention of the
West focuses, naturally, on nations that are actually or potentially hostile to the
West.

The non-Western nations, on the other hand, assert their right to acquire
and to deploy whatever weapons they think necessary for their security. They
also have absorbed, to the full, the truth of the response of the Indian defense
minister when asked what lesson he learned from the Gulf War: "Don't fight
the United States unless you have nuclear weapons." Nuclear weapons, chemical weapons and missiles are viewed, probably erroneously, as the potential
equalizer of superior Western conventional power. China, of course, already
has nuclear weapons; Pakistan and India have the capability to deploy them.
North Korea, Iran, Iraq, Libya and Algeria appear to be attempting to acquire
them. A top Iranian official has declared that all Muslim states should acquire
nuclear weapons, and in 1988 the president of Iran reportedly issued a directive
calling for development of "offensive and defensive chemical, biological and
radiological weapons."

Centrally important to the development of counter-West military capabilities is the sustained expansion of China's military power and its means to create
military power. Buoyed by spectacular economic development, China is rapidly
increasing its military spending and vigorously moving forward with the modernization of its armed forces. It is purchasing weapons from the former Soviet
states; it is developing long-range missiles; in 1992 it tested a one-megaton
nuclear device. It is developing power-projection capabilities, acquiring aerial
refueling technology, and trying to purchase an aircraft carrier. Its military
buildup and assertion of sovereignty over the South China Sea are provoking
a multilateral regional arms race in East Asia. China is also a major exporter of
arms and weapons technology. It has exported materials to Libya and Iraq that
could be used to manufacture nuclear weapons and nerve gas. It has helped
Algeria build a reactor suitable for nuclear weapons research and production.
China has sold to Iran nuclear technology that American officials believe could
only be used to create weapons and apparently has shipped components of
300-mile-range missiles to Pakistan. North Korea has had a nuclear weapons
program under way for some while and has sold advanced missiles and missile
technology to Syria and Iran. The flow of weapons and weapons technology is

generally from East Asia to the Middle East. There is, however, some movement in the reverse direction; China has received Stinger missiles from Pakistan.

A Confucian-Islamic military connection has thus come into being, designed to promote acquisition by its members of the weapons and weapons technologies needed to counter the military power of the West. It may or may not last. At present, however, it is, as Dave McCurdy has said, "a renegades' mutual support pact, run by the proliferators and their backers." A new form of arms competition is thus occurring between Islamic-Confucian states and the West. In an old-fashioned arms race, each side developed its own arms to balance or to achieve superiority against the other side. In this new form of arms competition, one side is developing its arms and the other side is attempting not to balance but to limit and prevent that arms build-up while at the same time reducing its own military capabilities.

Implications for the West

This article does not argue that civilization identities will replace all other identities, that nation states will disappear, that each civilization will become a single coherent political entity, that groups within a civilization will not conflict with and even fight each other. This paper does set forth the hypotheses that differences between civilizations are real and important; civilization-consciousness is increasing; conflict between civilizations will supplant ideological and other forms of conflict as the dominant global form of conflict; international relations, historically a game played out within Western civilization, will increasingly be de-Westernized and become a game in which non-Western civilizations are actors and not simply objects; successful political, security and economic international institutions are more likely to develop within civilizations than across civilizations; conflicts between groups in different civilizations will be more frequent, more sustained and more violent than conflicts between groups in the same civilization; violent conflicts between groups in different civilizations are the most likely and most dangerous source of escalation that could lead to global wars; the paramount axis of world politics will be the relations between "the West and the Rest"; the elites in some torn non-Western countries will try to make their countries part of the West, but in most cases face major obstacles to accomplishing this; a central focus of conflict for the immediate future will be between the West and several Islamic-Confucian states.

This is not to advocate the desirability of conflicts between civilizations. It is to set forth descriptive hypotheses as to what the future may be like. If these are plausible hypotheses, however, it is necessary to consider their implications for Western policy. These implications should be divided between short-term advantage and long-term accommodation. In the short term it is clearly in the interest of the West to promote greater cooperation and unity within its own civilization, particularly between its European and North American components; to incorporate into the West societies in Eastern Europe and Latin America whose cultures are close to those of the West; to promote and maintain cooperative relations with Russia and Japan; to prevent escalation of local inter-civilization conflicts into major inter-civilization wars; to limit the expansion of the military strength of Confucian and Islamic states; to moderate the reduction of Western military capabilities and maintain military superiority in East and Southwest Asia; to exploit differences and conflicts among Confucian and Islamic states; to support in other civilizations groups sympathetic to Western values and interests; to strengthen international institutions that reflect and legitimate Western interests and values and to promote the involvement of non-Western states in those institutions.

In the longer term other measures would be called for. Western civilization is both Western and modern. Non-Western civilizations have attempted to become modern without becoming Western. To date only Japan has fully succeeded in this quest. Non-Western civilizations will continue to attempt to acquire the wealth, technology, skills, machines and weapons that are part of being modern. They will also attempt to reconcile this modernity with their traditional culture and values. Their economic and military strength relative to the West will increase. Hence the West will increasingly have to accommodate these non-Western modern civilizations whose power approaches that of the West but whose values and interests differ significantly from those of the West. This will require the West to maintain the economic and military power necessary to protect its interests in relation to these civilizations. It will also, however, require the West to develop a more profound understanding of the basic religious and philosophical assumptions underlying other civilizations and the ways in which people in those civilizations see their interests. It will require an effort to identify elements of commonality between Western and other civilizations. For the relevant future, there will be no universal civilization, but instead a world of different civilizations, each of which will have to learn to coexist with the others.

Notes

1. Murray Weidenbaum, *Greater China: The Next Economic Superpower?*, St. Louis: Washington University Center for the Study of American Business, Contemporary Issues, Series 57, February 1993, pp. 2–3.

2. Bernard Lewis, "The Roots of Muslim Rage," *The Atlantic Monthly*, vol. 266, September 1990, p. 60; *Time*, June 15, 1992, pp. 24–28.

3. Archie Roosevelt, *For Lust of Knowing*, Boston; Little, Brown, 1988, pp. 332–333.

4. Almost invariably Western leaders claim they are acting on behalf of "the world community." One minor lapse occurred during the run-up to the Gulf War. In an interview on "Good Morning America," Dec. 21, 1990, British Prime Minister John Major referred to the actions "the West" was taking against Saddam Hussein. He quickly corrected himself and subsequently referred to "the world community." He was, however, right when he erred.

5. Harry C. Triandis, *The New York Times*, Dec. 25, 1990, p. 41, and "Cross-Cultural Studies of Individualism and Collectivism," Nebraska Symposium on Motivation, vol. 37, 1989, pp. 41–133.

6. Kishore Mahbubani, "The West and the Rest," *The National Interest*, Summer 1992, pp. 3–13.

John R. Bowen **NO**

The Myth of Global Ethnic Conflict

$\mathbf{M}$uch recent discussion of international affairs has been based on the misleading assumption that the world is fraught with primordial ethnic conflict. According to this notion, ethnic groups lie in wait for one another, nourishing age-old hatreds and restrained only by powerful states. Remove the lid, and the cauldron boils over. Analysts who advance this idea differ in their predictions for the future: some see the fragmentation of the world into small tribal groups; others, a face-off among several vast civilizational coalitions. They all share, however, the idea that the world's current conflicts are fueled by age-old ethnic loyalties and cultural differences.[1]

This notion misrepresents the genesis of conflict and ignores the ability of diverse people to coexist. The very phrase "ethnic conflict" misguides us. It has become a shorthand way to speak about any and all violent confrontations between groups of people living in the same country. Some of these conflicts involve ethnic or cultural identity, but most are about getting more power, land, or other resources. They do not result from ethnic diversity; thinking that they do sends us off in pursuit of the wrong policies, tolerating rulers who incite riots and suppress ethnic differences.

In speaking about local group conflicts we tend to make three assumptions: first, that ethnic identities are ancient and unchanging; second, that these identities motivate people to persecute and kill; and third, that ethnic diversity itself inevitably leads to violence. All three are mistaken.

Contrary to the first assumption, ethnicity is a product of modern politics. Although people have had identities—deriving from religion, birthplace, language, and so on—for as long as humans have had culture, they have begun to see themselves as members of vast ethnic groups, opposed to other such groups, only during the modern period of colonization and state-building.

The view that ethnicity is ancient and unchanging emerges these days in the potent images of the cauldron and the tribe. Out of the violence in Eastern Europe came images of the region as a bubbling cauldron of ethnonationalist sentiments that were sure to boil over unless suppressed by strong states. The cauldron image contrasts with the American "melting pot," suggesting that Western ethnicities may melt, but Eastern ones must be suppressed by the region's unlikable, but perhaps necessary, Titos and Stalins.

From John R. Bowen, "The Myth of Global Ethnic Conflict," *Journal of Democracy,* vol. 7, no. 4 (October 1996). Copyright © 1996 by Johns Hopkins University Press and The National Endowment for Democracy. Reprinted by permission of Johns Hopkins University Press.

Nowhere does this notion seem more apt than in the former Yugoslavia. Surely the Serbs, Croats, and Bosnians are distinct ethnic groups destined to clash throughout history, are they not? Yet it is often forgotten how small the differences are among the currently warring factions in the Balkans. Serbs, Croats, and Bosnians all speak the same language (Italy has greater linguistic diversity) and have lived side by side, most often in peace, for centuries. Although it is common to say that they are separated by religion—Croats being Roman Catholic, Serbs Orthodox Christian, and Bosnians Muslim—in fact each population includes sizeable numbers of the other two religions. The three religions have indeed become symbols of group differences, but religious differences have not, by themselves, caused intergroup conflict. Rising rates of intermarriage (as high as 30 percent in Bosnia) would have led to the gradual blurring of contrasts across these lines.

As knowledgeable long-term observers such as Misha Glenny have pointed out, the roots of the current Balkan violence lie not in primordial ethnic and religious differences but rather in modern attempts to rally people around nationalist ideas. "Ethnicity" becomes "nationalism" when it includes aspirations to gain a monopoly of land, resources, and power. But nationalism, too, is a learned and frequently manipulated set of ideas, and not a primordial sentiment. In the nineteenth century, Serb and Croat intellectuals joined other Europeans in championing the rights of peoples to rule themselves in "nation-states": states to be composed of one nationality. For their part, Serbs drew on memories of short-lived Serb national states to claim their right to expand outward to encompass other peoples, just as other countries in Europe (most notably France) had done earlier. That Balkan peoples spoke the same language made these expansionist claims all the more plausible to many Serbs.[2]

At the same time, Croats were developing their own nationalist ideology, with a twist: rather than claiming the right to overrun non-Croats, it promised to exclude them. Nationalism among the Croats naturally was directed against their strong Serb neighbors. When Serbs dominated the state of Yugoslavia that was created after the First World War, Croat resentment of Serbs grew. The most militant of Croat nationalists formed an underground organization called Ustashe ("Uprising"), and it was this group, to which the Nazis gave control of Croatia, that carried out the forced conversions, expulsions, and massacres of Serbs during the Second World War. The later calls to war of the Serb leader Slobodan Milosević worked upon the still fresh memories of these tragedies.

But the events of the Second World War did not automatically lead to the slaughters of the 1990s; wartime memories could have been overcome had Yugoslavia's new leaders set out to create the social basis for a multiethnic society. But Marshal Tito chose to preserve his rule by forbidding Yugoslavs from forming independent civic groups and developing a sense of shared political values. Political opposition, whether in Croatia, Serbia, or Slovenia, coalesced instead around the only available symbols, the nationalisms of each region. Tito further fanned nationalist flames by giving Serbs and Croats privileges in each other's territories—Serbs held positions of power in Croatia, and Croats in Belgrade. In the countryside these minority presences added to nationalist resentments. Tito's short-term political cleverness—nostalgically remembered by some in the

West—in fact set the stage for later slaughter. Resentments and fears generated by modern state warfare and the absence of a civil society—not ethnic differences—made possible the success of the nationalist politicians Milosević and Franjo Tudjman.

The Legacy of Colonialism

But what about Africa? Surely there we find raw ethnic conflict, do we not? Our understandings of African violence have been clouded by visions, not of boiling cauldrons, but of ancient tribal warfare. I recall a National Public Radio reporter interviewing an African UN official about Rwanda. Throughout the discussion the reporter pressed the official to discuss the "ancient tribal hatreds" that were fueling the slaughter. The official ever so politely demurred, repeatedly reminding the reporter that mass conflict began when Belgian colonial rulers gave Tutsis a monopoly of state power. But, as happens so often, the image of ancient tribalism was too deeply ingrained in the reporter's mind for him to hear the UN official's message.

What the African official had to say was right: ethnic thinking in political life is a product of modern conflicts over power and resources, and not an ancient impediment to political modernity. True, before the modern era some Africans did consider themselves Hutu or Tutsi, Nuer or Zande, but these labels were not the main sources of everyday identity. A woman living in central Africa drew her identity from where she was born, from her lineage and in-laws, and from her wealth. Tribal or ethnic identity was rarely important in everyday life and could change as people moved over vast areas in pursuit of trade or new lands. Conflicts were more often within tribal categories than between them, as people fought over sources of water, farmland, or grazing rights.

It was the colonial powers, and the independent states succeeding them, which declared that each and every person had an "ethnic identity" that determined his or her place within the colony or the postcolonial system. Even such a seemingly small event as the taking of a census created the idea of a colony-wide ethnic category to which one belonged and had loyalties. (And this was not the case just in Africa: some historians of India attribute the birth of Hindu nationalism to the first British census, when people began to think of themselves as members of Hindu, Muslim, or Sikh populations.) The colonial powers—Belgians, Germans, French, British, and Dutch—also realized that, given their small numbers in their dominions, they could effectively govern and exploit only by seeking out "partners" from among local people, sometimes from minority or Christianized groups. But then the state had to separate its partners from all others, thereby creating firmly bounded "ethnic groups."

In Rwanda and Burundi, German and Belgian colonizers admired the taller people called Tutsis, who formed a small minority in both colonies. The Belgians gave the Tutsis privileged access to education and jobs, and even instituted a minimum height requirement for entrance to college. So that colonial officials could tell who was Tutsi, they required everyone to carry identity cards with tribal labels.

But people cannot be forced into the neat compartments that this requirement suggests. Many Tutsis are tall and many Hutus short, but Hutus and Tutsis had intermarried to a such an extent that they were not easily distinguished physically (nor are they today). They spoke the same language and carried out the same religious practices. In most regions of the colonies the categories became economic labels: poor Tutsis became Hutus, and economically successful Hutus became Tutsis. Where the labels "Hutu" and "Tutsi" had not been much used, lineages with lots of cattle were simply labeled Tutsi; poorer lineages, Hutu. Colonial discrimination against Hutus created what had not existed before: a sense of collective Hutu identity, a Hutu cause. In the late 1950s Hutus began to rebel against Tutsi rule (encouraged by Europeans on their way out) and then created an independent and Hutu-dominated state in Rwanda; this state then gave rise to Tutsi resentments and to the creation of a Tutsi rebel army, the Rwandan Patriotic Front....

In these cases and many others—Sikhs in India, Maronites in Lebanon, Copts in Egypt, Moluccans in the Dutch East Indies, Karens in Burma—colonial and postcolonial states created new social groups and identified them by ethnic, religious, or regional categories. Only in living memory have the people who were sorted into these categories begun to act in concert, as political groups with common interests. Moreover, their shared interests have been those of political autonomy, access to education and jobs, and control of local resources. Far from reflecting ancient ethnic or tribal loyalties, their cohesion and action are products of the modern state's demand that people make themselves heard as powerful groups, or else risk suffering severe disadvantages.

Fear From the Top

A reader might say at this point: Fine, ethnic identities are modern and created, but today people surely do target members of other ethnic groups for violence, do they not? The answer is: Less than we usually think, and when they do, it is only after a long period of being prepared, pushed, and threatened by leaders who control the army and the airwaves. It is fear and hate generated from the top, and not ethnic differences, that finally push people to commit acts of violence. People may come to fear or resent another group for a variety of reasons, especially when social and economic change seems to favor the other group. And yet such competition and resentment "at the ground level" usually does not lead to intergroup violence without an intervening push from the top.

Let us return to those two most unsettling cases, Rwanda and the Balkans. In Rwanda the continuing slaughter of the past few years stemmed from efforts by the dictator-president Juvenal Habyarimana to wipe out his political opposition, Hutu as well as Tutsi. In 1990–91 Habyarimana began to assemble armed gangs into a militia called Interahamwe. This militia carried out its first massacre of a village in March 1992, and in 1993 began systematically to kill Hutu moderates and Tutsis. Throughout 1993 the country's three major radio stations were broadcasting messages of hate against Tutsis, against the opposition parties, and against specific politicians, setting the stage for what followed. Immediately after the still unexplained plane crash that killed President Habyarimana in April 1994, the presidential guard began killing Hutu opposition leaders, human rights activists, journalists, and others critical of the state, most of them Hutus. Only then, after the first wave of killings, were the militia and soldiers sent out to organize mass killings in the countryside, focusing on Tutsis.

Why did people obey the orders to kill? Incessant radio broadcasts over the previous year had surely prepared them for it; the broadcasts portrayed the Tutsi-led Rwandan Patriotic Front as bloodthirsty killers. During the massacres, radio broadcasts promised the land of the dead to the killers. Town mayors, the militia, the regular army, and the police organized Hutus into killing squads, and killed those Hutus who would not join in. The acting president toured the country to thank those villagers who had taken part in the massacres. Some people settled personal scores under cover of the massacre, and many were carried away with what observers have described as a "killing frenzy." The killings of 1994 were not random mob violence, although they were influenced by mob psychology.[3]

In reading accounts of the Rwanda killings, I was struck by how closely they matched, point by point, the ways Indonesians have described to me their participation in the mass slaughters of 1965–66. In Indonesia the supposed target was "communists," but there, too, it was a desire to settle personal scores, greed, willingness to follow the army's orders, and fear of retaliation that drove people to do things they can even now barely admit to themselves, even though many of them, like many Hutus, were convinced that the killings stopped the takeover of the country by an evil power. In both countries, people were told to kill the children and not to spare pregnant women, lest children grow up to take revenge on their killers. Americans continue to refer to those massacres in Indonesia as an instance of "ethnic violence" and to assume that Chinese residents were major targets, but they were not: the killings by and large pitted Javanese against Javanese, Acehnese against Acehnese, and so forth.

The two massacres have their differences: Rwanda in 1993–94 was a one-party state that had carried out mass indoctrination through absolute control of the mass media; Indonesia in 1965–66 was a politically fragmented state in which certain factions of the armed forces only gradually took control. But in both cases leaders were able to carry out a plan, conceived at the top, to wipe out an opposition group. They succeeded because they persuaded people that they could survive only by killing those who were, or could become, their killers.

The same task of persuasion faced Serb and Croat nationalist politicians, in particular Croatia's Franjo Tudjman and Serbia's Slobodan Milosević, who warned their ethnic brethren elsewhere—Serbs in Croatia, Croats in Bosnia—that their rights were about to be trampled unless they rebelled. Milosević played on the modern Serb nationalist rhetoric of expansion, claiming the right of Serbs everywhere to be united. Tudjman, for his part, used modern Croat rhetoric of exclusionary nationalism to build his following. Once in power in Croatia, he moved quickly to define Serbs as second-class citizens, fired Serbs from the police and military, and placed the red-and-white "checkerboard" of the Nazi-era Ustashe flag in the new Croatian banner.

Both leaders used historical memories for their own purposes, but they also had to erase recent memories of new Yugoslav identities, tentatively forged by men and women who married across ethnic boundaries or who lived in the cosmopolitan cities. The new constitutions recognized only ethnic identity, not civil identity, and people were forced, sometimes at gunpoint, to choose who they "really" were.[5]

Contrary to the "explanations" of the war frequently offered by Western journalists, ordinary Serbs do not live in the fourteenth century, fuming over the Battle of Kosovo; nor is the current fighting merely a playing out of some kind of inevitable logic of the past, as some have written. It took hard work by unscrupulous politicians to convince ordinary people that the other side consisted not of the friends and neighbors they had known for years but of genocidal people who would kill them if they were not killed first. For Milosević this meant persuading Serbs that Croats were all crypto-Nazi Ustashe; for Tudjman it meant convincing Croats that Serbs were all Chetnik assassins. Both, but particularly Milosević, declared Bosnian Muslims to be the front wave of a new Islamic threat. Each government indirectly helped the other: Milosević's expansionist talk confirmed Croat fears that Serbs intended to control the Balkans; Tudjman's politics revived Serbs' still remembered fears of the Ustashe. Serb media played up these fears, giving extensive coverage in 1990–91 to the exhumation of mass graves from the Second World War and to stories of Ustashe terror. This "nationalism from the top down," as Warren Zimmerman, the last U.S. ambassador to Yugoslavia, has characterized it, was also a battle of nationalisms, with each side's actions confirming the other's fears.

If Rwanda and the Balkans do not conform to the images of bubbling cauldrons and ancient tribal hatreds, even less do other ongoing local-level conflicts. Most are drives for political autonomy, most spectacularly in the former Soviet Union, where the collapse of Soviet power allowed long-suppressed peoples to reassert their claims to practice their own languages and religions, and to control their own territory and resources—a rejection of foreign rule much like anti-imperial rebellions in the Americas, Europe, Asia, and Africa. Elsewhere various rebellions, each with its own history and motivations, have typically—and erroneously—been lumped together as "ethnic conflict." Resistance in East Timor to Indonesian control is a 20-year struggle against invasion by a foreign power, not an expression of ethnic or cultural identity. People fighting in the southern Philippines under the banner of a "Moro nation" by and large joined up to regain control of their homelands from Manila-appointed politicians. Zapatista rebels in Chiapas demand jobs, political reform, and, above all, land. They do not mention issues of ethnic or cultural identity in their statements—indeed, their leader is from northern Mexico and until recently spoke no Mayan. Other current conflicts are raw struggles for power among rival factions, particularly in several African countries (Liberia, Somalia, Angola) where rival forces often recruit heavily from one region or clan (giving rise to the notion that these are "ethnic conflicts") in order to make use of local leaders and loyalties to control their followers.[5]

Ethnic Diversity and Social Conflict

This brings us to the third mistaken assumption: that ethnic diversity brings with it political instability and the likelihood of violence. To the contrary, greater ethnic diversity is not associated with greater interethnic conflict. Some of the world's most ethnically diverse states, such as Indonesia, Malaysia, and Pakistan, though not without internal conflict and political repression, have suffered little interethnic violence, while countries with very slight differences in language or culture (the former Yugoslavia, Somalia, Rwanda) have had the bloodiest such conflicts. It is the number of ethnic groups and their relationships to power, not diversity per se, that strongly affect political stability. As shown in recent studies by political scientist Ted Gurr, and contrary to popular thinking, local conflicts have not sharply increased in frequency or severity during the last ten years. The greatest increase in local conflicts occurred during the Cold War, and resulted from the superpowers' efforts to arm their client states. (The sense that everything exploded after 1989, Gurr argues, comes from the reassertions of national identity in Eastern Europe and the former Soviet Union.)[6]

By and large, the news media focus on countries racked by violence and ignore the many more cases of peaceful relations among different peoples. Take Indonesia, where I have carried out fieldwork since the late 1970s. If people know of Indonesia, it is probably because of its occupation of East Timor and its suppression of political freedoms. But these are not matters of ethnic conflict, of which there is remarkably little in a country composed of more than three hundred peoples, each with its own distinct language and culture. Although throughout the 1950s and 1960s there were rebellions against Jakarta in many parts of the country, these concerned control over local resources, schooling, and religion. An on-again, off-again rebellion where I work, on the northern tip of Sumatra, has been about control over the region's vast oil and gas resources (although the Western press continues to stereotype it as "ethnic conflict").

Cultural diversity does, of course, present challenges to national integration and social peace. Why do some countries succeed at meeting those challenges while others fail? Two sets of reasons seem most important, and they swamp the mere fact of ethnic and cultural diversity.

First there are the "raw materials" for social peace that countries possess at the time of independence. Countries in which one group has been exploiting all others (such as Rwanda and Burundi) start off with scores to settle, while countries with no such clearly dominating group (such as Indonesia) have an initial advantage in building political consensus. So-called centralized polities, with two or three large groups that continually polarize national politics, are less stable than "dispersed" systems, in which each of many smaller groups is forced to seek out allies to achieve its goals. And if the major ethnic groups share a language or religion, or if they have worked together in a revolutionary struggle, they have a bridge already in place that they can use to build political cooperation.[7]

Take, again, the case of Indonesia. In colonial Indonesia (the Dutch East Indies) the Javanese were, as they are today, the most numerous people. But they were concentrated on Java and held positions of power only there. Peoples of Java, Sumatra, and the eastern islands, along with Malays and many in the southern Philippines, had used Malay as a *lingua franca* for centuries, and Malay became the basis for the language of independent Indonesia. Islam also cut across regions and ethnicities, uniting people on Sumatra, Java, and Sulawesi. Dominance was "dispersed," in that prominent figures in literature, religion, and the nationalist movement tended as often as not to be from someplace other than Java, notably Sumatra. Moreover, people from throughout the country had spent five years fighting Dutch efforts to regain control after the Second World War, and could draw on the shared experience of that common struggle.[8]

One can see the difference each of these features makes by looking next door at culturally similar Malaysia. Malays and Chinese, the largest ethnic groups, shared neither language nor religion, and had no shared memory of struggle to draw on. Malays had held all political power during British rule. On the eve of independence there was a clear fault line running between the Malay and Chinese communities.

The Importance of Political Choices

But these initial conditions do not tell the whole story, and here enters the second set of reasons for social peace or social conflict. States do make choices, particularly about political processes, that ease or exacerbate intergroup tensions. As political scientist Donald Horowitz has pointed out, if we consider only their starting conditions, Malaysia ought to have experienced considerable interethnic violence (for the reasons given above), whereas Sri Lanka, where Tamils and Sinhalese had mingled in the British-trained elite, should have been spared such violence. And yet Malaysia has largely managed to avoid it while Sri Lanka has not. The crucial difference, writes Horowitz, was in the emerging political systems in the two countries. Malaysian politicians constructed a multiethnic political coalition, which fostered ties between Chinese and Malay leaders and forced political candidates to seek the large middle electoral ground. In Sri Lanka, as we saw earlier, Sinhalese-speakers formed a chauvinist nationalist movement, and after early cooperation Tamils and Sinhalese split apart to form ethnically based political parties. Extreme factions appeared on the wings of each party, forcing party leaders to drift in their directions.

But political systems can be changed. Nigeria is a good example. Prior to 1967 it consisted of three regions—North, South, and East—each with its own party supported by ethnic allegiances. The intensity of this three-way division drove the southeast region of Biafra to attempt to break away from Nigeria in 1967, and the trauma of the civil war that followed led politicians to try a new system. They carved the country into 19 states, the boundaries of which cut through the territories of the three largest ethnic groups (Hausa, Yoruba, and Igbo), encouraging a new federalist politics based on multiethnic coalitions. The new system, for all its other problems, prevented another Biafra. Subsequent leaders, however, continued to add to the number of states for their own political reasons. The current leader, General Sani Abacha, is now adding to an already expanded list of 30 states; this excessive fragmentation has broken up the multiethnic coalitions and encouraged ethnic politics anew. A similar direction has been pursued by Kenya's Daniel arap Moi, who has created an ethnic electoral base that excludes most Kikuyus, increasing the relevance of ethnicity in politics and therefore the level of intergroup tensions.

What the myth of ethnic conflict would say are ever-present tensions are in fact the products of political choices. Negative stereotyping, fear of another group, killing lest one be killed—these are the doings of so-called leaders, and can be undone by them as well. Believing otherwise, and assuming that such conflicts are the natural consequences of human depravity in some quarters of the world, leads to perverse thinking and perverse policy. It makes violence seem characteristic of a people or region, rather than the consequence of specific political acts. Thinking this way excuses inaction, as when U.S. president Bill Clinton, seeking to retreat from the hard-line Balkan policy of candidate Clinton, began to claim that Bosnians and Serbs were killing each other because of their ethnic and religious differences. Because it paints all sides as less rational and less modern (more tribal, more ethnic) than "we" are, it makes it easier to tolerate their suffering. Because it assumes that "those people" would naturally follow their leaders' call to kill, it distracts us from the central and difficult question of just how and why people are sometimes led to commit such horrifying deeds.

Notes

1. Two of the most widely read proponents of the view I am contesting are Robert Kaplan, in his dispatches for *The Atlantic* and in his *Balkan Ghosts: A Journey Through History* (New York: St. Martin's, 1993), and (writing mainly on large-scale conflict) Samuel P. Huntington, in "The Clash of Civilizations?" *Foreign Affairs* 72 (Summer 1993): 22–49. My concern is less with the particular difficulties of these writers' arguments, about which others have written, than with the general notion, which, as with all myths, survives the death of any one of its versions.

2. See Misha Glenny, *The Fall of Yugoslavia* (New York: Penguin, 1992), for a balanced and ethnographically rich account of the Balkan wars. On recent tendencies in European nationalisms, see especially Rogers Brubaker, *Nationalism Reframed: Nationhood and the National Question in the New Europe* (Cambridge: Cambridge University Press, 1996). Brubaker makes the important point that "nationalism" should be treated as a category of social and political ideology, and not a pre-ideological "thing."

3. Among recent overviews of massacres in Rwanda and Burundi, see Philip Gourevitch, "The Poisoned Country," *New York Review of Books*, 6 June 1996, 58–64, and René Lemarchand, *Burundi: Ethnic Conflict and Genocide* (Cambridge: Cambridge University Press, 1995).

4. That there were memories, fears, and hatreds to exploit is important to bear in mind, lest we go to the other extreme and argue that these conflicts are entirely produced from the top, an extreme toward which an overreliance on rational-choice models may lead some analysts. Russell Hardin's otherwise excellent *One for All: The Logic of Group Conflict* (Princeton: Princeton University Press, 1995) errs, I believe, in attributing nothing but rational, self-aggrandizing motives to those leaders who stir up ethnic passions, ignoring that they, too, can be caught

up in these passions. The cold rationality of leaders is itself a variable: probably Milosević fits Hardin's rational-actor model better than Tudjman, and Suharto better than Sukarno. In each case, it is an empirical question.

5. The same points could be made concerning the religious version of "ancient hatreds," such as Muslim-Hindu relations in India. However peaceful or conflictual "ancient" relations may have been (and on this issue there continues to be a great deal of controversy among historians of South Asia), the often bloody conflicts of the past ten years in India have been fueled by ambitious politicians who have seen boundless electoral opportunity in middle-class Hindu resentment toward 1) lower castes' claims that they deserve employment and education quotas, and 2) the recent prosperity of some middle-class Muslims. See the penetrating political analyses by Susanne Hoeber Rudolph and Lloyd I. Rudolph in the *New Republic*, 22 March 1993 and 14 February 1994, and a historical and ethnographic study by Peter van der Veer, *Religious Nationalism: Hindus and Muslims in India* (Berkeley: University of California Press, 1994).

6. See Ted Gurr, *Ethnic Conflict in World Politics* (Boulder, Colo.: Westview, 1994).

7. See Donald L. Horowitz, *Ethnic Groups in Conflict* (Berkeley: University of California Press, 1985), 291–364.

8. I would propose "dispersed dominance" (a situation in which each of several groups considers itself to dominate on some social or political dimension) as a second important mechanism for reducing intergroup conflict alongside the well-known "cross-cutting cleavages" (a situation in which one or more important dimensions of diversity cut across others, as religion cuts across ethnicity in many countries). "Dispersed dominance" takes into account social and cultural dimensions, such as literary preeminence or a sense of social worth stemming from putative indigenous status. It is thus broader than, but similar to, political mechanisms such as federalism, when these mechanisms are aimed at (in Donald Horowitz's phrase) "proliferating the points of power." It is the empirical correlate to the normative position articulated by Michael Walzer in *Spheres of Justice* (New York: Basic Books, 1983) that dominance in one sphere (or dimension) ought not to automatically confer dominance in others.

POSTSCRIPT

Are Cultural Rivalries and Ethnic Conflicts the Next Great Threats to International Security?

Examining the causes and trends in conflict is a difficult enterprise. Perhaps no area in world politics has been studied and analyzed more than conflict. Arguing that certain forms of conflict are on the upswing or downswing is difficult because we do not have the benefit of historical context. Looking back on the twentieth century, for example, we can clearly see the increasing scope and impact of war; deaths and weapon destruction increased at virtually every stage. Determining the likelihood that ethnic conflicts will dominate the security agenda in the coming years, however, is difficult to evaluate.

The sheer ferocity of ethnic conflicts in the past decade in places like Rwanda, Bosnia, Kosovo, Chechnya, Angola, Afghanistan, and Israel and Palestine seem to support Huntington's thesis that ethnicity and culture will define the battle lines between groups. Yet is culture at work or simply political power? The passion of the combatants may mask the more Machiavellian goals of leaders and individuals.

One element is certain. As the centralized power and influence of large imperial states like the USSR and others diminishes, fault lines of conflict that may exist between people in various regions are more readily exploitable, like those in Yugoslavia by former Serb president Slobodan Milosovich. This means that such conflicts are indeed more likely, as leaders take advantage of paranoia, animosity, and fear to create an "other" against which a people may rally, at least for a short time. Whether this is part of a major global trend in ethnic conflict and cultural divides or merely political opportunism is still open to question.

Literature on this topic includes Farhang Rajaee, *Globalization on Trial: The Human Condition and the Information Civilization* (Kumarian Press, 2000); Daniel Patrick Moynihan, *Pandemonium: Ethnicity in International Polictics* (Oxford University Press, 1994); and Stephen M. Walt, "Building Up a New Bogeyman," *Foreign Policy* (Spring 1997).

Contributors to This Volume

EDITORS

JAMES E. HARF is a professor emeritus of political science at Ohio State University, where he continues to teach courses in international affairs, global issues, and American government. He is coauthor of *World Politics and You*, 5th ed. (Brown & Benchmark, 1995) and *The Politics of Global Resources* (Duke University Press, 1986). He also coedited a four-book series on the global issues of population, food, energy, and environment, as well as three other book series on national security education, international studies, and international business. His current research interests include the world population problem and its regime. As a staff member of the Presidential Commission on Foreign Language and International Studies, he was responsible for undergraduate education. He also served for 15 years as executive director of the Consortium for International Studies Education, a group of colleges and universities devoted to the improvement of international studies education.

MARK OWEN LOMBARDI is a professor in and chair of the Department of Government and World Affairs at the University of Tampa. He is coeditor of *Perspectives on Third World Sovereignty: The Post-Modern Paradox* (Macmillan, 1996), and he has authored several articles on such topics as African political economy, U.S. foreign policy, and curriculum reform. Dr. Lombardi is a member of numerous associations, including the International Studies Association, the African Studies Association, and the National Committee of International Studies Programs Administrators. He is director of International Programs at the University of Tampa and a former executive director of the U.S.-Africa Education Foundation. His teaching and research interests focus on the areas of world politics, U.S. foreign policy, African politics, and Third World development.

STAFF

Theodore Knight   List Manager
David Brackley   Senior Developmental Editor
Juliana Gribbins   Developmental Editor
Rose Gleich   Administrative Assistant
Brenda S. Filley   Director of Production/Design
Juliana Arbo   Typesetting Supervisor
Diane Barker   Proofreader
Richard Tietjen   Publishing Systems Manager
Larry Killian   Copier Coordinator

368

AUTHORS

PETER L. BERGER is the University Professor of Sociology and Theology and director of the Institute for the Study of Economic Culture at Boston University in Boston, Massachusetts. He has also taught at the New School for Social Research, where he earned his M.A. and Ph.D.; Rutgers University; and Boston College. He was awarded the Mannes Sperber Prize in 1992 for significant contributions to culture, and he is the author of *Redeeming Laughter: The Comic Dimension of Human Experience* (De Gruyter, 1997).

JANE T. BERTRAND is a professor in and chair of the Department of International Health and Development in the Tulane School of Public Health and Tropical Medicine. She earned her Ph.D. in sociology from the University of Chicago and has published over 50 peer-reviewed journal articles. Her areas of expertise include international family planning, applied research, and information-education-communication.

LEON F. BOUVIER is an adjunct professor of demography at Tulane University in New Orleans, Louisiana, and a senior fellow of Negative Population Growth, a national organization that was founded to educate the American public about the detrimental effects of overpopulation on the environment and people's quality of life. He is coauthor, with Lindsey Grant, of *How Many Americans?* (Sierra Club Books, 1994).

JOHN R. BOWEN is the Dunbar Van Cleve Professor and chair of the Social Thought and Analysis Program at Washington University in St. Louis, Missouri. His research is concerned primarily with the role of cultural forms (religious practices, aesthetic genres, legal discourse) in processes of social change. He earned his Ph.D. from the University of Chicago in 1984, and he is the author of *Muslims Through Discourse: Religion and Ritual in Gayo Society* (Princeton University Press, 1993).

LESTER R. BROWN is founder, senior researcher, and chairman of the board of directors of the Worldwatch Institute, a research institute devoted to the analysis of global environmental issues. He launched the institute's annual *State of the World* and *Vital Signs: The Trends That Are Shaping Our Future* reports, and he is the founding publisher of the bimonthly *World Watch*. He earned his M.S. in agricultural economics from the University of Maryland in 1959 and his M.P.A. in public administration from Harvard University in 1962. His many books include *Eco-Economy: Building a New Economy for the Environmental Age* (W. W. Norton, 2001).

WILLIAM J. CARRINGTON is an economist at the U.S. Department of Labor's Bureau of Labor Statistics.

LEE A. CASEY has served in the U.S. Department of Justice and now practices law in Washington, D.C.

ROBERTA COHEN is a Foreign Policy Studies guest scholar at the Brookings Institution, where she has also been codirector of the Project on Internal Displacement. A former senior adviser to the representative of the UN secretary general on internally displaced persons, she has been a consultant to the United Nations, the World Bank, the Refugee Policy Group, and the International Human Rights Law Group. She earned her M.A. from Johns Hopkins University in 1963, and she is coauthor, with Francis M. Deng, of *Masses in Flight: The Global Crisis of Internal Displacement* (Brookings Institution Press, 1998).

FRANCIS M. DENG is a Foreign Policy Studies senior fellow of the Brookings Institution. A former Sudanese ambassador to the United States, Scandinavia, and Canada, he has also served as the UN secretary general's special representative on internally displaced persons. He earned his LL.M. and his J.S.D. from Yale Law School in 1965 and 1968, respectively. He is coeditor, with Terrence Lyons, of *African Reckoning: A Quest for Good Governance* (Brookings Institution Press, 1998).

SETH DUNN is a research associate and a climate/energy team co-leader at the Worldwatch Institute. He has also been a consultant to the Natural Resources Defense Council and a research assistant with the Yale Center for Environmental Law and Policy. He is coauthor, with Christopher Flavin and Jane A. Peterson, of *Rising Sun, Gathering Winds: Policies to Stabilize the Climate and Strengthen Economies* (Worldwatch Institute, 1997).

CHRISTOPHER FLAVIN is president of the Worldwatch Institute, where he is responsible for overall management and fundraising, leads the institute's management team, and represents the institute before a broad range of audiences around the world. He also heads the institute's climate and energy team, and he is cofounder of the Board of the Business Council for Sustainable Energy. He is the author of *Power Surge: Guide to the Coming Energy Revolution* (W. W. Norton, 1994).

THOMAS L. FRIEDMAN is one of America's leading commentators on world affairs. A two-time Pulitzer Prize–winning journalist for the *New York Times,* he is the author of the international best-seller *The Lexus and the Olive Tree: Understanding Globalization* (Farrar, Straus & Giroux, 1999).

GARY GARDNER is director of research at the Worldwatch Institute. His research interests include agricultural resource degradation, materials use, global malnutrition, and the dynamics of social change. He earned an M.A. in politics from Brandeis University and an M.A. in public administration from the Monterey Institute of International Studies.

JEFFREY E. GARTEN is the William S. Beinecke Professor in the Practice of International Trade and Finance and dean of the School of Management at Yale University. An expert in finance and international trade, he was undersecretary of commerce for international trade from 1993 to 1995, and he currently writes a monthly column for *Business Week* on major challenges facing global business leaders. He has also been on the faculties of New York University and the Columbia Business School, and he is the author of *The Mind of the CEO* (Perseus, 2001) and *The Big Ten: Big Emerging Markets and How They Will Change Our Lives* (Basic Books, 1997).

ROSS GELBSPAN was an editor and reporter at the *Philadelphia Bulletin*, the *Washington Post*, and the *Boston Globe* over a 30-year period. In 1984 he was a corecipient of the Pulitzer Prize for public service reporting.

BRIAN HALWEIL is a staff researcher at the Worldwatch Institute, where he researches issues related to food and agriculture, including organic farming, biotechnology, hunger, and water scarcity. His work has been featured in national newspapers, such as the *L.A. Times, Christian Science Monitor*, and the *New York Times*. He earned B.S. degrees in Earth systems and in biology from Stanford University.

DON HINRICHSEN is an environmental reporter who specializes in covering the developing world. He is also a consultant on population for the United Nations, principally the UN Population Fund. He is the author of *Coastal Waters of the World: Trends, Threats, and Strategies* (Island Press, 1999).

PETER HUBER is a senior fellow at the Manhattan Institute's Center for Legal Policy. His articles on science, technology, environment, and the law have appeared in such journals as the *Harvard Law Review* and the *Yale Law Journal*, and he is a regular columnist for *Forbes* magazine. He is the author of *Hard Green: Saving the Environment From the Environmentalists* (Basic Books, 2000).

SAMUEL P. HUNTINGTON is the Albert J. Weatherhead III University Professor at Harvard University, where he is also director of the John M. Olin Institute for Strategic Studies. He is the author of *The Clash of Civilizations and the Remaking of World Order* (Simon & Schuster, 1996).

JOHN ISBISTER is a professor of economics at the University of California, Santa Cruz, where he has been working since 1968. His past research has been in economic development, demography, and immigration, and his current research focuses on ethical problems in economics. He is the author of *Promises Not Kept: The Betrayal of Social Change in the Third World*, 4th ed. (Kumarian Press, 1998).

ROBERT C. JOHANSEN is a senior fellow and a professor of government and international studies in the Joan B. Kroc Institute for International Peace Studies at the University of Notre Dame. He specializes in issues of international ethics and global governance, the United Nations and the maintenance of peace and security, and peace and world order studies. His scholarly articles have appeared in such journals as *World Policy Journal, Third World Quarterly*, and *The Journal of Peace Research*, and he is coeditor of *The Constitutional Foundations of World Peace* (State University of New York Press, 1993).

JEAN M. JOHNSON is a senior analyst in the Division of Science Resources Studies at the National Science Foundation in Arlington, Virginia, an independent U.S. government agency responsible for promoting science and engineering. She is the author of *The Science and Technology Resources of Japan: A Comparison With the United States* (DIANE, 2001).

ROBERT A. JORDAN is a columnist for the *Boston Globe*.

JERRY KANG is an acting professor of law at the University of California, Los Angeles. His teaching and research interests include civil procedure, Asian American jurisprudence, and cyberspace. He earned his J.D. from Harvard Law School in 1993, and he has also worked for the National Telecommunications and Information Administration.

EDWARD N. LUTTWAK is senior fellow of preventive diplomacy at the Center for Strategic and International Studies. He has also served as a consultant to the Office of the Secretary of Defense, the National Security Council, and the U.S. Department of State. He is a member of the National Security Study Group of the U.S. Department of Defense and an associate of the Japan Finance Ministry's Institute of Fiscal and Monetary Policy. He is the author of *Turbo-Capitalism: Winners and Losers in the Global Economy* (Simon & Schuster, 1999).

N. GREGORY MANKIW is a professor of economics at Harvard University, where he has been teaching since 1985. He is also a research associate and director of the Monetary Economics Program for the National Bureau of Economic Research, associate editor of *Review of Economics and Statistics,* and a columnist for *Fortune* magazine. His many publications include *Monetary Policy* (University of Chicago Press, 1996).

DAVID MASCI is a staff writer for *CQ Researcher.*

ROBERT S. McNAMARA was president of the World Bank Group of Institutions until his retirement in 1981. A former lieutenant colonel in the U.S. Air Force, he has also taught business administration at Harvard University, where he earned his M.B.A. He became president of Ford Motor Company in 1960, and he served as secretary of defense from 1961 until 1968. He has received many awards, including the Albert Einstein Peace Prize, and he is the author of *In Retrospect: The Tragedy and Lessons of Vietnam* (Random House, 1995).

ADIL NAJAM is an assistant professor in the Department of International Relations and in the Center for Energy and Environmental Studies at Boston University, where he has been teaching since 1997. His research interests include sustainable development and political ecology, global trade and environment negotiation and policy, and environmental security. He is the author of *Environmental Negotiation in an Unequal World: Converting Threats Into Opportunity* (Zed Books, 2001).

MARK W. NOWAK is an environmental writer and a resident fellow of Negative Population Growth. His writing has appeared in national newspapers, magazines, and environmental journals, and he has contributed to several books on population, immigration, and the environment. He is a former executive director of Population-Environment Balance and a long-time advocate of U.S. population stabilization.

PETER G. PETERSON is chairman of the Blackstone Group, a private investment bank; chairman of the Institute for International Economics; deputy chairman of the Federal Reserve Bank of New York; cofounder and president of the Concord Coalition; and chairman of the Council on Foreign

Relations. He is the author of *Gray Dawn: How the Coming Age Wave Will Transform America—And the World* (Crown, 2000).

DAVID PIMENTEL is a professor of insect ecology and agricultural sciences at Cornell University, where he has been teaching since 1955. He is a member of a number of professional societies, including the Ecological Society of America and the American Institute of Biological Sciences, and he served as consulting ecologist on the White House staff in 1969–1970. His many publications include *Ecological Integrity: Integrating Environment, Conservation and Health,* coedited with Laura Westra and Reed F. Noss (Island Press, 2000).

MARK C. REGETS is a senior analyst in the Division of Science Resources Studies at the National Science Foundation in Arlington, Virginia, an independent U.S. government agency responsible for promoting science and engineering.

DAVID B. RIVKIN, JR., has served in the U.S. Department of Justice and now practices law in Washington, D.C.

DAVID ROTHKOPF is an adjunct professor of international and public affairs at Columbia University, where he earned his B.A. He has also been managing director and a member of the board of directors of Kissinger Associates, chairman and CEO of International Media Partners, and acting undersecretary of commerce for international trade and deputy undersecretary of commerce for international trade policy development for the U.S. Department of Commerce.

JULIAN L. SIMON (1932–1998) was a professor of economics and business administration in the College of Business and Management at the University of Maryland at College Park. His research interests focused on population economics, and his publications include *The State of Humanity* (Blackwell, 1995) and *The Economics of Population: Key Modern Writings* (Edward Elgar, 1997).

MAX SINGER is president of The Potomac Organization, Inc., a public policy consulting and research firm in Chevy Chase, Maryland. He has also served as president of the World Institute in Jerusalem and of the Hudson Institute, a policy research organization now located in Indianapolis, Indiana, which he cofounded. He is coauthor, with Aaron Wildavsky, of *The Real World Order: Zones of Peace/Zones of Turmoil,* rev. ed. (Seven Bridges Press, 1996).

BAKER SPRING is the F. M. Kirby Research Fellow in National Security Policy at the Heritage Foundation, where he examines the threat of ballistic missiles from developing countries and U.S. national security issues. He earned his M.A. in national security studies from Georgetown University.

EHUD SPRINZAK is a professor of political science at Hebrew University in Jerusalem. He has also been a senior scholar at the United States Institute of Peace.

FRANCIS R. STABLER has worked as a systems engineer on the introduction of technology in the defense and automotive industries for over 30 years. He is currently a technology planner for General Motors.

PAUL STARR is a professor of sociology at Princeton University and coeditor of *The American Prospect.* He is also director of the Century Institute, founder of the Electronic Policy Network, and president of the Sandra Starr Foundation.

JOE STORK is advocacy director of Human Rights Watch/Middle East, a nongovernmental organization established in 1978 to monitor and promote the observance of internationally recognized human rights in Africa, the Americas, Asia, the Middle East, and among the signatories of the Helsinki accords.

MICHAEL TOBIAS is the author of more than 25 books and the writer-director-producer of over 100 films, including the acclaimed 28-part series *A Parliament of Souls* and the 10-hour miniseries *Voice of the Planet.* He has also published over 200 articles and essays in such journals as *Mother Earth News, The New Scientist,* and *Discovery.* Among his books are *A Day in the Life of India* (HarperCollins, 1997) and *A Vision of Nature: Traces of the Original World* (Kent State University Press, 1995).

BRIAN TUCKER, a former chief of the CSIRO Division of Atmospherics Research in Melbourne, Australia, is now a senior fellow of the Institute for Public Affairs.

UNITED NATIONS ENVIRONMENT PROGRAMME (UNEP) was organized to provide leadership and encourage partnership in caring for the environment by inspiring, informing, and enabling nations and peoples to improve their quality of life without compromising that of future generations. The executive director of UNEP is Klaus Töpfer, undersecretary general of the United Nations.

AL J. VENTER, an author and a journalist, is a Middle East correspondent for Jane's *International Defense Review.* With over 30 years' experience in that region, he has done a series of studies on nuclear and biological warfare pertaining to Iraq, Iran, Syria, Algeria, Egypt, Sudan, and other countries. He also writes on issues pertaining to water in that part of the globe.

Index